Theorising Chinese Masculinity
Society and Gender in China

This book is the first comprehensive analysis of Chinese masculinity. While there is a vast Eurocentric scholarship on gender and sexuality, there has been little work addressing these issues within the Chinese context. Kam Louie uses the concepts of *wen* (cultural attainment) and *wu* (martial valour) to explain attitudes to masculinity. This revises most Western analyses of Asian masculinity that rely on the *yin-yang* binary. Examining classical and contemporary Chinese literature and film, the book also looks at the Chinese diaspora to consider Chinese masculinity within and outside China. Its use of a largely indigenous framework to analyse Chinese masculinity makes it an exciting addition to this burgeoning field.

Kam Louie is Professor of Chinese Studies, Asian Languages and Studies Department, University of Queensland. He is the author or co-author of more than ten books on Chinese culture.

To my brothers and sisters
Bigg, Keith, Edward, Anne and Maria,
And to the memory of
Kwan-yee

Theorising Chinese Masculinity
Society and Gender in China

Kam Louie
University of Queensland

CAMBRIDGE
UNIVERSITY PRESS

CAMBRIDGE UNIVERSITY PRESS
Cambridge, New York, Melbourne, Madrid, Cape Town, Singapore, São Paulo, Delhi

Cambridge University Press
The Edinburgh Building, Cambridge CB2 8RU, UK

Published in the United States of America by Cambridge University Press, New York

www.cambridge.org
Information on this title: www.cambridge.org/9780521119047

First published 2002
This digitally printed version 2009

A catalogue record for this publication is available from the British Library

National Library of Australia Cataloguing in Publication data
Louie, Kam.
Theorising Chinese masculinity: society and gender
in China.
Bibliography.
Includes index.
ISBN 0 521 80621 6.
1. Masculinity – China. 2. Men – China. I. Title.
305.310951

ISBN 978-0-521-80621-3 hardback
ISBN 978-0-521-11904-7 paperback

Contents

Acknowledgements

In the ten years that it has taken me to write this book, numerous institutions and individuals have helped me. The University of Queensland, the Australian Research Council and the Chinese Studies Center in Taipei have provided me financial and institutional support. The UQ Playhouse, Rainworth Primary School and Brisbane State High School, by looking after my children so ably, have provided me valuable time and peace of mind to research. I have benefited from the professionalism and helpfulness of the staff at Cambridge University Press, and Carla Taines' meticulous editing has greatly improved the text. I am also grateful to my family, colleagues and friends who have listened to and commented on my ideas about what it means to be a Chinese man. In particular, I should thank Mark McLelland, Morris Low, Bonnie McDougall, Cheung Chiu-yee, Peter Cryle, Zhong Xueping, Susan Brownell, Li Jinyu, Song Geng, Mabel Lee, Geremie Barmé, Keith McMahon, Anne McLaren, Helen Fong, Carole Tan, Carl Hinze, Allan Luke, Lisa O'Connell, Bob Hodge, Chen Ping, Mary Farquhar, Wai Wai Lui, Andrew Gosling, Alan Walker and Ray Kitson, and the anonymous readers for CUP and the publications listed below for providing me with assistance, materials and advice. As always, my indebtedness to my wife Louise Edwards cannot be expressed in words. She wrote parts of chapter 1 and made insightful criticisms on the entire manuscript. No analysis of men or women is complete without some reference to the other, and Louise's research on women has been a constant source of inspiration for this project on men.

Earlier versions of parts of some chapters have appeared in the following: chapter 1: 'Chinese Masculinity: Theorizing *Wen* and *Wu*' (co-authored with Louise Edwards), *East Asian History* 8 (1994); chapter 2: 'Sexuality, Masculinity and Politics in Chinese Culture', *Modern Asian Studies* 33.4 (Cambridge University Press, 1999); chapter 3: 'Sage, Teacher, Businessman: Confucius as a Male Model', in Shiping Hua (ed.), *Chinese Political Culture* (Armonk, NY: M.E. Sharpe, 2001); chapter 5: 'The Macho Eunuch', *Modern China* 17.2 (Sage Publications,

1991); chapter 7: 'Constructing Chinese Masculinity for the Modern World', *China Quarterly* 164 (Oxford University Press, 2000), and 'I Married a Foreigner: Recovering Chinese Masculinity in Australia', in Wenche Ommundsen (ed.), *Bastard Moon: Essays on Chinese-Australian Writing, Special Issue of Otherland* 7 (2001). Every effort has been made to trace and acknowledge copyright. I would be grateful to hear from those copyright holders I have not been able to contact.

1   Introducing *wen-wu*:
Towards a Definition of Chinese Masculinity

The Chinese characters for *wen* and *wu*. (Calligraphy by Kam Louie)

As we enter the twenty-first century, the proposition that race and gender are fundamental analytic categories in both academic and popular discourses is beyond dispute. Momentous social and political movements like the post-World War II Civil Rights campaigns in the USA and the numerous national independence struggles around the world highlighted injustices perpetrated on the basis of skin colour. Similarly the feminist movement has raised public consciousness about inequities based on gender. Feminist and postcolonial studies have refined and reinforced each other's methodologies such that the 'woman' and 'native' categories claim equal prominence with the now highly scrutinised 'Other'.[1] The insights and new knowledges to be gained from using gender as a tool for examining 'the natives' is clearly evident in Chinese studies. Since the 1980s a number of important works have been published discussing the position of women in Chinese society.[2] However, despite the attested interest in gender in China, there is an important lacuna in this work – masculinity. In effect, 'gender' has become synonymous with 'woman' because of the failure to focus on masculinity.[3]

Until the early 1980s, gender studies in the West was also equated with women's studies. Since this time, literature on men and masculinity has grown exponentially. While history everywhere has been mainly 'his-story', it is only in the last twenty-odd years that 'he' has been problematised and masculinity as a cultural construct theorised. Many perspectives approaching the problem of masculinity have been advanced, but there is still no comprehensive theorising of a universal set of defining characteristics of masculinity. In an influential cross-cultural study of masculinities, David Gilmore has produced a set of core masculine attributes such as self-direction and discipline which seem universal. However, he also notes that many variations exist along the cross-cultural continuum of male images and codes.[4] These variations prevent a theoretical structure that satisfies a definitive universal masculinity from being formulated. Instead, what has been produced is a plethora of apparently different kinds of masculinity, almost always from a Western perspective, ranging from the 'mainstream' – such as the profeminist or mythopoetic[5] – to those from the 'outside' – such as gay or black.

The poverty of theory on the generic man is understandable given the fact that 'man' as a universal signifier for huManity has not been questioned until recent years and the specificity of men's actual lives is so diverse even just in the Western world.[6] Empirical evidence suggests support for the social constructionist model of masculinity which argues that 'the meaning of masculinity is neither transhistorical nor culturally universal, but rather varies from culture to culture and within any culture over time'.[7] Nonetheless, a failure to theoretically reconstruct and deconstruct models of masculinity, whether they be 'Eastern' or

'Western', would only perpetuate the myth of a supra-sexual 'mankind',[8] placing all other kinds in the margins.

Even if we are to provide 'perspectives' on masculinity,[9] these perspectives should take account of non-Western possibilities. For China in particular, a general theoretical approach is important because, as Edward Said has argued, the Orient is feminised to such an extent that it 'is penetrated, silenced, and possessed'.[10] In some respects, under the Western gaze, the portrayal of Chinese men seems to confirm this thesis. Images of Chinese men on billboards in the streets of Beijing or Hong Kong as well as in the American media do not conform to the 'macho' stereotype of masculinity currently circulating in the West.[11] In keeping with Orientalist tradition, Western descriptions of Chinese sexuality focus mainly on Daoist bedroom techniques and exotica such as bound feet and aphrodisiacs. Until very recently, there were very few academic studies devoted exclusively to Chinese masculinity. As Susan Mann opines, the poverty of studies on Chinese men is particularly vexing because 'bonds among men were key to success and survival for rich and poor, elite and commoner, in Chinese history'.[12] The limited published studies of Chinese men are at their best when focusing on the non-mainstream such as homosexuality.[13] Similarly, books designed for the lay readership tend to provide anecdotal stories of unusual or sexually dysfunctional men.[14] By 2000, there existed only one scholarly book in English that dealt exclusively with 'mainstream' masculinity.[15] However, this book concentrates on the psychological state of men who feel 'besieged' in post-Mao China.[16] Masculinity is also a subject that occupies at least half of Susan Brownell and Jeffrey Wasserstrom's forthcoming reader.[17] But most of the essays in their book take an anthropological or historical approach, and 'evoke a sense of how femininity and masculinity in China are constructed and performed as *lived experience*'.[18] All these studies are invaluable for enhancing our understanding of Chinese masculinity, but as yet, there are no books that attempt to systematically conceptualise the theoretical underpinning of Chinese masculinities in general terms. The present book will fill this gap by developing broad paradigms facilitating the theorisation of Chinese masculinity.

Rather than analysing the representations and performance of Chinese masculinity as 'lived experience', my objects of analysis are the concepts, icons and symbols which have evolved as a consequence of that 'experience'. In this regard, my approach emerges from within a social constructionist schema. As social constructs, icons and symbols are rarely stable. My aim is to develop paradigms – primarily Chinese but also Western – that will enable us to generalise these evolving constructs in their proper contexts. Thus, while I examine social constructs as icons, symbols and paradigms, I am fully aware that they can be discussed as discourses, so that contained within each, we have contradictory and subversive elements that in turn change the constructs themselves. Furthermore, while I do not adopt an empirical method, I am informed by insights derived from the social sciences. In addition to Susan Brownell's work, a number of excellent anthropological and sociological accounts of gender and sexuality (mostly female) in China have appeared in recent years.[19] Their informants range from factory workers to university professors, and the problems discussed are as diverse as these participants. However, to date no study has explored one of the single most important Chinese paradigms explaining the performance of gendered identities – in particular masculinity – the dyad *wen-wu* (cultural attainment–martial valour).

Despite its importance, the *wen-wu* construct has received very little attention in discussions of Chinese gender or masculinity.[20] This chapter outlines some of its main features. The different manifestations and implications of *wen-wu* as a defining feature of Chinese masculinity will be discussed in the rest of the book. While I have glossed the term as 'cultural attainment–martial valour' above, this rendition is only very approximate. I will elaborate on the definitions later in this chapter. I first should emphasise that by advancing an indigenous definition of masculinity, I do not pretend that the mind–body, mental–physical, cultural knowledge–martial arts dichotomies implicit in the *wen-wu* dyad are the sole preserve of the Chinese conceptualisation of masculinity. Variations of the *wen-wu* paradigm could be applied to other cultures, particularly those in East Asia.[21] For example, the Japanese author Yukio Mishima aimed to achieve an idealised balance between the literary and the martial in his regimen of building bodily strength before committing *seppuku*.[22] Similarities with other cultures are less direct, but some such as the ancient Greek and Roman are renowned for stressing both body and mind,[23] with others such as Jewish culture emphasising the intellectual aspect.[24]

Again, while I utilise comparisons with other cultures, my project never strays far from its China focus. Cross-cultural studies are simply better left to comparative anthropologists.[25] However, intensive case studies such as this current book can supplement more general observations across cultures. For example, David Gilmore relates the beginnings of his study of comparative male images to his discovery of the Andalusian *machismo*, which he 'believes exists to a degree in many societies'.[26] Yet, while machismo forms an integral part of his descriptions of many masculinities ranging from the Mediterranean to the Indian, he believes that the Chinese performance of masculinity 'is often manifested more subtly than in the macho societies'.[27] However, contrary to popular belief, machismo is highly visible in Chinese culture when viewed through an appropriately 'cultured' lens, as chapters 2, 5 and 8 reveal below. Before I outline the main features of *wen-wu*, two interrelated points should be made explicit. The first is related to the importance of including masculinity in so-called 'gender' studies and the second is why we need to conceptualise Chinese masculinity as an independent category.

Sexual Difference

The importance of including studies of masculinity in the valuable work being carried out on sexual difference in Asia is paramount. Previous histories of the world, including China, have frequently been criticised for being dominated by the narration of events that were of male concern. But in effect the 'maleness' of these events remains undisclosed. As stated above, because the writing of these histories has always portrayed 'man' as the universal, normative subject, the effect has been a neat deflection of any analysis of male dominance by having the man as 'male' evade the spotlight. It is the intention of this current project to remove the normality of Chinese 'maleness' as subject. To problematise the notion of masculinity within patriarchal society is to bifurcate the two concepts – masculinity is not patriarchy but rather part of the discourse of a gender order that has been constructed within a patriarchal society. In this respect masculinity requires closer examination.

By focusing on masculinity we can 'sexualise' men in the same way androcentric scholarship and some feminist-inspired scholarship sexualised women. This is important for studies of China because Chinese men are often depicted in both the West and China as less 'sexual' and more 'intelligent' than both black and white men.[28] In the literary domain, this view is particularly apparent in comparisons of the chivalric traditions, as we shall see in the next chapter. In recent years, popular texts in the West such as advertisements have begun to sexualise the Chinese male body. However, these glossy presentations, with the objects commonly in vulnerable and passive poses, only confirm Said's view that the Orient has been metaphorically feminised. They are consumer products for the eyes of the (Western) buyer, and are not intended to reflect the worldview of the objects themselves.

In this chapter, a general paradigm for the Chinese masculine ideal is proposed in order that the actual representations and implications of this ideal can be better understood. Stereotypical male types such as the effeminate scholar and the macho soldier will be examined in the next four chapters, while the impact and transformations of *wen-wu* over space and time will be analysed in chapters 7 and 8. In this chapter, I aim only to provide a model that captures the Chinese masculine ideal. *Wen-wu* is introduced from the outset because it is central to all discussions of Chinese masculinity.

Because it captures both the mental and physical composition of the ideal man, *wen-wu* is meant to be constructed both biologically and culturally. Clearly my position here is one which rejects the early feminist theorists' division of sex and gender whereby the former was regarded as referring to the biological aspects of masculinity and femininity and the latter to the cultural aspects.[29] While these theories developed from the need for feminists to counteract biological reductionism, they are themselves in danger of reducing everything to cultural determinism. Culture does have marked effects on the physical development of the biological body,[30] as is evident in the effect of modern technologies upon men's bodies. The effects of body-building and weight-lifting on the male form are evident.[31] In the sexuality stakes, the drug Viagra literally produces physical changes in the user and this in turn produces psychological and 'cultural' changes.

Our biological bodies therefore also shape our cultural-psychological beings. While idealists such as Stoltenberg may suggest that the penis is not significantly different from the clitoris,[32] such suggestions are too simplistic to explain male/female differences. For men, a notion of self draws upon and interacts with the ideals, stereotypes and models of masculinity circulating in society. But it is also drawn from a man's experience of how his sexual pleasure is produced and his prowess perceived. Male sexuality may be socially constructed, but our bodies do more than passively accept the culture inscribed upon them – they alter and transform themselves in response to their environments and generate patterns of change within cultural trends.[33]

This concept of 'mutual referencing' and 'mutual interactiveness' explains changes in perceptions of 'manliness' and 'the manly physique' across the lengthy Chinese past. Van Gulik notes the ideal of masculine beauty changes over the dynasties and relates this to the fluctuating importance of physical activities. Men of the Tang period 'cultivated a virile, even martial appearance. They liked thick beards, whiskers and long moustaches and admired bodily strength. Both civilian and military officials practised archery, riding, sword fighting and boxing, and proficiency in these arts was highly praised.'[34] Van Gulik continues by contrasting the Ming and Qing with previous dynasties saying,

> Instead of the middle-aged, bearded men of the T'ang and Sung periods, ardent lovers are now preferably depicted as younger men without beard, moustache or whiskers. At that time [Ming] athletics were still admired, young students practised boxing, fencing and archery, and riding and hunting were

favourite pastimes. Thus bodily strength was one of the recognized attributes of a handsome man. They are depicted as tall and broad shouldered, and the nudes of the erotic albums show them with heavy chests and muscular arms and legs ... Under the Manchu occupation the martial arts were monopolized by the conquerors, and as a reaction the Chinese, and more especially the members of the literary class, began to consider physical exercise as vulgar and athletic prowess as suited only to the 'Ch'ing barbarians,' and Chinese professional boxers and acrobats. ... The ideal lover is described as a delicate, hyper-sensitive youngster with pale face and narrow shoulders, passing the greater part of his time dreaming among his books and flowers, and who falls ill at the slightest disappointment.[35]

The male body, then, is culturally inscribed within discourses of masculinity and as such is much more than a product of *perceived* 'essential' biological difference. At the same time, it also determines that culture and discourse interact in subtle and dialectical ways.[36] Recognising that biology as well as culture is vital for the study of masculinity is especially important for the disclosing of Chinese masculinity because I argue that both race and ethnicity are essential for understanding how the concept is constructed. Van Gulik has already made some conjectures on the implications of Han–Manchu differences on masculinity. In recent years, anthropologists have researched the Han-minority dialectic on questions of gender.[37] Han-minority interaction and its significance for masculinity will be briefly discussed in chapter 7. However, as readers of this book are most likely to be based in English-speaking countries, and Western impact remains the most important foreign influence on Chinese living in and outside China, I will concentrate on how this impact affects the constructions of Chinese masculinities. Both chapters 7 and 8 deal mainly with Chinese perceptions and representations of masculinity in the context of the 'yellow–white' interactions.

From Machismo to *yingxiong haohan*

Men's studies are burgeoning in Western universities, reflecting a growing popular interest in the topic. The appearance of increasing numbers of 'men's' magazines such as *FHM, GQ* and *Men's Health* attests to this cultural shift.[38] But these courses and magazines deal exclusively with European and American cultures and primarily adopt a contemporary vision. It is my goal to broaden this discussion to include Chinese masculinity. Subaltern studies have convincingly demonstrated the partiality and even the insularity of many Western feminist paradigms by revealing their inapplicability to women of Africa or Asia.[39] Similarly we can show that male dominance is manifested and perpetuated in a multitude of ways beyond the Western model. Indeed, if female subordination has a multiplicity of forms, then male domination must necessarily be capable of similar variance.

It is clear from even the briefest visit to China that contemporary Chinese sexuality is constructed differently from that of the West.[40] This is particularly evident when one looks at the construction of masculinity. Western stereotypes of the 'real man' have described the Occidental male as forming his notion of male-self within images of toughness, courageousness, and decisiveness. An adventuresome spirit, a proclivity to violence, a tendency towards physical rather than oral expression of thoughts and a callous attitude to sexual relations would also be important components of a Western male's self-image.[41] This is not to say that Western notions of masculinity are clear-cut or static, or that all, or even many, Western men really want to live in 'Marlboro Country'. Indeed, ideals of the 'real man' are changing, and hardly a month passes without some book being published or television documentary being screened exhorting men to behave in very different ways.[42] While some white men may feel there is a 'masculinity crisis'[43] and attempt to reorient themselves as 'sensitive new age guys' of the Steve Biddulph mould or neo-masculinist macho men of the Robert Bly type,[44] men of colour ask 'why is this men's movement so white?'[45] In particular, Chinese men living in Western countries, whether straight or gay, feel keenly the difference skin colour makes to their sense of identity and masculinity,[46] and their sense of alienation finds no relief in these new 'men's movement' groups. I will indicate in chapters 7 and 8 the degree to which the Chinese diaspora has contributed towards such changes.

The application of the contemporary Western paradigm of the 'macho man', whose power is made manifest in brute physical strength and unerring silence, to the Chinese case is largely inappropriate, because while there is a macho tradition in China it is not the predominant one. Thus, the Chinese tradition of macho hero represented in terms such as *yingxiong* (outstanding male) and *haohan* (good fellow)[47] is counterbalanced by a softer, cerebral male tradition – the *caizi* (the talented scholar) and the *wenren* (the cultured man). This is not found to the same degree in contemporary Western conceptions of maleness. Moreover, it will become apparent as we discuss the *wu* heroes later that, unlike the contemporary West, in the Chinese case the cerebral male model tends to dominate that of the macho, brawny male. While the philosophers of ancient Greece, the English gentlemen in colonial times or the recent computer nerds do provide alternative models of masculinity, these images have not been described as desirable and attractive in the same way that the *wenren* have been depicted throughout Chinese history.

The Western paradigms of masculinity are thereby largely inappropriate to the Chinese case: their application would only prove that Chinese

men are 'not quite real men' because they fail the (Western) test
of masculinity. On a cross-cultural survey where Western visions are
adopted as the norm, Asian men can be described as inadequate. For
example, Sun Longji's study of masculinity concludes that Chinese men
are effectively eunuchs and proposes that the ideal masculine form is that
of the Latin American and Mediterranean male.[48] It is as if the opposite
of 'masculinity' is not 'femininity' but 'impotence' within the matrix
of cross-cultural comparisons. In this schema, the West sets the 'normal'
and 'natural' standard of masculinity and it is against this template that
other cultures are compared. This analytical path is clearly misleading.
The point should rather be to develop questions or paradigms that are
generated from within the Asian context rather than to simply mimic
work designed for the West a decade earlier and conclude that Chinese
men are feminised or neutered.[49] This is what I will attempt to do in
this book.

From *yin-yang* to *wen-wu*

In discussions of Asian sexuality, the most commonly invoked 'Chinese'
paradigm is that of *yin-yang* in a notion of the harmony of opposites. Within the common superficial appreciation of *yin-yang* theory,
femininity and masculinity are placed in a dichotomous relationship
whereby *yin* is female and *yang* is male.[50] This binary operation is similar
to the Pythagorean opposition between light–dark, male–female, right–
left and so on. Real men are supposed to have plenty of the *yang* essence.
For example, in a recent handbook for men, which covers a wide range
of material from sexual etiquette to fatherhood, the first section begins
by explaining that what 'makes a man a man' is his possession of a strong
yang essence (*qi*), defined vaguely as 'determination, strength and good
self-control'.[51] We will return to these qualities, especially the last one, in
later chapters.

The difference between the Pythagorean opposites and *yin-yang*
theory is that in the latter, both essences are regarded as being in constant
interaction where *yin* merges with *yang* and *yang* with *yin* in an endless dynamism. This suggests that every man and woman would embody
both *yin* and *yang* essences at any given moment and during sexual
intercourse, the two sexes exchange sexual essences. For the male, the
ideal situation is one where he absorbs *yin* essence from the woman,
without losing his precious *yang* essence to her. For the woman the
reverse is true – she must absorb the man's *yang* essence without losing
her *yin* essence. This sexual vampirism implies some form of expand-
ing capabilities wherein one maintains one's original essence (which in
men would be *yang* and in women *yin*) and yet holds the potential to

absorb additional essences that expand vitality and natural powers.[52] This renders the reductionist understanding of *yang* being male and *yin* being female only partially accurate. Indeed, since both sexes can be either or both *yin* and *yang*, the performance of sexual difference is not wholly explained by *yin-yang* theory. However, in a cross-cultural analysis one could propose that Chinese masculinity is ultimately more all-encompassing than Western masculinity as a result of this acceptance of the merger of *yin* and *yang* essences in one corporeal form.

By asserting that both men and and women embrace both *yin* and *yang* at any particular point in time, this paradigm has proven to be so all-encompassing that it effectively maps the universe on a sexual male–female grid. In this study, I want to isolate general categories which serve as coordinates for maleness only. Discarding *yin* and *yang* is crucial because the potential for interminable interactiveness implicit within *yin* and *yang* prohibits gender specificity. Incisive theorising of masculinity is inhibited by the fluidity of the *yin-yang* binary because each statement should equally be applied to femininity as well. However, the gender order implied by the Confucian strictures on social organisations, clearly placing male above female, implies that the mutuality of *yin* and *yang* must have been counteracted with an alternative sex-specific discourse legitimising and naturalising the imbalance in power between the sexes.[53]

The Chinese paradigm that serves as a prompt to further analysis of masculinity alone is the binary opposition between *wen*, the mental or civil, and *wu*, the physical or martial. These terms have numerous meanings. The *Great Chinese Dictionary* lists 26 definitions for the word *wen*,[54] with the core meanings centring around literary and other cultural attainment. Herrlee G. Creel seems to have captured the gist of its import when he states that *wen*

> appears to have originally had the sense of 'striped' or 'adorned', and it may be by extension from this that wen came to mean 'accomplished', 'accomplishment' and even 'civilization': all of those adornments of life that distinguish the civilized man from the untutored barbarian.[55]

Wu also has over twenty definitions listed in the *Great Chinese Dictionary*, with the core meanings centring around martial, military, force and power.[56] In a recent book on the history of the *wuxia* (the chivalrous *wu* fighter), Chen Shan contrasts the *wuxia* with the European knights and the Japanese samurai. He believes that the adherents of *wu* fight for righteousness (*yi*) and are loyal to men in their group and eschew women. By contrast, the European knights have more aristocratic values and fight for religious or other more lofty ideals, and the samurai retain a military spirit (*bushido*) and are loyal to their *daimyo* or lord.[57] Chen Shan postulates that in the Zhou Dynasty, men who had *wu* (martial arts) expertise dominated the *shi* (the upper classes). They were known as the *wushi*. It was only after Confucianism took hold that *wen* became progressively more dominant for the upper classes, resulting in *shi*'s later association with 'scholar-officials'.[58]

The claim that sometime in the legendary past, *wu* was dominant over *wen* may be romanticised utopian reconstructions on the part of those who specialise in *wu*. Nevertheless, it is indisputable that either *wen* or *wu* or both *wen* and *wu* were perceived to be essential for men of substance. This *wen-wu* paradigm is particularly relevant to understanding masculinity because it invokes both the authority of the scholar and that of the soldier. Chinese masculinity, it will be shown, can be theorised as comprising both *wen* and *wu* so that a scholar is considered to be no less masculine than a soldier. Indeed, at certain points in history the ideal man would be expected to embody a balance of *wen* and *wu*. At other times only one or the other was expected, but importantly *either* was considered acceptably manly. The Confucian *Analects* presents this dichotomy to us in the phrase: 'There is no man who does not have something of the way of *wen* and *wu* in him.'[59] *Wen* and *wu* refer specifically to the ancient Kings of the Zhou – known by their posthumous titles King Wen (*Wen Wang*) and King Wu (*Wu Wang*). Their personality traits and governing techniques developed to signify the way of culture and the way of force. *The Book of Rites* describes their differences as 'King Wen used culture to rule and King Wu used military power'.[60] Their relationship has long been perceived as dichotomous and ubiquitous and has consistently been referred to in relation to national government and self-cultivation.

The sexual specificity, that is the unique maleness of the dichotomy *wen-wu*, becomes even more apparent when it is juxtaposed with *yin-yang*. This point is elaborated in chapter 5. Here, it should be noted that while men and women can both be discussed in terms of *yin* and *yang*, the *wen-wu* dichotomy is applied to women only when they have transformed themselves into men. Women cannot otherwise be productively discussed in terms of *wen* or *wu* for both these aspects of official social life were explicitly denied women with varying degrees of rigidity over the broad sweep of the Chinese past. While in their private residences women could engage in scholarly activities or swordplay and archery, it is primarily in fantasy novels such as the influential Qing novel *Jinghua yuan* (*Flowers in the Mirror*) that such skills can actually be publicly recognised. Here we read of young women warriors who avenge wrongs, and of talented women scholars who achieve official recognition through examinations for women held under the auspices of Empress Wu.[61]

That there were 'geniuses' among women in traditional China is beyond question.[62] But in practice, the construction of femininity for Chinese women used such Amazons and female scholars only as part of an unachievable fantasy realm that ultimately confirmed their own space in the 'inner' private world.[63] Those who stepped beyond these strictures were still contained within the notion of the 'exemplary woman' whose imitation of manly traits served to reinforce the 'superiority' and 'normality' of masculine ideals. Thus, the public corporealisation of *wen* and *wu* necessarily occurred in the male sex. Donning male attire therefore usually precedes the women's temporary forays into the male arena. This is the case with all the *Jinghua yuan* Amazons who are repeatedly assumed to be boys. Another classic literary representation of the woman warrior is Hua Mulan, who dressed as a man for over ten years during her military forays. Interestingly, such women 'appear *even more* feminine and conventional when they return to their female roles than they did before they assumed male guise'.[64] As well as these *wu* ideals, we also have the romanticised tragedy of Zhu Yingtai, who wears the manly scholar's robes to participate in formal studies.

In all such cases, the woman's *wen* or *wu* achievements are acknowledged only if they publicly demonstrate that they are men, however superficially or transiently. Official recognition of *wen-wu* achievements is most commonly through passing the civil service examinations (the *wenju*) and the military service examinations (*wuju*).[65] Both were only available for men. Thus, *wenren*, literally '*wen* people' can only be translated as 'men accomplished in *wen*' or 'cultured men'. It was assumed that women who achieved excellence in *wen* were abnormal. And they probably were, given the social discrimination they had to overcome in traditional China. In the same way, the *xia* were men heroes. Women fighters, and there are many in literature, are specified as the *xianü*, and they are usually fantasies more than reality for most of Chinese history. I must emphasise again that the above does not imply that women did not excel in the literary, martial, or any other cultural accomplishments. The point is rather that *wen-wu* is concerned primarily with conceptualisations of cultural constructs. As cultural constructs, *wen* and *wu* realms are the public preserve of men, and women who dare to venture in must do so in a manner which will further prove the exclusivity of male rights implicit in this construct.

While women are not part of the *wen-wu* paradigm, neither are men from non-Chinese races. This does not imply that non-Chinese were not considered masculine but rather that their masculinity was sexualised to reveal their animal barbarism. Western men were perceived to be civilised men stripped of their civilisation – men of animal instincts and animal sexual drives. Frank Dikötter describes early Chinese perceptions of Western men as having four testicles and an excess of body hair. Both characteristics imply a highly sexualised notion of masculinity.[66] This sexualisation of 'the other' is similar to Victorian-era portrayals of colonised peoples, 1960s white portrayals of blacks as being highly sexual, or current visions of homosexual men as being more promiscuous. Indeed, much of the feminist project has been concerned with elucidating the manner in which men sexualised women as other. Thus, *wen-wu* was not perceived as applicable to men outside the Chinese cultural realm because it contains within its matrix a masculine sexuality of self-affirming, civilising difference. It is thus an ideal construct with which to analyse Chinese masculinity.

In the above discussion, I have provided a paradigm that unravels the way the Chinese have hitherto conceptualised masculinity. The coordinates of this paradigm can and do change with social transformations. Clearly, it is not immutable. For example, as globalisation progresses and Chinese men interact with the outside world more closely and intensely, the racial and cultural reference points of *wen-wu* are also rapidly changing. The world dominance of American media means that the Western masculine ideals represented in many of the American images are becoming more and more commonly accepted in China. Conversely, the influx of Chinese students and migrants to America, Europe and Australia has impacted on Western concepts of maleness. And the popularity of martial arts films such as those by Bruce Lee and Jackie Chan has also subtly changed notions of manly valour and machismo in the West. These issues will be discussed in detail in chapters 7 and 8.

As well as gender, racial and ethnic considerations, *wen-wu* has very significant class implications. In the dual aspects of national government and self-cultivation, *wen-wu* can be applied to a broad range of social classes as a paradigm for conceptualising maleness. It is not exclusively a paradigm of maleness for the elite man whereby masculinity is conflated with social power. Such a conflation establishes all men as powerful and all women as powerless and is thereby too simplistic. Men (especially Chinese men) can have less power relative to elite women (especially white women), but they are still clearly male. Therefore, insofar as masculinity is applicable only to men, it is something more than social power because it signifies a potentiality for ultimate power in a way that femininity does not.[67]

In *Jinghua yuan*, Empress Wu (the only woman in the entire history of China to have been enthroned) is described in the fictionalised version of her radical challenge to male dominance as a reincarnation of a fox demon. Moreover, her drunken edicts for the hundred flowers to bloom in the dead of winter precipitates the unusual events in the novel. Her rise to power and subsequent imperial decrees are therefore presented as an inversion of the natural order. And this order is only restored when other talented women rebel against her. Thus, while gender need not be conceived within a rigid 'oppressor–oppressed' rubric, it does imply a different potentiality for power and social control – masculinity incorporates the right to 'the final say' while femininity incorporates 'the final confirmation of assent'. In the untangling of class from gender, *wen-wu* can serve as a useful paradigm since it is equally applicable to the male elite and the male masses, as will become evident below.

Wen is generally understood to refer to those genteel, refined qualities that were associated with literary and artistic pursuits of the classical scholars, and can thereby be partly analysed as a leisure-class masculine model. This type of masculinity is best typified by the image of groups of men writing poetry for mutual amusement or to mark a memorable occasion. Nonetheless, the elite affiliations of *wen* are not exclusive, because a broad range of social classes aspired to scholarly attributes. This is exemplified by the Wang Mian ideal of the peasant-turned-scholar in the Qing novel *Rulin waishi* (The Scholars).[68] All Chinese men, regardless of social standing, had the right to aspire to high-ranking civil posts through the examination system.

Similarly the *wu* attributes of physical strength and military prowess were not the sole preserve of the masses since they were cultivated by large sections of male society – from elite Tang polo players to Qing street acrobats. This breadth of scope is revealed in the ambiguity of *wu* philosophy. *Wu* was conceived as embodying seven virtues which together 'meant the degree of military authority sufficient to make further engagement unnecessary'.[69] The seven virtues are those qualities that 'suppressed violence, gathered in arms, protected what was great, established merit, gave peace to the people, harmonized the masses and propagated wealth'.[70] *Wu* is therefore a concept which embodies the power of military strength but also the wisdom to know when and when not to deploy it.

While Confucius embodies *wen* in the popular imagination, an equally famous and probably more popular icon, Guan Yu (or Guan Gong), embodies *wu*. Revered as the *wu* god in temples and shrines throughout the Chinese world (often alongside Confucius as the Paragon of Teachers and *wen* god), Guan Yu is a famed general from the Three Kingdoms period (220–280AD), immortalised in the classic novel *Sanguo yanyi* (*The Romance of the Three Kingdoms*).[71] The implications for Chinese masculinity of these two icons will be examined in some detail in the next two chapters. The dichotomy between *wen* and *wu* can incorporate a broad range of social phenomena and men. Thus in direct contrast to the *wu* of Guan Yu is another major character from *Three Kingdoms*: Zhuge

Liang who is credited with the wisdom and learning of the civil minister. In the other classic novel centred on men's heroic exploits, *Shuihu zhuan (All Men Are Brothers)*,[72] we have Wu Song famed for his drunken slaughter of a tiger (*wu*) and Wu Yong for his strategic acumen (*wen*). The figures of Confucius, Guan Yu and Wu Song are analysed in the following chapters as exemplars of *wen* and *wu* ideals.

In schemes devised by myth-makers, it is significant that there is usually a character standing between and above the poles of *wen* and *wu*. Just as in the *yin-yang* scheme the most perfect being is one who has harmonised the two categories, so in the *wen-wu* scheme the man above other men must possess both attributes. This trilateral configuration applies to all classes. For example, among the ruling class in the novel *Sanguo yanyi*, Liu Bei the king stands above Zhuge Liang the prime minister and Guan Yu the general. In *All Men Are Brothers*, Song Jiang the bandit-chief stands above Wu Song the murderer-turned-bandit and Wu Yong the school-teacher-turned-bandit. In the early years of the Chinese People's Republic, this triadic structure had Mao Zedong above Liu Shaoqi the administrator (*wen*) and Zhu De the general (*wu*). The supreme leaders are consistently promoted as holding both *wen* and *wu* in their masculine identity.

Leadership and *wen-wu*

Traditionally, it was perceived that a balance between the two styles of masculinity should be achieved for the ideal continued successful and long-term national and self management. Good government by rulers and good personal governance for men as individuals as well as in their management of their families were perceived as the balancing of these two forces – often portrayed as complementary opposites. The *Zuozhuan* provides us with many examples of the aristocrat who was skilled in both the art of war and the literary and philosophical arts. For example, the archetypal Confucian good ruler, Duke Zhou (Zhou Gong), was a skilled warrior as well as a skilled practitioner in the civilian arts. Confucius, the *wen* god renowned for his philosophical and literary skills, was also a proponent of archery and charioteering and encouraged the development of these *wu* arts in his students' education.[73] As early as the Han Dynasty, Sima Qian had already spoken of the custom of having the *wen* officials lined up on the east side of the imperial court and the *wu* officials arrayed on the west side.[74] The Emperor, of course, sits in between and above the two groups. This custom survived into the twentieth century.

The numerous four-character expressions and idioms that have a sustained popularity throughout Chinese history attest to this mutual reinforcement and difference within unity. For example, it is stated in the

'Jie lao' section of the *Han Feizi* that: 'The country must have *wen* and *wu*, the officials ruling must have rewards and punishments.'[75] Similarly, the *Shiji* has the phrase: '*Wen-wu* used in concert is a long term strategy.'[76] These sorts of early phrases were followed by a host of sayings such as '*Wen* and *wu* are complete in every respect' (*wen wu shuang quan*), '*Wen* and *wu* are all encompassing' (*wen wu liang quan*), '*Wen* and *wu* are the all encompassing talents' (*wen wu quan cai*), '*Wen* and *wu* combine everything' (*wen wu jianquan*), 'The completeness of *wen* and *wu*' (*wen wu jianbei*) and 'Employ *wen* and *wu* in concert' (*wen wu bing yong*): all refer to the importance of having both *wen* and *wu* to achieve successful government of nation, family and self.

The Tang scholar Lu Chun, cited in McMullen's work on the cult of the Tang war god Qi Taigong, demonstrates the ideal of a balance between *wen* and *wu*. Lu Chun argues that this balance was achieved during the Spring and Autumn period but was lost during the Warring States period when the military became increasingly exclusive and professional, distancing itself from the civil bureaucracy. The situation in the Spring and Autumn period is described as: 'The officers of the armies were the same as the ministers; those who held the great levers [of administration] were the supreme commanders [of the armies].'[77] Lu Chun's ideal vision of an official during the Tang then was of a man who 'goes out a General and returns as a scholar' (*Chu jiang ru xiang*).[78]

During the Qing dynasty, the Manchu rulers' need to display competency in both *wen* and *wu* is evident in Jonathan Spence's account of the Kangxi Emperor. To win approval from the Han elite, Kangxi was concerned to present himself as capable in both *wen* and *wu* skills and respectful of the needs of both the military and the cultural sections of the elite.

> The Kang-hsi Emperor thus inaugurated the first of those great literary projects for which the Ch'ing dynasty is justly famous; this was a measure of his feelings of confidence and stability: having been '*wu*', the military conqueror of Wu San-kuei and Galdan, he would now also assure his reputation as '*wen*', the literary Emperor, proving his appreciation of the Chinese poetic tradition despite his non-Chinese ancestry.[79]

Thus, while not all men would necessarily be able to incorporate high levels of skill in both *wen* and *wu* attributes, the truly great men would. The need to Sinicise themselves in terms of *wen-wu* is also evident in Qianlong, as Angela Zito brilliantly demonstrates in her analysis of a series of Qianlong portraits.[80] Ideal masculinity can be either *wen* or *wu* but is at its height when both are present to a high degree.

Moreover, the display of the balance between *wen* and *wu* was an important signifier of moral and cultural attainment and thereby served to legitimate one's rule. Public executions, parading of prisoners and shows of military strength served to justify and ensure the continued right to rule, but this display of *wu* in itself was not enough. Emperors also legitimised their reigns by invoking respect for their cultural achievements (their *wen* attributes), premised upon narratives of China as a culturally superior and advanced nation. In this context *wen* and *wu* became major tools for displaying and maintaining imperial power.

Thus we see the display of *wen* power in steles, scrolls and banners of the calligraphy of society's leaders, particularly the Emperor. In contemporary China, Mao Zedong's calligraphy is featured prominently as the symbolic expression of his control of the (masculine) *wen* power.[81] It is still common to hear people say that women's calligraphy never truly captures the real essence of the art. Women are regarded as lacking the ability to exude the inner strength required to produce powerful character forms. The famous calligraphers of traditional and contemporary China and Taiwan are all men. Calligraphy, because it is part of the display of *wen* power and closely linked to masculinity, lies beyond the grasp of non-men. Male leaders of every persuasion and historical period therefore try to demonstrate both *wen* and *wu* prowess. That is, all ambitious males strive for both *wen* and *wu*, and those who achieve both are the great ones. Lesser men may achieve only one or the other, but even this partial success will bestow upon them the aura of masculinity and the right to rule over a certain domain, however small. Mao Zedong, in his poem 'The Snow', claims that none of the founding emperors of China's great dynasties, such as the Han and Tang, were truly great because, although they each conquered China with their military might, they lacked the 'literary achievement' and 'artistic grace' so important in a leader among leaders.[82]

Wen's Primacy over *wu*

While the ideal masculine image achieves a harmony between *wen* and *wu*, this is not to say that the relationship between *wen* and *wu* is, or always was, one of equality. Indeed the relationship between the two forces has been one of dynamic opposition as well as harmony. An extract from the *Analects* shows that right from the beginning of Chinese philosophical thought, *wen* was considered superior to *wu*, despite each having its place in the ordered Confucian state. In his discussions of music and virtue Confucius clearly shows his preference for the non-*wu* path. As D.C. Lau has stated, the connection between music and poetry (*wen*) was intimate because although not all music would have words, all poetry could be sung. Lau argues that this connection makes Confucius' statements on music equivalent to his statements on *wenxue* as a whole.

'Confucius required of music, and, by implication, of literature, not only perfect beauty but perfect goodness as well.'[83]

The Confucian preference for *wen* over *wu* is then revealed by the phrase: 'The master said of the *shao* that it was both perfectly beautiful and perfectly good, and the *wu* that it was perfectly beautiful but not perfectly good'.[84] *Shao* is the name of the music of Sun who ascended the throne after the abdication of Yao and was chosen for his virtue. On the other hand, the King of Wu ascended the throne through brute military force and his music was known as *wu* or military. Thus *wu* is inferior to *wen* as representing the need to resort to force to achieve one's goals. Similarly, an extract from the Confucian classic *Spring and Autumn Annals* says: 'The virtues of *wen* are superior, the greatness of *wu* is lower, and this has always and will always be the case.'

That the Confucians prioritise *wen* above *wu* is only to be expected, since Confucius is the god of *wen*. In chapter 3, we will look further at the significance of Confucius. Here, it is important to note that the Chinese word '*ru*', originally denoting a Confucian scholar, can now refer to any scholar. Because of this, in the written text at least, *wen* has in most cases taken primacy over *wu*. While the relationship between the two masculine ways can be fraught with tension, by the later part of the Tang Dynasty civil ministers were sneering at the illiteracy and brute strength of the military ministers.[85] The supremacy of the *wen* during this period is also revealed by McMullen's discussion of canonisation titles. The *wen-wu* dichotomy was reflected in the titles of canonisation which appeared in both single and double character designations. 'In this context they were mutually exclusive. Even though, in other contexts, it was a T'ang ideal that an individual civil or general service official should combine *wen* and *wu* …'[86] The separation of the canonisation designations made manifest a hierarchy which granted 'supreme prestige' to those ministers who were granted the *wen* character designations. Those granted the *wu* designations were recognised as different and inferior.[87]

This hierarchy of talents meant that *wu* became associated with non-elite masculinity at various points in China's past, while *wen* was often a more elite masculine form. This was not always the case as McMullen has pointed out. In the Spring and Autumn period, warfare was the preserve of the Zhou nobility.[88] This may account for the unity between *wen* and *wu* in the one official, whose scarcity has been lamented by scholars since – from Lu Chun to Huang Kuanzhong. Huang mentions that in the Eastern Jin soldiers were of the same class as slaves and in the Song the phrase 'A good piece of metal does not become nails and a good man does not become a soldier' (*Hao tie bu da ding, hao nan bu dang bing*) was prevalent.[89] *Wu* was then related more to the non-elite men who had less social power while *wen* is more clearly the masculinity of the elite. But both are theoretically equally achievable and ordinary men can aspire to *wen* attributes just as elite men could aspire to *wu* ones, as the Manchu rulers did in the Qing.

The differences between *wen* and *wu* males are also apparent when one considers the relationship each has with women. While romances of scholars and beauties are common themes, indicating a closeness of *wen* to women, the *wu* hero shows his strength and masculinity by resisting the lure of feminine charm. In contrast to Western 'real men' who always get the girl, the *wu* hero must contain his sexual and romantic desires. This important difference will be further explicated in the next chapter on the *wu* god Guan Yu. In chapter 5, I use the example of Wu Song to show that the readers of *All Men Are Brothers* and *Jin Ping Mei* (*The Golden Lotus*) recognise Wu Song to be a 'real man' when he is desired by the amorous Golden Lotus.[90] Furthermore, Wu Song becomes a *real* 'real man,' when he rejects her advances. Containment of sexual and romantic desire is an integral part of the *wu* virtue. By contrast to the *wu* male's necessary rejection of women, the *wen* male usually more than fulfils his sexual obligations to women.

Participation or success in the imperial examinations was a respected part of the masculine image and signified a desirability and sexual power that has led to countless 'scholar-beauty' (*caizi jiaren*) romance tales. The requirement that candidates travel to imperial examination centres gave rise to opportunities for chance meetings with women, as in the case of Scholar Zhang and Cui Yingying.[91] The archetypal *caizi*, the trainee *wenren* Scholar Zhang, is discussed in chapter 4. The 'talented scholar' won the girls in Imperial China and moreover, like the macho male of the contemporary Westerns, had the power to relinquish them if it became inconvenient without threatening to damage his future desirability. However, unlike the *wu* hero whose total rejection of women reflects moral strength, the scholar who wins the woman must follow through his obligations if he is to be a successful *wenren*. The abuse of this power, by careless abandonment of wives and lovers, elicits disapproval and possible punishment for the *wen* hero. The archetypal bad husband Chen Shimei, who is executed for abandoning his wife and children after gaining first place in the imperial examination, provides a good illustration of this principle.[92]

The split between *wen* and *wu* continues today. In the People's Republic of China the *wu* ideal has achieved increased prominence through the Communist leadership's bid to promote the peasant or working-class 'hero' and more recently by images of masculinity from the West. Both these trends have seen the strengthening of the *wu* type of masculinity in movies, novels and plays.[93] Li Cunbao's novel, later made into a movie, *Gaoshan xia de huahuan* (*The Wreath at the Foot of the*

Mountain), represents an early 1980s projection of the camaraderie, loyalty and self-sacrifice of the military.[94] The 1986 film *Hong Gaoliang* (*Red Sorghum*) reveals the influence of traditional *haohan* images and contemporary Western 'macho man' on Chinese culture. The central male figure is rude, brutal, murderous, and uncouth, but also strong and decisive and invincible – surviving a daring attack on the Japanese. Similarly, the tales of the 'root seekers', such as those by Jia Pingwa, whose writing we will examine more closely in chapter 5, have aptly been described as 'Chinese Westerns'.[95] Many of these tales are conspicuous for their descriptions of tough, frontiersmen who deal out the same tough treatment to nature as they do to women, in a manner akin to the American pioneers of the 'wild west'.[96]

Men in stories such as those noted above are considered *wu* even though many are not soldiers. *Wu* is therefore not entirely a military activity, in the same way that *wen* is not just a scholarly attribute. Wu Song for example is more an outlaw than a soldier. More recently, the manifestations of *wu* can be seen in the Chinese diaspora through kung fu films such as those featuring Jet Li and and Jackie Chan. These and other popular actors like Bruce Lee routinely portray working-class heroes whose daring exploits are carried out not only in China and Hong Kong, but in the West. The influences of *wen-wu* on the world stage are subtle but unmistakable, and I will return to this phenomenon in the last chapter. Despite the increasing credibility of *wu*, it is still possible to see that the power of the softer, more refined intellectual masculine form lives on in the daily expression of self by Chinese men. For example, in contemporary Taiwan, the continuing strength of *wen* values is evidenced by the listing of political candidates' highest educational attainment in briefings for televised electoral coverage. The high number with doctoral qualifications contrasts sharply with contemporary Western candidates who, if in the rare instance that they hold a doctorate, would emphasise their 'sporting' mass appeal or military service rather than their elite education. Education in its *wen* sense is a feature with popular appeal to a Chinese electorate for it symbolises the 'right to power', whereas it can be a liability to candidates in many Western countries such as Australia.

Generally speaking, the dynamic tension between the poles of *wen* and *wu* permits the production of a varied number of possible expressions of male self. The dichotomy *wen-wu* has a sufficiently ancient and sufficiently recent enough history to provide us with a base for the development of theories of Chinese masculinity, both in relation to Western masculinity and Chinese femininity. The unproblematised incorporation of Western models of male sexuality previously applied generates the inadequate conclusion that Chinese men are less than 'real men' (see the discussion of this phenomenon in chapters 7 and 8). Similarly the adoption of the *yin-yang* model of Chinese sexual difference imposes a fluidity of 'essence' that cannot elucidate the specificity of masculinity with a sufficient degree of depth. The *wen-wu* dichotomy overcomes both of these theoretical quandaries. Finally, the additional problem of incorporating class differentials into gender analyses is addressed within the *wen-wu* matrix. Inequality between the social power of men of different classes can be explained through the *wen-wu* dichotomy without resorting to the reductionist tendency which connects masculinity directly with elite social power.[97]

Having put forward the rationale and justifications for adopting an indigenous theoretical construct to analyse Chinese masculinity, the more interesting questions of significance and impact will need to be answered. To do this, I propose to examine in some detail the *wen-wu* icons Confucius and Guan Yu, drawing out the sexual and political significance of how their masculinities are constructed. While the Chinese dyad *wen-wu* forms the basis of our analytic framework, a repetition of traditional Chinese theories and clichés about Chinese sexualities clearly will not take us beyond a recounting of existing gender and class ideologies which have served to perpetuate the world's most resilient culture for hundreds of years. Therefore, the following analysis uses Western methodologies such as semiotics and psychoanalytic theory as well as Chinese methodologies. Because I will be looking at representations of masculinity, most of the sources are literary texts that have produced iconic and paradigmatic male figures. Although the commentaries examined are mostly in the Chinese language, the texts themselves are such important works that translations are usually readily available. Some, such as *The Romance of the Three Kingdoms* examined in the next chapter, are classics that have been translated numerous times already.

2   Portrait of the God of War Guan Yu: Sex, Politics and *wu* Masculinity

Illustration from an 1890 edition of *Sanguo yanyi*, showing Guan Yu reading a Confucian classic. Note the bundle of books on the floor and the great sword carried by his lieutenant – symbols of *wen* and *wu* – in the foreground.

In the last chapter, I indicated that *wu* characteristics are easier for the Western reader to identify as masculine traits because they are manifested in behaviour such as bravery, mateship and physical strength. The Chinese model most closely associated with the *wu* man is the *yingxiong* (hero). This chapter examines the composition of the Chinese hero and projects it onto the sexual-political plane, in order to unravel the sexual and political tensions of *wu* masculinity that have traditionally been stitched over by a moral exterior. It is necessary to make explicit the sexual and political dimensions of *wu* masculinity because the Chinese warrior-fighter is often depicted as having no romantic feelings whatsoever. He is supposed to be motivated solely by worthy causes, and not by his own individual passions.

Existing scholarship on the Chinese hero reflects these asexual characteristics – some writers link the hero with Chinese concepts of chivalry,[1] and others discuss the hero as 'revolutionary' and 'mass-based'.[2] None point to the importance of the politics of sexuality in understanding the dynamics of the *wu* 'hero'. Traditionally, both Chinese and Western scholarship have casually dismissed the Chinese hero's sexuality. It was asserted that, in contrast to Western chivalric romances, where love is often the most important inspiration for heroic deeds, love (and by implication sex) in traditional Chinese chivalric tales 'plays no such important part'.[3] This sort of interpretation simultaneously emerges from and reinforces the mentality outlined in the previous chapter in which Chinese men are said to be less sexy than white or black men.

The apparent desexualisation of the Chinese hero continued into the present, though through the careful selection and processing of images, producers of both Western and Chinese popular icons have succeeded in constructing seemingly asexual images such as Grasshopper in the television series *Kung Fu* and the enduring Lei Feng of the People's Liberation Army. The failure of critics to identify the erotic when describing these purportedly asexual images has meant they have contributed to this process of neglecting a vital dimension of the formation of Chinese masculinity.[4] Ironically, those who disclaim the Chinese hero's sexuality have only heightened sensitivity to sex. In the last few years, Sinologists, partly inspired by Western feminist criticism, have begun to explore issues of men and sex in both traditional and contemporary Chinese literature.[5] Other scholars such as Keith McMahon have examined the issue of male sexuality in Ming-Qing texts which had until his publications been marginalised or ignored.[6]

In this chapter, I will add to this re-evaluation of Chinese expressions of masculinity by analysing the *wu* god (often translated in English as the God of War) Guan Yu in sexual and political terms. Guan Yu is of paramount importance for the *wen-wu* construction of masculinity because 'in China Confucius is worshipped as the greatest man of scholarly learning, and Guan Yu as the greatest man of military prowess'.[7] Guan Yu's image is ubiquitous inside China as in the various diasporic communities, easily recognised by his trademark red face and fierce expression, but his significance is much harder to see and describe. In his day, Guan Yu (160–221AD) was only one of many military leaders at the end of the long and prosperous Han Dynasty (206BC–220AD) and the beginning of the chaotic 'Three Kingdoms' (Sanguo) period (220–280AD). He was probably illiterate and made no attempt to save 'China' or serve any emperor against any foreign enemy. Yet over the next 1,600 years his status rose steadily, such that by the Ming Dynasty he achieved the status of an imperial god (*Guan sheng dadi*). It is difficult to find any parallel figure in Western narratives of power and rulership. He is perhaps a combination of St George and St Peter, Robin Hood and Daniel Boone, El Cid and Ned Kelly, John Wayne and Arnold Schwarzenegger, but the analogies are far from exact, and the combination though unique is never stable. However, one feature in his personality is constant – his immovable self-control. In modern terms, he would be an epitome of 'cool'.

This chapter will restore passion and desire in this immortal Chinese hero, who has hitherto been seen as driven solely by either lofty ideals such as loyalty or alternatively by animal savagery. The failure to recognise the sexuality inherent in *wu* lies partly in the dominance of a reading that regarded sexuality as being fundamentally hetero-erotic. This assumption implicitly regarded displays of affection between men as non-erotic. However, our perception of the *wu* hero changes dramatically if we read the texts from a perspective where bisexuality is taken as the norm and where homo-eroticism is privileged over the hetero,[8] as was the case in Tokugawa Japan and ancient Greece.[9]

There is no doubt that homosexuality has featured quite dramatically in various creative arts, including literature, over the entire period of Chinese history.[10] While homosexual behaviour is not always easy to define,[11] it is nevertheless often associated with physical contact by the people involved. Other, less visible, relationships may involve more profound emotions and feelings, but are often overlooked in discussions of male intimacy. For example, closeness and attraction between men can stem from social relationships such as patronage, fraternity, camaraderie and even rivalry. These relationships generate feelings of possessiveness, jealousy and desire (even if subconscious) between the heroes and oftentimes these are more intense emotions than those that are generated through just sex alone. In order to avoid the difficulties of defining the exact constitution of 'homosexuality' and in order to encompass the 'unbrokenness of a continuum between homosocial and homosexual',

I will employ Eve Kosofsky Sedgwick's concept 'homosocial desire'.[12] This concept also suggests ways that Chinese studies can contribute to the field of gender studies by providing further evidence of its effectiveness outside a Western context.

Sedgwick's model is particularly illuminating here because it provides 'a strategy for making generalisations about, and making historical differences in, the *structure* of men's relations with other men'.[13] This strategy enables us to juxtapose the two sets of materials relating to Guan Yu while at the same time acknowledging their differences. In this respect, what *counts* as sexuality will depend very much on the genre or historical period, and there is no question that the literati novel tends to elide sexuality generally while the cycle of popular tales is more explicit in descriptions of erotic and emotive behaviour. However, the structure of the homosocial continuums remains a constant, albeit a constant which is culturally contingent.

As stated earlier, Guan Yu is a perfect model to illustrate the *wen-wu* masculinity principle because he is placed alongside Confucius in temples as the *wu* god with Confucius (who is studied in the next chapter) as the *wen* god. By denying any sexual/romantic desire in the *wu* hero, writers (who by default are *wen* men) have successfully projected an image of men with more physical prowess (and generally also from the lower classes) as having no compassion or other human feelings. Nevertheless, Guan Yu's image is ambiguous enough to be read in multiple and unintended ways by those not so enamoured by refined sensitivities. Thus, Guan Yu is worshipped mostly by the masses whereas Confucius is more highly regarded by the elite. While the literary manifestation of Guan Yu is best known in the classic novel *Three Kingdoms*,[14] the Guan Yu mythology is an amalgam of his more memorable performances from both the novel and a whole cycle of stories and legends of the Sanguo period.[15]

Portrait of a Sexualised Warrior

Scholars such as Van Gulik have already pointed out that descriptions of coitus in traditional Chinese classics on sex are often couched in terms of military battles.[16] The converse is also true: military and political manoeuvres can be read sexually. Such a figurative reading can be applied to the entire novel. For example, the warriors speak of having 'lost their bodies' (*shishen*) when forced to serve bandits militarily just as do women who describe their unwilling loss of virginity or chastity. Another common expression, 'rather die than be humiliated' (*ning si bu ru*), can be read both politically and sexually. While such readings remain highly metaphorical, *Three Kingdoms* is ultimately a narrative on political and military warfare at whichever level it is read, and the most valued commodities in such a realm are the displays of manly prowess. Therefore, with or without a sexualised reading, *Three Kingdoms* provides a good case study for performances of masculinity. The novel has a cast including hundreds of heroes, but Guan Yu emerges paramount as the archetypal 'real hero', the god of *wu*.[17]

As the epitome of the *yingxiong*, Guan Yu is described as having only 'bright and clear' feelings and as being 'unmoved by beautiful women or treasures'.[18] Despite this subtextual taboo, all commentators have neglected a 'sexual' reading of his persona. Restoring his sexual identity refutes the orthodox image of the 'asexual he-man' in Chinese elite culture. Another reason for focusing on Guan Yu is that while he is unique, he is also the best model for purposes of generalisation to broader cultural norms. He is the most glorified and worshipped of all characters in Chinese history and literature.[19] Over the seventeen centuries since his death, he has been honoured by rulers of successive dynasties with official titles such as lord, king and god.[20]

This canonisation as the essential embodiment of *wu* both perpetuated and reflected his accumulating popularity among ordinary people. Thousands of temples have been erected in his honour. Today, he is one of the most popular gods both in China and abroad. As well as the many temples, little shrines in his honour can be found in Chinese restaurants from outback Australia to metropolitan New York. His popularity reaches all social groups, including anti-establishment organisations – for example, the Triads take him as their patron saint. In other mass-appeal media,[21] including operas, comic books and story-telling, the adventures of Guan Yu and his fellow-heroes from *Three Kingdoms* still provide endless entertainment for old and young alike.[22] The Guan Yu image is an integral part of Chinese culture and the Chinese conception of masculinity. However, in contrast to the numerous posthumous titles and temples bestowed on Guan Yu, there is no single study devoted to examining the implications his image has for the construction of male sexuality and power.

This scholarly silence is not a consequence of the original construction of Guan Yu by those who created the image. For example, masculinity and power are highlighted in the novel itself, in the famous dialogue between the prime minister Cao Cao and Guan Yu's sworn brother and lord Liu Bei, in which they discuss the characteristics of a hero (*yingxiong*). Cao Cao describes the *yingxiong* as having huge ambition – no less than aiming to rule the world. More significantly, Cao Cao also gives an oblique illustration of the true nature of a hero: like a dragon, he is able to be at ease in the universe and to shrink and extend at will. This characteristic is neither new nor startling, Cao Cao merely repeats a phrase that was a cliché even for his time.[23] However, it is the symbolic significance of the qualities repeated here which are of interest. Dragons not only refer to power and control, but more importantly, by the description of its expandable penile quality, they also invoke a specifically male potentiality.[24] The author of the novel, through Cao Cao, thus proposes a concept of the *yingxiong* as a combination of specifically phallic masculinity with power – particularly the power to rule. The fact that this definition is enunciated by Cao Cao is significant because he of all the characters in the novel exploits and enjoys power most overtly.

Cao Cao in this passage concludes that he and Liu Bei are the only true *yingxiong* of that time, yet this judgement is pronounced by an unreliable source. Moreover, although Cao Cao was historically the most powerful person in the Three Kingdoms era and probably the most able leader of men, in the minds of its Chinese readers, the novel's depiction of him as a villain (*jianxiong*), plus the numerous popular images of him as tyrant, disqualify him as a 'real hero'. Similarly, although Liu Bei is cast as the true king in the novel, he too has been referred to as a villain (*xiaoxiong*), and many critics have seen him as an insincere politician not worthy of emulation. In *wen-wu* terms, neither man is supposed to excel in *wu*. By contrast, one of the most enduring myths about Guan Yu the *wu* icon is that he is incapable of treachery and villainy and he is the only person whom Cao Cao holds in the highest regard throughout the novel. However, while Cao Cao and Liu Bei are sexually active, the sexual significance of Guan Yu's apparently chaste and upright behaviour remains hidden and needs to be teased out.

An examination of Guan Yu's physical appearance is instructive. The popular depiction of him as a well-built general with a long beard and a red face is in keeping with the brief description of his appearance when he is first mentioned in the novel: 'he was nine feet tall, with a two-foot beard and a deep red face'. The first item mentioned is his extraordinary height. All the heroes in *Three Kingdoms* tower above the common soldiers. Size as a measure of power and manliness seems to be universal and needs little elaboration.[25]

The next characteristic is his two-foot-long beard. Facial and other bodily hair is equally a universal standard for manhood. In *Three Kingdoms* itself, Guan Yu's beard is honoured by Cao Cao who bestows on him the title 'lord with the beautiful beard' (*meiran gong*) and presents him with a pouch to cover it. We are thereby informed that the beard is out of the ordinary, but its links to masculinity are not made clear.[26] However, hair (in this case the imposing beard) is linked in the popular imagination much more closely to masculinity. According to folklore, Guan Yu's beard is the metamorphosis of a little dragon.[27] The dragon motif appears repeatedly in description of Guan Yu's physical appearance.

The third feature in his appearance – the red face – is not only characteristic to Guan Yu but to masculine heroes in general (for example, in Chinese opera masks). The novel itself only mentions it in passing, but in popular folklore, it is the centre of many myths and legends. One legend tells of Guan Yu saving a woman from rape by killing the assailant. Guan Yu then washes his face to disguise himself, using sacred water provided by the Heavenly Queen Mother. The process of washing in this sacred water gives Guan Yu's face the red colour for which it has become famous. In *yin-yang* terms, water is extremely *yin* (female), while red is the most *yang* (male) colour – thus the ultimate *yin* spirit is transformed into an amplified *yang* essence by the supreme goddess' intervention.[28]

Guan Yu's red face immediately signifies a strong *yang* (male) essence. It is, in this case, the most conspicuous symbol of his masculinity, so much so that the red face has become the symbol of the God of War. However, this indicator of masculinity is a consequence of a virtuous act of one man killing another for molesting a woman. The sexual overtones are carried through with baptism by sacred water (the essential female fluid) of the supreme goddess. The tale is infused with sex and sexuality that are entirely omitted in the *Three Kingdoms* version.

The Woman as Foil

The association of male power with sexuality is found not only in Guan Yu's physical attributes. The sword he wields, which is known by his name (*Guan dao*), is also described as the 'green dragon sword' (*qinglong dao*). Weapons such as swords are universally used as indicators of penile potency,[29] and the sword in this case has reiterated and emphasised the connection by invoking the dragon motif. There is no historical evidence that Guan Yu had ever wielded a big sword: as with his red face, it is a creation of later story-tellers that has achieved permanence.[30] The sword symbolises a narcissistic power which only becomes manifest in the context of a woman in the role of a foil – the body upon which male potency writes itself.

The sexual significance of the sword is clearer only at the popular level by story-tellers in their recreation of the fate of Diao Chan, the most alluring of all women in the Three Kingdoms cycle. In popular imagination, Diao Chan's tale is the epitome of the homily 'heroes find beautiful women the most difficult hurdle to overcome' (*yingxiong nanguo meiren guan*). However, Guan Yu overcomes her. In one Yuan Dynasty play, Diao Chan is presented to Guan Yu by his younger 'brother' Zhang Fei after her husband Lü Bu dies, but instead of accepting her as the spoils of war, Guan Yu kills her with his sword.[31] Again, the decapitation of Diao Chan does not appear either in the historical records or in the novel itself, but is propagated through mass media such as operas and story-telling.[32] The association of ultra-masculine symbols (red face, beard and sword) with sexual antagonism towards women has found the most direct expression in popular forms. The historical records and the novel, both mainly read by the Confucian literati, have chosen to reproduce an oblique and subtle representation of the evils which occur when the masculine is overcome by the feminine.

In the novel itself, Guan Yu has no contact with Diao Chan although she appears very early, before Guan Yu and his two brothers have established themselves as major characters. She is, however, the source of strife between the tyrant Dong Zhuo and his adopted son in a manner which is in keeping with traditional admonitions regarding the dangers posed by beautiful women. She is presented as a gift to Dong Zhuo by his enemies in order to create jealousy between Dong and Lü. Her charm and cunning finally provoke the desired result and Lü Bu kills his adopted father Dong Zhuo. Lü Bu and Dong Zhuo are at the beginning of the novel a most formidable pair: even in terms of size, Dong Zhuo is portrayed as so bulky that he can hardly walk while Lü Bu is a huge man even among the big heroes. As a tyrant who has complete power over the court and the feudal lords, Dong Zhuo is the most powerful politician who is feared and hated by those under him. His adopted son, Lü Bu, whose manly prowess is demonstrated by his ability to simultaneously engage in combat the three brothers Liu, Guan and Zhang, is without doubt the best fighter in the novel.

Although Lü and Dong possess more power and valour than anyone else in the Three Kingdoms cycle, they are never regarded as true heroes. Both men are perceived as having little moral fibre, which is signified by their succumbing to women. This is illustrated in the final siege that ultimately costs Lü Bu his life. His mistake is described as being that 'he listens to the words of his consorts and not to the plans devised by his generals'.[33] In the popular tradition, the fear that women (and children) may pose as threats to male homosocial bonds is told in much more brutal fashion. For example, in the opening of the *cihua* story about Liu Bei's adopted son Hua Guansuo, Guan Yu proposes that he and Zhang Fei slaughter their wives and children to ensure their loyalty to Liu Bei.[34]

Thus, although manifestations of power such as physical size, martial skills and sheer brutality are indicators of *wu* masculinity, in themselves they are not sufficient to make the 'real' *yingxiong*. Another necessary condition must be the ability to withstand feminine charms. C.T. Hsia's observations about the *All Men Are Brothers*[35] heroes are equally applicable to Guan Yu: 'Precisely because of their sexual puritanism, these heroes harbour a subconscious hatred of women as their worst enemy, as a teasing reminder of the unnaturalness of their heroic self-sufficiency'.[36] The 'dark side' of this ability to resist women is one where the source of the attraction, the woman, is eliminated altogether in unrestrained misogyny. As is shown in *All Men Are Brothers*, the hatred of women often degenerates into bloodthirsty displays. In *Three Kingdoms* itself, the heroes' misogyny is not as explicit. However, the popular treatment of the relationship between Guan Yu and Diao Chan, in which Guan Yu kills the heroine for the simple reason that he does not want to be tempted, is a classic illustration of such a misogynist phenomenon. This quality whereby violence is necessarily enacted on beautiful women most vividly differentiates the *wu* hero from the knights and heroes of Europe.

Where *yin* and *yang* are perceived as being in constant mutual interaction, with one ascending and the other declining, sadistic violence against women serves as a potent sign of masculine prowess. However, in the novel itself this is not made explicit. It is the popular forms of the tale that reveal a significance deeper than a mere sexual tug of war. Descriptions of sexual violence attributed to the lower classes seem to be particularly acute and vivid even in contemporary fiction, a point which we will discuss further in chapter 5. One explanation could be that the display of power by brute force is the easiest option open to people without other kinds of power. In this way, class and gender converge. Thus, in the novel itself, sadistic acts are committed by women – people who have no direct political power.[37] In the same way, men who perform the most sadistic acts, such as the *wu* heroes Yang Xiong and Wu Song in *All Men Are Brothers*, are also those from the lower classes.[38]

It could of course be argued that the extreme action of eliminating the woman as the target of desire only acknowledges the degree to which sexual desire dominates the action and the actor. In the Confucian literati version, that is the novel, control of this desire is expressed in a more oblique manner. Guan Yu has no dealings with Diao Chan, lest refinement in the hero be soiled by association with a courtesan. Such women can be treated as merchandise. They do not form obvious links between men except as commodities. However, women who are wives or sisters of men of equal status are connections between men which can transcend commercial relationships.

Desire for Women and the Incest Taboo

The novel's most famous depiction of relationships between men and women of the same social status is in the episode where Guan Yu guards his sisters-in-law while they are under house arrest in Cao Cao's camp. Here, Guan Yu is supposed to have guided his sisters-in-law in their search for the women's husband, Liu Bei. His observance of propriety is such that he never enters their living quarters, and keeps vigil outside their door every night, reading a book by candlelight. Statues of Guan Yu, the god, now show him holding either his sword or a book, so that he has not only been elevated since his death to a god, but has also incorporated scholarly attributes. As we will see in the next chapter, Confucius the *wen* god and icon is often said to have both *wen* and *wu* qualities. Similarly, Guan Yu as a *wu* god to be worshipped is often given *wen* attributes. It is significant that his scholarship (and it is Confucian scholarship that is referred to here)[39] has been included in the episode narrating his chivalric treatment of women of his own social status.

This episode is often cited to illustrate Guan Yu's proper behaviour towards such women. Throughout the ordeal of searching for Liu Bei, which includes what for Guan Yu is the disgrace of being Cao Cao's 'guest', Guan Yu's foremost concern is that the women should not suffer any indignity. He himself keeps the proper distance expected for relations between a man and his sisters-in-law. If this were the end of the story, the hypothesis that the most venerated he-man in Chinese culture is indeed a 'cool character' who has complete control over his desires would be sustainable. However, a later episode in the novel holds clues to an alternative interpretation that reflects a highly sexualised masculinity.

In this episode, Guan Yu's obsession with his sisters-in-law is shown obliquely in terms of political power. Not long before his tragic death in Jingzhou, Guan Yu dreams that he is bitten in the leg by a black bull-sized boar and wakes up in fright. As Moss Roberts points out,[40] this incident in the dream alludes to a story in the classic *Zuozhuan*, in which Wuzhi murders his first cousin, the Duke of Qi, with the help of Qi's wife. With the deed accomplished, Wuzhi plans to assume the duke's title as well as marry his widow. As cousins are considered brothers, it was a case of fratricide.[41] The dream thus symbolises Guan Yu's subconscious desire for Liu Bei's kingdom and his women and it points to fraternal betrayal through adultery with a sister-in-law. This revelation throws a completely different light on his ostentatious loyalty to his brother and propriety towards his sisters-in-law.

Throughout the ages, critics have insisted that Guan Yu's loyalty to his brother Liu Bei as expressed in his treatment of his sisters-in-law should be emulated as a model of rectitude.[42] However, the dream points to a more sexualised reading. Guan Yu himself is obviously very upset after his dream. His whole identity, both in the novel and in the many myths and legends about him, depends upon the maintenance of a heroic image, one that is untouched by ordinary feelings, from the pain of having poison dug out of his bones without anaesthetics to the desire for beautiful women such as Diao Chan. The dream brilliantly questions the ability of this military hero to control his fears and desires. The accepted reading is that it indicates Guan Yu's secret ambition to usurp his brother's political power. However, if the political and sexual are read as coordinates leading to the same portrait of a hero, then an additional reading is also possible.

In the context of the novel, the intimation of incestuous desires in Guan Yu, even in a disguised form, has to wait until his ego has become so large that it is overpoweringly self-destructive. As some critics have pointed out, Guan Yu was by the time of his impending capture and death extremely arrogant and proud. Earlier on, he may have been prepared to deliver his sisters-in-law to his sworn brother with their chastity intact. But by the time of the dream, he had himself gathered political might. As governor of the pivotal province of Jingzhou, he had designs of even greater power and grandeur. The dream sequence can certainly be read as a lesson in the immorality of wanting, even in a dream, to usurp power from one's older brother and king.[43] It is equally revealing when read as the hidden agony of a man who spends his life repressing his desires, whether they be sexual or political.[44]

However, such a psychological reading does not invalidate the sustained veneration for Guan Yu felt by all classes of people over the centuries. As the epitome of the *wu* hero, Guan Yu's success in driving his desires for women and political power into his subconscious serves the same social function as having no such desire at all. It is easy to see why successive rulers have made him a god. Their subordinates' self-imposed suppression of the urge to usurp power would serve them well. In the Three Kingdoms story cycle, this urge is cleverly associated with incest, defined in this case loosely to include lust for one's sister-in-law, an act much frowned on throughout Chinese history. In stories about heroism and brotherhoods, where the brothers are not related by blood but by love and affection, taboos need to be extra strong to prevent disasters such as those which befell the tyrant Dong Zhuo and his son Lü Bu, whose father and son relationship is cemented by oath rather than by blood.

Love Between Brothers

If we take incest as a possible element in the relationship between Guan Yu and his sisters-in-law, then the excessive distance between himself and the women takes on added significance. In the Three Kingdoms mythology, the most eulogised bond is that between the brothers Liu Bei, Guan Yu and Zhang Fei. This brotherhood gives the story its popularity. If Guan Yu or any of the heroes show any emotions in the Three Kingdoms, it is their intense feelings for each other. Their public affection for each other is extremely emotional, sometimes with disastrous consequences.[45]

To most critics and redactors of the story, such emotions symbolise brotherhood in all its proper glory. It is supposed to be the epitome of *yi*. Or, as many have said, a more horizontal loyalty that is different to *zhong* – the loyalty between the ruler and subject. This brotherhood has been interpreted as sterile in sexual terms, because homosocial desire is not raised as an issue in the scholarly interpretations of the novel or the Three Kingdoms myth.[46]

Yet, more popular literary genres make explicit the sexual dimension of such 'brotherly love' in the Three Kingdoms heroes. For example, in the stories that the renowned Qing poet and scholar Yuan Mei collected, one in particular explicitly relates the homosexual relationship between the general Zhou Yu and his lord Sun Ce as self-evident.[47] Attachment between men has always been seen as the primary human bond in novels such as *Three Kingdoms* and *All Men Are Brothers*. But as 'the register of heroes', these novels shun any description of explicit homosexual or heterosexual behaviour. These less than 'manly' activities are only elaborated on in novels such as the *Jin Ping Mei* or in short stories such as those recorded by Yuan Mei.[48]

It would be foolish to assume from this that the 'man's world' lacked any kind of sexual or erotic feelings – an assumption apparently held by traditional and modern critics. It is more likely that homosocial desire in the literati novel genre such as *Three Kingdoms* is described in symbolic terms. For example, in the very first chapter, Liu, Guan and Zhang conduct the celebrated brotherhood ceremony. Their peach garden pledge has since been widely imitated.[49] It is, for example, re-enacted in the first chapter of the sexually explicit novel *Jin Ping Mei*. According to Eberhard, the peach, especially the peach blossom, has definite sexual connotations,[50] and it is worth noting that Zhang Fei in his invitation to Liu and Guan mentions that his peach garden was just blossoming.

Once homosocial desire is accepted as a primary value in the Three Kingdoms cycle, then the behaviour of the men in relation to *yi* becomes much more meaningful. For example, the expression 'sleeping together in the same bed and loving each other like brothers' (*Qin ze tongchuang, en ruo xiongdi*) is used very frequently to describe the love between the three brothers.[51] However, because sexual penetration is not explicitly specified, this expression is rarely read sexually. Moreover, it would seem that although the literati view does not permit homosexual relations to blossom among the brothers, the non-literati folklore, such as the stories collected by Yuan Mei, takes homosexuality between the heroes in the novel for granted. Brothers 'sharing the same bed' can thereby be read as signifying more than just fraternal closeness. In a number of places in the novel, Liu Bei and other heroes are said to 'share the same bed' (*tongta*).[52] While it has always been common for people in China to sleep in the same bed (most often with each person sleeping head to toe) and doing so does not automatically mean they are having sex, the term *tongta* has been used with sexual denotation for centuries. Furthermore, it is often used to indicate a sexual relationship that is highly hierarchical.[53] As early as the Song Dynasty, we have instances where the lord 'orders' a subordinate to 'share the same bed' with him.[54]

While explicit descriptions of homosexual relations do not occur in the novel itself, this conforms to its taciturnity regarding any kind of explicit sexual narrative, hetero or homo. We may deduce the emotional closeness achieved by the heroes when we compare the novel's characters' behaviour and ways of viewing each other before and after they 'share the same bed'. For example, Liu Bei seems to share his bed with many of his subordinates, especially with his young literati advisers. The descriptions of Liu Bei holding hands with his counsellor Xu Shu and the emotional farewell between them display an intensity of feeling between them that cannot be explained by Confucian etiquette:

> His tears fell like rain and Xu Shu also wept. But when the last goodbyes were said and Xu Shu had gone, Liu Bei stood gazing after the little party and watched it slowly disappear ... One of the trees shut out the travellers from his sight and he pointed at it saying 'I wish I could cut down every tree in this area'. When asked why he felt like this, he replied, 'Because they hinder my sight of Xu Shu'.[55]

The intensity of the relationships between the men in the novel are even more easily seen in the jealousies which result from sleeping together. It is well-known that after Liu Bei sleeps with Zhuge Liang, the most talented strategist in the Three Kingdoms, Guan Yu and Zhang Fei both sulk. For example, in the episode after Liu Bei first 'shares his bed' with Zhuge Liang, both Guan Yu and Zhang Fei are resentfully unco-operative, an attitude noted by Zhuge Liang himself.[56] They do not seem to like any of the men that share Liu Bei's bed. Moreover, the relationship that Liu Bei has with his subordinates who have slept with him seems always to be cemented and said to be as close as that between brothers. Very talented men such as Zhuge Liang, Xu Shu and Zhao Yun seem happy to serve under him after spending a night with him. The 'sharing of beds' is not restricted to Liu Bei and his men. In the novel itself, there are several devoted pairs of men: the Sun Ce–Zhou Yu and Sun Quan–Lu Su pairs are classic examples. It is worth noting here that at least one partner in the pairs is a *wen* man. The erasure of sexual desire in these texts seems more complete with the *wu* heroes.[57]

While the novel does not provide explicit descriptions of sexual contact when the men sleep together, neither does it give descriptions of sexual relations between the heroes and women. Yet, no reader would question the implied sexual relationship between Lü Bu and Diao Chan. The heterosexual orientation of most readers leads them to take sexual contact in these relationships for granted. In the end, the interpretation of these relationships depends very much on the writing and reading strategies one wants to adopt. It is significant that in the case of the Three Kingdoms heroes, there are plenty of signifiers to enable the strategies to translate from the sexual/erotic to the political/military plane.

The affection between men has, not surprisingly, been the inspiration for much creative work in traditional China. Throughout the ages, the romantic image of these men, handsome and 'talking and laughing', has haunted artists and poets alike.[58] However, the sexual undertones are inevitably even more subdued and refined in the more elevated genres such as poetry and essays. Notwithstanding differences between genres, one reading has been generally accepted: the naturalness and primacy of affection between men above all other human emotions. It is this understanding that gives meaning to the importance of overcoming the challenge posed by the intrusion of women.

Thus, the Three Kingdoms, like other stories which posit models for manly behaviour, makes it clear that love between men, whether it be erotic or otherwise, is the only noble emotion. Heterosexuality is at best a distraction. Furthermore, if it is taken too seriously, it is destructive to the ideal brotherhood of the *yingxiong* and must be eliminated. Relationships of loyalty, of either the *zhong* or *yi* kind, are only applicable between men. It is significant that it is only men who perform acts of *yi*, never women (unless, of course, it is an *yi* suicide similar to those carried out by servants and animals). The loftiness of *yi* implies that men who practise it observe its exclusive nature, whether it be a one-to-one or a group exclusivity. Furthermore, they also observe the decorum that is associated with *yi*. Therefore, no matter how attached they are to each other, it is important to appear to be completely self-controlled and exempt from the orgiastic indulgence of their polygynist alter egos.

Some Brothers are More Equal than Others

In the more orthodox and Confucian retelling of the Three Kingdoms, the sexual, particularly homo-erotic, workings of the monogamous hero's mind are again best illustrated in the person of Guan Yu. While Liu Bei does not seem to have any problems with sleeping with other men, there are no indications throughout the novel that Guan Yu shares his bed with other men.[59] His relationships with men are as intensely controlled as his relationships with women, and they are equally proper. This propriety and intensity make him the most suitable exemplar for a morality which elevates self-denial. Again, ancient Greece also provides such ostentatious shows of virtue:

> Thus Xenophon's Agesilaus not only 'kept at arm's length those whose intimacy he did not desire', but kept from embracing even the boy he did love; and he was careful to lodge only in temples or in a place where 'all men's eyes became witnesses to his rectitude'.[60]

As Foucault points out, such a display of abstinence 'was the visible mark of the mastery they brought to bear on themselves and hence of the power they were worthy of exercising over others'.[61]

However, in traditional Chinese literary criticism, Guan Yu's displays of righteousness in places and situations where 'all men's eyes became witnesses to his rectitude' have not been explained in terms of desire and power.[62] On the contrary, they are normally explained in terms of *yi*, a concept which is supposed to encase ideas of loyalty, faithfulness, friendship and honour. The idea of *yi* is so central to the novel that the title itself, *Sanguo yanyi*, can be translated as 'The *Sanguo* as an Explication of *Yi*'.[63]

As a central Confucian virtue, *yi* has attracted numerous explications, and the difficulty of arriving at a consensus of meaning is seen in the common division of the term into 'great *yi*' (*da yi*), 'little *yi*' (*xiao yi*), etc. Yet, many critics, especially contemporary ones, have continued to insist that the loyalty and obligations between men when they are bonded by *yi* were originally meant to be mutual. That is, the *yi* bond between sworn brothers in famous scenes such as the peach garden ceremony in *Three Kingdoms* and the brotherhood ceremony in *All Men Are Brothers* was an egalitarian one, where all brothers were meant to love and honour each other on an equal footing.

Many critics claim that this *yi* quickly deteriorates into a vertical loyalty where some men rule and others serve. The unequal *yi* bond is seen in expressions such as *yipu* (loyal servants) and *yima* (loyal horse).[64] This unequal bond is particularly evident in the case of Guan Yu. After he dies, his underlings either commit suicide or are killed and his horse refuses to eat and dies. It is often argued that the transformation of the notion of *yi* is most clearly seen in the more common expression *zhongyi*, where the *zhong* unambiguously denotes a vertical loyalty.[65] This hierarchical relationship can be read on a homosexual plane as well. While the *yi* between the three brothers Liu, Guan and Zhang is, as indicated above, exclusive and jealously guarded, the fact that the two younger brothers submit to Liu politically means they also play the submissive role homosexually. While Liu can establish *yi* bonds (often meaning sleeping together) with other talented men, Guan and Zhang must remain totally faithful to the dominant Liu. They have underlings who remain faithful to them, but if they establish any *yi* bonds with those on a political/sexual status equal to Liu, the whole notion of *yi* is called into question.

The unequal sexual relationship between men and women is mirrored here. Sleeping together, as in the case of women 'losing themselves' to men, means surrendering. It is a bond, but an extremely hierarchical bond, and by no means equalises the differences between men as it is supposed to do. And just as in cases of marriages designed to cement or balance powerful allies and enemies, the sexual and 'fraternal' relationships between the men in the novel are, more often than not, based on considerations of political power rather than on any emotions which are 'horizontal'. The righteousness which is supposed to be in *yi* is thus inherently linked with the right to wield power and alternatively the willingness to submit to another's power. By projecting himself as the embodiment of *yi*, Guan Yu is compelled to surrender himself to Liu Bei totally.

The clearest illustration of the repercussions of *yi* in terms of power and homosocial relations is the triangular matrix consisting of Guan Yu, Liu Bei and Cao Cao. Although historically a man of great talents, Cao Cao is portrayed throughout the novel and all the associated stories and plays stemming from it as most lacking in *yi*. This portrayal predates the novel. According to Su Dongpo, the most famous poet of the Song Dynasty, the true self of a man reveals itself most clearly at the point of death. Su Dongpo accuses Cao Cao of being an immoral human being (*bailun renwu*) on the grounds that on his deathbed, in front of his sons and grandsons, he wept and made arrangements to leave property to his various consorts.[66] That he wept is no problem: everybody weeps copiously in the novel; the crime is that he bestows goods to his women on such a public occasion. In a world of masculine bonds, where other kinds of bond are considered worthless, the show of feeling towards women in this solemn hour cannot be forgiven. Although Cao Cao spent his life manipulating others, the deathbed scene is singled out by Su Dongpo as particularly repugnant, as he involves women in the affairs of men.

This action breaks the male bond that is meant to be exclusive – thus confirming the view that Cao Cao was not a *yingxiong* despite his many accomplishments. By contrast, Liu Bei's deathbed scene is written as a moving farewell to his men, particularly Zhuge Liang, who is entrusted to nurture his son and complete the military enterprise they have been engaged in for some decades. Not a woman is in sight. More importantly, it depicts Liu Bei, who has both *wen* and *wu*, as a man who manipulates the political scene right to the last. Liu Bei is a worthy man for real heroes to follow, as illustrated by his ability to retain the unreserved loyalty of both Zhuge Liang, universally acknowledged as the personification of *wen* qualities in Three Kingdoms, and Guan Yu, the carrier of *wu* essence. While we have shown above that Guan Yu's devotion to Liu Bei has its ambiguities, Guan's relationship with Cao Cao is no less full of conflicting desires and allegiances.

The episodes in which Guan Yu sojourns in Cao Cao's camp and Guan Yu releases Cao Cao at Hua Rong Pass are given very intensive and comprehensive treatment by critics as illustrations of Guan Yu's *yi*. Starting with Mao Zonggang (fl. 1660), whose commentary on the *Three Kingdoms* is generally regarded as the authoritative exegesis of the novel, critics have attempted to excuse Guan Yu by inventing different kinds of *yi*. Thus, Mao imagines that Guan Yu, in his dilemma on whether to kill Cao Cao, reasons that 'if others kill him, then they are performing an *yi* act; but if I kill him, then I am not acting according to *yi*'.[67] In the same way that a heterosexualised reading of Guan Yu's relationship with his sisters-in-law has both political and sexual dimensions, this episode, though always read militarily and politically, can also take on a sexual reading. Although Cao Cao in the novel is highly sexualised, there is no indication that Guan Yu is ever attracted to him. By contrast, Cao Cao is attracted to Guan Yu even on their first encounter when Guan Yu is a mere archer. As a haughty man who is enamoured of Liu Bei since their first encounter, Guan Yu does not form any other emotional ties with either men or women throughout the novel. As is expected of a *wu* hero, he has succeeded in suppressing both his hetero- and homosexual desires. Even family ties have been obliterated for the sake of *yi* ties with his 'brother' and 'king'. Although he is married and has children, there is no mention of any kind of interaction between him and his wife (or wives) or children. He is thus, for Liu Bei, the perfect mate.

Guan Yu's loyalty and faithfulness to Liu Bei in his dealings with other men are a homosexual reflection of the suppression and control of his heterosexual feelings witnessed in the episode concerning the sisters-in-law. For example, Guan Yu takes the presents offered by Cao Cao on his knife, and not by hand. He also puts Cao Cao's gift of fine clothing on top of that which was given to him by Liu Bei, thus his body would not be soiled. It is significant that other men in *Three Kingdoms*, notably Liu Bei, show very effusive displays of fondness to each other by bodily contact such as holding hands and embracing each other. Such manifestations of emotion seem to be totally absent in Guan Yu.

Given Guan Yu's fame as someone dedicated to *yi* and his concomitant absolute loyalty to Liu Bei, his release of his brother's arch-enemy, Cao Cao, at Hua Rong Pass is one of the most memorable episodes in the novel. The episode tells how, after Cao Cao's army is decimated by Liu

Bei at the Battle of the Red Cliff, Cao Cao flees for his life with a few retainers. He is forced to traverse Hua Rong Pass, which is guarded by Guan Yu. But instead of capturing or killing him, Guan Yu releases Cao Cao to repay a past favour. This magnanimous action is not to be reciprocated and Cao Cao is to be the nemesis of the three brothers. The episode thus contrasts different manifestations of *yi* and how they affect political fortunes.

This whole episode, however, is a fabrication designed to highlight Guan Yu's moral rectitude. There is no such event in the historical records, and even in the anecdotal *pinghua* stories, the tale is related quite differently.[68] Critics throughout the centuries have been able to expound on this episode as an illustration of the conflicts between private and public *yi* and how it only heightens the *yi* of Guan Yu. Thus, it is often said that Guan Yu epitomises the expression 'for the sake of the greater *yi*, one must annihilate kin bonds' (*da yi mie qin*).

However, if we read this episode on a sexual and emotional plane as in the earlier episode invoking his sisters-in-law, we can see that, by his exaggerated formality towards Cao Cao and his subsequent release of the latter, ultimately Guan Yu has betrayed Liu Bei. Like other kinds of passionate devotion between two people, theirs is meant to be totally exclusive. By inserting this episode, the story-tellers have managed to heighten the tensions created earlier when Guan Yu, in his devotion to Liu Bei, refuses to wear Cao Cao's present of clothes close to his body. As in his public displays of virtue when escorting his sisters-in-law, in his relations with Cao Cao, Guan Yu also behaves so that 'all men's eyes became witnesses to his rectitude'. These public displays are also pregnant with (homo) sexual overtones.

No matter how much ink is used attempting to exonerate his release of Cao Cao, the fact remains that Guan Yu has 'betrayed' Liu Bei. It should be remembered that in discussing the notion of the *yingxiong* earlier, Cao Cao had identified himself and Liu Bei as the only true *yingxiong*. If Guan Yu is attracted by Liu Bei's heroic qualities, it seems logical that he should also have similar feelings for Cao Cao. The erotic elements of these feelings are revealed in his refusal to touch Cao Cao's presents lest they soil his body. They are also revealed in his extremely exaggerated rejections of Cao Cao's overtures of admiration and affection.

Mao Zonggang in his summation of the release episode has Guan Yu referring to Cao Cao as a 'bosom friend' (*zhiji*).[69] Contemporary critics inadvertently take the idea of Guan Yu's feelings for Cao further into the sexual realm when they note that Guan Yu was obligated to Cao Cao because when he was detained by the latter, he was allowed to preserve his chastity (*jiecao*).[70] In order to excuse Guan Yu's behaviour in releasing Cao Cao, his libido is often said to have been sublimated into the 'greater loyalty' (da yi), which is presumably devoid of ambiguous human foibles. Furthermore, as we have observed above, the subtext regarding Cao Cao is that no matter how powerful and heroic he may appear, his relationship with women disqualifies him as a real yingxiong. As the embodiment of yi, therefore, Guan Yu could not be seen to surrender himself (in all senses of the word) to Cao.

Guan Yu's inflexibility and his exaggerated sense of his own importance may ultimately spell a tragic personality,[71] but his posthumous political career, where so many emperors throughout the ages have conferred on him titles of lord, king and god, indicates a personal triumph unparalleled by any historical or literary figure. Without doubt, Guan Yu is an extremely contradictory and ambiguous icon whose boundaries shift and blur over time. However, the indeterminacy of this icon allows the possibility of its continual transformation to accommodate particular historical audiences. It also permits a re-positioning of the icon to suit the text in which it is situated. In this chapter, I have attempted to read the icon in two contexts: the literati novel and popular texts such as opera. I have also tried to dissect the icon with two powerful applications – the erotic and the political. These two applications 'necessarily obscure and misrepresent each other – but in ways that offer important and shifting affordances to all parties'.[72]

The eroticism of wu heroes like Guan Yu is certainly hidden – often deliberately so. In the literati novel in particular, all sexual signifiers are carefully obscured. However, even though the desexualisation of Guan Yu in the novel indicates a strategy of 'containment',[73] this strategy can nevertheless be deconstructed. Despite the erotic and political opacity of the Guan Yu icon, its boundaries often stray into realms of desire and power because of its unrelenting insistence on a 'structure of men's relations with other men'. This structure, encompassing both the novel and popular images, may try to 'misrepresent', but the misrepresentations, when seen in terms of the management of desire, betray a clever repression of political ambitions. Guan Yu's single-minded loyalty to his lord and head of the family is rewarded by his achieving the unique status of the ultimate yingxiong in the novel and wu god in myth. But those who lionised and canonised him have also demonstrated by very powerful sexual signifiers that any suggestion of disloyalty, even as oblique and subconscious as a dream (in the case of the novel), would bring personal tragedy and national disaster. The sexual and political forces which underpin the structure of homosocial desire in Guan Yu's relationship with Liu Bei and Cao Cao provide excellent illustrations of strategies for ideological and social control.

Finally, the construction of the Guan Yu icon and its relationship to the Liu Bei image, who as elder brother represents familial authority and as lord the power of the state, are enlightening in the *wen-wu* schema. As stated earlier, Liu Bei does not excel in either *wen* or *wu*. However, he *does* possess plenty of both attributes – enough to qualify him as family head and king. Guan Yu's claim to embodying all the qualities of *wu* may elevate him to godly status, but in practice, he needs to submit to a 'lesser man' because of his lack of *wen*. While both men embody desirable ideals in the Chinese masculinity schema, Guan Yu as the ultimate *wu* icon can only take a subordinate position to Liu Bei who has more *wen* qualities. The intricate ways in which *wen* dominates *wu* in the masculinity stakes will be examined in the next chapter in a discussion of the *wen* god Confucius.

3　Confucius as Sage, Teacher, Businessman: Transformations of the *wen* Icon

This portrait of Confucius is attributed to the artist Wu Daozi (c. 750 AD).
The caption states, 'Confucius, The Foremost Teacher, Giving a Lesson'.
Note the sword tucked under his arm.

Having examined the *wu* icon Guan Yu and its redaction in contemporary times in the previous chapter, I now explore the constructions of *wen* and its reconstitution in the modern world. I do this by tracing the changes undertaken by *wen* masculinity as embodied in the scholar-intellectual (*wenren*, or man of letters) ideal, as exemplified by the *wen* god Confucius. I am therefore once more analysing ideals and social constructs rather than 'real' men. As shown in the previous two chapters, the ideal man is one with both civil and military (*wen-wu*) accomplishments. This chapter focuses on the *wen* half of this dyad. After establishing the significance of the *wen* god Confucius in this Chinese masculinity framework and its relationship to both sexes, the chapter will outline how Communist scholars have constructed Confucius as a progressive educationalist so that his 'modern fate' is not a terminal one. In the final part of this chapter, I will examine the icon in the last two decades of the last millennium.

I will show that in the 1980s and 1990s, *wen* ideals have been fundamentally transformed, and can now be seen as encompassing commercial expertise. Confucius as capitalist entrepreneur turns the traditional understanding of *wen* on its head. From being a moral and political force, the *wen* icon now embraces an economic component as well. If this thesis is correct, constructions of Chinese masculinity have undergone a revolution the implications of which are truly cataclysmic. The 'real man' in China today need not have the *wen-wu* attributes as they are traditionally understood – he may in fact have neither. Successful *wen* masculinity can now be measured by the acquisition and flaunting of trappings such as the size and power of mobile phones and laptop computers. The Chinese male ideal is moving closer to the image of young executives found in in-flight magazines read by the international jet-set. The fact that the image of a successful young executive may also be an ideal sought by women indicates that gender boundaries are becoming increasingly blurred. I will return to this issue in later chapters. In this chapter, I intend to focus on the changing significations of the *wen* icon Confucius.

Confucius and the Chinese Masculinity Framework

As I have indicated above, throughout China and the communities of the Chinese diaspora, Confucius is worshipped as the *wen* god and Guan Yu as the *wu* god in temples. Thus, Confucius is known as the '*wen* sage' (*wensheng*) and Guan Yu the '*wu* sage' (*wusheng*) and Confucius temples are also known as '*wen* temples' (*wenmiao*). Guan Yu is more popular in the temples, comics, operas and other forms of mass culture,[1] and Confucius is much more highly revered by the elite, with his teachings forming the basis of formal education in China until this century. While these two icons represent the dual ideals of Chinese masculinity, Confucius is the one which must be deconstructed if we are to understand the components of manhood which are sought by men who operate mainly with their minds. They are the ones who have inherited the functions of the traditional scholar-gentry class.

Of course, the proposition that both academic attainment and controlled physical prowess are necessary ingredients for manhood may also be applicable to other cultures. As Andrew Nathan has convincingly shown, attempts to prove empirically that Chinese culture is unique are far from conclusive,[2] and I certainly do not want to imply that Chinese masculinity is an exception to this general principle. The objective of this chapter lies elsewhere. While Confucianism has for centuries been seen by both Chinese and European scholars as the very essence of Chineseness and Confucius the personification of this essence, recent interpretations of the philosopher and his philosophy have moved closer to a universalistic rather than a particularistic position. Confucius has frequently been invoked for nationalistic purposes, but the traditional strategy of equating him with Chineseness may quickly become outdated in the computer age. In this latter context, the icon representing him will be unreadable even with the latest applications and platforms because notions of Chineseness are increasingly being dispersed and blurred.

Traditionally, Confucius was regarded as a sage (shengren). Such status, although sought as the ultimate goal by the neo-Confucians, was understood to be beyond the capabilities of the average man. For the last two millennia, most Chinese men aspired instead to the Confucian ideal of the junzi. The word junzi appears in the Analects 106 times. Roughly translated as 'gentleman', 'refined man' or 'virtuous man', it is for our discussion best rendered as an 'exemplary person'.[3] The close relationship between the junzi and wen is reiterated several times in the Analects. By contrast, junzi is not usually associated with the wu aspect of masculinity.[4] One of the best-known expressions linking junzi and wen occurs in verse 27, book VI of the Analects, where Confucius says 'the junzi is well-versed in wen'.[5] A more elaborate description occurs in verse 18, in which the Master explains that 'when a man has more zhi than wen, he will be vulgar. If he has more wen than zhi, he will be a pedant. If he has a well-balanced mixture of these two qualities, he is then a junzi'.[6] Most commentators agree that zhi is a relatively straightforward concept. It is the basic or innate substance which makes up a man.[7] Through the process of education and enculturation using wen, a man with the right amount of the zhi substance will turn into a genteel junzi. Wen thus encompasses all the qualities that sublimate nature into culture.

In practical terms, *wen* is the product of a proper education. It is said that Confucius taught four subjects: 'cultural refinement (*wen*), moral behaviour (*xing*), loyalty (*zhong*) and faith (*xin*)'.[8] Since the last three are ethical concepts, we can assume that the skills that we know he taught – literature, music, archery, charioteering, writing and mathematics – belong to the category of *wen*. During the Communist era, these qualities became the ingredients upon which debates on education were based. Here, I should reiterate that in general, the accomplishments which Confucius considered to be preconditions to *junzi*-hood apply only to men.

As a model for men, the *junzi* is contrasted with the *xiaoren* (inferior man). The *Analects* contrasts the *junzi* and *xiaoren* in numerous places. Of most interest to us is the declaration by Confucius that 'the *junzi* understands the importance of morality (*yi*) and the *xiaoren* understands the importance of profitability (*li*)'.[9] In the context of the Spring and Autumn and Warring States period, this is an important pronouncement. The biggest challenge to Confucians at that time was Mozi, who unashamedly advocated profit and utility as desirable goals. The Confucian hatred for the utilitarian profit motive continued right into the twentieth century, with merchants and business people theoretically placed almost at the bottom of traditional Chinese society in terms of social status. One of the most striking illustrations of this Confucian outlook can be found in the Qing novel *Rulin waishi* (The Scholars).[10] In this novel, the ostentatiously unambitious but talented Wang Mian is held up as the ideal man, and all the scholars and officials who lust after power, privilege and money in the novel are portrayed as despicable fakes. In many ways, Wang Mian is the reincarnation of Yan Hui, Confucius' favourite student (a perfect *junzi* who has also been posthumously canonised as a sage), who died without achieving office, wealth or fame.

This does not mean that Chinese masculinity was depicted as asocial and apolitical, traits normally ascribed to the Daoists. Wang Mian did not actively seek office, but he gave advice freely to the ruler. Confucius, too, in his lifetime was said to have wandered from state to state looking for a kingly patron so that he could offer counsel. In contemporary terms, he was a political lobbyist. By definition, having *wen* implied the ability to work with one's verbal skills: thus the *wenren* influenced social events through rhetoric and not necessarily social action. The *wenren* saw himself as the moral and spiritual guide to society. Certainly, Confucius sought only the company of the mighty and shunned the common folk, the *xiaoren*. Interestingly, in the same statement in which Confucius admonishes his followers to shun the *xiaoren*, he also directs them to keep women at a respectable distance.[11] Women are thus another class of people who are considered troublesome and who should be eschewed. Since masculinity is often associated with sexuality and is also often analysed in terms of its relationship to femininity, it is important that this issue be clarified for Confucius and the *wen-wu* framework.

Confucius and the Sexes

I have shown in the last chapter that the *wu* ideal has a multitude of defences against women, such that in the popular imagination the *wu* god Guan Yu would rather decapitate a beautiful woman than be tempted by her. This is also true of all the sadistic murders of women in the classic novel *All Men Are Brothers*.[12] By contrast, in the typical 'scholar and beauty' (*caizi jiaren*) formulation of male–female affairs discussed in the next chapter, the scholar always beds the girl. One would thus expect the *wen* god to be surrounded by women. But this is simply not the case – Confucius is never presented in the company of women.[13] In traditional stories, *wen* men indeed consort with women in ways not possible for *wu* men, but this situation is not meant to be read as the ideal. Indeed, although the *caizi jiaren* genre is by definition the romance between talented men and beautiful women, there are also hundreds of love stories in which the scholar learns the folly and dangers of attachment to women. In these stories, the women are often prostitutes, demons or fox-fairies who use their wiles to bewitch and ruin their men. Thus, the impeccable Wang Mian has a significant man and a significant woman in his life, but the man is his old peasant mentor and the woman is his old mother. He does not marry and has no romantic attachments.

Traditionally, the exclusivity of *wen-wu* in the male domain was taken for granted: women were barred totally from entering *wen-wu* sites such as the Hanlin Academy and the military establishments. Those who did, such as Zhu Yingtai who tried to gain recognition for *wen* accomplishments by entering a scholarly academy, had to do so dressed as men. Tragedy usually ensued. Similarly, women who were good at *wu*, such as the woman warrior Hua Mulan, had to conceal their sex in order to receive credit for their accomplishments. Once these women applied rouge and adopted feminine attire again, all their *wen-wu* attributes disappeared. In the words of Joseph Allen, the 'dressing and undressing of the Chinese woman warrior' is not 'primarily the story of military action but rather of returning home'. All the different versions of the Hua Mulan story are 'tales of domestication'.[14] *Wen-wu* is a male quality, and is never conferred on women. If women were to worship at the feet of a Confucius idol, it would be for their sons' success at examinations. This is not a problem but for the fact that when writers talk about 'the concept of man', it is often confused with the concept of humankind, with man as a gendered person endowed with sexual desire and needs being ignored.[15]

Indeed, as we observed above, Confucius himself has unambiguously classed women with the *xiaoren*, a species to be avoided. He would rather have women kept far away than have them offering sacrifices at his feet. In descriptions of his life which we find in the *Analects*, Confucius seems to live up to his principles in this regard. All of his disciples and associates are men, and in his teachings all exemplars are male. He seems most at ease and happy in the company of men, and displays his grief most manifestly at the death of Yan Hui, his favourite student. The only time this homosociality is challenged is when he visits the beautiful Nanzi, and his outspoken disciple Zilu immediately shows his displeasure, prompting protestations of innocence from the Master.[16]

The homosociality and misogyny which characterise the *wu* god Guan Yu can thus also be found in the *wen* god, albeit in a different form and in a less dramatic way. It may seem self-evident that Confucius' philosophy is male-centred, but scholars have assumed that Confucian concepts are not gendered. In the *Analects*, the detested *xiaoren* is mentioned 24 times, mostly counterposed to the *junzi*. But in keeping with the neglect of women in Confucius' time, there is no reference to women as a group. The paucity of instruction regarding women from the Master leaves a lot of room for extravagant interpretations. Some have even tried to argue, as recently as a couple of years ago, 'that the teachings of Confucius are similar to those of some Feminists'![17] The justification for such pious assertions usually rests on the argument that Confucius advocated the notion '*ren*'. In its written form, '*ren*' is 'composed of two parts, the figure of a person and the numeral two, and so we render it into English as "person to person care" or just "care" to be brief'.[18] In this instance, the authors are targeting a Western audience, which is presumably sympathetic to Chinese culture but not its sexist tendencies, so Confucius is presented as a caring, loving man.

However, for Chinese scholars whose most important audience was for many years the Chinese Communist Party, the question of Confucius' attitude towards women is not of primary concern. After all, the CCP explicitly puts women's liberation as secondary to class liberation. The major preoccupation of the CCP has been the assumption and continuance of political power: women were welcome only in as far as they helped to achieve this goal. Similarly, in the *Analects*, which was written with the explicit aim of creating states ruled by wise men and peopled by *junzi*, women virtually do not exist. By default, this omission has led to a patriarchal system that was only attacked on this basis during the May Fourth movement early in the twentieth century. The next significant period in which women received attention came with the establishment of the PRC. In the new spirit of sexual equality of the early 1950s, some of the more strident critics of Confucianism such as Cai Shangsi with his

May Fourth style onslaught on Confucius as misogynist and elitist were promoted.[19] However, the most damaging Communist criticism of Confucius in the 1950s and 1960s came from younger scholars such as Zhao Jibin and Yang Rongguo. Their concerns were not with gender, but with class. Their writings show that, contrary to the common belief that Confucius had discovered humanity in his notion of 'ren', he had only worked on behalf of the ruling elite of his time. The 'people' in 'ren' did not extend beyond the ruling class.[20] Thus, they argued that even for his time, Confucius was politically reactionary, so even the essence of his thinking (as opposed to the concrete manifestations of Confucianism in Chinese history) should not be emulated in the new China.

This very critical assessment of Confucius gained strength in the early 1960s. From the Cultural Revolution until the late 1970s, it reigned supreme. In such an anti-traditional environment, Confucius clearly could not be restored to his former glory. As an icon, he only signified a superfluous fossil from a bygone era, hardly a model for men to imitate. Yet, it was also obvious that the tenacity of *wen* as a predominant male virtue could not be so easily erased. Many scholars who had spent years learning the Confucian classics depended on the acceptance of these classics as canon for their authority and privileged positions. Therefore, whenever it was politically permissible, they wrote in defence of Confucius. Mao Zedong's instruction to 'sum up our history from Confucius to Sun Yat-sen and take over this valuable legacy' was reiterated *ad nauseam* to justify the continuing need for traditional Confucian values.[21]

Nevertheless, while influential philosophers such as Feng Youlan valiantly attempted to find a place for Confucius in the new China, these attempts only served to further demystify the *wen* god. In their arguments that Confucius had made a valuable contribution to world culture through the discovery of 'ren' as loving the ordinary person, philosophers such as Feng Youlan expanded great efforts trying to prove that Confucius was not advocating class oppression but building a Chinese-style humanism. This argument was very attractive, and even in the 1980s, some scholars were still trying to prove that Confucius' humanism was superior to that of the Europeans.[22] But, if at best he was a humanist, it would be impossible to restore to him the godly status traditionally accorded him.

Indeed, in the first thirty or so years of the PRC, the propaganda apparatus was geared to producing new male prototypes for national adulation. These were the peasant-worker-soldier models, which are best illustrated by the Daqing worker Wang Jinxi and the Dazhai peasant Chen Yonggui. For a soldier hero, we have the ubiquitous Lei Feng. These were men whose images dominated the media in the 1960s and 1970s as encapsulating the socialist ideal. Ostensibly dedicated, selfless and simple-minded, they confound all former notions of masculinity in terms of *wen* and *wu*. The worker-peasant-soldier icons did not share the passions or ambitions which characterise the traditional *wen* or *wu* gods. Their complete lack of sexual desire and interest in women was the only conspicuous commonality between them and the previous prototypes. In this climate where traditional *wen-wu* values were under sustained attack, intellectuals had to find a new mode of operation as reformed *wenren* in the new society.

In fact, in the early decades of the PRC, there were very few *wen* models which were congruent with traditional norms. Intellectuals are notoriously difficult to fit into a class schema, and attempts to valorise intellectuals in the aftermath of the Cultural Revolution produced nerd-heroes such as the mathematician Chen Jingrun. Although some women reputedly found these awkward individuals desirable as marriage partners, they were so insipid that they were hardly likely to inspire too many followers. In a sense, even though the scholars of old achieved fame by passing examinations through rote learning and aspiring to official positions, at least in the ideal, they were meant to be thinking beings with a rich inner life. With Lei Feng and the other new male models, whose heroism depended on being small parts of a bigger machine, unthinkingly and willingly performing mindless chores, traditional respect for education and culture had to withdraw from the scene. The new ideal did not advocate excelling in either *wen* or *wu*, which requires a certain degree of self-control and control over others. In effect, between 1949 and 1976, the new class analysis positively discouraged any form of individuality that did not manifestly advance the good of the worker-peasant-soldiers, and produced heroes who were anti-intellectual and hence anti-*wen*.

Confucius as Teacher and Scholar

Therefore, it was of utmost urgency for intellectuals of the *wenren* mould to justify their social usefulness on the new political scene. They did so in two stages. I will discuss the more orthodox effort first. With the changed social situation in the early years of the PRC, it was obvious that Confucius could no longer be invoked as 'the Sagely King, the Everlasting Teacher, the Protector of the People and the High Priest of the World'.[23] However, almost all evaluations of Confucius since the PRC was established have contained at least a paragraph or two praising his contribution to education, except for a couple of years during the anti-Confucius campaign of 1973–74. The new *wenren* in socialist China could hardly claim to be members of the 'labouring masses', so teaching and research provided an important vehicle for staking a claim to socialist construction. Being a teacher is a legitimate and worthy profession, and the 'paragon of teachers' (*wanshi shibiao*) is, of course, Confucius.

Apart from one's parents, teachers were traditionally most revered and esteemed. Mao Zedong himself declared that he wanted to be remembered as a teacher. His statement was unlikely to have been modesty or self-effacement, but rather was a strategic use of a long-held veneration for teachers. As stated earlier, the idea of Communist leaders fulfilling the role of exemplars of moral conduct accords well with the 'Confucian philosophy of education [which] is the notion of education by example'.[24] Calls to 'inherit' Confucius' ideas on education and praise for his role as a scholar and teacher were routine in any discussion of Confucius before the Cultural Revolution. Thus, as early as 1954, several articles appeared in the leading intellectual national newspaper *Guangming ribao* extolling Confucius as an educationalist.[25] The first, by Xu Mengying, claimed that Confucian education encouraged people to practise benevolent government by teaching 'the way of the *junzi*'.[26] Interestingly, Xu tried to argue that Confucius had extended the meaning of *junzi* beyond a simple reference to the aristocracy, to an implied broad code of behaviour. Thus, it would have relevance in contemporary socialist China.

The idea that the *junzi* was just someone who loved the people, and who therefore should be emulated in socialist society, was stressed even more vigorously during the Hundred Flowers Movement, when a whole book was published on Confucius as an educator. Written by Chen Jingpan, an academic in education at Beijing University, the book presents Confucius as an educator who used the models of the sage (*shengren*) and gentleman (*junzi*) to enlighten his students.[27] His method was based on the idea of self-cultivation (*xiuyang*). The use of the term *xiuyang* is important, as it is the basic tenet used by Liu Shaoqi in his book *On the Self-cultivation of a Communist Party Member*, which first appeared in 1939.[28] By showing that Communist leaders such as Liu Shaoqi had extensively employed Confucius as a source model for the new socialist man, academics and intellectuals attempted to show that their idol had relevance for the new society. It is true that the revival of Confucian values had the blessing of very powerful leaders such as Liu Shaoqi and Zhou Yang, who organised the well-publicised commemoration of the 2440th anniversary of Confucius' death in 1962. However, these people unfortunately also belonged to the faction that lost power during the Cultural Revolution. During this time, their Confucian leanings were also vigorously attacked.

Despite these attacks, Confucius maintained some significance throughout the Communist period. Even the anti-Confucius campaign of 1973–74 saw a huge resurgence of interest in Confucianism, as evidenced by the hundreds of articles and books about Confucius as well as the thousands of meetings held to 'criticise' him. Cartoons and descriptions from this period depict a weakling who looks like the decrepit scholar Kong Yiji painted so poignantly by Lu Xun in 1919. But because he was held up as a 'negative example' (*fanmian jiaocai*), the 'positive man' was presumably everything which was contrary to these representations. The depiction of Confucius as a weakling may also have been a reaction to the 1960s, when attempts were made by sports educators to show that he was a robust and physical person. Extracts from the *Analects* describing him as tall and strong were quoted as evidence that he combined the *wen* type of education with physical education (as *wu*).[29]

Thus, those who wanted to promote Confucius claimed that he did not neglect the physical. This assertion attempted to justify 'inheriting' him in the new socialist China, where model men and women were supposed to engage in manual labour. The aversion of *wen* men for physical labour in traditional China is well-known. Confucius in the *Analects* explicitly discourages his students from participating in productive labour which he regards as not worthy of the *junzi*. *Wen-wu*, like many other ideological constructs, is about self-control and control of others. Thus, *wu* implied not just physical strength, but how that strength was used. Productive labour such as that of peasants was considered unskilled work not worthy of *wu*. Just before the Cultural Revolution, some academics such as Li Yinnong had abandoned the pretence that the model male must be the worker-peasant-soldier. Li claimed that Confucius had made a greater contribution to Chinese civilisation than had the peasants he chastised.[30]

It is not surprising that during the Cultural Revolution Confucius was most vehemently attacked for his educational ideas. In the new China, where 'feudal' ways were meant to be abandoned, it was difficult to salvage the philosopher most closely identified with those ways. As we have seen above, education was the one area where many intellectuals felt Confucius could still provide a model. Through education, and its associated *wen* values, the Chinese literati of the past and intelligentsia of the present could continue to acquire a sense of meaning and power in society. This became patent as soon as the Cultural Revolution ended. The first piece of literature to question 'gang of four' policies, Liu Xinwu's 'Class Teacher', was about education.[31] Immediately after its publication, writers associated their own sexuality and masculinity with the power of the pen. This could be seen from short stories such as 'Glasses'[32] and the controversial novel *Half of Man Is Woman*,[33] which link political power, sexual potency and desirability closely with education, knowledge and other *wen* achievements.

Wen masculinity was experiencing a phenomenal comeback in the early 1980s, and Confucius was once more elevated to a supreme position. His status as the paragon of teachers was used as a signal that this was a man worthy of imitation. Throughout the 1980s and 1990s, it was generally agreed that a crisis of faith, especially among the young, was haunting China. It was felt that there was a moral vacuum after the disillusioning experiences of the Cultural Revolution. Thus, even as early as 1980, Confucian moral education was proposed as a means of filling this gap. This proposal was reiterated many times. Again, Confucius was held up as a man upon whom young people could model themselves. Thus, by highlighting the perception that the moral and educational situation had reached a crisis point, Confucius as *wen* god was used again to justify the privileged positions of scholars and intellectuals as indispensable elements of the social fabric.

By the early 1990s, Confucius and Mao Zedong were paired as the two greatest educators in Chinese history, one ancient, one modern. In a significant article on this topic, Xu Quanxing, a member of the CCP Central Committee Party School, argues that Mao Zedong had on numerous occasions wanted to be remembered as a teacher. Furthermore, he quotes Mao Zedong praising Confucius in many of his speeches and writings. One of the most interesting quotations from Mao Zedong is his assessment of Confucius in a talk in 1938. After eulogising Confucius, Mao asks rhetorically: 'why didn't Confucius become a Communist? That's because the masses those days did not want him to be a Communist: they wanted him to be a teacher. But today, the masses want us to be Communists.'[34] That is to say, if Confucius had been alive in the 1930s, he would have been a Communist leader. Such claims are almost clichés; what is remarkable about this one is the manner of its deployment in supporting the arguments about the paramount importance of the ancient sage for Chinese culture.

Critics like Xu Quanxing are not merely debating the merits of Confucian education. As a professor of the Communist Party School, Xu leaves little doubt as to the political motive behind his article. He concludes with a short comment to the effect that although Confucius' influence on Mao Zedong was generally positive, it also had a negative aspect. The biggest shortcoming in Confucius' educational thought, according to Xu Quanxing, is his 'emphasis on ethics and disregard for materiality' (*zhong renlun, qing wuli*).[35] Because of this, Chinese thinkers throughout the ages, including Mao, have paid insufficient attention to material and economic progress. By contrast,

Deng Xiaoping rectified this bias in Mao Zedong. He [Deng] spoke about the importance of education for achieving modernisation and catching up with the highest international standards. He pointed out that science and technology were the key to the four modernisations, and education provided the foundations.[36]

Presumably, if Confucius lived in the 1990s, he would be more than just a Communist leader: he would be a Communist entrepreneur!

Confucius as Entrepreneur: 1980s and 1990s

Given the fact that for centuries Confucius had been associated with the scholar class and seen to be hostile to commerce and monetary concerns, it seems inconceivable that he could be portrayed as a business guru. Yet, as I will show in the following discussion, this is precisely what happened. As stated above, attempts to resuscitate the traditional image of the *wenren* as the conscience and guardian of Chinese values were often made by enshrining Confucius as the paragon of teachers. These attempts to privilege the social positions of the scholars, which had proven so successful in previous centuries, could have continued into the twenty-first century. The 'contemporary neo-Confucianists' (*dangdai xin rujia*)[37] such as Tang Junyi and Tu Wei-ming would certainly not have been averse to such a turn of events. For example, the *Journal of Confucius and Mencius Research* (*Kong Meng xuebao*), which has been distributed since 1961 by the Confucius and Mencius Society in Taiwan, continues to propagate the same traditional Confucian values. In North America, academic associations such as the Canadian Culture and Regeneration Research Society, which publishes the quarterly *Cultural China* (*Wenhua Zhongguo*), have also been formed to revive traditional Chinese culture in the new world order. Significantly, since the mid-1980s, some 'contemporary neo-Confucianists' outside China have attempted to modernise and internationalise Confucianism by linking Confucian education with the economic prosperity in East Asia.[38] Studies of cultures in the social sciences have also projected Confucian values as a 'dynamic dimension' in promoting economic growth.[39]

In the PRC, a similar shift in emphasis has also taken place. Since 1978, there has been a major national or international conference on Confucius or Confucianism every year, indicating an unprecedented enthusiasm for the philosopher and his philosophy.[40] In the beginning, the conferences were held to repudiate the 'gang of four' criticisms of Confucius. Very quickly, however, they became events for his adulation. The fact that the venue was almost always in Qufu, Confucius' birthplace, and held on his birthday, made the intentions of these conferences even more transparent. Thus, at the 1984 gathering, a ceremony was held to unveil Confucius' statue as well as to establish the Chinese Confucius Foundation, whose director was Kuang Yaming, the former president of Nanjing University. Kuang was a staunch Communist, and at the same time, a good Confucian. He was then about to release his new book calling for the 'inheritance' of Confucius and his ideas.[41]

In the same year, the International Confucian Association was established in Beijing, with Singapore's former prime minister Lee Kuan Yew elected honorary director. Lee Kuan Yew's role was a clear signal that Confucianism was seen as not merely compatible with, but an important ingredient for building a modern society. Since then, numerous international conferences have been held to commemorate Confucius, with most foreign participants coming from East and Southeast Asia. The economic growth of the Asia-Pacific region throughout most of the 1980s and 1990s generated increasing interest in the search for 'Asian values', of which Confucianism was an integral feature. In quick succession, a series of articles appeared showing how Confucianism had been essential for modernisation in industrial countries in East Asia such as Japan and Korea.[42]

Scholars and intellectuals who for many years had called for the 'inheritance' of Confucius' educational thought were understandably very quick to cash in on the economic boom in East Asia in the 1980s and early 1990s. As early as 1979, the link between Confucian values and the quest for wealth and industrialisation was expressed implicitly in the immensely popular prize-winning short story 'Manager Qiao Assumes Office' by Jiang Zilong.[43] In the fields of philosophy and political commentary, this link was made explicit by the mid-1980s. By the 1990s, the message was very forcefully promoted.[44] From a sagely adviser to kings and statesmen everywhere, Confucius has been turned into a management consultant, whose words set the benchmark for good business practice.[45] His morals are held up as exemplary because they are supposed to promote production and profit.

However, as pointed out earlier, the *Analects* unambiguously states that 'the *junzi* understands the importance of morality (*yi*) and the *xiaoren* understands the importance of profitability (*li*).' Thus, throughout Chinese history, good Confucians such as the neo-Confucian Zhu Xi eschewed talk of profit and business. This aversion to money and commerce would have to be resolved if the *junzi* model were to succeed in an era which measured success in economic terms. Confucians throughout the ages were supposed to have placed morality above profits and utility, whereas the Mohists took the reverse position. This is a major reason that Mozi has generally been ignored throughout history, including during the Communist period.[46] Interestingly, in the economically driven social climate of the 1980s, it was felt that this premise needed to be reassessed. Articles which discuss the relationship between ethics and utility usually conclude by arguing the need for some degree of morality in an age where 'money is all'.[47] By 1989, when three international conferences were held in China to commemorate the 2540th anniversary of Confucius' birth, scholars were keen to connect Confucius' views on the profit motive to the modernisation of China, saying that both *yi* and *li* were important in this age of rapid economic growth.[48] Kuang Yaming, in an influential paper 'On Confucius' *yi-li* and Economic Affairs', contended that on close examination, Confucius did not really stress *yi* above *li*. In fact, his highest ideal was 'the Great Commonwealth' (*datong shijie*), in which *yi* and *li* were in harmony and in unity.[49] The reason Confucius highlighted the conflict between *yi* and *li* was that he realised 'the Great Commonwealth' was difficult to accomplish in his time. He emphasised *yi* so that an ethical society could at least develop first.

Therefore, by the end of the 1980s, there was a concerted effort to show that Confucius' ideas were beneficial to economic growth. As well as the appearance of many articles devoted to the relationship between Confucian ethics and business management, a number of conferences were held to examine traditional Chinese morality and the market economy.[50] Using the generally accepted view that the central core of Confucius' teaching is '*ren*', and that '*ren*' meant the discovery of humanity in human relationships, scholars tried to show that this emphasis on the centrality of men was the essential element that had been missing in modern management.[51] Furthermore, it is often argued that there is a close connection between Confucian and socialist economic morality, so that in a developing socialist market economy, Confucian ethics should be used to combat the corrupting influence of the lust for money.[52] This view was even more appealing because of the belief that first the Cultural Revolution and then modernity had had a dehumanising and alienating effect on the people, especially the young.[53]

Once more Confucius was eulogised and promoted as a model for the young. More importantly, he was celebrated as the person who outlined a method whereby management can be carried out efficiently by humane cadres and managers. In a very detailed article, Beijing University economist Zhao Jing argued that Confucius' management techniques could be adopted by capitalist and modern enterprises. The thrust of his argument was aimed at 'leaders' in both industry and politics. In particular, he claimed that those who emphasised politics a few years earlier were people who 'did not understand our national character', who wanted to rush straight ahead with communism without checking whether this was a realistic move or not.[54] Zhao acknowledged that Confucian lack of attention to the economic structure of nations had a negative impact on China. However, he believed that if Japan and Korea could modernise by adopting Confucius' management techniques, China could too. 'Moral management' became a motto under which many writers advocated the return of Confucius in the new industrial China.[55]

Throughout the 1990s, the powerful forces of industrialisation and consumerism have pushed cultural artefacts, including masculinity, into the marketplace as commodities.[56] Scholars and writers have therefore had to satisfy consumers instead of each other. Their metamorphosis entailed a similar re-invention of their alter ego, Confucius. The *wen* god is thus re-interpreted as someone who did not suppress the profit motive, but who merely advocated righteousness (*yi*) as a means by which the *junzi* could have a moral standard to which to aspire (once he became economically successful).[57] In the present climate where luxury items are flaunted and unashamedly taken as signs of success, the Confucius icon has been stood on its head. Scholars such as Zhao Jing discuss the moral management techniques of Confucius with the ultimate aim of nurturing a generation of leaders who follow the reformed Confucius.

This does not mean, of course, that *wen* has been erased from the masculinity matrix. The new consumer society has unquestionably brought huge dilemmas for intellectuals and artists who cling to traditional ways. 'Tradition' here refers not only to tradition from Imperial times, but the Communist tradition as well. In 1999, as part of a forum on heroes in the Chinese Youth League journal *China Youth*, the merits of Bill Gates are compared with those of Pavel Korchagin, the most influential literary character from the Soviet era.[58] Not one of the comments dismissed Bill Gates, and some agreed that he is 'a successful businessman' and a 'realistic model'.[59] It would have been inconceivable even a decade earlier for a Party organ responsible for the political instruction of the nation's young to praise the world's richest man as comparable to Korchagin. Business success is now clearly a primary aim of moral-political education. The reconstruction of Confucius has provided a tremendous morale boost for the *wenren* who now 'wade into the ocean of business dealings' (*xiahai*). By claiming that the venerated sage had over a couple of thousand years ago discovered the secret to a humane leadership style suitable for the twentieth century, these men can indulge in finance and at the same time feel morally superior. They are the new *junzi*.

The commodification of intellect and morality had already been given a traditional (as in Imperial old ways) and rationalised foundation in the early 1980s. This was seen most vividly in the eulogy of the Manager Qiao-style masculinity following the publication of 'Manager Qiao Assumes Office' in 1979. However, Manager Qiao saw himself as uncompromisingly Communist. Both he and his wife are Soviet trained. By 1999, casting Bill Gates as a hero and as the most successful of enterprise managers, old Communist values are questioned and found wanting. Most importantly, Chinese men's, particularly businessmen's, nationalist and masculine pride can be restored after so many years of uncertainty and anguish. Confucius can still be retained in the pantheon of Chinese gods as one of the most enduring icons. The Chinese search for wealth and power has produced some curious consequences in relation to this icon. It is now quite proper for graduates of commerce to hold their graduation ceremonies and have their photos taken at the Confucius temples. The efficacy of relics connected with the *wen* god is now measured not by the virtues they inspire, but by how much cash they generate. For example, money-making from tourism ventures that link Qufu and Confucius is highly topical and greatly trumpeted.[60]

As the world becomes more accessible and interdependent through travel and finance, China will change and become more international in outlook. The Confucius icon will change with it. Given the divergent number of Confuciuses we have contended with in the past fifty years, the man is indeed the consummate chameleon. In order for us to 'inherit' (*jicheng*) his teachings, Confucius has been variously interpreted as sage, scholar, teacher, restorationist and business guru. Confucius as business-man is the last word on him. For example, in late 1998 and 1999, when parts of East Asia were having problems economically, journalists were quick to blame Confucius for the 'five basic human relationships' which had apparently led to hierarchy and lack of rule of law and transparency, resulting in an 'Asian eclipse'.[61] Like it or not, the word 'Confucius' will continue to be shorthand for Chinese culture no matter how this culture is interpreted.

Although discussions of Chinese culture generally do not make gender issues explicit, the implicit perspective of such discussions is usually a male (*wen-wu*) one. More specifically, as the *wen* god, Confucius will continue to exemplify this particular aspect of male culture. The *wu* component of masculinity is also changing and becoming more international, as can be seen in martial arts films such as those of Bruce Lee, Jackie Chan and Samo Hung. Thanks to cyberspace, images and models are available to many different cultures instantaneously. Constructions of Chinese masculinity will need to be continually altered and modernised if they are to have meaning and relevance. By the same token, the basic *wen-wu* structure will also need to be transformed if it is to be maintained as a 'national characteristic'. As long as the man (and, progressively, woman as well) in question is Chinese, it does not matter whether he is to be a multinational entrepreneur or civil servant, his personality will be said to have qualities which are consonant with the *wen* god Confucius. In this way, although *wen* has never before been rendered as business acumen and managerial skills, that unlikely interpretation seems to have been achieved in recent times.

4   Scholars and Intellectuals: Representations of *wen* Masculinity Past and Present

Scholar Zhang and the maid Hongniang from *The Story of the West Wing*. The scholar's masculinity remains uncompromised by his apparent deference to the maid. From Chen Hong, *Guoju gushi*, vol. 2, Taipei: ROC Council for Cultural Affairs, Executive Yuan, 1991, p. 72. Reproduced with permission.

Having traced the changing interpretations of Confucius as the *wen* icon in the previous chapter, I now examine the personification of traditional and contemporary *wen* ideals in a representative selection of archetypal characters from fiction and drama. Scholar Zhang, from the Tang story 'The Story of Yingying' and the Yuan drama *The Story of the West Wing*, is useful for analysing traditional *wen* masculinity. For a contemporary counterpart, I analyse the character Zhang Yonglin in three influential novels of the 1980s, *Mimosa, Half of Man Is Woman* and *Getting Used to Dying*, all by the controversial writer Zhang Xianliang. Both the Scholar Zhang and Zhang Yonglin stories are semi-autobiographical. Writers, dramatists and readers embrace these stories as drawing on 'real' people's experiences and as such, the analysis of these fictional constructions of *wen* masculinity reveals how Confucian teachings are supposedly embedded in real individual lives.

These stories exemplify *wen* masculinity, too, because the stereotypical *wen* man in traditional China is most popularly equated with the scholar characters in the countless romances featuring talented scholars and beautiful women (the *caizi jiaren* stories).[1] It is these fictional scholars who give concrete expression to qualities of talent in the *junzi*. These scholars and intellectuals would on the surface appear to personify the teachings of Confucius. Yet, more often than not, they are portrayed as wilfully deviating from Confucian orthodoxy, giving rise to the impression that theory is diametrically opposed to practice. For example, Confucius equates women with lowly people (*xiaoren*) who should be kept at arm's length, but the scholars in literary and artistic dimensions usually have two basic aims in life: to be successful in the civil service examinations and to win a beautiful woman (or women). This chapter addresses some of these discrepancies between Confucian theory and practice by examining two prototypes of the scholar–beauty romances.

According to the compilers of a recent collection of romantic (*yanqing xiaoshuo*) stories, the *caizi jiaren* genre 'commenced at the end of the Ming Dynasty and only began to decline after the Qianlong reign in the Qing Dynasty'.[2] However, as the compilers of another monumental collection of romantic fiction remarks, 'where there is human society, there is human romance'.[3] While the *caizi jiaren* genre did indeed reach its peak in the Ming-Qing period, its prototype extended as far back as the Han Dynasty (206BC–220AD),[4] and its ideological message permeated all layers of Chinese society right into the twentieth century.

The Scholar in the Tang Dynasty

The best illustration of early representations of the male lovers from among the precursors to the *caizi jiaren* genre is the Tang Dynasty tale,

'The Story of Yingying'. As Minford and Lau note, 'This classical tale, which is supposedly autobiographical, is without doubt the single best-known love story in Chinese literature'.[5] Written in the *chuanqi* style,[6] this story is only a few pages long, yet it has influenced conceptions of scholarly romances for centuries. One of the most prominent re-presentations of this story is the Yuan Dynasty drama *The Story of the West Wing* by Wang Shifu.[7] Moreover, the literary style of this play was one of the most imitated in the Ming and Qing dynasties.[8] Although as a result of early twentieth century language reforms, the story is no longer used as a model for writing, its ideological impact continues through to the present. I will show that between the Tang and Yuan dynasties, two very different ideals of masculinity emerged. Yet, both ideals reveal that *wen* is more important than *wu* in the masculinity stakes. Most import-antly, both versions unambiguously point to the understanding that beautiful women are attracted to talented students (*caizi*) who are not yet *wenren* but who aspire to be so. The women act as connoisseurs, cheerleaders, and sometimes sponsors of the budding male talents.[9] By the 1980s, Zhang Xianliang was able to pontificate on this phenomenon with great gusto.

As we have observed, men aspired to *wen* accomplishments because the *wenren* traditionally implied success at the civil service examinations that gave access to privileged official positions on the imperial bureaucracy. While there was a general overlap between the literati and officialdom (and therefore power), this was not always the case. Infrequent though it may be, the literati could find their access to officialdom greatly diminished under certain socio-political conditions. The term '*wenren*' underwent some changes between the Tang and the Yuan dynasties. Martin Huang summarises that change succinctly when he notes that:

> In the Tang and the Northern Song periods, the distinction between *wenren* and *shidafu* (scholar-official) was not particularly significant because most *wenren* were in one way or another admitted into the official world and many of them were members of the *shidafu* class (e.g., Su Shi [1037–1101]). This situation began to change dramatically in the Yuan dynasty (1271–1368) when the Mongol rulers ranked the literati almost at the bottom of the scale of social classes and restricted their role in politics.[10]

Martin Huang points out that after the Yuan Dynasty, the identity of the *wenren* was under more pressure to change. 'By the eighteenth century the alternative of being a *wenren* was further challenged by the gradual blurring of distinctions among the social classes, especially those between literati and merchants.'[11] The implications of the merchant challenge (real or imagined) for *wen-wu* masculinity will be examined more closely in chapter 7. The point that needs to be stressed here is that in the Tang Dynasty, the notion of a scholar-official class was a lot less problematic than during the Yuan, when traditional scholars lost access to officialdom and the concomitant power and privilege. I will show in this chapter that despite this loss, the essential idea of the superiority of the *wenren* persists. As we saw in the previous two chapters, the *wenren* is a man who has been *wen*-ised – someone who is educated and cultured. This was an important process for development into the Confucian *junzi*. Furthermore, like men who have *wu*, the most important criterion for attainment of *junzi*-hood is self-control. Thus, like the *wu yingxiong*, the *wenren* should be able to resist women if they get in the way of his cultural attainment, which in practical terms is success in the civil service examinations.

All the *caizi jiaren* stories revolve around the theme of winning the woman and passing the examinations, though not necessarily in that order. The term '*caizi*' (talented scholar) reveals the intent of these stories. According to the early dictionaries *Shuowen* and the *Jiyun*, the primary meaning of '*cai*' refers to the basis of plants or the innate essence of people,[12] much like the *zhi* referred to by Confucius. And, as Confucius had indicated, a man needs both *wen* and *zhi* to become a *junzi*. The *wen* civilises the *zhi* that is in all men. Thus, a *caizi* has talent, often talent of a creative sort such as composing poetry. But of course that innate talent amounts to nothing if it is not civilised, educated or cultured (that is, *wen*-ised). The *wen*-ising process is one where the *caizi* learns more orthodox pursuits to enable him to pass the examinations and take on social responsibilities.[13] The *caizi jiaren* story is therefore about the realisation of the boy-talent into the *wenren* and *junzi*, who is recognisably manly and socially admired.

If *junzi*-hood is the ultimate prize that all men should seek, and sexual temptation is the hardest obstacle to overcome, the *wen* man has as much at stake as the *wu* man in controlling sexual desire. Yet, the mechanisms by which he controls this desire are diametrically opposed to the method of abstinence adopted by the *wu* heroes. While the *wu* masculinity reinforces ideologies of 'brotherhood' and loyalty to other men, to rein in aggressive competitiveness among the men, Cao Pi of the Three Kingdoms period had already recognised the general principle that '*wen* men despise each other' (*wenren xiangqing*).[14] This expression has become an extremely common idiom used to describe the relationship between intellectuals. Though apparently physically weaker, the *wen* man appears more competitive than the *wu* man, and he is more adept in justifying the gratification of his sexual desires while simultaneously asserting that he has 'self-control' in his dealings with men and women. 'The Story of Yingying' and *Story of the West Wing* are classic illustrations of this phenomenon.

Written by one of the best-known Tang poets and statesmen, Yuan
Zhen (779–831), 'The Story of Yingying' belongs to the Tang *chuanqi*
genre. It describes a young man named Zhang, who 'was agreeable and
refined, and good looking, but firm and self-contained, and capable of no
improper act'.[15] In one of his travels, he seeks shelter in a monastery,
where a widowed Mrs Cui is also staying with her young son and a
daughter, whose name is Yingying. A mutiny of the troops stationed
around the monastery erupts just at this time. Scholar Zhang knows
some officers nearby and he writes to them to come and protect the Cui
family. When order is restored, Mrs Cui invites Scholar Zhang to dinner
to thank him for saving the family. He meets her daughter Yingying,
whose beauty is 'so radiant it took the breath away'.[16] Scholar Zhang
immediately falls in love with her. With the help of Yingying's maid
Hongniang, Zhang exchanges love poems with Yingying and within a few
nights, they become lovers. Some time later, Zhang leaves for the capital
Chang'an to take the examinations. Separated by distance, they exchange
love letters. In the capital Zhang shows Yingying's letters to his friends.
Despite their apparent mutual affection, Zhang is resolute in refusing
to marry Yingying. A year after his departure Yingying marries someone else. Zhang also takes another woman as his wife. Later, Zhang
attempts to meet Yingying during a journey through her town. Yingying
declines to see him and instead sends him a couple of poems about
being forsaken.

In his discussion of the story, James Hightower concentrates on
establishing whether Yuan Zhen is the narrator, the author or both.
Hightower is not concerned with the implications for masculinity as such.
However, he 'is reluctantly led to the conclusion: the author of the story
was Yüan Chen [Yuan Zhen], who wrote it out of his own experience
and intended it both as self-justification and warning'.[17] Hightower's
scholarship is impeccable, but having tried unsuccessfully to read the
story ironically or as an indirect attack on a prominent statesman,
he seems unwilling to accept his own well-argued conclusion. He is
reluctant to accept the story as an objective narration of Yuan Zhen's own
experience. He seems puzzled that the young protagonist, who 'is rather
strait-laced, self-consciously and self-righteously moral, not easily influenced by his friends', could so easily repudiate a sweet and beautiful girl
like Yingying 'on grounds of expedient-morality'.[18]

This assessment of Scholar Zhang was based on modern Western
notions of morality and expediency. If we read the story as a straightforward account of a pre-marital affair between two good-looking and
talented youngsters from good families, then the outcome is the best
that one could wish for. Indeed, 'His contemporaries for the most part
conceded that Chang had done well to rectify his mistake' in the act of

abandoning Yingying.[19] Zhang's mistake was to have lost control over his sexual desire manifested in his pre-marital sex with Yingying. He regains control over his desire by rejecting the source of that emotion – Yingying. Even Yingying understands this perfectly in one of her rare utterances: 'To seduce someone and then abandon her is perfectly natural, and it would be presumptuous of me to resent it.'[20] Though by the end of the story Yingying claims to have lost her looks and feels ashamed before Zhang, she is at least alive and married. Two other highly influential fictional heroines from the Tang *chuanqi* stories, Miss Ren and Huo Xiaoyu, paid with their lives for their love and devotion, like so many other beautiful women.[21]

Yingying enabled Zhang to prove his masculinity. First, his sexual conquest of her proves his physical prowess. Second, his rejection of her after he sits the examinations demonstrates he has learnt a successful lesson in male self-control. We are told right from the beginning that Scholar Zhang is not only good-looking, but 'firm and self-contained'. But when he first sets eyes on Yingying, he is instantly infatuated with her beauty and attempts, through Hongniang, to seduce her. His self-control and firm vision for examination success ahead therefore waver in the face of female beauty. However, when Yingying comes to see Zhang and upbraids him for trying to take advantage of her by substituting 'seduction for rape', he simply 'went back over the wall to his quarters, all hope gone'.[22] Yet, it is Yingying who then goes to his bed a few nights later, uninvited. At no stage is there any indication that Scholar Zhang fails in his self-control. When he finally decides to abandon her, Zhang's professed reason (his 'remarkable farrago', according to Hightower) is a standard excuse given in practically all traditional romances: 'It is a general rule that those women endowed by Heaven with great beauty invariably either destroy themselves or destroy someone else … I have no inner strength to withstand this evil influence. That is why I have resolutely suppressed my love.'[23] This misogynist outlook is consistent with Scholar Zhang's initial adherence to single-minded self-cultivation towards *junzi*-hood. He suppresses his love for the woman to demonstrate his success in moving along the path to scholarly self-control. Yingying is merely a device through which Zhang can prove his *wen* masculinity. And it is this self-control that his friends and generations of *wenren* since have wanted to emulate.

As I have argued earlier, proof of self-control is a crucial prerequisite for the control of others. It is also a necessary condition for mastery of *wen-wu* skills. The *chuanqi* story is written in *wenyan*, a language that only an elite population would be able to read in the Tang Dynasty. Indeed, many were written for the enjoyment of small circles of friends. The morality so explicitly enunciated in 'The Story of Yingying' was therefore

likely to have been accepted by the literati reader as representing the
author's genuine ethical position, devoid of satire and self-mockery. If
Martin Huang is correct, the literati in the Tang period were relatively
self-assured about their own belief systems. By the Yuan and Ming,
however, the social position of the literati was not so secure, and the
scholars saw themselves (along with the courtesans that populate fictional
writing) as 'marginal members of society'.[24] The *caizi*'s suppression of
sexual desire in order to attain some form of enlightenment and possibly
junzi-hood therefore became a much more ambiguous project.

The *caizi* as Not-yet-realised *junzi*

Story-telling also became a more sophisticated art form, so that complex
ideas, both moral and emotional, were developed more fully, especially
since novels were beginning to become more acceptable as a literary
genre. In his analysis of Li Yu's *The Prayer Mat of Flesh (Rou putuan)*,[25]
Robert Hegel demonstrates convincingly that this novel can be read as
a masterpiece of satire, in which Li Yu ridicules the scholar-gentry class
humorously but mercilessly.[26] Hegel's translation of the protagonist's
name (Weiyang Sheng) as 'Not Yet Spent' is particularly apposite. Right
from the beginning of the novel, Not Yet Spent reveals that he has a
great mastery of the *wen* skills, and he claims that his ambition is to be
the greatest *caizi* in the world and to marry the most beautiful *jiaren*.
However, by unrestrainedly seeking sexual gratification, his conduct is
unbecoming and he never does reach *junzi*-hood. The surgical removal
of 'his' gigantic penis at the end of the novel may symbolically take away
the root of desire, but that enlightened state is a ridiculous rendition of
the Buddhist doctrine of the elimination of desire – he has still not yet
mastered the secret of Confucian self-discipline.

While the *caizi jiaren* formulation can be constructed in more
ambiguous and complex ways, and Li Yu has done that brilliantly, most
audiences and readers would not have had the time and expertise to
deconstruct what they saw and read. They would have simply wanted
to be entertained and have their fantasies and longings verbalised. This is
especially the case for the less serious reader, who most likely treated art
and literature as a salve for the tired soul. For example, *The Prayer Mat of
Flesh* has always been seen primarily as pornography and only secondarily
as social satire. The popularity of the *caizi jiaren* genre since the Yuan
rests mainly on its feel-good storyline, and not on the profundity of social
analysis it provides to its readers. Yet its popularity does mean that whatever messages it carries are accepted by, or at least exposed to, a broader
audience than the Tang *chuanqi* tales. This is certainly true of Yuan drama
(*zaju*), which can be seen as the popularisation of literati concerns and

ideals. Plays and operas were appreciated by the 'masses' in ways that literature was not – especially those written in the classical style such as 'The Story of Yingying'. One would therefore expect the ideologies of the Yuan *zaju* to be very different to those of the Tang *chuanqi*. Yet, an analysis of Wang Shifu's play *The Story of the West Wing*, which is derived from 'The Story of Yingying', will show that the *wen-wu* manifestations are made more specific and concrete, but the assumptions and logic remain the same.

The plot of *The Story of the West Wing* is basically the same as 'The Story of Yingying'.[27] However, there are some significant additions and alterations. For example, Mrs Cui is now strongly opposed to the union between the young lovers, while the maid Hongniang develops into a most memorable and witty character who is instrumental in bringing the lovers together. The most momentous change is the resolution of the romance: in *West Wing*, Scholar Zhang and Yingying marry and live happily ever after. Many writers have celebrated this major about-face in the conclusion as a triumph of young love against feudalism. In more academic language, the changes can also be seen as the ascendance of sentiment (*qing*) over rationality (*li*).[28] Both *qing* and *li* are Confucian concepts, and the interplay between them was central to philosophical debates in Chinese history and the rise of neo-Confucianism. In the context of *wen-wu* masculinity, of course, rationality is essential. Sentiment, especially the sexual kind, is exactly what the *junzi* and *yingxiong* need to guard against. Yet in the play, Scholar Zhang swoons, weeps and kneels to not just women (and that's horrible enough), but the maid Hongniang. As Song Geng observes,

> The portrayal of the lovesick scholar in the play verges on caricature. This, on the one hand, can be ascribed to the traditional parody on the pedantic scholar in the Chinese literary scene; on the other hand, it can also be viewed as a self-caricature of the uselessness of the frustrated Yuan literati.[29]

It is a caricature which finds resonance in much of Ming-Qing fiction, as we have seen in the case of Not Yet Spent above.

Despite Scholar Zhang's deviations from the guidelines of proper *junzi* conduct in his dealings with women, he does find happiness and is even rewarded with being the top candidate in the examinations (whereas in the Tang story, he fails). This could be explained by the fact that the Yuan version is a performance genre targeted at the lower classes so the scholar does not have to adhere so strictly to Confucian morality.[30] While Scholar Zhang is not yet a *junzi*, his *caizi* credentials are still intact. Like his progenitor, he is good-looking and has ambitions to pass the civil service examinations for an official career. Unfortunately, he falls short in his ability to be 'firm and self-contained'. It is this deficiency which suggests to both Western and Chinese audiences that the *xiaosheng* role, of which Scholar Zhang is a classic example, lacks masculinity.[31] The evidence that having little self-discipline would lead to a failure to gain access to power seems indisputable. However, why are there so many images of weak but desirable *caizi* such as Scholar Zhang since the Yuan? It is unlikely that the *wenren* in the last millennium really gave up all claims to *wen-wu* ideals of masculinity and power and privilege.

The Story of the West Wing shows that while the original Tang story unmistakably points to self-control as a prerequisite to manhood, the *caizi* in *West Wing* does not need that core value and still succeeds. The audience for the play was not the literati class alone – the play is aimed at a broader audience of merchants, artisans, townspeople, peasants and so on. Also, by the Yuan Dynasty, the social position of the literati was lowered and they were plagued by insecurities and uncertainties, so that their self-portraits were almost caricatures. However, *wen* still takes precedence over *wu* and the *West Wing*, like so many of the *caiji jiaren* stories featuring frail and sensitive scholars, only serves to consolidate the *wenren* (even if he has not yet made it to being a *junzi*) as the most masculine of men. Unlike the Tang story in which Scholar Zhang is the only significant male character, the *West Wing* has several notable stereotypical male roles. Early in the play when the monastery is surrounded by the rebel soldiers, Scholar Zhang sends a letter to General Du Que for assistance. To deliver the letter when the monastery is surrounded takes great courage and fighting skills. The task is entrusted to a brave and strong monk Huiming, who accomplishes the task. Du Que leads an army of 5,000 men to the monastery and saves the Cui family. As Song Geng points out, 'the letter is composed in exquisite and elegant language ... A frail scholar who cannot fight himself, Student Zhang has "a million soldiers in his breast", because he is the holder of textual power.'[32] It is interesting, too, that his heroic deed is achieved with the help of two *wu* heroes, the military general (*yingxiong*) and the loyal and brave monk (*haohan*). *Wen*'s commanding position over *wu* is naturalised in the play.

Two other male characters in the play demand our attention. They are Zhang's rivals for Yingying: the rebel General Sun Feihu and the scholar Zheng Heng. With the help of the *yingxiong* General Du, both are vanquished. This pair of villains contrasts starkly with Du and Zhang, also a pair of men representing the *wen-wu* dyad. The difference is that Du and Zhang symbolise legitimate and correct *wen-wu*: Du is a general in the imperial army and Zhang is a *caizi* who achieves the title of *zhuangyuan* by taking first place in the imperial examinations. By contrast, Sun and Zheng are pseudo *wen-wu*: Sun is a rebel and Zheng does not study well and achieves nothing despite having a rich and powerful family background. Both are punished for their failure to live up to the *wen-wu* ideals.

This brief discussion of *The Story of the West Wing* confirms the proposition reached by scholars such as Van Gulik and Martin Huang that by the Yuan-Ming dynasties the literati felt less secure about their social positions than in previous times. In fact, C.T. Hsia believes the transformation of Scholar Zhang was already taking place by the time story-tellers in the Northern Song were retelling the story. He asserts that 'their rather unsophisticated audiences could not have stomached the tale as Yuan Chen wrote it and would have wanted either a more tragic ending or a happier one, with the caddish hero duly transformed into a devoted lover'.[33] The play also indicates that the scholars were more competitive with other men for access to political power and social acceptance, and this competition is most vividly illustrated by the rivalry over claims to the woman. Winning the woman is therefore not just a sexual conquest, but an affirmation of social and moral righteousness. Through such creative justifications, we can see that even though many have lost political power, the literati's faith in the superiority of *wen* values remained strong. Scholar Zhang of the *West Wing* may have lost the 'firm and self-contained' resolve of his previous self in Tang times, but in the end, the two are the same person.

Scholar Zhang is still a *caizi* whose *wen* credentials only need to be formalised by the examination process. The understanding is that as a *wenren*-in-training, his self-control can be indulged a little. Indeed, in some cases, the *caizi* has to learn self-control by indulging himself while young. But once he is married and passes the examinations, he would be expected to be a full-fledged *wenren*, and not remain a wavering, emotional *caizi*. In this light, it makes sense to categorise *West Wing*, yet not so much the Tang *chuanqi*, as a *caizi jiaren* romance, because whereas in its Tang counterpart, the scholar loses his way but, in rejecting the temptations of a woman, regains his self-control, this is not the case in the Yuan *zaju* version. Even as a *caizi* in the Yuan play, however, Scholar Zhang has *wen* (both literary and moral) pretensions, and he is still considered superior to men who are only good at the martial arts and men who are less talented in literary pursuits. The difference is that in having less resolve the *caizi*'s fantasies are more exaggerated. Furthermore, to be a *caizi* means that even if he shows indifference to mundane pursuits such as passing examinations, he always passes them anyway.[34] The *caizi* therefore can have his cake and eat it too: he beds the woman and is successful in the examinations without having to leave her. Such a formula is standard for the *caizi jiaren* genre because the audiences were mostly non-scholars, so that success in examinations remained in the realm of fantasy, and the tensions between self-control and self-gratification did not demand such total resolution.

The Contemporary *wenren*

With the image of the traditional talented scholar explained in terms of the *wen-wu* paradigm, the contemporary constructions of masculinity of intellectuals can now be discussed within the traditional *wenren* framework. I will do this by looking at the male protagonists in the trilogy of semi-autobiographical novels by the controversial writer Zhang Xianliang (b. 1936): *Mimosa* (1984), *Half of Man Is Woman* (1985) and *Getting Used to Dying* (1989). Throughout the late 1980s and 1990s, these novels, especially *Half of Man Is Woman*, were seen as emblematic of the new sexual openness in China. All three novels have been translated and are widely available in the West. One of the major reasons for Zhang Xianliang's popularity in the last two decades of the twentieth century is his depiction of Chinese sexuality in China and by 1989 (in *Getting Used to Dying*) abroad.

While the Western reader – and many Chinese readers in the twenty-first century – will find his descriptions of sex contrived and hackneyed, it has to be remembered that Zhang Xianliang wrote at a peculiar time. Many critics agree that he 'speaks movingly of the plight of the country's intellectuals'.[35] More importantly for our purposes, as a self-professed intellectual, his writing reveals many of the concerns of the modern-day *wen* man. China is changing rapidly and some of the concerns raised in the three novels under discussion are dated. But I will show that the fundamental issues of masculinity raised in Zhang's novels stem from traditional times, and they continue to remain constants in the construction of *wen* masculinity thereafter. The unusual historical juncture under which Zhang Xianliang's novels were produced directs most critics' attention to 'labour-camp' life or/and its ramifications for the male protagonist's relationship with women.[36] The narrators' insecurities, sense of self-importance, impotence and misogyny are then explained in terms of labour-camp or totalitarian politics.

I argue that the unusual political conditions mask the constancy of *wen* masculine traits portrayed, causing readers and Zhang himself to wonder if the government had castrated 'China's entire intellectual community'.[37] I am, of course, not belittling the suffering or injustice that may have been inflicted on intellectuals in the first thirty years of Communist rule. And I agree that peculiar period may have produced some very warped personalities. However, the self-identity of the *caizi* and the *zhishifenzi* (the modern intellectual) do have basic similarities that outweigh the impact of changed social or political positions. In the same way that the Scholar Zhang of the Tang Dynasty is unmistakably the same Scholar Zhang of the Yuan Dynasty, Intellectual Zhang in Zhang Xianliang's semi-autobiographical trilogy is yet another metamorphosis of the classic *wenren*.[38] That reduplication process is explicable and most easily revealed by unravelling the *wen-wu* matrix in the ways it orders the mind–body dichotomy and how that affects man–woman and man–man relationships.

The title of one of his very first stories, 'Flesh and Soul', already makes the demarcation between the body and the mind.[39] This short story is about a young man who, despite being wrongfully accused of being a rightist and sent to a state farm, elects to remain a herdsman rather than go abroad to inherit his father's fortunes. The main thrust of the story does not directly articulate *wen* and *wu* transformations. However, the title does reflect the principle that spiritual and mental concerns take precedence over the material and corporeal. *Mimosa* and its companion piece *Half of Man Is Woman* elaborate on this principle most eloquently. In *Mimosa*, the intellectual protagonist Zhang Yonglin, who is the narrator-protagonist for both novels, is released from a labour camp in 1961 to work in a state farm. Despite his emaciated condition, he is befriended by Mimosa, a young ethnic minority woman who feeds him from her secret store of grain and other food provided by the men who admire her beauty. Zhang Yonglin cannot catch animals or make furniture for her, but she loves to listen to his stories and ideas. Until Zhang's appearance, Hai Xixi, a strong and handsome Muslim carter at the farm, is her favourite among her suitors. As Mimosa shows her preference for brains over muscle, the two men get into a fight which neither wins. Zhang Yonglin emerges as the victor by default, and Hai Xixi runs away. That night Mimosa lavishes her love on Zhang as a victorious hero. When Zhang becomes passionate, however, Mimosa advises him to study hard and promises that they will marry when the difficult times are over. But before that happens, Zhang Yonglin is accused of having been instrumental in Hai Xixi's escape and is imprisoned. When he is released six years later, he discovers that Mimosa has returned to her home in Qinghai with her daughter. The novel ends in Beijing in 1983, when Zhang Yonglin, at a conference in the Great Hall of the People, remembers how the simple folk such as Mimosa helped him become a successful person.

Clearly the narrator is remembering 'Mimosa' as a symbol of the labouring people who nurtured him back to health and success. That abstraction is misleading. As Gang Yue points out, as well as being a 'replica of the feeding mother',[40] Mimosa is illiterate, displays no class consciousness, belongs to an ethnic minority and has an illegitimate child. If anything, her image 'provides a powerful subversion of the people'.[41] Nonetheless, it is true that her role in the story is to feed Zhang Yonglin and urge him to study so that he becomes a full man. Food is so much part of her identity that in the scene where they declare love to each other, instead of 'darling' (a term apparently unfamiliar to her), she asks him to call her 'rourou' (meat) and she would call him 'gougou' (puppy).[42] Zhang Yonglin notes that:

> Though gougou was a term of endearment, it was a far cry from my old romantic notions. The form her love took and the terms of endearment she used rather embarrassed me – they seemed so laughable. Though I didn't want her to sense the gap between us, I was only too well aware of it myself.[43]

There is no reason to doubt Zhang's sincerity in his romanticised vision of the role of the people and women. However, as he reminds us throughout, there is a gulf between him and them, 'a gulf that could never be bridged'.[44] Nevertheless, it is interesting that in the revelations about his reactions to the problematic terms of endearment, he cites gougou rather than rourou as laughable. In practice, Mimosa is tantamount to a piece of meat on which he, as a scholar who cannot fend for himself in the harsh conditions of the farm, feeds. She is only a source of food for him and her two-year-old daughter: the other men in fact provide her with provisions, and that's why she has plentiful supplies. Interestingly, he feeds on her as a piece of flesh to his heart's content, but he does not sleep with her. This seems to hark back to the *wu* men in the *Three Kingdoms* and *All Men Are Brothers*. Zhang Yonglin is nothing of the sort. He is not coitophobic, he is just sublimating his sexual energies until he and she are ready. She is aware of this and, like the good woman in traditional fiction, urges him to adhere to this path.

She wants him to sublimate because: 'You're a scholar, you must study. So long as you study I don't mind slaving away until I'm blue in the face.'[45] Thus, like the *caizi* of old, he is very much at home with a beautiful woman who is prepared to suppress her own sexual desires so that he can study without any burdens. He reads and thinks; she cooks and sews. To Zhang as much as to the traditional *wenren*, this is a picture of a perfect familial life. For this utopia to be truly perfect, it needs to be an ideal that the woman also desires. Thus, the narrator observes that:

> It was evident from her radiant face that she enjoyed this atmosphere. And this enjoyment dated from her childhood – she thought it right for a woman to have a man studying beside her. Chinese women down the ages have always had this beautiful fantasy.[46]

The *caizi jiaren* vision that women throughout the ages had apparently coveted is therefore painted as alive and well even in the harsh conditions of the state farm.

This ideal is even more forcefully asserted in the relationship between the men. In the first business transaction he has after he leaves the labour camp, Zhang tricks a poor old peasant into selling him five catties of carrots below their real value by his deftness with mental arithmetic.[47] Throughout the novel, not only does Mimosa respect him for his learning, but even his male rivals defer to him as a clever and learned man. The narrator's acceptance of Mimosa's readiness to sacrifice herself to him, the scholar, is not particularly surprising given his understanding that 'Chinese women down the ages have always had this beautiful fantasy'. Significantly, Hai Xixi, the Muslim carter whose physical prowess and moral scruples make him a perfect *wu* counterpart to Zhang's *wen*, also defers to his assumed superiority as a scholar. He not only yields Mimosa to Zhang, but he 'shows his forgiving manly style [*nanzihan zuofeng*]',[48] and leaves behind a hundred catties of soy beans for the couple before he runs away. He reassures Zhang that he had secretly grown the beans himself because: 'I know you scholars don't eat stolen food. I'll tell you where it comes from.'[49] Thus the scholar's superiority in the moral sphere is taken for granted.

When Zhang asks him to take some with him, Hai's response is 'No! Wherever I am I won't go without food. I'm not like the two of you, a woman and a scholar ...'.[50] This parting remark is a *wu* man's resigned acceptance of the general principle that lovers would naturally be 'a woman and a scholar'. Hai Xixi, being a Muslim, had tried to woo Mimosa. Had he been a decent traditional Chinese *wu* man of the *yingxiong* or *haohan* mould, he should not even have bothered. How times change! I will show in the next chapter some of the changes the Communist revolution has made to *wu* masculinity. It is irrelevant whether discussion centres on the intellectuals or the peasants: the precedence of *wen* over *wu* remains a constant. Underneath all the soul-searching and self-doubt, the intellectual's sense of self-identity as superior to all and above the tangles of sexual desires also remains constant. In this novel, Zhang Yonglin does not need to cast Mimosa aside, as did the Tang Dynasty Scholar Zhang. Nevertheless, our PRC Intellectual Zhang is conveniently separated from Mimosa, enabling him to forge ahead in his career in the capital. To show his ability to win a woman and then abandon her in the new political framework, we need to look at the sequel.

Half a *wen* Man is Still a Hero

Zhang Yonglin's tortuous biography continues in *Half of Man Is Woman*, where Zhang finds himself in a labour camp in 1967. Every night the prisoners swap stories of dreams where they copulate with ghosts, as their sole diversion from the bleak surroundings. In this sex-starved environment, Zhang Yonglin comes across a woman prisoner bathing in a creek, getting a clear view of her sensuous naked body. She also sees him but lets him continue to gaze at her. Eight years later, Zhang Yonglin is released and works herding goats in a state farm. The Party secretary, Cao Xueyi, arranges for a woman, Huang Xiangjiu, to come and help him. It is the same woman he had seen bathing years earlier. She has since been married and divorced twice. Before long, they are given permission to marry by Cao Xueyi. On their wedding night, Zhang finds that years of denial have made him impotent and wants to divorce, but she refuses. Discovering later that Huang is having an affair with Cao Xueyi, in frustration and bitterness, he buries himself in Western and Chinese philosophy. A flood at the farm gives Zhang Yonglin the opportunity to become a hero, and Huang Xiangjiu that night is especially attentive to him: finally he gets his erection and from being 'half a man', becomes 'whole'. Having regained his potency, he treats Huang Xiangjiu with open contempt while she responds with renewed tenderness and affection. But he is determined and leaves her, at a time that coincides with the end of the Cultural Revolution and the re-emergence of intellectuals.

While his resolve to leave a woman who has made him 'whole' to pursue his manly ambitions would make the Tang Scholar Zhang proud, Zhang Yonglin's actions in this novel prompted one of the biggest debates regarding sexual morality in contemporary Chinese literature. Some Chinese critics call him a 'fake *junzi*' for his behaviour, while others regard both his original impotence and subsequent desertion of Huang Xiangjiu as reflections of the political climate of that era.[51] Some also see the interweaving of sex and politics in this novel as an allegory for the 'castration' of Chinese intellectuals in the Mao regime.[52] Whether one interprets Zhang Yonglin's behaviour towards the heroine as the result of moral or political struggles within or outside of himself, it is difficult not to come to the conclusion that 'women are employed as the site within which a man's struggle is staged'.[53] Indeed, in her review of the novel, Marsha Wagner states that: 'The novel is a fascinating psychological study of misogyny.'[54]

It does seem that the portrayal of Huang Xiangjiu in this novel is far less sympathetic than that of her counterpart Mimosa in the prequel. Although Mimosa is a single mother and she flirts with other men, her chastity is highlighted. By contrast, Huang Xiangjiu is divorced twice and after she marries Zhang Yonglin has an affair with the cadre Cao Xueyi. Zhang Yonglin therefore has some justification in abandoning her so he can play a larger role as in nation-building. However, it remains true that like Mimosa, Huang is responsible for bringing Zhang back to health. As the personification of the Communist Party, Cao Xueyi is far too powerful for Zhang to take him on physically as he had done with the labourer Hai Xixi. It is significant, though, that it was during the flood that Zhang emerges as the hero. He is a good swimmer and Cao cannot swim. As we will see in the next chapter, the ability to conquer water can be read as the ability to control female forces since water is *yin* in the *yin-yang* scheme. It is precisely after the flood episode that Zhang finds his sexual potency again and has total power over Huang Xiangjiu. It is also at this time, when he can finally 'make it' with Huang sexually and she loves him fully that he decides to leave her.

It is this ungrateful behaviour that many critics find puzzling if not immoral.[55] However, in the context of the *wen-wu* schema and the example set by the Tang hero Scholar Zhang, Intellectual Zhang's actions are comprehensible and natural. The Tang Scholar Zhang simply asserts that Yingying would be a dangerous woman to have around if he were to succeed in life. As her twentieth-century reincarnation, Huang Xiangjiu is explicitly depicted as untrustworthy through her affair with Cao. As I have argued, by the Yuan Dynasty the literati had lost so much political authority that they were portrayed as weaklings. This partly explains why the Yuan Dynasty Scholar Zhang ends up marrying Yingying when his Tang Dynasty self had enough resolve to leave the woman. The reduced status of intellectuals in the early years of the Communist regime can certainly be used to explain why Intellectual Zhang cannot do much to punish Party Secretary Cao for having an affair with his wife. However, there is a 'spiritual victory' of sorts in the flood episode. It is clear after this that Huang Xiangjiu is totally devoted to Zhang and she considers the Cao affair to have been a mistake. Nonetheless, by the end of the story, the Cultural Revolution has ended and Deng Xiaoping has returned to Beijing. Intellectuals have regained some of their lost power and privilege. By the reckoning of the traditional *wenren*, it is to be expected that Zhang would leave, 'because Huang Xiangjiu has now become an obstacle to his further psychic emancipation by trying to confine him to the life she has at her command'.[56]

The general rule that beautiful women 'invariably either destroy themselves or destroy someone else' laid down by the Tang Scholar Zhang is now explicitly given a political and psychological dimension. By arguing that Zhang's treatment of women (sexual desire) is only the same as his treatment of men (political ambition), critics such as Kwok-kan Tam can claim that in order to achieve emancipation, Zhang 'must break away from the power game underlying the intricate and twisted relationships between him and Huang Xiangjiu, as well as between him and Cao Xueyi'.[57] For Zhang, therefore, women and men are to be dominated and then transcended.

In traditional China, the literati competed directly with each other for political power (as well as beautiful women). Even during the Yuan

Dynasty, those who succeeded, as the play *West Wing* so eloquently showed, were portrayed as moral and had *wen* attributes whereas the losers were shown to be corrupt and without cultural and literary talents. Success at the civil service examinations was a normal path to political power. In the twentieth century, this system broke down. Nonetheless, intellectuals still competed for recognition and privilege by claiming moral superiority like the deposed traditional Confucian officials. And when they could not, they sought the traditional route of 'transcendence' by following the Legalist Han Feizi's advice that one should simply flee if one can't win.[58] Often, the retreat into one's mind and running away amounted to the same action.[59] And in many cases, women were used as a site through which the superiority of the intellectuals' moral and mental powers was revealed.[60] However, in the mighty Chinese political machine that has waged intermittent but thorough campaigns against 'elite culture' since 1949, it has often been difficult for scholars to directly compete for supremacy in the bureaucracy or government. Accordingly, many have taken the 'flight' option.

Zhang Xianliang's *Getting Used to Dying* is a good illustration of a story where the protagonist is physically detached from his usual abode and at the same time lives a life mostly in his mind. The narrator is nameless but he refers to himself by the first, second and third personal pronouns, accentuating further his split personality. Although the narrator is not named, his memories of prison camps and the concerns expressed in the novel point to its autobiographical nature, so that it could be seen as the third of a trilogy following *Mimosa* and *Half of Man Is Woman*. Indeed, some critics state that 'given its subtexts, it is not difficult for us to tell he is none other than Zhang Yonglin' and proceed to address the narrator as such.[61] Although the novel is written in a 'modernist' mode so that historical periods, places and voices are unclear, making it difficult to chronicle times and people exactly, the plot is relatively simple. The narrator is a former political prisoner in China who has had several near-death experiences. His novels have made him world-famous and he travels to America and France, where he has sex with several women, including an ex-lover from China, a Taiwanese woman, a French woman studying Chinese and a Vietnamese prostitute. However, every time he reaches orgasm, he is terrified by an intrusive image – a gun lodges a bullet into his brain.[62] At the end of the novel, he goes back to a village in China, to a former lover who is clearly an aged Mimosa or Huang Xiangjiu. This is the only time in the novel that women and sex are not associated with death and a bullet in the head. Thus, while it can be said that in the global competition for sexual dominance, 'to screw foreigners is patriotic',[63] the nationalist agenda must ultimately triumph. The narrator explains his going back to an aged peasant as his brand of 'patriotism'.[64]

The reincarnation of Zhang Yonglin in this novel is no longer impotent. Like some of the other better known novels in the 1980s and 1990s,[65] the protagonist's sexual exploits with multiple partners are highlighted to show his desirability, yet this man is unhappy. Nonetheless, his competitiveness with other men vis-à-vis women has become even more pronounced. Indeed, as if the numerous heterosexual affairs are not enough to convince him (and the reader) that he is now no longer 'half a man', one of his lovers who has married an American reassures him, 'Don't be jealous. He may be a white man, but that thing of his isn't any bigger than yours. And in bed, he's not up to you.'[66] By going international, he now has a much bigger range of men whom he can outwit and outperform.[67] The superiority of the Chinese intellectual is indicated in a number of places, usually by the criterion that they alone know the real China. In the 1990s, immensely popular television soap operas such as *Beijingers in New York* and *Foreign Babes in Beijing* unambiguously correlated sexual 'conquest' of white women with national revival,[68] so that: 'The victory that Chinese men are able to score with foreign women symbolizes not only the resurrection of Chinese masculinity but also a triumph of the Chinese nation itself.'[69]

In reality, of course, sexual competition with other Chinese is much more immediate than that with white males. Thus, descriptions of rivalry with overseas Chinese are given more intense and detailed treatment in the novel. For example, on one occasion, his cousin Qiao (rendered as Joe in the Avery translation used here), who is a very successful businessman in America, graciously flatters him by saying that had his whole family been brought to America by his uncle earlier, he would be doing even better. Zhang's reaction reveals his competitive nature in no uncertain terms. He muses,

> Yes, if we had brought the whole family to America I would certainly be doing better than you. In America, anyone can be a success, start with bare hands and set up a family, not only commercially minded Chinese. On the mainland in China, on the other hand, sons of certain families were looked down on as the 'enemy class'. Years later they were belatedly made 'intellectuals with a contribution to make to the Four Modernizations'. But these sons, every one of them, had to have been extraordinarily talented just to stay alive. Do you know that?
>
> Neither he nor Joe spoke during the drive home. Emotions that fate had played with so lightly were set rigidly on their faces, to the point that they didn't dare look at each other. Several days later Joe brought Jenny [Joe's Korean mistress] to see him and, with a woman in between, they were able to talk. Only where sex was concerned could the two men feel equal.[70]

Like other *wen* men throughout Chinese history, Zhang looks down on 'commercially minded Chinese'. The people with 'extraordinary talents' are those with intellectual pretensions. In another part of the novel, he quotes a Communist Party member friend who has just visited the Louvre in Paris and who makes the observations that 'without nobility there is no art. I mean nobility in the broadest sense. A country that cannot produce a nobility of the spirit is a country that is doomed.'[71] Despite this faith in the nobility of spiritual matters, economic reforms in the early 1980s had produced a whole literature about the relationships between Party functionaries, managers and intellectuals. This movement followed Jiang Zilong's 'Manager Qiao Assumes Office' in 1979,[72] and by the 1980s, it became known as 'reform literature' (*gaige wenxue*). It was so pervasive that many writers who otherwise had no interest in commercial matters wrote about these economic reforms. Zhang Xianliang, for example, had written a novel discussing the nature of manhood in the era of reform.[73] By the 1990s, the tendency towards globalisation and commercialism had affected intellectuals in more personal ways. As we saw in the last chapter, even Confucius was re-interpreted as a business guru, and many writers had also waded into the sea of business dealings (*xia hai*). Zhang Xianliang himself had become the manager of two large enterprises by the mid-1990s.[74]

By traditional definitions, the *wenren* should not be a businessman, not even a part-time businessman. However, I should reiterate that our concern is more with the constructions of the *wen-wu* man rather than what men actually did or do. As chapter 7 will show, the changing constructions of the *wen* man as a result of Westernisation had already begun in the early twentieth century. The transformation of *wen* to include business acumen reached its peak in the 1990s, as was demonstrated in interpretations of Confucius in the previous chapter. The idea that Confucian business ethics could be valued in Western management practices has also been proposed for business students in the West.[75] In Marxist terminology, the economic base must interact dialectically with the ideology for both or either to change. However, no matter what changes occur, the *wen-wu* constructions seem to maintain a few basic principles. From the Tang Dynasty until now, *wen* men continue to hold the high moral ground and claim to be a spiritual aristocracy. The *wen* man always attracts women, whether he is a *caizi* on his way to the capital, an inmate in a labour camp or a visiting writer in Paris. As well as providing him with food and sex, the women serve one other very important function. In all cases, to be successful, the *wen* man must have control over others because of his superior intelligence, but more importantly over himself. Until he learns that, he remains a *caizi*, becoming a *wenren* and *junzi* only when he has matured. What better way to demonstrate this self-control than to bestow on or withhold sex from the woman at will? In this way, the *wen* man is similar to the *wu* man.

More importantly, as the narrator of *Getting Used to Dying* observes in the quotation above, men can only relate to each other through women and sex. It should be remembered that he makes that observation as a result of self-generated rivalry with his cousin Qiao. He feels his material circumstances are, as a historical accident, not as auspicious as his cousin's, but that women will help to equalise them. That could be read in two ways: that women provide the topic or medium for conversation, or that women, too, are a competitive prize for the better man. The second reading is as plausible as the first given that what we have shown is that while *wu* masculinity is most concerned with male loyalty, solidarity and brotherhood and so on, *wen* masculinity seems to bring out competition, chauvinism and self-centredness in men. This is curious since *wu* masculinity is meant to be warlike and physical, *wen* masculinity is meant to be bookish and cultured. On the other hand, it is logical that if *wen-wu* is all about control, then *wen* must have as its primary motivation dominance over *wu*. In this way, although women often serve as the conduit linking men together, masculinity is foremost a construct that signifies the linkages and differences between men. The next chapter will further investigate this phenomenon by analysing more closely *wu* masculinity with class. This way, the uses of masculinity as a measure for socio-political power are even more evident.

5　The Working-class Hero: Images of *wu* in Traditional and Post-Mao Fiction

Wu Song Slaying the Tiger. The *wu* hero overcomes women in the same way he subdues beasts – by killing them. From Shi Nai'an and Luo Guanzhong, *Outlaws of the Marsh* (trans. Sidney Shapiro), Hong Kong: Commercial Press, 1986, p. 171. Reproduced with permission.

This chapter discusses the constructions of *wu* masculinity in contemporary China by focusing on a short story by the influential writer Jia Pingwa. Before doing this, I should clarify a few important aspects of *wu*. As indicated in the last three chapters, the social, economic and political power accompanying success in the civil service examinations meant that *wen* is associated with the masculinity of the powerful while *wu* is more a 'working-class' masculine ideal. By 'working-class', I am not referring to the Marxist notion of the proletariat or any kind of industrial urban worker.[1] In the case of China, this *wu* hero is more likely to be a poor and lower–middle peasant.

The *haohan* in Traditional China

Although the *wu* ideal is best illustrated by the god Guan Yu, we have seen that over the centuries the Guan Yu icon has been elevated to such a high status that he cannot be called 'working-class'. Even when he was alive, he was a powerful general, and he became a god in death. His godly status underscores the fact that he is an ideal, one that is beyond the reach of mortal men. He is a hero of the *yingxiong* variety – men who had political ambitions as well as a desire to be 'real men'. For examples of the types of heroes who come from the lower echelons of society and whose social mobility is very limited, we will have to look at the *haohan* variety. C.T. Hsia glosses the *haohan* hero as 'good fellow'. This literal translation is quite apt, as 'fellowship' in certain conditions 'exalts the ideal of friendship to the point of usurping the language of brotherhood'.[2]

Those conditions are found in *All Men Are Brothers*. Here, the 108 Liangshan heroes are outlaws who would take 'a knife in the ribs for a mate'[3] and who live at the margins of society. Apart from their leader Song Jiang, whose intention all along is to rejoin the regular forces and serve the emperor,[4] they have no expectations of achieving high office politically or socially.[5] Thus, while both *yingxiong* and *haohan* exemplify the *wu* ideal, the *haohan* is more likely to be from the underprivileged classes and to remain so. Typical occupations include monks, convicts, foot soldiers, peasants and fishermen. Of the more notable 'good fellows' in *All Men Are Brothers*, Wu Song, Lu Zhishen, Lin Chong, Li Kui and Yang Xiong are some of the most memorable. Among them, Wu Song is probably the 'best fellow' of all. Wu Song has all the important characteristics to warrant being endowed with 'Wu' as a surname, and Song (meaning pine, usually taken as a symbol for longevity and steadfastness)[6] as a given name.[7] His name connotes a man of immutable *wu* spirit. Before we look at the contemporary Chinese working-class hero, I will introduce the traditional understanding of a rough-and-ready *haohan* through the figure of Wu Song.

Wu Song is destined to be an outlaw. Even if he were to be in the regular army, he would remain a low-ranking officer. It is inconceivable that he would be 'classy' enough ever to be a general. Also, there is no attempt, even in popular representations seen in operas, comics or clay figurines, to give him any *wen* attributes by making him read a book, as had been the case with Guan Yu. Nevertheless, he is arguably the most popular and most beloved hero in Chinese folklore. All Chinese children, for example, are familiar with the details of chapter 23 of *All Men Are Brothers*, 'Wu Song Kills a Tiger on Jingyang Ridge'.

In this episode, Wu Song is on his way to see his elder brother when he passes the Jingyang Ridge. Before he climbs the hill, he stops at a tavern to have a drink. This particular inn makes its own potent liquor – it has the reputation of being so intoxicating that no man can cross the ridge after drinking three bowls of it. In typical *haohan* fashion, Wu Song downs not three, but eighteen bowls. As he is about to embark on the trek across the ridge, the tavern-keeper warns him that there is a tiger on the loose. This tiger had already killed nearly 30 strong men. Wu Song ignores the man, thinking he is only trying to scare people into spending the night in his inn. However, as he proceeds a little further, he sees an official notice confirming the tiger story. His reaction is illuminating: 'if I go back, he will ridicule me for not being a *haohan*. I can't go back.'[8] Fearful that his *haohan* status would be publicly questioned, he risks his life.

As he proceeds and just before the tiger appears, we are told that 'a wild gust of wind blew', signalling that this was not an ordinary animal. The tiger jumps, side-swipes and slashes at Wu Song but misses each time. Wu Song then strikes at the tiger with his staff but in his haste snaps the staff on a big branch, and he is left holding only a short piece,

> Lashing itself into a roaring fury, the beast charged. Wu Song leaped back ten paces, and the tiger landed in front of him. He threw away the stump of his staff, seized the animal by the ruff and bore down. The tiger struggled frantically, but Wu Song was exerting all his strength, and wouldn't give an inch. He kicked the beast in the face and eyes, again and again. The tiger roared, its wildly scrabbling claws pushing back two piles of yellow earth and digging a pit before it. Wu Song pressed the animal's muzzle into the pit, weakening it further. Still, relentlessly clutching the beast by the ruff with his left hand, Wu Song freed his right, big as an iron mallet, and with all his might began to pound.[9]

Wu Song lands fifty or sixty blows on the beast and beat it with his broken staff until it lay dead.

The action of killing the tiger, though described with an economy of words, is nevertheless vivid and detailed. We know the beast is amazingly ferocious before it even appears, and it takes Wu Song dozens of kicks and blows with his fists to subdue it. In each sequence of the action, we are presented with descriptions not only of the physical environment, but of Wu Song's psychological state as well. After the tiger is dead, the exhausted Wu Song is horrified to be confronted by two more tigers leaping out of the dry grass. He exclaims that he is finished. These tigers turn out to be hunters in tiger skin disguised to hunt the man-eater. They, like the reader, marvel at Wu Song's bravery and strength. These details help stress Wu Song's heroism. If, as Zhou Guangkuo points out, Wu Song had despatched the tiger easily, without fear and without exertion, his heroism would not be as pronounced.[10] In fact, in the novel itself, another 'good fellow' Li Kui kills four tigers in chapter 43, but he does it so precisely and effortlessly that there is no lasting impression of what took place, and Li Kui is not known as the tiger killer.

The tiger-killing episode refers to two of Wu Song's traits that established him as a *wu* hero above the average *haohan* found in *All Men Are Brothers*. First, his tolerance for alcohol is highlighted. All heroes consume large quantities of alcohol. In the novel, the heroes repeatedly meet each other in taverns and inns, and whenever they congregate, a show of gluttony (for meat especially) and insobriety (for alcohol) is obligatory. To demonstrate how he excels in this ritual, Wu Song drinks alone, and a great deal of fuss is made about the strength of the wine. To top it off, he kills a man-eating tiger when he has consumed six times the amount that would intoxicate the average man. Second, killing is routine for the *yingxiong haohan*. Wu Song himself conducts 'an orgy of murder' in chapter 31, where he slaughters an entire family – men, women and children. In this massacre, 'we follow the movement of Wu Song's dagger as it smites someone right in the face and cuts into the armchair in which he is sitting, or as it slashes another below the ear and through the neck'.[11] The savagery of such atrocities would be too gruesome for the more sensitive readers. By contrast, the tiger-killing episode is appealing to audiences of all ages because it combines alcohol with unrestrained killing – not of toddlers and young girls – but a dangerous man-eating tiger.[12]

Chinese children know Wu Song through this tiger-killing episode. However, adults are more fascinated by the events in the next three chapters of the novel following Wu Song's battle with the tiger. Wu Song goes to his elder brother's (Wu the Elder) house. Short, ugly and nicknamed 'the three incher' (*san cun ding*), Wu the Elder is married to Golden Lotus (Pan Jinlian). Golden Lotus' wanton behaviour and her fate make her the most unforgettable female character in *All Men Are Brothers*, if not in all Chinese literature. Her sexual relationships resonate so strongly with the idea of a loose woman that her name has since been incorporated into the Chinese language to mean just that. This fascination with Golden Lotus is centuries-old. The three chapters from *All*

Men Are Brothers have been expanded into one of the greatest, and some would say most pornographic, novels in world literature, *The Golden Lotus* (*Jin Ping Mei*).[13] This novel provides perceptive insights into the social life as well as the perceived threat of the merchant class to literati sexuality in late Ming China. In chapter 2, I examined how merchants have been incorporated into the *wen-wu* paradigm in the 1990s via Confucius. I will investigate the integration of merchants and business classes into the masculine amalgam further in chapter 7. Here, the focus is on Wu Song. In both classic novels the broad outlines of Wu Song's relationship with Golden Lotus and the other main characters remain the same.

When she is first introduced to her brother-in-law, Golden Lotus' thoughts are 'if I could have a man like that I wouldn't have lived in vain!'[14] As soon as she is alone with Wu Song, she tries to seduce him. In a *wu* gesture that would make Guan Yu proud, Wu Song pushes her away so violently that she is nearly knocked off her feet. He then proceeds to lecture her on the proper behaviour between siblings-in-law. After this, Wu Song warns his brother about her and he distances himself from this enticing sister-in-law from this point on. Soon after, Wu Song goes on a mission for nearly two months and when he returns, he finds that Golden Lotus has been having an affair with Ximen Qing, a profligate who together with Golden Lotus has poisoned Wu the Elder. The adultery and the murder give Wu Song an excellent justification to embark on a vengeful rampage wherein he beheads the two adulterers and offers the severed heads as sacrifices to his brother's memorial tablet. This episode illustrates most vividly the taboos associated with coveting one's brothers' wives and the duty of 'brothers' to police the wives' chastity.

Wu Song's sadistic savagery on his sister-in-law's body is the reverse of his previous displays of decorum and his apparent lack of sexual interest in her,

> While [Wu Song's] two feet pinned down her two arms, he ripped open the bodice covering her breasts. Faster than can be told, he placed the tip of his dagger beside her breast and twisted it once. Holding the knife in his mouth, he used both hands to dig open her chest and pulled out her heart, liver, and five entrails and placed them as an offering before the spirit tablet. Then with one swipe of his dagger, he cut off that woman's head and blood flowed over the entire floor.[15]

As Maram Epstein aptly points out, this 'horrific variation of a rape' demonstrates that Golden Lotus 'is no longer a woman but an emblem of the dangers associated with transgressive desire'.[16] Sexual transgression is an unforgivable sin. To show to the public his purity in this regard, Wu Song has to exhibit his wrath with a ferocious vengeance. As in the case of Guan Yu, the vehemence of denial hides a sexual desire that is forbidden for the *wu* man. In this case, intimations of coveting one's sister-in-law make the desire even more taboo. The ferocious expression of Wu Song's repressed sexuality is typical of traditional fiction's representation of a working-class hero with plenty of *wu* and almost no *wen* – someone who can only control his moral universe through brute strength and self-discipline.

Wu in Contemporary China

The understanding that *wen-wu* is a continuum along which masculinity can be correlated with class was never questioned in traditional times. Those with more *wen* belong to a higher class, but having minimum *wu* is better than no masculinity at all. And to be a really powerful man, it is essential to have both *wen* and *wu*. In gender terms, those without *wen* or *wu*, the women, have no political power at all. Such at least is the accepted ideology: men take public office and women are not supposed to participate in public life and are therefore kept out of political power games. In reality, of course, life was not that simple. Even though fictional representations such as the Wu Song stories do reinforce the simple formulae of *wen* = more power, *wu* = less power, and women = no power, it is clear that through the depiction of their destructiveness, women can also be represented as wielding tremendous personal power.

This picture was largely accepted until the twentieth century, when, as I show in the next chapter, women began to write about love and sex in increasing numbers. These women authors have appropriated aspirations and grievances that were traditionally perceived as exclusively male preserves. As I show in chapter 7, Western imperialism and Japanese aggression also had their impact on the Chinese male identity. The chaos that ensued was so great that by the mid-twentieth century, China (with the help of the Western powers) closed its doors and tried to forge its own destiny in a make-believe world of working-class heroes who conformed to a list of rigid ideologically determined characteristics.[17] When China re-opened its doors in the late 1970s, Chinese women were even more critical of their men. It was obvious that, as well as being unhappy with the social system, some women were also influenced by the more feminist rhetoric of the early 1970s, especially that of the anti-Confucius movement in 1973–74. They were particularly disparaging about the perceived weakness of the male gender, declaring that there were no 'real men' in China. Sun Shaoxian, in her study of Chinese 'feminist literature' in the 1980s, observed that 'because of this despair at not being able to find real men, feminist literature had reached a depressingly low point'.[18] Zhang Jie has perhaps best epitomised this feeling in her sneering description of an apparently successful male cadre, who was reclining on a red sofa, one leg over the armrest and the buttons of his trousers undone to reveal the kind of colourful underpants usually worn only by women.[19]

The assessment that, beneath a thin veneer of masculinity, Chinese men were repulsively feminine may have arisen from the influence of Western conceptions about the nature of the 'real man'. For example, the young feminist Fan Yang, in her discussion of the male/female dichotomy, also talked about 'the rise of the feminine and the decline of the masculine (*yin sheng yang shuai*)'. She claims that compared to men of other cultures, the Chinese seem to have had part of their masculinity 'castrated' and that, even on the screen, strong male characters like those portrayed by Alain Delon were not to be found.[20] Overseas Chinese too felt that 1980s China lacked 'real men'. The popular and widely read Hong Kong writer Sun Longji uses a version of Freudian psychology and structuralism to conclude that Chinese men everywhere were being feminised, that: 'Whether it is in Hong Kong, Taiwan or the Mainland, the tendency towards the "eunuchisation" (*taijian hua*) of the Chinese male has become a universal phenomenon.'[21]

Fear of eunuchisation may be a response to male prerogatives lost through changes in sex-role behaviour resulting from the destabilisation of the traditional social order. Consequently, a new style of fiction emerged that depicted men in hyper-masculine roles such as hunters, primitive tribesmen and rough frontiersmen. The irony is that while in China the avant-garde was seeking the macho 'real man' by appealing to popular Western symbols and images, in the West itself, critics had already long since discredited the macho man myth.[22] Some feminists were already accusing the postmodern sensitive man of 'slithering between hetero- and homosexuality, blackness and whiteness, masculinity and femininity' in order to 'get a bit of the other'.[23] More pertinent for our project, Chinese masculinity can be constructed differently to contemporary Western masculinity, even though that difference is constantly evolving.

The complaint that China, compared to the West, lacks 'real men' is misplaced. What is disturbing about such laments is that the definition of 'real men' is so strikingly similar, whether it is given by men or women. If it is true that those who define also control, then the concurrence of views by writers of both sexes suggests a trend which will further widen the gender divide, as both sexes seem to have fixed notions of the true nature of the 'real man' and the 'real woman'. Moreover, it seems that in order to counter the accusation that China lacks real men, evidence must be produced to show that some Chinese men are not only tough and inflexible, but that these characteristics were innately Chinese, and not imported from the West. This is in fact what has happened: the 'root-seeking literature' (*xungen wenxue*) phenomenon, which was the most significant literary movement in the 1980s, can be seen as a response by young Chinese male writers to the accusation that they are pseudo-men.

In his book on the various genres of writing that appeared in China in the 1980s, Cao Wenxuan devotes an entire chapter to the rise of the 'tough man' (*yinghanzi*).[24] The basic characteristics of these heroes, according to Cao Wenxuan, are a cold exterior toughness, and a spirit that can be obliterated but not defeated. Cao provides many examples from the current literature to illustrate these characteristics. Indeed, literature is not the only domain where male images seem to fit the specifications of the 'tough man'.[25] Other types of creative work such as the film *Red Sorghum* (*Hong gaoliang*) and popular songs of the late 1980s, such as those of the 'Airs of the Northwest' (*Xibei feng*), also extol 'masculine' traits of toughness and strength. Not surprisingly, these specifications are no different to those of the *wu* qualities we have discussed above. In the rest of this chapter, I will concentrate on one story by the 'root-seeking' writer Jia Pingwa, 'Human Extremities', as a typical response by such writers.[26] In examining Jia Pingwa's glorification of machismo in terms of gender and class and how they relate to the concepts of social power and control, we find that he has indeed sought and found the cultural roots of Chinese masculinity.

Because we will be concentrating on one particular story, it may be helpful to begin with a summary of 'Human Extremities' and the circumstances surrounding its production. The story was published in the Shanghai literary journal *Wenhui yuekan* in October 1985, under the title '*Renji*'. Zhu Hong has translated this as 'How Much Can a Man Bear?'[27] I prefer a more literal translation because, although the story is written by a man about men, I believe the author is attempting to make a statement about people of both sexes, much as André Malraux has done in his *The Human Condition*.[28] It is only in this double-gendered context that the text itself is a powerful declaration of the burdens of human existence in general.

The story takes place in Shangzhou, a county which is not very far south of Xi'an, the site of the ancient capital Chang'an, a district that provides the setting for most of the literary pieces by Jia Pingwa. He has written a novel with *Shangzhou* as its title, as well as a series of essays and short stories specifically on the customs and manners of Shangzhou. The title of his most famous novel, *Feidu* (*Defunct Capital*),[29] refers explicitly to this city. 'Human Extremities' is set in the Cultural Revolution and its aftermath. It opens in 1969, with two peasants, Guangzi and Lamao, who have been bond-brothers since birth and are so close that when they become young men they live together. Indeed, they were betrothed to each other before birth by their parents and would have been married had they not been of the same sex. In the first two years of the Cultural Revolution, they make a living castrating pigs. In 1969, during a huge flood, they rescue a delicate and beautiful young woman, Liangliang, from the raging waters. We learn later that she is the daughter of a teacher from another town. While Guangzi is out the next morning castrating pigs, Lamao has sexual relations with the woman, who acquiesces to his advances because she feels obliged to 'return his favour'. Guangzi is furious and cannot forgive Lamao for debasing himself and 'acting like an animal'. Lamao in despair commits suicide. Liangliang disappears. Guangzi, in his grief at losing Lamao, gives up the castrating trade and, for three years, lives like one possessed. During this period, he performs mourning rituals, such as preparing three meals a day for the dead Lamao.

At the end of three years, during a famine, Guangzi meets another woman, Baishui, who is a peasant reduced to begging for survival. She is gang raped by the village men who call themselves 'revolutionaries', and she becomes pregnant. Guangzi pities her and marries her. A child, Tiger, is born. However, unknown to Guangzi, Baishui is already married, and two years later her other husband shows up and snatches her away. We are told that not long thereafter she dies from mistreatment. For three years, Guangzi, though again stricken with grief, single-handedly raises Tiger, 'acting as father and mother'. Gradually, he returns to normal and begins castrating pigs again.

By this stage in the story, the Cultural Revolution is finished and many people are released from prison. Guangzi by accident comes across Liangliang again, who, as it turned out, had just been released from a wrongful imprisonment. She has been transformed from a delicate woman into a tough and single-minded avenger seeking revenge for her-self and her father. Her suffering, she claims, has made her a 'crusader, neither man nor woman'. We also find out that a baby was born from her sexual encounter with Lamao and that before she went to prison, Liangliang had to give the baby away and was never to see her again. She and Guangzi decide to marry, and over the years they both work hard to save enough money for her to go to Beijing to reverse the verdict on her father. After much hardship, this is done and many officials are repri-manded for their wrongdoings. Liangliang herself then takes over her father's old teaching position in a nearby town. She and Guangzi have to live separately because he is unable to become accustomed to town life. Tiger goes to her school. Liangliang dies a few years later. At her funeral, everyone, including Tiger, thinks that Guangzi is very callous because he shows no sorrow. After this, Guangzi never mentions her name again, becomes more and more withdrawn, and, in his dotage, dreams of Tiger and Liangliang's missing daughter getting together as man and wife.

The protagonist of the story, Guangzi, has all the characteristics of the *haohan*. He is tough, silent to the point of being callous, and, though almost destroyed physically, never once compromises his moral scruples. His masculinity is portrayed most vividly just before he rescues Liangliang:

> When they reached a spot farther upstream, they also stripped naked. They warmed up their chests and bellies with their own urine and then plastered their groins and genitals with mud ... Guangzi was perfectly at home in water and, holding a cutting knife between his teeth, he slipped down into the water.[30]

The description in this passage very clearly points to a man whose actions are highly physical and daring. His nakedness is not described in detail, but the description is sufficient to direct our attention to his manhood. At this stage of the story, Guangzi and Lamao are still in the prime of their lives, with no previous knowledge of women. This is also the only time in the story that Guangzi is described as a good swimmer. If we take the classical symbolism of water as signifying the *yin* (female) in the *yin-yang* dichotomy, it is significant that a woman is plucked from the water by Guangzi who, as a virgin, is 'perfectly at home in water'.

While Guangzi enters the water without fear, the episode also tells us that he nevertheless literally protects his penis from the chill of the water by rubbing mud on it. In the traditional 'five elements' theory (*wuxing*), of course, earth is the neutral element in the *yin-yang* matrix, thus it neutralises these two poles.[31] The symbolic implications go further. The excess of water is deadly, and in the story, we are told that floods do occur frequently and the flooded river carries not only goods washed down from upstream, but also death and sorrow. In this case, although the woman it sweeps down is plucked from certain death, she is also the catalyst for much sorrow and, for Lamao, premature death. While the men tried to protect themselves against the feminine natural disaster, they could not escape the calamity brought about by a 'delicate' woman carried down by water, the ultimate combination of the *yin* essences.[32] This episode is particularly interesting when contrasted with the *wen* man Zhang Yonglin's subduing the flood and his woman discussed in the previous chapter. Whereas the *wen* man's conquering of *yin* essences brings potency and power, the *wu* man's encounter with them brings only sorrow.

The fact that Guangzi goes into the water with a knife between his teeth is also significant. The knife, of course, is a singularly lethal symbol for *wu* masculinity. We have seen that the *wu* god Guan Yu's knife is so important to his persona that it is always near his person and even has several names. In contemporary narratives, the knife is equally potent as a male symbol. For example, in many of the stories in the 'Strange Lands and Strange Tales' series by another influential 'root-seeking' author, Zheng Wanlong, the heroes are experts at doing battle with knives. Although guns are carried, it is knives which are prominent when these characters show their masculine prowess. An unsheathed knife, like an erect penis, can bring both punishment and reward. Those who are proficient with knives face danger and death 'like real men'. In one instance, the hero Shen Keng kills a bear with a knife and in the process also dies. However, when he is separated from the deadly embrace with the bear, his face is found to be as calm as ever, showing not a trace of fear or sadness.[33]

As well as being a symbol of pain, or having the ability to inflict pain, the knife in the case of Guangzi performs a double function. The next time it is mentioned, his knife is used to 'cut free the bloody knot of flesh' that is the reproductive organs of a male pig. The sexual connotations of the functions of heroism gained from knife-wielding is not lost on Zheng Wanlong. In another story from the 'Strange Lands and Strange Tales' series, the hero, Chen Sanjiao, captures a bear and cuts it open with a knife: 'The knife went in through the throat, opening up the body all the way down. Blood and guts came rushing out, and the balls also got smashed.'[34]

Thus, the knife conjures up images of both potent masculinity and the destruction of this masculine potency. It is a phallic symbol which, at this point in 'Human Extremities', Guangzi controls without any problems. By the flick of a knife, he is able to free Liangliang from certain death in the tangle of weeds that have trapped her under a torrent of water. However, it must be remembered that this is at the beginning of the Cultural Revolution, a time when everything was turned upside-down. And in the conventions of 'root-seeking' fiction, it was a time when the rough-and-ready he-men were all-powerful, a time when *wu* masculinity dominated *wen* sensibilities. As a strong peasant at the prime of his life, saving a defenceless woman without thinking, Guangzi is very much a *wu* of the *haohan* mould. Like the intrusion of women in the lives of the classical *wu* heroes, however, the appearance of Liangliang confounds the blissful existence of the two brothers.

Lamao hangs himself, not because he is ashamed of raping Liangliang, but because his 'brother' insinuates 'that he was no better than a beast'. Wu Song, too, asserts that he is 'not some wicked immoral animal' when he repulses Golden Lotus' seductive moves.[35] Like Eve in the Garden of Eden, who brought disaster upon mankind, Liangliang unwittingly spoils the virginal gaiety and quasi-marriage of the 'brothers'. Although

Liangliang also loses her virginity and suffers by giving birth to a child that she must abandon, her reaction to being virtually raped is matter-of-fact, and, having performed her role as foil to the men in the narrative up to this point, she literally walks out of the scene for ten years.

The focus is on the brothers' horror at what has taken place. Lamao takes his own life because he had let the 'organs which make him restless' take over his emotions. In Guangzi's eyes, Lamao's loss of self-control has made him no better than an uncastrated pig. Like the heroes of *All Men Are Brothers*, Guangzi and Lamao were devoted to each other and lived a relatively carefree harmonious life, where they had little need for self-discipline. As C.T. Hsia points out, for working-class heroes such as Wu Song, who have no restraints in terms of alcohol consumption and killing people, sexual abstinence became the only proof of their self-control.[36] In this case, Lamao has not only shown that he was incapable of self-control, but he has also betrayed the implicit homosexual relationship between himself and Guangzi by sleeping with Liangliang, who should have been Guangzi's woman because he saved her.

By having sex with his brother's woman, Lamao has committed the most atrocious crime against the code of brotherhood found in all traditional stories of heroism. As noted above, Guan Yu is careful to let the whole world see that he is honourable in his relations with his sisters-in-law and Wu Song is a hero among heroes for a similar reason. Such notions of brotherly ties have in recent years re-emerged as a dominant theme in much Chinese fiction, particularly when writers talk about their experiences among the peasantry.[37] A much used expression to describe this bond is '*ge'ermer bang*', literally 'the gang of brothers'. While the bond between men has so far been only in a Platonic light, the strength of the bond is never questioned, and it is precisely because these relationships are not supposed to get enmeshed in apparent sexual wantonness and jealousies that they are seen as manly.

Guangzi's violent reaction against Lamao's sexual act swings from a punishing rejection of his 'brother' to an equally extreme pathological form of repentance after the latter's suicide.[38] Guangzi's dedication to the memory of Lamao harks back to traditional mourning reserved for one's parents. It is a show of grief that goes beyond that afforded by custom to husband and wife, a relationship which Guangzi and Lamao would have enjoyed, had they been born boy and girl. Thus, although Lamao exerts power over Liangliang during his sexual act with her, the incident itself spells the apparent loss of his power. For Guangzi, the three-year mourning ritual is ostensibly carried out to expiate his role in Lamao's death. In the context of the story, it is also a statement that the penalty for association with wanton sexuality must be paid; in this case, the cost is the temporary loss of power and control.

The playing out of sexual desires is thus a power game, and the winning or losing of this game is partly determined by the sex of the players. Those in authority, the 'real men', are seen to remain in the dominant position of control, and they can either give or withhold sexual pleasure/power while women's sexual pleasure remains dependent on husbands, lovers, or rapists. However, this sexual power, although vested in men, can only continue if the men show that they have control over it. The fates of Golden Lotus and Ximen Qing in *All Men Are Brothers* are clear examples of what happens to both men and women if they cannot rein in unbridled lust. Here, by succumbing to his desire over Liangliang, Lamao has, by his own estimation, become no better than a beast or a woman. Liangliang is less affected because the traditional ethic depicts her, and all other women, as less in control and thus less responsible. Only 'real men' are able to master their desires, whereas women and pseudo-men become slaves to their lust.

For example, the next woman to appear in Guangzi's life, Baishui, is also raped, although this time brutally and by a gang of 'revolutionaries'. However, her sexuality seems heightened by this experience, and she unashamedly forces herself onto Guangzi in the middle of the night in the same way that, in traditional times, ghosts and fox-fairies made their way into unsuspecting story-tellers' beds.[39] Baishui's apparent inability to control her feelings is seen in the context of her utter helplessness and lack of self-respect. When told by Guangzi to leave, she exclaims that she has nowhere to go and that: 'I am an evil woman. I deserve to die.'[40] It would seem that in the patriarchal world described by writers such as Jia Pingwa, the loss of virginity/chastity deprives the woman of the only commodity with which she can buy sexual and moral legitimacy. One path open to such women is that used by fox-fairies and prostitutes: sex as a weapon for power over men. But this magical power is always only temporary, while the men are 'bewitched'. The challenge to 'real men' is whether they can resist this charm.

There is another more final and drastic option open to women. It is one of protest suicides and suicide pacts like that described in the 1985 short story 'Five Girls and One Rope', in which five young women simultaneously hang themselves rather than getting married.[41] The period in which this story is set is indeterminate. It suggests that the circumstances in the past that caused female suicides have remained unchanged today. Just as with the suicides of 'virtuous women' in traditional times, female deaths of this sort, even now, are condoned, or viewed sympathetically as understandable behaviour, although the situation that has brought the suicide about is condemned. By taking charge of their lives for this last, and only, time, women become honorary men, albeit dead men: they gain self-discipline and power over their desires, which the 'beast' Lamao is unable to do. And when he too redeems himself by taking his own life, his 'brother' Guangzi honours him by observing the three-year mourning ritual.

The *wen* Man and the Macho Eunuch

Male sexual abstinence *per se* is not seen as virtuous; it has to be a denial that is self-imposed. Those men who lack the capacity to put this self-control into practice are seen as objects of pity and scorn. Throughout Chinese history, the mythology surrounding eunuchs is thereby highly uncomplimentary. They are seen as greedy, temperamental, and cowardly.[42] In many instances, eunuchs are equated with women, who are also seen as lacking the capacity for discipline and self-restraint. For example, *The Book of Songs* over 2,500 years ago stated that:

Chaos in the world does not come from Heaven
But it is born of women;
Those who cannot be taught and instructed
Are the women and eunuchs[43]

The popular imagination is fuelled by many tales of the wide variety of 'aphrodisiac and herbal concoctions, constant massage with *yin*-essence and quasi-sexual gymnastics'[44] which the eunuchs were supposed to have indulged in to try to 'regain their manhood'. Their alleged sadism, with all its sexual connotations, is further proof that eunuchs are not 'men'. Historically, eunuchs are perceived as gaining power not through the usual *wen* route of passing the civil service examinations, nor through the *wu* route of military service. If they became powerful, it was through the favouritism of inept and corrupt emperors rather than merit. In the traditional *wen-wu* context, therefore, the eunuch is doubly despicable. When filtered through the Confucian matrix, the externally imposed inability to exercise self-control over their own sexualities is transformed into the inability to have offspring. In the text we are examining, this Confucian corollary of defining manhood with insemination carries interesting complications. Here, it is Lamao who has a girl by Liangliang and the 'revolutionary' rapists who impregnate Baishui with Tiger. By contrast, Guangzi, the hero of the story who has all the characteristics of a macho man, has somehow become a functional eunuch.

At this point we must look beyond Hsia's insight that some men need to prove their manhood by self-imposed celibacy. Why is this self-control so necessary? The answer lies in the Confucian quest for 'self-control and returning to righteousness' (*keji fuli*). This precept was meant to be the key to entering the class of gentleman (*junzi*), whose role it is to rule over

women and other men. Self-control is thus a fundamental prerequisite
for control over others. This principle seems to apply not just in a Confucian schema, but in most other cultural systems as well. The sexual
gymnastics attributed to popular Daoism, and Tantric Buddhism in
which ejaculation is delayed or withheld, is another extension of this
control. To be able to exercise discipline over one's sexual desires is therefore more than an exercise in self-discipline, it is a necessary criterion for
gaining political power, as well as moral and spiritual superiority. Self-
control seems to be universally hailed as a leadership quality. As Foucault
points out,

> In order not to be excessive, not to do violence, in order to avoid the trap of
> tyrannical authority (over others) coupled with a soul tyranized by desires, the
> exercise of political power required, as its own principle of internal regulation,
> power over oneself. Moderation, understood as an aspect of domination over
> the self, was on an equal footing with justice, courage, or prudence; that is, it
> was a virtue that qualified a man to exercise his mastery over others. The most
> kingly man was king of himself.[45]

In the Confucian framework where having offspring is so essential,
Guangzi's tragedy is his childless status. It is a signifier indicating that
an important ingredient for being a whole man has been castrated. This
incompleteness disqualifies Guangzi from attaining the 'kingly way'. His
status, as a disqualified man, is particularly significant when compared
to that of Liangliang. In the beginning of the story, when the Cultural
Revolution is at its height, Liangliang is literally swept under by the
political storm, and has to be rescued by Guangzi and Lamao. Essentially
she is raped by the peasant Lamao, who is intoxicated with his power.
And the girl born of that union is, like the so-called lost generation of the
Cultural Revolution, entrusted to a peasant and is never heard of again.
However, when the verdict on her family is reversed after the Cultural
Revolution, Liangliang regains her family's status and prestige, and it is
Guangzi who cannot enter that privileged realm. He remains a peasant
until the end of his life.

The subtext of the story indicates, then, that self-control over one's
own sexual desires is a necessary, but not sufficient, condition for posses-
sing the 'kingly way'. Both Guangzi and Lamao belong to the peasantry
and, although they sometimes travel around the villages castrating pigs,
their status as poor peasants remains unchanged. Therefore, no matter
whether their sexual behaviour is saintly or bestial, they cannot be seen
to be 'kingly'. For peasants such as Lamao and the 'revolutionaries',
the only way they can get any control whatsoever is through macho
brutishness. But this unleashing of carnal energies, which puts them in
a dominant position, is in times of relative peace inevitably ephemeral.

While brutal strength can be a sort of *wu* prowess, it is not the Guan Yu sort of *wu*. Guan Yu is a deified general, and as I mentioned in chapter 2, he is most often depicted as reading a book, so that his *wu* is seen as *refined*. It is more a Wu Song sort of 'working-class' *wu* that can be praiseworthy sometimes, but never allowed to be elevated to a leadership position. By contrast, those who come from the educated (*wen*) classes can always legitimate their political positions. The effeminate Confucian scholar is just as assured of his leadership role as the woman Liangliang, daughter of a teacher, the ultimate *wenren*. What they have in common is both self-control and the right class background.

Thus, the self-control that makes one a leader is only transferred from the sexual realm to the political realm when the person involved comes from the educated class. This is especially conspicuous in stories by writers such as Zhang Xianliang who are obsessed with being a member of the intellectual elite. As the previous chapter has shown, almost all of Zhang's stories are about male intellectuals who, through mastery of their sex drives, regain a political power lost in the Anti-rightist Campaign or the Cultural Revolution; the women are there to facilitate this process.

In 'Human Extremities', it is significant that Liangliang, a woman, inherits the position of teacher from her father. Having come from an intellectual background, there is nothing illogical about this, except that she is not a son. The story makes it quite clear, however, that in the process of regaining this status, Liangliang has lost her gender characteristics. We are told in many places that she is 'neither man nor woman'. By being sexually neutral, Liangliang can presumably take political power. However, this admission has a Confucian twist that damns the woman for her sex. By assuming male characteristics and not playing the role assigned her, we are told that no matter how hard she tried, Liangliang could not bear Guangzi a child. She effectively becomes a female eunuch. Women assuming political power is thus interpreted as an unnatural phenomenon bound for failure as much as eunuchs taking control.

The Cultural Revolution is not mentioned very often in this story, but it is clearly seen to be responsible for producing the chaos in the sexual and political spheres. As Guangzi muses at the beginning of the story, 'What had the world come to! How filthy the villagers' minds were! This came of evil times.'[46] This is a very common theme in much of the literature in the late 1970s and 1980s. 'Scar literature' is really another name for literature about mistaken political labels, and almost all seductions and rapes in that literature are carried out by *wu* men who do not or should not have political power. In most cases, they are peasants or workers or, if they are cadres and army officers, they are portrayed as villains who have been wrongly invested with political power by a previous regime, whether it be the Guomindang or the 'gang of four'.

The problem is not whether Chinese men behave like women or eunuchs. It is whether such images generate a sense of political might or a sense of the ridiculous. In a survey conducted among young women in China, of the men who have been popular in the Chinese imagination, Jia Baoyu of *The Dream of the Red Mansions* was voted the least desirable male among them.[47] His effeminate behaviour, far from making him attractive, repels many.[48] Historically, this has not always been the case as evidenced by his popularity among his cousins and servants in Prospect Garden. As noted in chapter 1, by way of explaining this phenomenon, scholars like Van Gulik have argued that the process of the feminisation of Chinese men began in the Ming Dynasty and that by the Qing Dynasty, because the Han Chinese reacted against the martial arts which were dominated by the Manchu conquerors, 'The ideal lover is described as a delicate, hyper-sensitive youngster with pale face and narrow shoulders who falls ill at the slightest disappointment.'[49]

However, if we analyse this image in *wen-wu* terms, it is clear that this 'hyper-sensitive youngster with pale face and narrow shoulders' is a traditional image of a *wen* scholar. Baoyu may be physically weak, and he would be happy to confess that he has no *wu* skills. However, it is not at all clear that the women in traditional times found him an ideal lover because of his looks. It is more likely that they were attracted to his 'hyper-sensitivity' and, most importantly, his social status and its concomitant power. Furthermore, he was only an 'ideal lover' for a certain class of men and women: those who favoured *wen*. Those from the lower classes would have been attracted to the *wu* image, represented by men such as Guan Yu and Wu Song, and in the contemporary age, by action men such as Bruce Lee, Jackie Chan and Chow Yun Fat, as we will see in chapter 8.

In China, stories such as 'Human Extremities' show that the aggressive reassertion of the macho image is just that: it is an image of the working-class hero, stripped of political and economic power, trying to assert himself. In a relatively stable political order where violence is not the legitimate path to authority, however, these heroes could only achieve the *haohan* status. *Wu* virtues could only go so far. It is significant that most stories of this category of *wu* men are written by former 'educated youth' who came back from the villages to find the Cultural Revolution and peasant ways denounced. In the 'evil times' of the Cultural Revolution, they were, as 'educated youth', hailed as heroes. When, in the late 1970s, the Cultural Revolution program was totally negated, the political capital they once possessed was transformed into a liability. The returned 'educated youth' needed to rationalise their sojourns in the mountains and villages for their own peace of mind if not for political legitimacy.

In order to justify their rural experiences, men such as Han Shaogong, Zheng Wanlong and Jia Pingwa have appealed to nationalism by writing about 'cultural roots' and situating these roots in rugged and backward areas. In the process, a certain masculinity has emerged, one which draws its inspiration from notions of the 'good fellow' (*haohan*) in classical literature and village-based China. Unfortunately, such notions often contradict present policies, because the 'good fellows' of traditional fiction, like those found in *All Men Are Brothers*, are also products of 'evil times'. They are certainly not the intellectual type glorified by the post-Mao leadership. As with its traditional predecessors, therefore, 'root-seeking' fiction is full of ambiguities, and the resolution of these ambiguities switches from the political to the sexual depending on current governmental and social concerns.

The aftermath of the Cultural Revolution has seen tremendous social changes. These changes have, on the whole, been in the direction of a more 'normal' social structure. As Michael Kimmel points out in another context,

> The articulation of new versions of masculinity ... suggests the ways in which larger structural changes set in motion those microsocial processes that led women to redefine their roles, the critical events that provoke the historical 'crises' of masculinity.[50]

The problem in the Chinese case is that, in trying to resolve the gender inequalities they faced, women are re-assigning traditional roles for both men and women, roles from which the Cultural Revolution was just beginning to struggle to break free.[51] Chinese men have followed suit and have again internalised sex-roles which have traditionally benefited men, especially the *wen* men. In the process of 'the rectification of names', writers have been very efficient in not just restoring the old political order, but the old gender hierarchies as well.

Just as sexual dominance can be transferred into the political realm, political and economic power can also be perceived as sexual prowess. When powerful men such as Henry Kissinger observe that power is an aphrodisiac, they are merely reinforcing an ideology perpetrated by those with political and economic might. For the last 150 years, Chinese intellectuals have, on the whole, professed the desire to resist Western state and economic imperialism. Yet, cultural imperialism, especially media imperialism with its images of masculinity and femininity, has been objected to only on moral and political grounds. If those who denigrate Chinese male sexuality would only look at studies of the 'real men' in the West itself, they would see 'that beneath the macho posing and the bedroom performance, many [Western] men have unsure and conflicting feelings about their sexuality'.[52]

Regardless of how men feel about their sexual adequacy, in the fiction of the 1980s there are male characters who seem to fit the description of 'real men' made by Cao Wenxuan, and who are not macho eunuchs in the way we have described Guangzi. These are the men created by urban-based cadres such as Wang Meng, Jiang Zilong, and Li Cunbao. Although managers like Qiao Guangpu (the protagonist of Jiang Zilong's 'Manager Qiao Assumes Office') are macho, they are in no way eunuchs. In fact, they are very Confucian: they are educated, in official positions, and have children.[53] Their power and attractiveness come from the political, economic, and military clout they wield, and not knives and other weapons. Even when the heroes are members of People's Liberation Army, their 'manly qualities' are not seen to reside in their guns and cannons, but in their devotion to their army units, comrades, and families. Indeed, their military weapons are sometimes deliberately described as faulty.[54]

After over a hundred years of modernisation and 50 years of Communist rule, Chinese writers seem to be continuing to follow the traditional ordering of gender and *wen-wu* patterns and their relationship to class and power. This process, however, is not a linear one. Dialectical transformations are at work. For writers such as Jia Pingwa, who have given us the new working-class heroes such as Guangzi, the reaffirmation of the Confucian motto '*keji fuli*' (restraining oneself and returning to the rites) is not total. Unlike the peasant 'brothers' in *All Men Are Brothers* who delight in sadistic violence, Guangzi, as a model for a 'real man' of peasant origins, consciously shuns violence and abhors the rapes endured by Liangliang and Baishui. Guangzi's behaviour as a gentle and supportive spouse also contrasts sharply with previous heroes like Wu Song, who either do not marry or treat their wives like slaves.

The Cultural Revolution, with its working-class heroes, may have had a lasting effect on representations of the 'real man'. Guangzi, though coming from the class with the least political power, seems to have had some of his more unpleasant masculine qualities feminised. Furthermore, his self-control is shown to be more than just sexual. Throughout the story, he is described as able to observe all the self-discipline required of the real man in the Confucian sense. The fact that Guangzi, the peasant, is seen to be approaching the *junzi* in traditional terms indicates that the process of the 'rectification of names' (*zhengming*) in the post-Mao era is incomplete. While the images of the working-class heroes during the Cultural Revolution were too unrealistic and incongruous to the traditional *wen-wu* structure to be successful as models for behaviour, the portrait of Guangzi as a 'real man' is certainly not as brutish and unthinking as those of the Imperial and May Fourth periods.

However, this does not mean that the Chinese tradition has now been disrupted and that fundamental relationships between gender, class, and power have changed. On the contrary, the story makes it perfectly clear that women of whatever background can never be real 'leaders of men' and that peasants such as Guangzi can never compete for political power with the intellectuals. Control by lower class women and men thus remains attainable, albeit briefly, only along the feminine–masculine axis. The domination they exert over men and women who are more 'feminine', however, will only last as long as they remain physically powerful. Stories such as 'Human Extremities' seem to suggest that class domination is a much more permanent and powerful means of control than is gender.

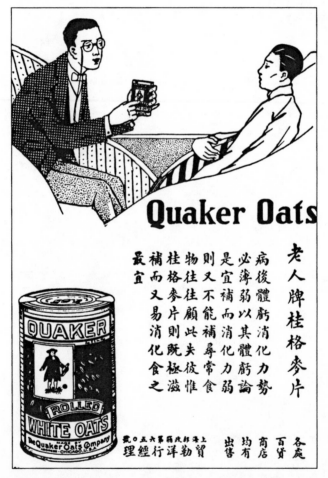

Advertisement showing a young Westernised man urging an ailing youth in traditional Chinese clothing to eat American Quaker Oats. From *Liang you* (The Young Companion), Shanghai, December 1927, p. 36. Reproduced with permission of the National Library of Australia.

I began this book arguing that Chinese masculinity needed to be theorised and studied more systematically and intensively because although Chinese gender and sexuality have received attention, the focus has been mostly on women. Even when writers protest that women have been 'silenced',[1] the spotlight remains fixed on their plight. With the emergence of a 'women writers' industry' in the last two or three decades of the twentieth century,[2] conversations about or by the 'silenced' gender became almost deafening. However, in the same way that many men use women as a measure for their own worth, women are also concerned about their relationships with men even when they are talking about themselves. Gender and sexuality are only comprehensible if the various genders and sexualities are correlated with each other and not in isolation.

As stated in earlier chapters, since men generally controlled the ideological mechanisms for social formations, they were mainly responsible for the constructions of social ideals, including masculinity. *Wen-wu* was thus defined in such a way that it was applicable to men only and for male advantage over women. Women were simply not part of the *wen-wu* domain. Certainly, in the literary canon, women's voices were mostly transmitted by (often defective) male amplifiers. To retrieve women's 'muffled' voices from amidst the noise and then to hear their commentary on men is not always easy. In the twentieth century, women began to take control over some of the ideological apparatus and as a result their voices have been increasingly unmediated and therefore are more audible. In the second half of the century in particular, women increasingly participated publicly in many forms of media such as literature – but their marginal status is still evident from critics' habit of identifying the authors' professional role as having added 'freak value as a woman writer'.[3] My intention here is not to adopt the attitude that women writers have a greater claim to truth because they are women. Or, to rephrase David Wang, I do not want to give the impression that by emphasising woman writers' and readers' capacity of grasping female problems in this chapter, I am attempting to reduce feminism to a simple dialectic of male vs. female.[4] However, I do think it is important in a book on masculinity to examine how women construct manhood. Not only are the various male ideals they construct important for showing us 'what women want', they also further illustrate that *wen-wu* is a social construct that is constantly being manipulated for the purposes of those who control the means to do so.

In this chapter, I argue that when modern Chinese women write,[5] men are portrayed as objects of desire.[6] Men are objects to be gazed at and assessed. As a consequence, under the pens of the women writers, masculinity is associated with a whole array of characteristics such as youthful innocence, sexual naiveté, tenderness and exotica – characteristics which traditionally have been associated with femininity, and not with *wen-wu*.

Naturally, since the objects under consideration are desirable men, it is inconceivable that *wen-wu* should not manifest itself in one form or another. This chapter examines these forms by analysing the signature works of three representative women fiction writers, Ding Ling (1904–1985), Ru Zhijuan (b. 1925) and Wang Anyi (b. 1954).[7] The works are 'Miss Sophia's Diary' (1928),[8] 'Lilies' (1958)[9] and *Brocade Valley* (1987).[10] Separated from each other by 30 years, they are chosen because they represent the attitudes of three generations of women in post-Imperial China. All three stories deal with the thoughts and feelings of young women in moments of great socio-political change.

The 'modern' woman in Ding Ling's 'Miss Sophia's Diary' faces the dilemma of the May Fourth generation which, wanting to abandon traditional norms, yearned for a glorified Europeanised individualism that promised a modern mode of living.[11] The heroine has abandoned traditional values, but it is not clear what alternatives are available to her. The second story, Ru Zhijuan's 'Lilies', is set during the historical turning point of the civil war between the Nationalists and the Communists. That is, between the 'modern' and Communist periods. Here, the protagonist's sympathies are unambiguously with the Communists, and the reader knows that victory for the Communist cause was a historical fact. The last story is situated during a time when Communist ideals were all but swept aside by the disillusioning impact of the Cultural Revolution and its aftermath. It heralds the hedonistic consumer culture of the 1990s and beyond.

I have chosen these three stories as representative studies of Chinese female constructions of men because all three were written quite self-consciously by women about their changing perceptions of male–female relationships. The male protagonist in the first story is an overseas Chinese. He embodies all the yearnings for Western things characteristic of the May Fourth period. The second male protagonist is a young soldier, a typical hero of the early Communist decades. The lover in the third story is a writer who has an extra-marital affair with the narrator. His moral ambiguity makes him even more of an idol in the uncertain time of the late twentieth century. All three stories became controversial and influential almost as soon as they appeared, reflecting the social concerns of their respective times. All three have been translated and critiqued extensively in Chinese and English. However, most of the criticisms have focused on the female subjectivities of the authors. I will highlight instead not only their descriptions of male–female relations, but more particularly, the attributes of their male protagonists.

Ding Ling and the Westernised Man

I'll begin with Ding Ling's 1928 story. Written at a time when Western imperialism was humiliatingly successful in China, it describes a period when Chinese men were totally demoralised. As I will discuss in chapter 8, the then current expression 'sick man of East Asia' is still bitterly remembered today. Some of the best writers of the 1920s and 1930s such as Lu Xun, Yu Dafu and Guo Moruo depicted Chinese men as physically decrepit and morally unworthy. Both authors and the characters they created share one trait which was common at that time: a tendency towards romanticism. Part of this trend for romantic yearnings, as will be seen in the next chapter, was to imitate Western ways. Most of the influential writers of this period had studied modern ideas in Europe, America or Japan. Nevertheless, they were insecure about their immediate career prospects and China's future. Thus, this 'romantic generation' often indulged in sentimentalism and narcissistic self-pity. In fact, stories from this time ritualistically describe the man as unable or unwilling to look after himself and family. Thus, the women often die or are sold as prostitutes or wet-nurses.[12]

The 'disappearance' theme for women is not confined to Chinese literature,[13] nor is it confined to women only. However, as Bonnie McDougall points out,

> the tendency of male authors to project death or suffering on women characters reflects the dominant concern of male authors for the fate of males. Women characters often disappear or die; when they figure as tragic protagonists, their unhappy end is frequently the occasion for reflections on male anxieties; and a female protagonist frequently serves as a symbol for a male-centred project.[14]

Whether it is the man or woman who disappears, modern Chinese literature written by men generally does portray the women as victims.[15]

The depiction of women as victim in the May Fourth was merely a modern rendition of an old theme. Despite the writers' sympathetic gestures and expressions of indignation at women's fate, their writing on the whole echoed similar sentiments expressed in traditional fiction. In numerous pre-modern narratives, women are portrayed as wronged by the men and/or sacrificed for the men's good. The self-sacrificing role performed by women in traditional tales often reached such superhuman proportions that they were depicted as having supernatural powers.[16] The deification of women as supernatural spirits enabled authors to create 'a symbol of the good wife that is upheld in Chinese society'.[17] Their celestial status provides the rationale for impossible standards. Though these women seem to take centre stage in the narratives, that position only allows their self-effacing virtues to be manifested for emulation by all women. With the emergence of women writers, however, a different perspective is provided. Women writers to a large degree also specialise in describing their own needs and desires, but their attitudes to and evaluations of the men differ dramatically from earlier male authors' depictions of men. This chapter will examine some of the fundamental differences between male and female characterisations of the *wen-wu* ideal.

When Ding Ling's 'Miss Sophia's Diary' first appeared in 1928, critics read it as a pioneering text enunciating the desires of modern, young women. Some likened it to 'a bomb shell thrown on the deadly quiet literary scene'.[18] The diary in question is very simple, covering a few months between December and March. As her name implies, Sophia is a modern, Westernised young woman. All the major characters in the narrative are also Westernised young men and women. She has left her family and lives alone in a hotel room. Her story is therefore one possible answer to Lu Xun's speculation on the future for Ibsen's Nora if she leaves home. Indeed, Sophia's life is not a happy one. She suffers from tuberculosis and is unable to engage in regular work or studies, and she indulges in introspection and fantasy. She keeps a diary in which she records the shifts and turns in her illness and the fluctuations in her moods. A young man by the name of Weidi is infatuated with her, but she feels that he does not understand her and takes pleasure in playing on his emotions. Her own feelings are aroused by Ling Jishi, a business student from Singapore, and the diary details her feverish and sometimes ambivalent desire for this man. To be nearer to him she moves to a damp hostel room even though that aggravates her illness. The diary ends when Miss Sophia realises her greatest desire: to feel Ling's full red lips on hers. Although she feels victorious, the kiss also makes her feel degraded. Full of self-pity, she decides to leave Beijing for the south.

According to Amy Lai, Ding Ling has fashioned 'another form of "silence" in the "The Diary of Miss Sophie", which signifies the deadlock of the female self' because Sophia ends up in despair and leaves for the south and terminates the diary.[19] If we consider that the diary is the work of a woman and the subsequent noisy discussions about it are also mainly by women, that conclusion is hardly justified. In what is often considered the first feminist story in modern Chinese literature, Ding Ling employs a technique that enables the narrator to indulge her feelings and emotions in a most narcissistic manner. Miserable she may be, silent she is not. Mercilessly, she dissects and ridicules all those around her. The diary format allows her to treat all her relationships purely in egotistical terms – we are left in no doubt that the world is only meaningful because of Sophie's intervention. In particular, she puts the two men in her life – Weidi and Ling Jishi – under close scrutiny and frankly discusses their significance in her mental landscape.

I will discuss Weidi first. He is typical of the kind of excessively sentimental, dependent male found in May Fourth fiction. Translated literally, the name Weidi means 'Little Brother Wei'. In Chinese, people often call others close to them 'brother' or 'sister'. However, considering the amount of space critics such as Tani Barlow have spent discussing the importance of Sophia's name in terms of its European origins and significance, it is surprising that little is said about Weidi's name beyond the fact that it signifies intimacy. What kind of intimacy is signified here? Contrary to the 'younger' signification of '*di*', Weidi is four years older. Not only does he not mind being called 'Younger Brother', but he calls Sophia 'Jiejie', or 'Older Sister' rather than by her name. Moreover, while he is about 25, his behaviour is extremely juvenile, and he often sulks and bursts into tears if Sophia is mean to him.

Such an over-sensitive, self-centred young man might have been endearing in Ming-Qing fiction (like Jia Baoyu), or even in the modern fiction of male writers like Yu Dafu, but in the eyes of a modern Chinese woman, this type of man is not only unromantic, but downright irritating. In her introduction to Weidi, Sophia describes his excessive demonstrations of affection and remarks that she 'ended up pitying him because he's so easy to exploit and because he has such a gift for doing the wrong thing in love'.[20] She manipulates Weidi's jealousy of Ling Jishi and allows him to read the diary. But after reading it, he displays only more self-pity and sniffles, 'I don't like that tall guy', referring to Ling Jishi. However, as Lydia Liu points out, when Ding Ling wrote 'Miss Sophia's Diary', she was endeavouring to assert herself (via the female narrator), 'not as someone's daughter, sister, lover or friend but as an autonomous subject'.[21] Sophia's diary is about Sophia, not about Weidi or Ling Jishi. Despite Weidi's essential self-centred personality, his continual protestations of being in love with Sophia run counter to the May Fourth ideals of individualism and freedom, and it is precisely the reason why a modern woman such as Sophia feels nothing but disdain for him.

This observation may seem self-evident. But contrast this to the way young women swoon over Jia Baoyu and other equally spoiled and hypersensitive young men in traditional literature, and the changed ideals for masculine attractiveness become evident. Jia Baoyu may like the company of girls and feminine things, but he is in control of his own life. As a boy and young man, he plays at being a girl, but as he matures, he still sits for the civil service exams and has a son before he departs for a life as a Buddhist hermit. Therefore, like Scholar Zhang of the Yuan drama *West Wing*, his seeming lack of control belies a *caizi* who can effortlessly perform *wen* tasks such as passing the civil service examinations. While he disdains the *wu* aspects of masculinity, there is never any question that his *wen* accomplishments are superb.

By contrast, in the 1920s, Weidi's petulant, sulky and resentful performances only make him look pathetic and silly. Baoyu in his more emotional days is only a young teenager, not 25 like Weidi. Moreover,

Weidi is four years older than the woman he fawns on. *Wen-wu* is not something that can apply to children and weak-kneed 'old men'. Unlike Baoyu and Scholar Zhang who show signs of literary accomplishment and therefore have claims to be a *caizi* (nascent *wenren*), Weidi, who is childish but not a child and tearful but not talented, is just despicable, especially to a 'modern woman' like Sophia. He has lost the ability to control Sophia, and his frequent tears are further evidence that he has also lost control over himself. No wonder, then, that 'in front of Weidi, it seems Sophia has turned into a man, and Weidi has turned into a woman who is full of worries and sadnesses'.[22]

The traditional *caizi* image clearly does not appeal to the modern woman. What is the alternative? As we will see in the next chapter, one ideal is a Westernised young man studying commerce. Such a man is also described in 'Miss Sophia's Diary'. He is the Western-educated Ling Jishi. In the beginning, Sophia finds him exotic and sexually attractive, partly because he is from outside of China. This is how she describes him when she first meets him:

> That tall guy is stunning. For the first time, I found myself really attracted to masculine beauty ... How can I describe the beauty of this strange man? His stature, pale delicate features, fine lips, and soft hair are quite dazzling enough. But there is an elegance about him, difficult to describe, an elusive quality, that shook me profoundly. When I asked his name, he handed me his name card with extraordinary grace and finesse. I raised my eyes. I looked at his soft, red, moist, deeply inset lips, and let out my breath slightly. How could I admit to anyone that I gazed at those provocative lips like a small hungry child eyeing sweets?[23]

If we changed the pronouns from 'he' to 'she' in this passage, we have a beautiful and sensual woman. Sophia's fantasies about Ling Jishi while highly erotic are non-sex specific. As Lydia Liu points out, 'Not only does the narrator objectify the man's "lips" as if they were pieces of candy, but she ignores the phallus and feminizes male sexuality by associating it with lips (labia).'[24] This man is not a man. He is, at least in the beginning, perceived of as an exotic, Western mirror image of a woman. More significantly, in terms of Chinese masculinity, both *wen* and *wu* characteristics have vanished. He is neither a scholar who could write classical poetry while drunk nor an expert swordsman who could fight an army single-handedly. He is a fantasy.

The sex reversal fantasy has its racial and cultural equivalents. May Fourth was a time when the Chinese were Occidentalising the West, when the stereotype for the West was that it was sexually liberated. When Sophia first meets Ling Jishi, she romanticises about him as a tall man from a strange land, a man who is alluring and seductive. He is not a tall and white man in reality, but coming from Singapore with a Western upbringing, he connotes for Sophia Britishness and exotica. Again, as Lydia Liu points out, 'Sophia's fantasy is not exactly about a Caucasian man but a Chinese man with a Caucasian man's sex appeal.'[25] Yet, when Sophia in the end does get to kiss those lips, why does she find him so disgusting?

Coming from the 'West', he does not have to have any of the restrictions that are part of traditional Chinese male *wen-wu* virtues. However, as an ethnic Chinese who is not 'really' Chinese, he is neither Eastern nor Western. A hybrid who shifts between the strict boundaries of race and nationality can offend as well as fascinate those who hanker after certainty. After the fantasies of kissing him and arousing him are realised, what lies below are what Sophia understands to be materialist pursuits of Western university students. The Occidentalism is self-fulfilling. In the beginning, Sophia actually asks him to teach her English, the language of the mysterious West. However, as he reveals himself to her more and more, she comes to realise that the only language he understands is that of success in career and money-making. In the eyes of the renowned male author Lao She – discussed in the next chapter – this attribute which is so hostile to *wen-wu* may still be portrayed as patriotic and manly, but to Sophia, the man is unworthy.[26]

Her disillusionment with and contempt for Ling Jishi are explicitly interpreted as a misguided attachment to Western notions of romantic love. For example, the 21 March entry is: 'All for that man's soft hair and red lips ... It was the chivalric European knights I was dreaming about. It's still not a bad comparison; anyone who looks at Ling Jishi can see it, though he also preserves his own special Eastern gentleness.'[27] The unreality of dreams of European chivalry and knights is made clear because this entry is followed by the revelation that same night that Ling Jishi is married and has had affairs in Singapore and frequents brothels. Sophia then declares that he cannot understand the nature of a woman's love and resolves to 'teach this college boy a lesson'.[28]

Thus, Ling Jishi may look like a knight in shining armour, but he's a fake. The day after this realisation she shows the diary to Weidi, who also fails to fathom her. She quickly goes the next step by kissing Ling Jishi and then leaves Beijing for the south. In kissing Ling Jishi's voluptuous lips, she has a sort of 'victory'. She is cured both of her fantasies of the European knight and of her pleasure on Weidi's dependence on her. She leaves them to seek her own health and ideals in a more congenial south.

Sophia's leaving for the south seems to suggest that, like the 'disappearing women' so prevalent in May Fourth fiction, there is a degree of 'self-erasing' as well as self-affirmation.[29] According to Feuerwerker, 'Sophie's struggles toward affirmation and understanding of the self through writing turn out to be self-defeating in part because the diary form, as she employs it, is revealed to be uniquely adapted for such defeat.'[30] This is one possible reading of the text, but it takes Sophia's protestations of having wasted time and energy writing the diary and her self-recriminations of having deluded herself by the looks of Ling Jishi too literally. Unlike so many other female characters in male-produced texts, her self-staged disappearance is the result of a positive choice to move to a better climate, and she laughs at the men as she does so, saying 'I've won, I've won'. As the diarist, she achieves a measure of independence by banishing the men from her mind and by ending the diary altogether. In her terms, the men are the ones who disappear.

More importantly, as the omniscient author, Ding Ling has produced a victory for women in the tug of war between the sexes that no other previous Chinese before had been able to achieve. In the past, male authors have often attempted to adopt the feminine viewpoint, but they inevitably speak in men's voices. Ultimately, the victimised women in their works serve as reminders of the failure of their men to protect them from the evils of a patriarchal system. The women's suffering only serves to reflect the concerns of men: their power, their *wen* and *wu* attributes. For Ding Ling's creation Sophia, the absence of traditional *wen-wu* masculinity in the men around her has little significance, but she finds them pitiable and loathsome. She is aware that the men have lost traditional *wen-wu* masculinity, but have not managed to gain the European knightly one. But instead of letting herself be the mirror of men's concern for their self-image, people around her serve as objects onto which she can assert her will. The development of modern Chinese 'women's literature' after Ding Ling shows that masculinity was often actively and publicly shaped and transformed by women.

Ru Zhijuan and the Soldier

According to Zheng Daqun, literature which investigated women's rights 'died a premature death' after the 1940s and was not revived until the 1980s.[31] This is correct only if we expect the literary material to explicitly refer to romantic or sexual relations or to female sexuality (*xing*). However, in terms of writings about male–female relations or literature about women's rights, plenty of stories were produced throughout this time, many with the specific purpose of promoting gender equality. The 'sexual levelling' was manifest in the hairstyles and fashions of both men and women, which seemed to become more similar.[32] As the energies of both sexes turned increasingly to social reconstruction and revolution, individual 'vanities' were positively discouraged. In the 1950s, this collectivist credo was generally accepted. Very tentative attempts to diverge from it occurred only during the Hundred Flowers period when some of the 'poisonous weeds' such as 'At the Precipice'[33] and 'Red Beans' were published.[34] These stories raised topics such as individual aspirations and sexual desires. They specifically talked about the roles men and women should play in this great socialist experiment: that they had a gendered and a social role. However, even these timid attempts at the revival of traditional and individualist gender and sexual roles were heavily criticised.

Such a puritanical environment gave outsiders the impression that the first decades of the PRC were devoid of the joys and sorrows of sexual, romantic and marital relations. The variations of courtship and marital and extra-marital relationships which provided the ingredients for traditional story-telling were now entirely at the service of national social and economic policies. Such restrictions made the creation of traditional love stories difficult if not impossible. But these were not traditional times. Women, for example, were writing in greater numbers, and the political dictate of sexual equality for once suited their collective yearning. Even though the political atmosphere was draconian, the propaganda art produced some truly remarkable pieces. Ru Zhijuan's 'Lilies' is one of the most sensitive 'love stories' to appear in the 1950s. Whether or not it is feminist, it is definitely a good illustration of how women looked at masculinity in the early decades of the People's Republic. The soldier in 'Lilies' typifies the heroes of this time, the most famous being the real-life soldiers Dong Cunrui (1929–1948) and Huang Jiguang (1930–1952).[35]

These models were extensively promoted so that the populace would emulate their selfless patriotic behaviour. They were generally fearless, frugal, and inevitably from the working-classes. In terms of an analysis of masculinity, they curiously had one thing in common: they were portrayed like the virtuous women of traditional China. That is, they were good-looking, extremely loyal (in the case of traditional women, loyalty to their lovers, but in these men, to their comrades) and most importantly, they die young. In fact, they die with their virginity intact, ensuring that they were devoid of any pollution and not tainted by any capitalist ideas. Like the young soldier in 'Lilies', model heroes such as Dong Cunrui and Huang Jiguang sacrifice their own lives for the sake of their comrades. Ru Zhijuan therefore had 'live' models on which to write her story. To emphasise this fact, Ru Zhijuan recounts that the soldier in the story is based on two actual soldiers she met when she was on the battlefield.[36] This 'life-like' character of Ru Zhijuan's early work is typical of the socialist realism of the 1950s, portraying ordinary 'typical' people demonstrating virtues consistent with current dogmas of the Chinese Communist Party.[37] Almost as soon as 'Lilies' first appeared in 1958, it was eulogised by Mao Dun,[38] and it established Ru Zhijuan's reputation as a great writer who could sensitively recreate the love between the army and the people.[39]

The story is set in the time of the Communist offensive against the Nationalists in the autumn of 1946. The narrator, a member of a theatrical troupe, has been sent to the front as a first-aid assistant. A young PLA soldier (so young that his status is a 'messenger', and not a regular fighter) is assigned to show her the way to the clinic, and she notes with sympathy his shyness and dedication. He fails to obtain bedding for the clinic from a newly married woman in the village although the narrator has no trouble getting a new quilt from her. While the soldier mumbles that the village woman is feudal in her attitudes, it is clear that the two young people are awkward in each other's company. Shortly after this exchange, the young soldier dies when he throws himself on top of a grenade in order to save his comrades. The bride wraps her new quilt, embroidered with lilies, around the dead soldier as his funeral shroud. Ostensibly on conventional themes such as the interdependence of the PLA and the ordinary people, the emotions shown by the soldier and the young bride hint at stronger, if hidden desires.

In the context of the 1950s when Ru Zhijuan wrote the story, whether the young bride feels any sexual attraction towards the young soldier is perhaps not so relevant. However, this death scene has broader significance for its implications about male–female relations. The quilt, we are told, is her bridal treasure that she has used only once or twice, if at all. It 'belongs' to her and her new husband who is away (presumably in the army, protecting their new home), and signifies their marital union and intimacy. That is why the onlookers are so horrified when she wraps the dead soldier in it as a burial shroud. Symbolically, she has united two men – her husband and her 'loved one' – by having them share her most cherished and personal possession. The story does not tell us what her husband's reaction would be, but its tenor clearly points to one permissible reaction: approval, grief, but most important, a sense of comradeship with the dead man. This new Communist twist is accepted as so normal that not one of the critics has referred to it. Yet, it is truly revolutionary in its assessment of the woman's role. Women have previously been portrayed as a threat to the brotherhood ideal. Men bonded against women. However, in this case, the woman acts as the mediator of the male bond. She is no longer the feared seductress who will destroy brotherly love, but is instrumental in the bonding process. Unsurprisingly, the story is written by a woman.

As I have pointed out elsewhere, 'the story deals with two potent sets of opposition, between men and women, and between traditional values and the new values of modern socialist China'.[40] Therefore, as well as the implied changes in gender roles, aspects of traditional patterns remain: men play soldiers and women play nurses or stay behind at home.

However, as well as the new role for the young bride discussed above, other significant changes could be seen in the triangular relationship between the narrator, the soldier and the young bride. Although this story is not in the form of a diary, it is told in the first person and the action is unambiguously told from the perspective of the narrator, who is the older woman. Thus, while a triangular relationship is described, the story, like 'Miss Sophia's Diary', is meant to be autobiographical and the omnipotent perspective of the female narrator is never in doubt. She controls and tells the story. Although Ru Zhijuan claims in 1980 that 'None of the characters or events in "The Lilies" are real, nor are they based on real people or events',[41] she notes in the same article that the soldier is a composite of real people she met.

It is with this understanding that the construction of the soldier becomes significant. Almost all the Chinese critics point to the soldier as loveable (*ke'ai*), innocent (*tianzhen*) and guileless (*hanzhi*).[42] Critics find him endearing mostly because he seems so sexually inexperienced and vulnerable. In the story, he is so shy that the first time the narrator speaks to him, 'his face swells up like Guan Gong'.[43] The allusion to the *wu* god Guan Yu invokes all the various elements of misogyny (perhaps gynophobia is a better word) that we have discussed in chapter 2. The soldier's relationship with the two women does seem to indicate that he wants no interaction with them, and when he is forced to engage them, he does so in a reactive and negative fashion. He literally keeps the woman narrator at a distance, to the point where she, as a liberated woman, gets angry. He again shows that trait when faced with the young bride, refusing to go back to her for the quilt.

However, we find that in both cases, his blushing in front of women is not a replay of the misogynist *wu* god Guan Yu, but embarrassment and bashfulness at not knowing how to talk to women. The new soldier was a *wu* man with all the traditional nastier aspects erased. In fact, his shyness in front of the women is resonant with the interactions between the 'talented scholars' (*caizi*) and 'beautiful women' (*jiaren*) in traditional stories. In the same way that beautiful young women in these stories engender feelings of protectiveness and possessiveness from the men, the soldier prompts maternal and sisterly affection from the older narrator, and subtle but deep romantic attachment from the young bride. From the reader's point of view, the resemblance with tragic heroines in traditional fiction is even more pronounced because the reader knows that he dies protecting his comrades. As Robert Hegel convincingly argues, his 'final conscious act transforms the character from comic bumpkin to ideal hero'.[44]

This sacrifice of his own life for the safety of his comrades – he throws himself on an exploding grenade – typifies the hero models of the 1950s and 1960s. This act is reminiscent of the sacrifices made by virtuous women in Imperial China, and it upstages even the brotherhood code of the *wu* god Guan Yu, who only agreed to die on the same day as his brothers, not before. Self-sacrifice was a virtue heavily promoted by the Communist propaganda of that time, and it is the single act that totally melts the hearts of the women in the story. In traditional romances, women kill themselves, or are killed, to receive high accolades for behaviour that is supposed to be emulated and adored. In early Communist propaganda literature, men also perform selfless acts to achieve hero status. However, men such as Dong Cunrui and Huang Jiguang die for the sake of other men. They remain sexless heroes. The soldier here seems to be like these men, but the fact that it is a woman writer who is describing him changes the nature of the masculinity matrix which takes him as a model. Like traditional virtuous women whose ghastly deaths titillated the sexual fantasies of men, we have here a virginal good-looking man who stirs deep emotions in the women. Shy he is, sexless he is not.

Sexual and gender reversals find parallels here in the subject–object relationship. Whereas in traditional literature, the men eye up the women, here the soldier is under the gaze of the two women. The narrator looks at him lovingly, referring to his solid build and his 'strapping shoulders' and 'the twigs in the barrel of his rifle ... put there more for ornamentation than camouflage'.[45] The young wife laughs at his embarrassment and causes him to tear his uniform. They enjoy teasing him, yet at the same time feel protective towards him, both before and after he dies. He is non-threatening sexually towards them, while they obviously cause him great discomfort. In this, he again behaves like coy young women in traditional tales, blushing and not daring to meet the eyes of the opposite sex.

The fact that the narrator is supposed to be telling the story in an objective manner makes her objectification of the soldier even more poignant. She takes command of the soldier from the beginning, though she is physically not as strong. This dominating role makes her more 'masculine' in the traditional sense. Not only is the narrator a woman, but the author, Ru Zhijuan, is also a woman. The two women in the story and the author each have the advantage that men have had for generations: the authority over the creation of an ideal and the telling of the story. Alas, the ideal man created, like ideal women of old, dies. Though the ostensible reason for that death is framed in political rather than gender terms, the concrete manifestations of its results do take it into the woman's world.

The female appropriation of the subjective voice enables sexual and gender reversals to go even further. In terms of the disappearing woman formulation, it is the man who disappears here. It is he who dies and will live in the women's hearts, and not the other way around as in traditional tales. Although he is a soldier (but a young messenger in the army), by having no cultural refinements or martial training, he is neither *wen* nor *wu* in the traditional sense. But he is clearly meant to be a hero, and he does warrant a place in the pantheon of real men. In the 1950s and 1960s, masculinity and gender roles changed dramatically, at least in the literature written by women. The promotion of the worker-peasant-soldier ideal had devastating consequences for traditional understandings of class and gender politics. *Wen-wu* masculinity had to be reconfigured. We have seen in earlier chapters how the transformations of *wen* and *wu* continue right into the twenty-first century. In the twentieth century, the most significant change to understandings of masculinity came with the emergence of women who could also participate in defining of this concept in the public arena.

In the early years of the Communist regime, under the pens of woman writers like Ru Zhijuan, young men are delicately constructed as loveable creatures, to be appreciated and adored by women, who take on active roles of perceiver, protector and creator, roles traditionally reserved for men. In 'Lilies', both women harbour maternal and sisterly concern for the young soldier as well as tender feelings which verge on romance. Those were the early Communist days when individual romance was discouraged and sexual feelings could not be expressed explicitly in print. Such a puritanical environment should be congenial to the *wen-wu* ideal. But in the eyes of the women, traditional understandings of this ideal are almost irrelevant. The power differentials between the classes and genders are meant to have changed, so that *wen* and *wu*, being so integral to these power relationships, would also need to be seen to have changed.

With hindsight, it is now relatively easy to see that much of the 'socialist realism' of the 1950s bore little resemblance to socialism or reality. Nonetheless, the constructions of the masculine ideal that were created at that time were laudable. Their impact lasted right into the 1980s. During the Cultural Revolution, in particular, women and peasants were emphasised as having mastered *wen-wu* skills in their own right. These were romantic ideals. After the disillusioning experiences of the Cultural Revolution, the ideals themselves were ridiculed as illusions. The backlash that followed had a tremendous impact on constructions of masculinity, as we have already seen. For women, ideal men also became a favourite subject of investigation, and I will focus on Wang Anyi, daughter of Ru Zhijuan, to see some of the models proposed.

Wang Anyi and the Writer

Similar to the May Fourth period when Chinese men had their egos shattered by Western imperialism, the 1980s was a time of great social upheaval in China. It was a time when men questioned everything about themselves, a time when, in Zhong Xueping's words, they felt that their masculinity was 'besieged'.[46] Even those who used brute strength to get their way were 'beleaguered'.[47] According to Margaret Hillenbrand, only by the use of strategic management of power relations such as that adopted by Zhang Xianliang would men be able to continue to dominate. Thus, even while men complained about being besieged, their response was an aggressive one, so that they projected themselves as wilful and overpowering, both mentally and physically.

For the women, this was a challenge. True, it was a time when revolutionary heroes no longer held any attraction. Men were no longer fighting an enemy and women wanted men who represented physical comfort and career prospects, not soldiers who get blown up and who blush at the sight of the opposite sex. The hero of 'Lilies' might have stirred the hearts of paedophiles and necrophiles, but the 1980s and 1990s were a cynical time, when this hero's coy behaviour would have been sneered at by many people. The 'wild men' in the writings and films by men in the 1980s were by contrast highly influential. These men had no revolutionary or patriotic fervour. Their displays of manliness came from their strength and their capacity to make money. They delighted in being bad or dangerous, and writing by women could be seen as providing ways to control the beasts the men had created.

As early as 1980, the older generation (represented by the mother in Ru Zhijuan's 'The Love of Daughters and Sons') already bemoans the fact that the younger generation were self-centred and lacked ideals.[48] In the early 1980s, one could still debate the relative merits of class and revolutionary standing versus material and corporate status. By the late 1980s and 1990s, a man's worth as being measured by having a career was no longer debatable. There were, of course, many other criteria for the ideal man, exemplified by the early simplistic choices drawn by Zhang Kangkang when her young female protagonists try to pick men of varying shades of brains and brawn (*wen-wu*) in stories such as 'Northern Lights'.[49] By the mid-1980s, the common lament from women writers was that 'there were no real men in contemporary China'.[50] It is in this climate of 'women's writing' that Wang Anyi wrote.

Wang Anyi's most famous work on 'what women want' is a trilogy on love and extra-marital sex published in the mid-1980s: *Love on a Barren Mountain* (1986), *Love in a Small Town* (1986) and *Brocade Valley* (1987).[51] In this chapter, I concentrate on the last novel because the male protagonists in *Brocade Valley* seem to encapsulate *wen* ideals perfectly. Although the novel is about a particular juncture in the life of the central female character, it, like the previous two stories, does an excellent job of looking at the male characters from her perspective. One is her husband, an intellectual who is mild mannered, does housework and tolerates her tantrums. The other is the ideal lover she meets at a conference: a writer who is intelligent, respected and sensitive to her needs. We know how Wang Anyi's mother Ru Zhijuan treats a soldier, a 1950s *wu* man, in 'Lilies'. I will show that in keeping with the changed times, the daughter now focuses on *wen* men, but the evaluation on masculinity still departs from that in traditional tales.

The heroine of *Brocade Valley* is an editor in a publishing house whose marriage has become routine and dreary. At a writers' conference in the glamorous mountain resort of Lushan she meets a famous novelist. She finds herself intoxicated by feelings of passion which have not stirred in her for a long time. After returning home to the same mundane surroundings, she waits for a letter from the writer. Her frustration grows as she fails to hear from him, but finally she realises that she was not so much in love with him as with the 'he' that their affair has created. To Western readers, the story is almost as boring as the heroine's life. Even to Taiwanese readers, 'this topic of extra marital affairs holds no special interest at all'.[52] Yet, Chinese literature since May Fourth had been so puritanical that some critics claim that Wang Anyi is 'one of the most daring woman writers since May Fourth'.[53] At the same time, this critic criticises Wang Anyi for having introduced 'overly dirty and unpleasant things' into the 'elegant halls of literature'.

Our focus is on the men in the story: in this case the husband and the lover. In some ways, the love triangle is similar to Sophia's situation with Weidi and Ling Jishi. The heroine's husband in this case is not a spoiled brat. On the contrary, he does a lot of the housework and puts up with her bad temper uncomplainingly. In contrast to Weidi's blustering enthusiasm, 'he bore everything in silence'.[54] Unfortunately for him, this was the wrong thing to do. 'Seeing his silent forbearance and prudent action, she felt sorry for him but even sorrier for herself.'[55] The husband in this story is not incompetent like Weidi, just boring. But his wife's reaction to him echoes the emotional upheavals of Sophia.

The story begins with the heroine waking up in bed next to her husband, and she takes a look at him:

> He lay on the bed, face up, arms and legs sprawled wide, occupying the half of the bed which she had just relinquished. The wind blew in the bamboo blind, shifting the morning sunlight; his body lay in the darkness one minute and bathed in light the next. Her mind also shifted from dark to bright and back again, as if it were on a swing going up and down, until she felt slightly nauseous. But he lay there without moving.
>
> At last, as if he'd heard some kind of summons in his dream, he made an abrupt dogpaddling movement with his limbs, turned over, and sat up cross-legged on the bed. At first he sat there blankly, his eyes staring into nothingness

as if in a trance. Abruptly he stretched out one hand and groped at the bedside cupboard. The first object his hand fell on was an earpick, and he proceeded to clean his ears. As the pick entered his ear, his eyes narrowed; a flicker of emotion passed his face – and finally some sign of life.[56]

At the end of the story when she comes back to him after her brief affair, this exact scene is repeated. He gets more pleasure from poking his own orifices than from contact with her. Even when they both got dressed and 'looked immaculate', 'they knew each other so intimately that there was no longer any possibility of mutual admiration'.[57] To the woman, the everyday man of her life is just that: mundane. Even if he puts on the shining armours of a European knight or uniform of a PLA soldier, she feels nothing for him but enervation.

The Lushan conference provides a break in this monotonous existence. Lushan is a famous and beautiful mountain resort, full of enchantment and postcard scenery. She is an editor whose job is to tidy up the creative work of writers. For the first time, she actually gets to meet some famous writers. The setting is perfect for her romantic feelings to be stirred. And she does indeed fall head over heels in love with a famous writer. It is not quite the same infatuation expressed by Sophia in regard to Ling Jishi. Times have changed. This young woman is not suffering from the 'spring fever'[58] of the May Fourth days, induced by the tubercular conditions of cramped and damp city life. She is not bewitched by a young 'foreign' student, but an older, married man. Nevertheless, the first night after meeting him, she fell asleep examining 'her actions and manner during the course of this day, like a student reviewing her conduct'.[59] In fact, throughout the conference, she kept feeling 'shy and naïve as a schoolgirl'.[60] By contrast, apart from being a well-known writer and a chain smoker, not much is said about him. He is, however, a considerate and attentive companion. For example, he helps carry her bag on a hike, walking on the side of the cliff so that she would not have to be afraid of the cliff-face.[61]

Of the men we have examined in this chapter, he is most like the scholars of the 'scholar–beauty' formulation in traditional romances. He is gentle, well-read, successful and charming. He has all the trappings of a *wen* person. In fact, he is a writer, and a successful one at that. She adores him for his fame and loves him for his verbal skills more than his knowing control of a host of situations such as walking on the right side of the cliff. Everything seems to fit the traditional or even May Fourth pattern. However, there is one major difference. As an editor, her job is to solicit manuscripts from people like him, and then to edit them. She can now rewrite him, and she can even delete him totally if she wants to. In short, she now has become the final arbiter of his manliness. And she can create him in any image she wants.

As Wang Anyi herself points out in another context, 'when a woman loves a man, it has nothing to do with the man's intrinsic worth. It is really about the realisation of her own ideals of love'.[62] As Peng Bin points out, the whole object of the affair is so that the young woman can take the image of the lover back with her to her boring marriage, an image that she can recall and play with at any time.[63] Interestingly, Wang Anyi in her discussion of how she came to write the story seems to assume that all marriages and husbands 'naturally' get stale.[64] By contrast, in this and other stories such as Zhang Jie's 'Love Cannot be Forgotten', it is assumed that it is much better to love an ideal in the mind, something you can treasure and not have to interact with in real life. Men are just boring once you get to know them. Thus, by having the woman go home and the man disappear from the scene altogether, the woman author/ narrator has the opportunity to shape and form the ideal to her heart's content.

Therefore, like Ling Jishi before Sophia kisses him, the ideal man is best when he is just a fantasy. These ideals are figures that live in the minds of the women, a bit like the fox-fairies and ghost wives that populate traditional ghost stories. In these early depictions of male–female relations, there are two archetypal women: the saint or the demon. Sometimes, one woman (or spirit) can begin with extreme evil intent on the man but end up being 'saved' and devoting her life to serving him. Most literary critics have concentrated on this type, whose function seems to provide a model for mortal women. These supernatural beings were no doubt figments of the imagination which served the men well. While there may have been subtle embellishments of these stories which presented the female sex more positively in their popular reincarnations such as operas and other performance art forms, the male = consumer vs. female = consumed template never changes.

One of the most interesting gender aspects about these traditional fantasies and ghost stories is that the sexy fox-fairies and ghosts are nearly always women. Of the hundreds of ghost stories about marital or romantic matters, very few are about ghost husbands. This fact illustrates in a most striking manner the immutable male-centred perspective adopted by the authors, who did not like to portray men (the likely gender of the authors) as angels or demons sacrificing themselves for women. The beautiful women (of whatever morals) are for their eyes and their consumption. Women internalise these images too, of course, but only as lessons on how to make themselves more desirable and consumable.

The three stories we have analysed show that it is only when women take over the role of myth-maker that we have ghostly lovers and husbands. Although the foreign student, the soldier and the writer in these stories are not fox-fairies or ghosts, the authors' intentions are clear enough. These men are artificial objects, designed to be rhapsodised over and treasured in the mind. They are all captured as fleeting phantoms, desirable perhaps, but not 'real men' who can be juvenile, boring or decay naturally before disappearing. The real thing is just not as good as a fantasy. Real men eat, drink and are not always merry. They fart, they burp, pick ear-wax and sometimes they refuse to disappear. Even the most victimised among them attempt to assert some degree of self-definition. Real men also play power games. In fact, for Chinese men, achieving *wen-wu* is tantamount to achieving power over both body and mind.

No wonder, then, that *wen* and *wu*, which depend so much on self-control and control over others, have been transformed beyond recognition in these female-created ideals. In these creations, the men may exhibit traces of *wen* and *wu*, but with the control component diminished or absent, they in no way invoke the kind of power and manhood inherent in the traditional Confucius or Guan Yu icons. Ding Ling's Singaporean student is a pseudo-foreigner who knows English (*yingwen*, literally the heroic *wen*). He may have none of the constraints placed on ordinary Chinese men. He may even be sexually tempting. But he cannot be *wen* or *wu* partly because he is a half-foreigner and *wen-wu* was at that time still preserved for Chinese men only. That's why if you kiss him, he tastes disgusting. Similarly, Ru Zhijuan's soldier may not have the misogyny of the *wu* heroes of the past and may be loveable, but that's because he has been feminised, seen most expressly in his weapon (his *wuqi*, literally the *wu* tool), which is decorated by flowers and other ornamental objects. More a boy than a *wu* hero, he dies without firing his gun at all. Wang Anyi's writer is a *wenren* by profession, and his demeanour is reminiscent of the *wen* scholars of the past. However, as we have seen above, the male scholars may not have changed, but the women have. They can now play the hegemonic game. The woman here is an editor, whose job is precisely to have control over these men's writings (the *wenzhang*, literally their *wen* pieces). The male protagonist is 'deliberately blurred' and becomes insignificant, but the female author 'imagines, produces, and wills the affair to re-create her selfhood'.[65]

The affirmation of selfhood by the women writers is framed in terms of the contest for power and dominance. By the second half of the 1990s, the female challenge to patriarchy had reached the point that their writings display an acute awareness of notions of the sexual politics of subjugation and oppression. In that context, the stories by the controversial writer Chen Ran (born 1962) are revealing. She has written a large number of stories about young women and their search for self-identity. Even though the female characters may be confused or victimised, they grow and assert their self-identity. Chen Ran's male characters are authority figures such as fathers, doctors and teachers.[66] These men may take advantage of young women sexually in Chen Ran's works, but whereas such abuse of authority in previous literature would show the woman as victim with no recourse to justice except as ghosts, Chen Ran's women characters grow and define themselves. By contrast, by abusing their power, the men relinquish any claim to being a *junzi* or leader of men. Ultimate power is denied them. In Chen Ran's stories, such men are not villains as much as pathetic figures that help the female protagonists grow.[67]

While traditional Chinese literature contains insufficient material written by women to enable us to easily comment on how women perceived and constructed *wen-wu*, there is enough in the modern period to make a few observations about their views. Generally, *wen-wu*, as traditionally understood, is not an overriding criterion for their constructions of the model man. *Wen* men, *wu* men and 'foreign' men are all treated with condescension or suspicion. Even if in real life the men may have more authority, in the mental games of their female creator, they are mere pawns. This is hardly surprising if, as is shown in this book, the central thrust of *wen-wu* is control: over self and others. The stories may be on themes of love and marriage, but the underlying problem is still one of sexual politics. And women want power as much as anyone. The danger in the rush to discover their 'true' identities apart from being someone's daughter, mother, lover, wife or friend is that, like the men they repudiate, they too may become alienated and self-objectified.[68] Traditional bonds such as the 'five human relationships' (*wu lun*) are incompatible with the modern world, but humans cannot exist without bonds.

In the rush to create new bonds, it is a pity that some women have taken the easy route by simply reversing the old ones. In her summation of the works by women authors of the 1980s and 1990s, Xiaojiang Li observes that: 'None of the stories follow the traditional romantic narrative. Women take the leading roles, men play second fiddle.'[69] In terms of subject–object relationships, women take on the active role and wield power and authority on the hapless male characters. However, as 'Miss Sophia's Diary' indicates, even from the woman's perspective, self-discovery and 'winning' do not necessarily lead to happiness. It should also be remembered that women writers and readers may be on the rise, but the impact they have on society as a whole is still relatively small. For example, the results of a 1998 survey of 500 Beijing households and 500 bookshop browsers show that of the top ten modern Chinese writers nominated by the respondents, not one is female.[70] True, the buying power of women consumers is now immense, but most prefer to read 'popular literature' by women writers with pen-names such as 'Huang

Who Loves Goodies' (Huang Aidongxi). This material deals with trivial, mundane matters and makes no pretensions about wanting to change the world.[71]

In the stories we have looked at, women manipulate their male characters in order to control them, but it seems the best outcome they can expect from this conflict is the realisation that they can do without the men, and take flight: either physically or into their minds. Or, as in the case of Ru Zhijuan, have the man die. Either way, the resolution is to get rid of the object of desire. By making men redundant, *wen-wu* also becomes superfluous. This abandonment of the cherished (by men) *wen-wu* schema is reminiscent of Lacan's analysis of the phallus as signifier. According to this analysis, in order to enter into the powerful patriarchal world, men trade their 'penis', that is, a man 'forfeits direct access to his own sexuality',[72] for the 'phallus', symbolising patriarchal power. They therefore experience a 'lack' in themselves. Women do not have to go through this 'castration' because they have never had a 'penis' anyway. However, this lack makes them more congenial to a more non-gender-specific symbolic system.

In the same way, by having been denied *wen-wu* in the old symbolic power structures, Chinese women can take or leave the remnants of traditional *wen-wu* attributes and not 'lack' anything in terms of their femininity. They have nothing to lose but a whole new world to gain. This chapter reveals some of the first steps towards that world. As I have indicated throughout this book, and to borrow Judith Butler's words, women have for centuries shown that they were able to 'do' *wen-wu* deeds. For recognition of a woman doer behind the deeds, however, women will need to do more than 'performatively' produce *wen-wu* results. They will need to take part in the production of 'the regulatory practices of gender coherence'.[73] I have demonstrated some of the effects of this process in this chapter. In the next two chapters, I will follow the trajectory of *wen-wu* as it traces a path in foreign lands, where, once again, *wen-wu* was not meant to be found.

7   Lao She's *The Two Mas* and Foreign Wives: Constructing *wen* Masculinity for the Modern World

A 1939 drawing by the famous artist Feng Zikai, showing the antiquated and decrepit scholar Kong Yiji begging outside a wineshop. From *Feng Zikai huihua Lu Xun xiaoshuo*, Hangzhou: Zhejiang renmin chubanshe, 1982, p. 175.

So far in this book, I have analysed the different ways *wen-wu* has been constructed by focusing on a number of contemporary paradigms and their traditional antecedents. I have also indicated that some modern Chinese women, consciously or unconsciously, have tried to denaturalise the gendered imperative whereby *wen-wu* is regarded as a male preserve. In the next two chapters, I move *wen-wu* onto an international matrix, with this chapter focusing on *wen* and the next on *wu*. For thousands of years during the imperial past, representations of the Chinese identity, including gender, were not seriously challenged by external images. However, in the twentieth century, to accommodate the effects of the globalisation process, Chinese identities were forced to modify themselves. Chapter 3 alluded to some of these modifications of the *wen* icon Confucius through a series of recreations and reincarnations during the last two decades of the twentieth century. This chapter resumes the examination of this re-interpretive process by comparing the *wen* identity in the first and last two decades of that century.

The beginning of the twentieth century was a chaotic time during which Chinese self-identity was badly shaken by the aggressive imperialism of the West and Japan. Although there are numerous studies on the impact of this aggression, almost nothing has been written on its effects on the Chinese constructions of masculinity.[1] Did East/West contact significantly change the male ideal? If so, how did the new image integrate traditional and Western gender configurations? This chapter analyses the ways in which a Western context alters Chinese intellectuals' reconstruction of these models to produce a new male *wen* prototype. One of the best representations of the interface between East and West is Lao She's (1899–1966) famous novel *Er Ma* (*The Two Mas*).[2] The 1920s was a time when many Westernised intellectuals such as Xu Zhimo were totally enamoured by European civilisation, to such an extent that Xu's influential friend Hu Shi once called for a 'wholesale Westernisation' of Chinese culture.[3] While there was a great diversity of masculine ideals in this period, the images presented in *The Two Mas* were in many respects typical of the Republican era. The upheavals in China during most of the twentieth century meant that the prophetic nature of these images is only becoming evident now.

The Historical Setting for the Novel

Lao She wrote the novel while he was teaching Chinese at the School of Oriental Studies,[4] London, between 1924 and 1929. Before he left China at the age of 26, Lao She had worked as a teacher for a number of years and was a practising Christian. As a writer, Lao She is best-known for his faithful and vivid descriptions of the residents of his home town, Beijing.

Almost all of his better known works are set in this city and address the concerns of its inhabitants. *The Two Mas* is unusual for the London location and the multi-ethnic nature of its characters.[5] Some critics claim that because of his relative maturity, Lao She's observations in *The Two Mas* are less emotionally and politically charged than most other writing at this time.[6] Indeed, Lao She had personally benefited from missionary help, and lived in relative comfort in London during a period of social chaos and patriotic fervour in China. *The Two Mas* can be interpreted as a text in which Lao She attempted to establish his nationalist credentials by writing a harsh indictment of British racism.

This was not a difficult exercise, given that in the early decades of the twentieth century, the overseas Chinese in London, like their counterparts in other parts of the world, were attributed a 'sinister repute'[7] for opium smoking and gambling. Moreover, 'the most recurrent note of disquiet in reports on Britain's Chinese was almost certainly their sexual relations with white women and girls'.[8] Even though investigations conducted by city councils and individuals such as George Wade found little substance to fears of sexual molestation by the Chinese, popular stories such as those by Thomas Burke titillated the British imagination by harking on this theme. Burke's 'The Chink and the Child', about a Chinese man's infatuation with a 12-year-old white girl and its tragic consequences,[9] was so popular that by 1936, three film versions of it were made.[10] While Burke was not always unsympathetic in his portrayals of the Chinese, his 'Tales of Chinatown' are filled with crime and menacing evil. In the British imagination, the Limehouse district provided the 'drug-filled settings'[11] which typified the Fu Manchu stories by Sax Rohmer. Fu Manchu, 'the yellow peril incarnate in one man',[12] has since become an omnipresent icon of the inscrutable and sinister Chinaman.[13] Such narratives meant 'that Britons of every age knew what to expect in their encounters with Chinese, and how to act in response'.[14]

Lao She's novel was thus produced in a politically and racially charged atmosphere vis-à-vis East/West relations. It could easily be read as a work of nationalist protestation by a miserable expatriate, similar to Yu Dafu's plaintive 1921 cry for China 'to get wealthier and stronger' in 'Sinking'.[15] However, the novel's thematic foci on interracial love and desire and the difference between old and new learning make it a perfect text for the study of the constructions of Chinese masculinity in a Western context. This chapter examines the composition of *The Two Mas*' three male protagonists in order to elucidate the ideological underpinning of the constructions of their masculinity directly confronted, as it was, by British prejudice.

The novel provides an interesting inventory of perceived injustices suffered by Chinese around the turn of the century. For example, in the novel, only two kinds of foreigner – missionaries and traders – are depicted as having any knowledge of China. Yet, to the former, even after many years' sojourn in China, the Chinese are no more than heathens whose souls need salvation; and the latter look down on the Chinese because they are incompetent in managing their money. These observations certainly seem to confirm the views expressed in the authoritative 8-volumed *Dictionary of Chinese Literature*, which characterises the novel as a narrative of prejudice endured by the overseas Chinese.[16] They also explain why some historians have used *The Two Mas* for the insights it yields about the Chinese intellectuals' dilemma in simultaneously loathing and loving China.[17] From a racial and nationalist perspective, the novel can definitely be read as a 'more or less tragic' statement with a 'patriotic message'.[18]

This chapter argues further that early last century, the Chinese male identity of the educated classes was threatened not only by the onslaught of Western values, but also by the emergence of more vocal women and working-class men in China itself. It was a time when the male identity was under tremendous pressure from cultural and gender challenges, but it was also a time before notions of hybridity were explained and valorised.[19] As we will see below, the mood of Chinese men therefore swung from depression to euphoria, both states being based on a nostalgia for a civilised past when China was great and *wen-wu* was exclusively Chinese and male. These mood changes continued for the next 70-odd years, a fact which may partly explain why to celebrate Lao She's centenary, *The Two Mas* was made into a 20-episode television series in 1999.[20] The many apparent parallels between the May Fourth era and the 1980s and 1990s galvanise the attention paid to this novel by the Chinese authorities. However, the significance and relevance of *The Two Mas* for the late twentieth century have their limits. Instead of feeling inadequate as Chinese nationals, as writers in the May Fourth Movement such as Lu Xun and Yu Dafu have demonstrated in their writings, Chinese men abroad in the 1990s often see their host countries as having a 'culture without culture'.[21] In fact, the rise of Chinese economic and political power in the international arena in the last two decades of the twentieth century had direct repercussions on the Chinese diaspora identities.[22] The second part of this chapter will examine the implications of these repercussions on *wen-wu*.

Class: The World of the Declining Scholar

As a result of the abolition of the civil service examinations in 1905, the position of scholars educated in the traditional manner declined very rapidly. This decline is best illustrated in literature by the character Kong

Yiji, whose classical learning only serves to make him a laughing-stock in the village.[23] Lu Xun probably created such a caricature deliberately to discredit the old-style *wenren*. Not only were they threatened by the disappearance of the social and economic base that had traditionally sustained them, but they were also besieged by their own successors. Among the younger writers and readers of that time, too, the archetypal Kong Yiji image struck a nerve because many – including Yu Dafu, Ba Jin, Lao She – were from wealthy families that had fallen on hard times.[24] The fear of ending up like Kong Yiji provided a strong incentive for intellectuals to re-invent themselves for the new era.

Part of that re-invention was to claim a mastery of foreign languages and knowledges. The adoption of the vernacular language and modern content in the education system as well as the thousands of students going abroad enabled a totally new style of scholar to emerge. Their model was the 'New Youth', whose understanding of the difference between the superior West and the inferior East was that the West valued youth whereas the East venerated age. Their mission was to get rid of the old and bring in the young.[25] The *wen* icon, Confucius, was fiercely attacked, and it appeared that the traditional scholar-gentry class really needed to 'close shop'.[26] Communist scholars would later tell us that enlightened writers such as Lu Xun wisely saw the inevitable victory of the working-class, symbolised by the rickshaw-puller.[27] The lionisation of the urban worker may have been a genuine recognition by left-wing intellectuals that the old scholar-gentry class was doomed, but it was obvious that the rickshaw-puller was never going to be a model for scholars as had been Wang Mian of *The Scholars* in traditional times.

Wen-wu was in tatters, but the young scholars stitched the bits and pieces back together again in such a way that it was still useable in the modern world. To do this, they utilised the social Darwinian notion of youth and strength replacing age and frailty as inevitable progress, so that the old-style *wenren* was represented as positively dangerous for the welfare of Chinese everywhere. This is a point repeatedly emphasised in *The Two Mas*. Ma Zeren, for example, is a most contemptible figure in the novel. Though hardly 50 years of age, he considers himself too old to engage in any form of productive and physical activity. He finds the most polite but implausible excuses to avoid helping others, including his ex-missionary benefactor Mr Evans, who wants to learn Chinese to translate some texts. Incredibly lazy and always looking for the easy way out, Ma Zeren is too proud to work at the London curio shop which his deceased brother bequeathed him. However, he furtively pockets little treasures and offers them to his landlady Mrs Winter in order to ingratiate himself with her. His political naivety and role as an extra in a movie that features unpalatable caricatures of the Chinese cause a riot against him in his shop. The potentially dangerous mob is pacified only because his hard-working shop assistant and part-time student, Li Zirong, knows how to control the trouble-makers. Yet, Ma Zeren sneers at Li Zirong for being vulgar and lacking in true learning.

While he perceives himself as restrained and venerable, Ma Zeren is indulgent with his sentiments and yearning for romance. In London, he quickly wins the heart of Mrs Winter. Even when his wife was alive, he sought the company of women and he fancies himself an attractive man. He looks down on physical labour, hates commerce in particular and daydreams about being an official back in China. He often drifts into an almost Daoist state of contemplation on the nature of beauty or regrets about unfulfilled ambitions of joining the bureaucracy. Such behaviour is supposed to be that of a *wenren*, and he luxuriates in it. However, in practice, it is clear that he is alienated from all those around him and he has no comprehension of the conditions of his existence. This is a brilliant portrait of a deluded *wenren* who is ripe for extinction, a most fitting candidate for finishing up as a Kong Yiji in an indifferent foreign land. The inevitable collapse of traditional *wen-wu* is even more compelling here because it occurs in an alien context, where norms and values are meant to compete in a social Darwinist struggle for survival.

In this light, Ma Zeren's son, Ma Wei, and the student Li Zirong stand out as counter-balances to Ma Zeren. They are young and prepared to replace Chinese ways with Western ones. Li Zirong in particular seems to have abandoned the whole *wen-wu* ideal, happily doing physical labour and studying for a business degree. While his class affiliations are neither capitalist nor communist, he explains European success in terms of business and hard work, not ethics. Interestingly, literary historians such as Zhao Xiaqiu do not nominate Li Zirong as the ideal figure, but Ma Wei.[28] Ma Wei is truly more of an antithesis to his father. Critics refer to him as patriotic and tragic. That may be true, but more importantly, he continues to operate, at least partially, within the traditional *wen-wu* paradigm, and he acts in ways which are consonant with those of the 'romantic generation'. He is highly sentimental, falls in love easily and hopelessly, is extremely patriotic, prone to hero-worship and tearfully demonstrates his sense of loneliness. However, the impetuosity of his melodramatic poses 'develop only into familiar stage gestures'.[29] While Ma Wei has certain qualities that are reminiscent of Scholar Zhang in *The Story of The West Wing*, what distinguishes him from the traditional *caizi* is his alienation from his father's generation.

Ma Wei's conscious separation from his father confirms Leo Lee's classic study of this generation. Lee points out that by the 1920s, the 'new' *wenren* was beginning to diverge from his traditional counterpart. Among the 'modern' fads favoured by the new-style *wenren*,[30] Leo Lee lists eight which were compiled by a social critic of that time. These include a conviction of his own genius, being amorous but lazy, having a penchant for modern fashionable clothes, and having both national and international friends. While Ma Zeren and his son Ma Wei are not writers and so do not fulfil some of the conditions such as contributing to journals or sponsoring new writers, they are both prime examples of the sort of men described by the list. The excessive displays of sentimentality, with a good dose of self-pity as exemplified by Yu Dafu's feelings of being 'a superfluous man castrated by advanced education',[31] give a heightened sense of helplessness. The 1920s were a time of mourning for the passing of one's own class, and a time to find ways to resurrect that class by manipulating old concepts such as *wen* and *wu*. The result can sometimes be tragic, and sometimes comic. By going international, the old scholars risked ridicule not just at home, but abroad. While having international friends was a precondition for being a 'new' *wenren*, its effect as demonstrated in *The Two Mas* would not have been welcomed by the intellectuals: in a foreign country, exhibitions of superfluousness and helplessness of the 'new' *wenren* are not just pathetic, they are also absurd.

Gender: A World of Foreign Women

This absurdity is most glaring when highlighted by the forces of love, sex and sentiment. In the 1920s, love and sex were popular and relatively openly discussed topics. It was a time, for example, when the publications of 'Dr Sex' were in great demand.[32] As Leo Lee points out, for the *wenren*, '[l]ove had become an over-all symbol of new morality, an easy substitute for the traditional ethos of propriety which was now equated with external restraint'.[33] Falling in love was indispensable as a signature for the new *wenren*. Both Ma Senior and and Ma Junior fall in love. The problem for them was the alien location they chose to perform this deed. They do not fall in love with sweet-natured, self-effacing and self-sacrificing Chinese girls of the Yingying type found in traditional fiction and drama: no such women existed in London. Instead, the Mas fall for foreign women who at best barely tolerate them. Situated outside the realm of a civilising *wen-wu* influence, these women cannot be measured against known cultural norms. For example, their more assertive behaviour could not be codified and made programmable within a *yin-yang* schema because as foreign women, they do not compute.

By Republican times, the traditional understanding that only men could master *wen-wu* was challenged by young women like Ding Ling. They took to publishing and political activity with gusto, showing that not only did they have *wen* accomplishments, but also they wanted the official recognition and power such accomplishments should yield.

Moreover, they deliberately and provocatively wrote about men as sex objects.[34] Even before 1911, Kang Youwei had already re-interpreted Confucianism to such an extent that in his *Great Commonwealth*,[35] he 'stresses the fundamental equality and right of independence of men and women'.[36] But that utopia referred to a distant future. After the Republic was established, and women became more educated and demanded more rights, sexual equality was not something to be granted by men, but claimed by women. In contrast to the traditional *caizi jiaren* formulation in which the scholar always wins the girl and his sexual dominance over the muscular *wu* man was never in doubt, *wenren* sexuality was constantly interrogated. As well as squirming under the gaze of women like the narrator in Ding Ling's 'Miss Sophia's Diary', men themselves were confessing all. For example, Lu Xun claimed that when faced with the onslaught of foreign might, Chinese men simply sacrificed their women.[37] This may explain the prevalence of woman as victim in May Fourth literature,[38] but what if there were no Chinese women to sacrifice?

The Two Mas describes the lives of Chinese men in London in the 1920s, where there were indeed very few Chinese women.[39] In the novel itself, no Chinese women are mentioned. Chinese masculinity, already besieged in China, is thus taken from its native context and abruptly forced to fend for itself, with no women whom it could sacrifice to fend off the ferocious foreign men. Moreover, for someone like Ma Zeren who is accustomed to the company of women back in China, the loneliness such an existence entailed would have compelled him to seek comfort from the foreign women around him. As a representative of the 'romantic generation', his son Ma Wei also flaunts his emotionality and sexuality. He quickly falls madly in love with the flirtatious Miss Winter. By having the father and son protagonists rent and share a house with the mother–daughter Winters, Lao She has constructed a situation in which interracial sexual attraction and romantic possibilities confront the protagonists daily. Furthermore, both Mas are educated and in the Chinese context are *wenren*. By contrast, the Winter women even by British standards are lower-middle class, ill-informed scatterbrains.[40] Two of the most fundamental ingredients for assessing masculinity – sexual desirability and marital attractiveness – are thus mapped onto the race and class axes in intriguing configurations.

In keeping with the novel's negative portrayal of the older generation, Ma Zeren's plan to marry with Mrs Winter is sad but farcical. If Ma Zeren was the righteous Confucian gentleman he professes to be, he should not even harbour romantic thoughts about a widow, let alone a widow from England. In one passage in the novel, he himself muses over life with Mrs Winter in China if they were to get married. The reverie of a misguided middle-aged man is bad enough, but the reality would have been much worse, if Han Suyin's descriptions of an interracial union in war-torn Republican China are to be believed.[41] Yet, Ma Zeren cannot escape from the daily temptations of the flesh and goes ahead with the plan. Unfortunately, he discovers that nobody would accept his plans to marry Mrs Winter and he cannot even buy a wedding ring without being greeted with disbelief and ridicule by the jeweller. For someone who can only think in clichéd terms about the attractiveness of traditional *wen* accomplishments, the jewellery shop episode stuns even the deluded Ma Zeren, who finally has to accept that traditional *wen* masculinity has no place in the new world. Tragically, class attributes such as education and refinement are not at fault here. The problem lies with the racial aspect of traditional *wen*, which, as I have noted in chapter 1, could be only part of a Chinese identity. Yet 'Chineseness' for the British at that time only conjured up images of an exotic people at best.

The romances between the Ma men and the Winters form the basis for the first Chinese novel-length romance between Chinese men and Western women. Love with foreigners was in fact one of the first topics to be broached by the new 'romantic generation' in Su Manshu's *Duanhong lingyan ji* (*Lone Swan*), but that relationship is between two (or three) Asians, and not between a Chinese and a European.[42] The various versions of the liaison between the celebrated late Qing courtesan Sai Jinhua and the German commander Count von Waldersee is note-worthy,[43] but in this case, the man is European and the woman is Chinese. These relationships do not go beyond the accepted gender and racial norms current in the early years of the twentieth century, where 'West' and/or 'male' equals power and 'Chinese' and/or 'female' power-lessness. By contrast, the large and salacious writings on the sexuality of Chinese men and their relations with white women in British literature of this time display sexual and racial anxiety of the most fundamental kind. They were 'governed by a range of desires, repressions, invest-ments and projections on the part of the white population ... [such that the Chinese are imputed to] have the power to lure white women into their dens'.[44]

The Two Mas can be seen as a reaction to and derivative of this lurid literature. The novel, in conformity with its English equivalents, con-structs the Chinese men as failing in their romantic quests. The difference is that the two Mas have *wen*. However, *wen* and *wu*, in their traditional configurations, were simply not factors that Europeans would even consider. The *wenren* may have mysterious sexual powers, derived from financial wealth or Confucian finesse, but these powers were perceptible only to Chinese of a similar class. To most Europeans, they were not visible, and the *wenren* were not seen as real men. Interestingly, the 'worker-student' hero of the novel, Li Zirong, seems to acknowledge but rejects not only this 'Western understanding', but the entire modern ethic of sexual equality and romance. Thus, he defends arranged marriages and happily waits to return to his 21-year old fiancée in China, an uneducated woman who only 'knows a few characters'. Li Zirong's philosophy on love and marriage is practical to the extreme. He explains to Ma Wei that many men in China are still ignorant and illiterate, and still cannot find suitable work. It is therefore illogical to educate women, who with literacy will read romantic nonsense and forget to look after their men. Quite literally, Li Zirong believes that 'cooking and doing the laundry are a woman's only responsibility'.[45]

Race, Ethnicity and Class

Like women, foreign men are kept out of the masculinity stakes in traditional China. In *The Two Mas*, the clash of civilisations produces new rules, but remnants of the old remain. As some critics have pointed out,[46] the British men in the novel are either hollow like the ex-missionary Mr Evans, drunken loud-mouths like the trader Alexander, or selfish bullies like the spoilt Paul. Even when it is a question of physical prowess, the British are depicted as all bluster and no match for the Chinese. The fight between Ma Wei and Paul, with the former ending up victor, is a clear illustration of this. Even the empty-headed Mary Winter, who is at most amused by Ma Wei's infatuation with her, was moved momentarily to let herself be kissed by him after the fight. Thus, ideals of masculinity are embedded within racialised narratives.[47]

Though less transparent, the novel also contains a mine of information on the issue of the relationship between ethnicity and masculinity.[48] In a number of passages, Lao She describes in detail the differences between the 'Chinatown workers' (the *Zhongguo cheng gongren*) and the *wen* type students (the *Zhongguo xuesheng*). London 'Chinatown' at that time was the Limehouse area, and the 'workers' were mostly seamen and laundry operators.[49] The use of the word '*Zhongguo cheng*' (Chinatown) by Lao She is therefore somewhat anachronistic by present-day understandings of the term. As indicated earlier, despite the numerical insignificance and the rapid turnover of the Chinese population in London in the first three decades of the last century, the term 'Chinatown' had a powerful fascination for the British of that time. It evoked feelings that 'beneath its calm dingy exterior there stir the same dark passions, instincts and racial tendencies which cause this mystic yellow people to be so misunderstood[,] feared and hated'.[50] Lao She's diatribe against the 'Chinatown Chinese' can therefore be seen as having been derived directly from or a reaction against such views.[51] The fact that these are contradictory motivations does not detract from the emotional intensity generated by the fictional characters in the novel, both for the author and the reader.

For Lao She, the students, and by extension the educated Chinese, are a class above the 'workers' in the Chinatown precinct. This Chinatown is one which 'brings shame to the Chinese'.[52] It is depicted as dirty and uncouth, thus validating the Orientalism of the British. Its inhabitants' alleged cultural and linguistic ineptness is blamed for feeding the inscrutable and sinister Fu Manchu syndrome.[53] The two Mas, like other educated Chinese, by contrast speak fluent English. Indeed, they communicate effortlessly with the locals as soon as they arrive in London, because as Christians, they had British friends before they left China (as was the case with Lao She himself). As Christians, they presumably also share a common ethos on which communication with the British can take place.

The only people with whom the Mas have problems communicating are the Chinatown workers, who, we are told, are Cantonese. Whether it is linguistically engendered or otherwise, the Chinatown workers are a truly incomprehensible and reprehensible lot. By the end of the novel, when they try to create a disturbance in the curio shop, they have been reduced to a pack who sneak around and produce funny 'sing-song sounds at the tail-end of every sentence – ooow, loou, ooow'.[54] The hero in this telling episode is Li Zirong, who has learnt to speak to them in Cantonese by sometimes acting as their interpreter. The villains in this case are thus not the British, but other Chinese, those with no *wen* or *wu* to recommend them. They are not portrayed really as men as such, but a faceless rabble with names like Ah Chou and Ah Hong (Ah Ugly and Ah Red).[55]

The only Chinatown Cantonese person who engages in conversation in any meaningful way is Manager Fan, owner of the Chinese restaurant regularly patronised by Ma Zeren. Interestingly, the name of his restaurant, the most prosperous in the Chinatown precinct, is Zhuangyuanlou (the Number One Scholar Mansion). Mr Fan provides a wonderful mockery of the name. In the traditional Confucian masculinity framework, merchants were the least desirable in terms of *wen-wu*. Doing business was certainly not one of the arts and skills Confucius promoted. In both Confucian and Daoist ideology, the ignorant peasant was often idealised, but, as we have seen in chapters 1 and 3, trade and profits have until very recently never been seen as compatible with *wen* or *wu*. This formulation operated also among the overseas Chinese, where money-making was disparaged.

Mr Fan succeeds in business, but by playing the Oriental clown: he incessantly gibbers ungrammatical platitudes to his customers. He smiles often, but that only accentuates his foolish looks because the perpetual grin on his face causes his eyes to squint (like a true Chinaman). However, he has business acumen, and at the end of the novel buys the shop from Ma Zeren at a bargain price. Thus, Mr Fan encapsulates the Orientalist notion – shared by traditional Chinese story-tellers – of the successful Chinese shopkeeper, a person whose aim in life is to make money and who does not care about the fate of China or the world, a man without principles and no *wen-wu* appeal whatsoever. Ma Zeren has misgivings about him because he is a 'merchant' (*maimai ren*),[56] but they nevertheless become good friends because Fan flatters him. While he is not as depraved, the portrayal of Mr Fan is reminiscent of the disgusting merchant Tai Fu in Thomas Burke's *Limehouse Nights*.[57]

Thus, the ignorance, cowardice and avariciousness attributed to the Chinatown Cantonese are congruent with the discourse on ethnicity and race adopted both by Lao She and by British writers of his time such as Thomas Burke. In common with all such ideological discourses, the concepts are not unambiguous or clear. Ma Junior and Ma Senior could be any of the Chinese ethnic groups. In fact, the novel tells us that the Mas were originally Cantonese, but Old Ma grew up in Beijing. Interestingly, he always tells people he is a Pekingnese, and admits to his Cantonese background only after Sun Yatsen's Cantonese government became more powerful and prestigious.

The significance of the depiction of the Cantonese compatriots is even more trenchant when we consider that Lao She himself was of Manchurian descent. As a child, he was witness to the hatred shown by the majority Han Chinese against his ethnic group, with influential revolutionaries inciting the crowd to believe that the Manchus were like animals, and 'should all be killed'.[58] Lao She would have also been aware, too, that such racist instigations were not simply rhetoric. Tens of thousands of Manchus were in fact massacred in cities such as Xian, Hankou and Hanyang. Manchus such as Lao She who lived in Beijing were saved from this fate, but they were required to assume Han identity by taking on Han surnames and quickly assimilating Han customs. However, as Vohra points out, even though Lao She submerged his ethnic identity, 'he never forgave or forgot all that transpired with his people in 1911'.[59] Vohra wrote this in 1974, but his assertion is confirmed by Lao She's semi-autobiographical work *Beneath the Red Flag*, which was first published posthumously in 1980.[60] This book gives a warm and candid description of Manchu life in the beginning of this century.

In *The Two Mas*, the treatment meted out to ethnic minorities is made more striking by the contrast between Chinese Han chauvinism and the educated Englishman's ability to take an interest in the non-mainstream. When Li Zirong tells Ma Zeren that a neighbouring shop has made a huge profit selling Mongolian and Manchurian books, Old Ma's reaction is dismissive and bigoted: 'Who would want to buy texts in Manchurian or Mongolian? Why buy those?'[61] Although he would have identified himself as Chinese in London, it is likely that with his sensitivities to ethnic differences, Lao She was able to knowledgeably and passionately describe the various ethnic groups of Chinese in London. He vocalises the distinction between race and ethnicity and the prejudice generated as a consequence of these categorisations most bitterly through Li Zirong,

> Cooking and washing clothes are the two big enterprises of Chinese overseas ... The Japanese who go abroad always set up bordellos; the Chinese go in for small restaurants and laundries. The difference between the two groups is that Japanese, in addition to their houses of prostitution, also operate shipping companies, banks, and other large businesses while the Chinese have nothing else.[62]

Historical accuracy aside, the lament that Japanese men were more successful in the control of both sex and money indicates that a subtle change in constructions of *wen-wu* has occurred. As I have shown in chapter 2, the connection between sex and masculinity had been unspoken and implicit in traditional China. Here, success in money-making and business is also accepted (however reluctantly) as evidence of manly success and accomplishment. This assessment is reiterated later when Ma Zeren and Mrs Winter decide to get married. When they try to buy a wedding ring, the shop assistant only shows them very cheap items. When Mrs Winter makes clear that they want a more expensive ring, the shop assistant apologises, 'I mistook this gentleman for a Chinese. I didn't realise he was Japanese.'[63] This final humiliation convinces Ma Zeren and Mrs Winter that there is no future in marrying a foreigner. It is also an instructive episode illustrating how one minority, the Japanese, can be used by the dominant group, the British, to oppress another minority group, the Chinese.

While Lao She takes care to highlight facets of incongruity between traditional *wen-wu* and British attitudes in the depiction of the two Mas and Li Zirong, he seems to have suppressed any sort of ambiguity when describing his compatriots from the Chinatown area. In the novel, the Chinatown people are like the mob described by Lu Xun in his preface to the collection *Call to Arms*: they are unthinking,[64] lacking in individuality and dumb. In this context, the difference between the Ma Wei versus Paul fight and that of the Li Zirong versus the Chinatown mob is enlightening. The former is a fight between two real men whereas in the latter, Li Zirong is portrayed in the manner of a Peking-opera *wu* warrior demolishing a rabble of no consequence. As positive protagonists, both Ma Wei and Li Zirong have *wen* and *wu*. Such characterisations are not problematic, but it is intriguing that compared to Paul, the Cantonese workers have even less *wen-wu*. The generalisation that foreigners are not eligible for *wen-wu* thus needs qualification. Compared to a middle-class foreigner, the Cantonese workers have even less to recommend them as men. Therefore, by the beginning of this century, class and ethnic differences were beginning to act as more powerful Othering mechanisms than racial ones.

The depiction of the workers from Chinatown as the Others whose language is incomprehensible and who have no distinguishing features contrasts markedly with the Mandarin-speaking embassy officials and students in London. These men do all the things men in traditional and modern novels do: they care about their country, they study hard and if necessary, they fight the good fight – in short, they have 'manly' emotions and behaviour patterns. By contrast, the Cantonese workers of Chinatown appear and behave as the faceless Chink, mentioned so often in the novel itself as inhuman monsters abhorred by the Orientalist narratives of that time.[65] While the Chinese abroad seem to share at least an 'imagined community',[66] therefore, Stuart Hall is correct to point out that despite the continuities and similarities, the many differences and disruptions within a diasporic group are 'unsettling'.[67] As Ralph Litzinger observes in the case of another ethnic and gender representation, it is not always the case that ethnic minorities are objectified and Orientalised. Ethnicity and gender are not categories that can be grasped easily through the mastery of research methodologies: 'They point not to the truth of social life, but to a never-ending cultural politics always informed by complex histories of production and negotiation by social actors in a wide range of different positions of power and authority.'[68]

Portrait of the Hero (*yingxiong*)

However, while concepts relating to gender and ethnicity are not fixed and remain elusive, it is possible to analyse how ideals in these realms are constructed. Having established which men have no *wen-wu* (and therefore do not count in the masculinity stakes), it is worthwhile to examine the construction of the ideal man, the hero, in this novel. As suggested above, Ma Wei is in many ways the representative of young men of the May Fourth generation. In his eyes, the hero is definitely Li Zirong. While Ma Wei is his father's son and needs to break away from tradition in order to find a path for himself, Li Zirong seems completely independent of traditional as well as 'modern' concerns. Ma Zeren despises him for being 'vulgar' and having no idea what learning is all about: he does not dream about becoming an official, and he is happy to do physical labour. In particular, Ma Zeren cannot understand why Li is so interested in the running of the curio shop as a business to make money, including happily dealing with the foreigners who have no cultural sensitivities.[69] He clearly does not fit into the definition of a *wen-wu* man by the traditional criteria. Yet, Ma Wei almost worships him, seeing him as someone 'who is not only an average person who could manage things and make money, but a perfect hero in both heart and mind' (*xinshen jianquan de yingxiong*).[70]

Li Zirong's preparedness to engage in business in order to make himself wealthy and China strong is not very different to the path advocated by the Self-strengtheners of Late Qing. Departing from the traditional Confucian aversion to business was not really that heretical by Republican times. What is remarkable in this case is that several decades after 'the last stand of Chinese conservatism',[71] Li Zirong is still seen by the traditional literati, as represented by Ma Zeren, as being 'vulgar' and 'common'. This disdain and mistrust of money was widespread throughout the twentieth century, when writers such as Mao Dun and Cao Yu often depicted businessmen and industrialists as immoral and exploitative. By comparison, Lao She quite emphatically states that the future of China lies precisely with young people who study and engage in business. He contrasts Ma Zeren's incompetence with Li Zirong's ingenuity and efficacy in numerous instances. Ma Zeren despises Li for his lack of *wen* accomplishments, yet Ma is at best a comical figure whenever comparisons are made. His sort of *wen-wu* is manifestly not appropriate to London, whereas Li Zirong's work practices and ambition to finish a business degree are painted as the only paths open for any young man interested in bettering himself and China.

As we have observed in chapter 3, *wen* has changed from traditional literati accomplishments to include business studies and profitable activities abhorred by the Confucians. In the novel, there are several places where the word 'hero' (*yingxiong*) is mentioned. Most of the time, it refers to businessmen who have succeeded in London. Ma Wei, for example, uses this term to describe his uncle who established the curio shop. Not all successful businessmen, of course, are heroic. Thus, the proprietor of Zhuangyuanlou Restaurant, Mr Fan, fits more the stereotypical merchant from traditional fiction. In the novel, Li Zirong is suggested in many places as the real *yingxiong*. His business acumen, his love of study and his ability to win a battle under difficult circumstances all add up to a man with the credentials for a renovated *wen-wu* hero. As representative of a shift in masculinity ideals, he is significant as he is prepared to continue to learn and study formally. It is not just any learning, and he does not learn so he can lead a moral life: he studies what is equivalent to an MBA and he studies quite unashamedly to make money.

Critics have pointed out that Li Zirong is not the ideal promoted by writers.[72] Rather, 'the ideal personality for modern Chinese youth is a combination of both Ma Wei and Li Zirong'.[73] Lao She himself has stated that 'Ma Wei had shortcomings, and did not totally live up to my ideal, and so I created Li Zirong as a supplement'.[74] The ambivalent attitude towards these characters by author and critics alike only testifies to a grudging respect which *wen* people at Lao She's time were beginning to accord the young businessmen who were starting to influence traditional images of masculinity. Therefore, the stereotypical portrayals of the three male protagonists in *The Two Mas* provide the reader with easy access to the main characteristics of Chinese masculinity which were apparently common among *wen* men in the West in Republican times.

Wen in the Contemporary West: The Case of Australia

Lao She's models of *wen* men abroad did not change significantly for most of the twentieth century. On the whole, it was assumed that the only way to succeed in Western countries was to amass a great deal of money.[75] And there were indeed many businesses which were very large and successful, especially in Southeast Asian countries. Cities such as Taipei, Hong Kong and Singapore became international centres of commerce and finance, and some Chinese businessmen became some of the richest and most powerful men in the world. In the People's Republic of China itself, however, money-making was for nearly 40 years considered capitalist and unpalatable. Furthermore, China had very little interaction with the Western world for most of that time. The version of *wen-wu* which was exported to the West was therefore from Southeast Asia. As the next chapter will show, the kinds of masculinity from this region, especially the film versions from Hong Kong, were strongly *wu* in orientation.

East/West interactions changed drastically after the Cold War ended. For example, many of those who emigrate now do so for business or education reasons rather than as labourers in search of work. Most have gone to America, but tens of thousands have also gone to other Western countries like Australia to study. In 1990 alone, one year after the 1989 Tiananmen Incident, there were over 13,000 enrolled in Australian English language courses.[76] Furthermore, a 1993 survey of 200 Mainland Chinese students in Australia found that over 60% had tertiary qualifications and 100% had secondary school education. In Chinese terms, these people would be classified as *zhishifenzi*, and were seen as having high *wen* accomplishments. However, the same survey shows that 80–90% of these students worked in jobs such as washing dishes in restaurants.[77]

Their academic achievements were not commodities they could carry across cultures. For many, the most urgent task was to re-activate the social recognition that they had earned in China. This partly explains why formal education, the key criterion for *wen-wu* accomplishments, is a goal to which most Chinese immigrants aspire. Even as entrepreneurs, they universally want tertiary qualifications for their children.[78] For the men at least, creating an acceptable *wen-wu* in the host country is tantamount to recovering a lost manhood. While the tendency to value academic excellence among the Chinese immigrants has been noted by many commentators, implications for masculinity stemming from this tendency remain unnoticed. I propose to briefly analyse the 'confessions' by these students in a collection titled *He Married A Foreign Woman*.[79]

I have chosen to scrutinise this book because it deals mostly with the love lives of *wen* men in Australia. While Australia is not in Europe or America, narratives of their romances are typical of those found in other Western countries, and they illustrate well how the fate of Chinese students in the West has changed since Lao She's time. The title story – the only one by Wu Li, the compiler of the collection – is an endearing account indicative of a success story of multiculturalism in Australia. The romance details Wu Li's quest for a marital partner in the first few years after he arrived in Sydney in 1989. The narrator is keen to marry and he goes to a marriage agency. Asked what sort of woman he wanted, he is very frank: a foreign wife who has an intense interest in Eastern culture and who can produce a child who will be educated in three languages and so on. However, when asked about his own circumstances, he reflects,

> What could I say? I could say that I had been a journalist in a Chinese newspaper, that I was a skilled orator, that I had organised many national events, that I was a good cook, that I didn't smoke and that I didn't drink. But all that belonged to a me that is no longer. Now, I am someone who knows no foreign language and has no status, someone whose job is a dishwasher in a restaurant. Which girl who grew up in a Western country would be interested in someone like me who has nothing to recommend him?[80]

His confession that 'all that belonged to a me that is no longer' is only partially correct. The qualities of not smoking or drinking and being a good cook are ones which presumably belong to a good husband, and he still has these qualities, and the success of his marriage subsequently testifies to this. But the academic and public qualities of writer, orator and organiser belonged to the past because in Australia, having no English language skills is to be castrated of *wen* attributes so valued in China. Without English, Wu Li becomes 'someone whose job is a dishwasher in a restaurant', and no woman would want to marry such a man. It is interesting, too, that his lament of his lack of desirability as a man in his adopted country is premised on his becoming a menial worker as dishwasher in a restaurant, even though he claims to be a good cook. Culinary skills can be an art and, in context, can signify a desirable masculinity, but washing dishes is categorised here almost as immoral. One can presumably be a famous chef without having to do mindless menial tasks, but washing dishes has nothing *wen* or *wu* about it.

However, like most of the students who left China in the 1980s and
1990s, Wu Li did have good educational qualifications and a good job
back in China. He is not the uneducated Chinese peasant who found
himself in racist Australia in the late nineteenth – early twentieth centuries. He has boundless confidence, and the eventual reclamation of
his former *wen-wu* identity is never in question. And even though the
marriage agency could not find what he wanted, he eventually finds
himself a wife. While the collection under consideration has several
accounts of cross-cultural marriages, Wu Li's romance with his wife is
given the most loving detailed treatment. Nobody reading it would doubt
their love for each other. It is also a most fitting example of the success
of multicultural Australia: he is from China and she is from Korea. She
is therefore 'foreign', but not Anglo Australian. The medium of communication between them is English, a 'foreign language' to both (Wu
Li has by this stage been in Australia for three years and has learnt 'a
little' English). From the descriptions provided, there seems to be no
difficulty in communication. If Wu Li had originally only counted
Anglo Australians as 'foreign' and is disappointed by ending up with an
Asian-Australian wife, it certainly does not show. His pride in his wife is
everywhere evident in the narrative. He relates how he learns common
Western habits of politeness such as saying 'please' and 'thank you' from
her while at the same time he revels in her 'impolite' discussions of sexual
techniques in public.

This pride takes on a *wen-wu* dimension right from the beginning. The
first time she invites him to dinner, his immediate observation is that
'she lives in Randwick, a place where higher intellectuals of Sydney
concentrate'.[81] The implication here is that although she herself is a
nurse, her associations are with the educated. And not just the ordinary
educated, but 'higher intellectuals', so that her class connections are also
admirable. As he tells her his old positions back in China and the twenty-
odd lowly jobs he has had to take up since arriving in Australia,

> She opened her surprised eyes and asked, 'you had such a good profession in
> China, why did you come here to be an odd job man?'
>   'Because I want to see the world. I want to have a richer experience of
> life!'[82]

This is not the sort of answer that could have been provided by any of the
tens of thousands of labourers who went abroad in earlier generations.[83]
From the nineteenth century until the 1970s, most Chinese who went
abroad were from the 'lower', non-educated classes, they occupied mostly
unskilled, exploited and back-breaking labouring positions.[84] At most,
these men could only claim a *wu* sort of masculinity, a fact reflected in

the ubiquitous presence of the *wu* god Guan Yu in overseas Chinese joss houses and the relative absence of the *wen* god Confucius in these temples.

In one of the most influential books on the Chinese students studying in America, Qian Ning notes that perhaps the most significant difference between them and intellectuals who remain in China is that they have developed a lively 'adventurous spirit'.[85] Thus, when some of them end up having to perform manual labour such as washing dishes in Chinese restaurants, they feel, as Wu Li does when such work is demanded of him, that it is beneath their true worth. Qian Ning adds, however, that for many, it is another kind of 're-education' which many intellectuals had undergone during the Cultural Revolution. The difference is that for the educated youth who went to the villages during the Cultural Revolution, there was a feeling that they were involved in 'an heroic tragedy of a political movement',[86] whereas working in manual jobs in Australia is neither heroic nor tragic. In both cases, the educated bounce back. With or without an 'adventurous spirit', the training which has enabled these men to claim mastery of *wen-wu* also enables them to learn the new skills to adjust to new circumstances. *Wen-wu* is highly resilient.

As well as Wu Li's own marriage, the book contains ten other cases of marriages. The book groups the theme of love and marriage into two parts. The first part contains six reports of 'successful' marriages and the second part contains five reports of 'failed' marriages. Of the Chinese partners in the six successful ones, three are men and three are women. One has married a Korean Australian, one a white African Australian, one an Italian Australian, one an English Australian and the other two white Australians of unknown origin. Not all of these are as wonderful as that between Wu Li and his Korean-Australian wife, and the one between the Italian Australian and his Chinese wife can even be regarded as lacking in passion. The degree to which the partners understand each other's individuality and culture also varies a great deal. Nonetheless, they are all excellent illustrations of working partnerships between different racial groups. By contrast, all the five reported 'failed' marriages are mono-racial Chinese ones.

Of course, this pattern may be a result of Wu Li's editorial bias. Nonetheless, these couples are not fabrications made up by him. The reports are all apparently true cases sent in by the people themselves, and at least three of the couples reported have their photographs printed in the book as well. These cases also contrast with illustrations put forward in books promoted by the Chinese authorities. Qian Ning's *Studying in USA*, for example, which is excerpted in *Xinhua wenzhai*, also features love and marriage prominently. Qian Ning speaks of problems faced by Chinese students and their marital break-ups. However, in the mono-racial example, the man's parents visit America after the break-up and the ex-wife 'pretends' that no divorce had occurred and acts the virtuous wife and daughter-in-law (and enjoys it). Husband and wife happily get back together again. When Qian Ning discusses interracial marriages, however, he cites an example in which a Chinese woman is bored because her professor husband knows no Chinese and neglects her emotional needs. Another example describes a Chinese man abandoned by his white American wife, who advises him to 'find a Chinese woman more suited to him'.[87]

In a study of Chinese students in Australia, Edmund Fung and Colin Mackerras note that: 'While the female students expressed no views on intermarriage, most male interviewees expressed a reluctance to marry an Australian woman.'[88] The reasons for the men's reluctance are similar to those that Qian Ning indicates for the Americans: Australian women are too bossy, too assertive, too promiscuous sexually and so on. Such prejudice is not very enlightening. However, what is illuminating about Fung and Mackerras' study is that the only student who has actually married an 'Australian'[89] seems to have a very happy marriage – to the extent that it 'had led to other members of his wife's family marrying Chinese'.[90] The suitability of Chinese men as partners is even more pronounced for the Chinese men born in the West. In one study of Asian-American men, Peter Chua and Diane Fujino found that 'US-born Asian men linked their masculinity with certain caring characteristics and were the only men's group willing to do domestic tasks'.[91] While such stereotypes of Asian men probably contain as much truth as the old Fu Manchu images, they at least signify an intention to be positive.[92]

Of course, it would be naïve to assume that interracial marriages are without problems. Carmen Luke and Allan Luke detail some of the complexities facing interracial families in their case studies.[93] Indeed, it could even be argued that in some quarters, advances in racial equality have prompted white supremacist backlashes.[94] In the unpredictable 'lived experience' of interracial relations, race definitely matters.[95] Nonetheless, the situation in the 1990s was not as grim as the beginning of the twentieth century, when the anti-miscegenation legal system in Australia actively persecuted white women who had relations with 'orientals'.[96] Even though they continued to 'experience unique forms of racism by association with persons of color',[97] the interracial marriages explored by Carmen Luke and Allan Luke are not significantly more disastrous than the 'average'. Indeed, unlike the older generations who seemed to have had more problems with issues of social acceptance:

All the couples we interviewed in their 20s and 30s spoke of their difference as a distinctive, affirmative and affirming characteristic: as 'half and half', as our 'own way', as 'a different way', as a 'third way'. Unlike some of their older counterparts who had lived through decolonisation and postwar reconstruction, none mentioned or seemed aware of the historical stigma towards interracial unions either in Australia or in their Asian countries of origin.[98]

Since Lao She wrote *The Two Mas*, there have obviously been many fundamental changes in attitudes towards Chinese–white romances. Many factors contribute to these changes. In terms of Chinese masculinity, the most significant factor leading to this new-found self-confidence is intricately bound up with the sort of men who are now coming to and growing up in Western countries such as Australia. They are educated. Within the Chinese cultural framework, they are regarded as having *wen*, a quality which secures their sense of masculine identity. Even though their English may need polishing, they have the will and self-confidence to succeed in the host country. This success is seen very much as part of a recovered manhood, and that manhood is measured in terms of *wen*, or academic success.

That *wen-wu* has found a place in the Western masculinity mosaic may be an inevitable conclusion to the changes that have taken place in definitions of manhood in Western countries in recent years. Taking Australia as an example, the diverse and radically different masculinities which have developed there are another reflection of the gradual acceptance of difference, both in terms of gender and culture. That acceptance is not yet total. For example, gay Australian Chinese men are only beginning to express themselves openly in public, and to a large extent, they are still Orientalised by the gay community.[99] Nevertheless, just as some of the best analyses of masculinity in the West are found in Queer Studies, so too the increased participation of Chinese gays in writing about gender and sexuality can only demystify Chinese masculinity further.[100] Furthermore, in the same way that business interests appropriate the celebration of sexual diversity in festivals such as the Sydney Mardi Gras, so too business and industry have embraced multiculturalism by having, for example, many choices of 'foreign language' channels on cable or satellite television. Some purists may denounce such mainstreaming as commercialism, but it is precisely the integration of difference into the commercial 'mainstream' that shows the success of sexual and cultural liberation movements in Western countries such as Australia throughout the twentieth century. As we enter the twenty-first century, the indications are that this process will continue to grow, and *wen-wu* will become an integral part of the fabric of global masculinity.[101]

8 Bruce Lee, Jackie Chan and Chow Yun Fat: Internationalising *wu* Masculinity

'The Coolest Man Alive', Chow Yun Fat, as Mark Gor in *A Better Tomorrow* (1986). Reproduced with permission of Cinema City Co. Ltd, Hong Kong.

This chapter explores how representations of *wu* have been transformed in the modern Western context by examining the impact of film superstars Bruce Lee, Jackie Chan and Chow Yun Fat. Through this process, I assess the ways Chinese notions of the martial half of *wen-wu* masculinity have evolved in dynamic interaction with Western (Hollywood) constructions of masculinity. The three actors under consideration are the only male Chinese entertainers who have 'made it' in the Hollywood scene. And the kung fu genre, recognisably Asian in origin, is also the only non-Western cinematic form which has achieved mainstream status in cinemas throughout the world.[1] Having a common origin in Hong Kong, the films of Lee, Chan and Chow provide ideal sites for tracing the trajectory of Chinese–Western interaction in the final decades of the twentieth century. While the PRC has reabsorbed it as a geographic entity, Hong Kong can, and does, represent itself as being traditional and modern, Chinese and Western as well as colonial and postcolonial. Likewise, all three actors have tried, and succeeded, in claiming a space in both the Chinese and American as well as many postcolonial consciousnesses.

Despite their undeniable status as popular icons, these superstars have until recently rarely featured in 'serious' academic discourse in China. In some ways, this is only to be expected. By definition, *wen* concerns are those associated with high culture and writing, and the literati would therefore understandably pay more homage to it than to *wu*, which was seen to matter less for gaining privilege and power. As Stanley Henning recently observed,

> In academia, the Chinese martial arts have been conspicuous by their relative absence from scholarly discussion, but when they have made an appearance it has usually been fleeting and in a muddle not much beyond what one sees in the bulk of martial-arts literature on the popular market. This can be seen in scattered writings at every step up the scholarly staircase to the pinnacle of sinology in Joseph Needham's *Science and Civilization in China*.[2]

It is true that there has been a rapid expansion of higher education since the 1970s, and that many disciplines such as human movement and leisure studies which had hitherto not been considered university subjects have now been incorporated into the curriculum. However, Chinese martial arts have on the whole been shunned as mainstream courses in academia, even though martial arts training schools and other kung fu paraphernalia have multiplied in both China and other countries.[3] This has not always been the case. As I have indicated in the Confucius chapter, the Master himself has stipulated courses on the *wu* skills of charioteering and archery as compulsory skills for the *junzi*. But by the

Tang Dynasty, the structure and importance of the civil service examinations had the effect of entrenching *wen* as the sole criterion for success, with *wu* relegated to a non-vital function. In chapter 5, we have examined the transformations *wu* has undergone in contemporary China and how it is still seen mainly as a working-class masculinity. In this chapter, I will investigate its constructions outside China.

For this analysis, kung fu films are an indispensable source of information. Unlike academia, the box office is not a 'scholarly staircase': it is a more democratic instrument that measures success by popular demand. Hong Kong (and its derivative Hollywood) films are ideal sites for unmasking Chinese masculinity in a global context. As Jenny Lau concludes in her comparison of Mainland Chinese and Hong Kong films, 'Although the Hong Kong films are satirical towards tradition and are apparently Westernised, they are still fundamentally Chinese'.[4] More importantly, for Western conceptions of Chinese masculinity, screen images were for a long time the only way in which most people were able to see representations of 'living' Chinese men and their daily activities. Hong Kong films have had a more 'popular' exposure to the West for over three decades. However, before the advent of kung fu movies, Chinese masculinity was represented mostly by non-Chinese men. As I have shown in the last chapter, by the beginning of the twentieth century, the marvels of Cathay as described by Marco Polo had long since given way to shadowy images of sin, drugs and pagan barbarism. The most popular and influential written texts describing a Chinese man are those by Sax Rohmer, who presents in detail 'a mental picture of Dr Fu Manchu, the yellow peril incarnate in one man' in *The Insidious Dr Fu-Manchu*. The mental image is supposed to be 'a person, tall, lean and feline, high-shouldered, with a brow like Shakespeare and a face like Satan, a close-shaven skull, and long, magnetic eyes of the true cat-green'.[5]

This is a striking spectre, but for anyone who has close contacts with real Chinese people, it is difficult to imagine how one could conjure up such an apparition as a Chinese man. Quite apart from the incongruities of having Shakespearian and Satanic looks, Sax Rohmer had obviously never noticed the colour of any Chinese person's eyes. Indeed, although numerous serials and movies based on the Fu Manchu stories were made throughout the 1920s and 1930s, not one of the actors was Chinese, and the most recognisable Fu Manchu role was performed by the renowned actor of horror movies, Boris Karloff. Therefore, for the first few decades of the twentieth century, American as well as European audiences were horrified and enthralled by sinister and dangerous yellow men on the screen who were in reality not Chinese at all. Real or not, the yellow peril terror struck at the heart of an insecure Western masculinity, because 'in episode after episode of the most sensational movies and comic strips, feral, rat-faced Chinese lusted after virginal white women. The threat of rape, the rape of white society, dominated the action of the yellow formula.'[6]

Even when the Chinese male figure is not a complete evil-doer, such as the protagonist in D.W. Griffith's filmic rendition of Thomas Burke's 'The Chink and the Child' discussed in the last chapter, his sexuality is unambiguously portrayed as perverse.[7] The protagonist, Cheng Huan, 'handles' the 12-year-old. He then kills her father who had sadistically beaten her to death. In this manner, Cheng Huan reinforces Orientalist notions of interracial sexual relations as inevitably linked with incest, sadism, paedophilia, necrophilia and murder. As Gina Marchetti points out, at the end of the story, orthodox racial and sexual order is upheld because 'Cheng Huan punishes himself symbolically for his transgression through suicide'.[8] Early Hollywood representations of Chinese masculinity were therefore a mixture of fear and loathing as well as a fascination with its imputed sexual perversity.

However, America was a more multi-ethnic society than Britain, and it was also more closely allied with China in World War II. By the 1930s and 1940s, slightly less loathsome and pathetic images of the Chinaman were appearing in America. For example, between 1925 and 1949, 48 feature films about 'Charlie Chan' (a totally American product) were made. Based on the six novels by Earl Derr Biggers, Charlie Chan is a detective who upholds the American legal system. He is famous for his 'proverbs', mostly beginning with 'Confucius says', spoken in pidgin English. Even though Charlie Chan was created 'as a refutation of the Fu Manchu characterisation of the Chinese' male, he is, as Gloria Chun says, 'devoid of any assertiveness and sexuality ... (and) self-effacing to a fault'.[9] The Charlie Chan symbol was created at a time when China was bullied by the Western powers and increasingly encroached upon by the Japanese. He is not a threatening figure. America could and did patronise the Chinese, so that even a 'positive' portrayal of a Chinese man was no more than a good-natured castrato whose favourite phrases are: 'I am so sorry. I have made stupid error. Captain – is it possible you will ever forgive me?'.[10] To add insult to injury, Charlie Chan, too, was never played by a Chinese actor.[11]

The fact that these male stereotypes were invented by non-Chinese for non-Chinese audiences can be seen by the way their masculinity was constructed. As noted in previous chapters, in the Chinese cultural context, all men by definition have some *wen* and/or some *wu*. Villains in Chinese culture such as Cao Cao might have been vilified for abusing their *wen* or *wu* attributes, but at least they had them. Other lesser beings, such as Ximen Qing, who were caricatures of men with *wen-wu*, were depicted as morally corrupt individuals who deserved to be punished. By contrast, the yellow peril images such as the evil incarnate Fu Manchu 'were often portrayed as beasts (wolves, rats, vultures and the like), the sort of animals that are strong, crafty, savage ... and malevolent'.[12] In Chinese folklore, the closest analogy would be the fox-fairies – a class of semi-human beings who are usually female, who, as we have seen in previous chapters, are generally denied *wen-wu* attributes.

While the Fu Manchu and Charlie Chan stereotypes are threatening or inscrutable to the Western mind, they would have been unintelligible in the Chinese masculinity schema. The *wen-wu* matrix simply cannot accommodate them as Chinese men. This is not surprising given that they are cultural and racial impersonators: there is nothing Chinese about them except the conspiratorial agreement on their designation between their creators and the audience. This agreement lasted right through the Cold War, the Vietnam War and, to a lesser extent, into the present time, in images such as the James Bond version of *Dr No*.

Western attitudes to Chinese men began to change in the 1960s and 1970s, when the anti-Vietnam War and Civil Rights movements dramatically changed perceptions of race and gender. These changes were a result of a number of social transformations in international relations. While they were vilified, the Vietnamese were grudgingly seen to be courageous fighters. Also, even though the East was still seen in an Orientalist fashion, at least Eastern mysticism was embraced by the hippies and some university professors. The rising might of the Japanese economy and the hosting of the Olympics in Tokyo in 1964 led to judo being admitted as an Olympic sport. Concomitantly, Asian martial arts gained increasing popularity.[13] Asian men were sometimes cast as physically empowered, so much so that the American public was happy to accept the idea of a half-Chinese man as hero in the form of Kwai Chang Caine or Grasshopper in the extremely popular TV series *Kung Fu* (first screened between 1972 and 1975).

The impact of this TV series cannot be overestimated. As well as using many homilies which come straight from ancient Chinese philosophy texts such as the Daoist classics, the series had the effect of carrying an anti-racism message. For example, in the episode 'Alethea' (15 March 1973), 9-year-old Alethea (played by a young Jodie Foster) befriends Caine. A man is shot and Alethea believes she saw Caine do the shooting. Caine is arrested and sentenced to death.

> When Caine is on the scaffold, Alethea stops the execution by claiming that she lied during her testimony, and only said that Caine was a murderer because he is Chinese. Caine is freed. Alethea is unhappy that she told a lie, but Caine

offers to take the lie away from her. To do this, he tracks down the two bandits and captures them.[14]

As always, Caine's mastery of kung fu restores a sense of justice and well-being to all viewers. At the same time, the series popularised martial arts to a Western audience, and it repeatedly hammers the message that the 'wisdom' of the East and the true worth of a Chinese man are misunderstood and not appreciated in America.

Enter the Dragon Bruce Lee

This is rather ironic because the idea of the *Kung Fu* series was apparently conceived by Bruce Lee in 1970. He proposed this project to the producers after his success in playing Kato in the series *Green Hornet*.[15] But much to his (and his fans') disgust, the role of Caine was offered to David Carradine, a white actor 'who doesn't know shit about martial arts'.[16] Maybe the producers were correct to assume that the American public was not yet ready to accept an 'Oriental' face as heroic or manly. In the long term, Hollywood's rejection of Bruce Lee at that point proved pivotal in the evolution of Chinese masculinity in the West. Bruce Lee went to Hong Kong and made four and a half movies in a matter of two or three years. And on Hong Kong soil, he was able to develop a masculinity model that was Chinese yet also embraced enthusiastically by a large movie-going audience in the West.

As Alex Ben Block, whose 1973 *Esquire* article helped herald the emergence of Bruce Lee in America, observed, Lee appealed particularly to young and dispossessed male audiences.

> Not just Asians but also young black African Americans or young minorities of all kinds, even for Caucasians who came from lower economic backgrounds, Bruce Lee was a hero. He represented someone who was able to break out of all of the things that seem to bind us in society and keep us from becoming a success.[17]

As a hero to the lower classes, Lee exacted revenge for personal grievances and achieved victory despite all odds – these attributes are major criteria for *wu* masculinity. The Bruce Lee screen persona has all three characteristics of loyalty, righteousness and mateship to justify him as a *wu* hero. In the context of the early 1970s, when the Chinese in the Mainland and the diaspora were desperately attempting to find international recognition, Bruce Lee had an added significance in terms of race and nationality.

Resistance to racial oppression is a central theme in all his movies. The film that launched him as a star is the 1971 *The Big Boss*. The Chinese title is *Tangshan daxiong*. *Tangshan* is the name given to China by overseas Chinese so the title resonates with sentiments of an 'Older Brother from The Home Country'. This semi-factual story described how a Thai Chinese helps his compatriots resist bullies in Thailand. The character played by Bruce Lee uses his kung fu skills to subdue the local gangsters who oppress Chinese workers. In his 1972 movie, *Fist of Fury* (*Jingwumen*), the Bruce Lee character is a disciple of the celebrated martial arts hero Huo Yuanjia, who fought the Japanese at the turn of the last century.[18] At his funeral, the Japanese bullies hold up a sign saying 'Sick man of East Asia'. After the funeral, Bruce Lee goes to the *dojo*, smashes the sign and says, 'now you listen to me, we are not sick men'. He then proceeds to defeat the Japanese karate experts, as well as a Russian martial arts master. In the same year, we see the Bruce Lee character, Tang Long, defeating Chuck Norris in the Colosseum in Rome in *Way of the Dragon* (*Menglong guojiang*). 1972 was a busy year for Lee, as he was also shooting *The Game of Death* (*Siwang youxi*), in which he fights the 7′4″ black basketball star Abdul-Jabbar.[19] Bruce was portrayed as vanquishing opponents of all colours and sizes.

Before *The Game of Death* was completed, Bruce Lee was offered the lead role in *Enter the Dragon* (*Long zheng hu dou*), which was to 'become the most famous martial arts movie ever'.[20] This movie, in which Lee disposes of an army of guards (both Asian and Caucasian) in unarmed combat, was not as financially successful as his other movies in Hong Kong.[21] However, it was the only Bruce Lee movie directed by an American and produced by a Hollywood studio (Warner/Concord). It launched Lee's fame internationally, so much so that even today the name Bruce Lee is synonymous with Chinese martial arts and his style still considered as the authentic and genuine kung fu. Interestingly, the movie 'was basically a remake of *Dr No* (1962), itself inspired by Sax Rohmer's Fu Manchu books'.[22] The difference, of course, is that instead of James Bond, the hero in this instance is a Chinese man. More importantly, he is played by a Chinese actor. For the first time in Hollywood, Chinese masculinity takes centre stage.

Ironically, Bruce Lee has been denounced by some Chinese academics who claim that he is in the same mould as Fu Manchu, Charlie Chan and Dr No. They argue that his image is wooden and lacking in masculinity.[23] They contrast the Bruce Lee characters in the movies with James Bond, who is always desired by beautiful women and who does not hesitate on screen to fulfil their desires. The allegation that Bruce Lee does not exude masculine sexuality deserves some attention because it is a common charge against Chinese men who are otherwise successful. First of all, it should be noted that in almost all of Bruce Lee's fight sequences, he makes a point of stripping his clothes off as much as decorum permits, displaying a spectacular body that is graceful yet hard. The physicality of his body must be interpreted in its historical context, and not simply dismissed as 'wooden'. As Yvonne Tasker observes, 'The hardness of Lee's body and of his star image emerges from a history of softness, a history of images in which both Chinese men and women had been represented as passive and compliant.'[24]

More significantly, in his movies, the Bruce Lee character does form romantic attachments to young women, played by beautiful starlets such as Maria Yi and Nora Miao. What he does not do on screen is consummate the romances in any explicit manner. But considering the intended Hong Kong and Southeast Asian audiences of that time,[25] the kisses and hugs which do occur were already going as far as public morals allowed. To these audiences, there was no question that the looks in the actresses' eyes demonstrated a desire for Lee's body just as strong if not stronger than the Bond girls' flirtations with 007. If the dynamics of *wen-wu* sexuality were to be applied to the Bruce Lee screen persona, his masculine sexuality becomes patently clear.

Like the *wu* heroes in traditional narratives, even when the women around him are concerned about him, the Bruce Lee characters do not romance these beauties like a *wen* scholar would do: he always attends to his social obligations first. These obligations involve displaying extreme loyalty to his teachers, avenging family and mates, and remaining untainted both morally and sexually. Such righteousness and incorruptibility make him more prudish than the European knights and the Three Musketeers. But as a martial arts expert, he has already gone much further than the *wu* heroes such as Guan Yu from the *Three Kingdoms* and Wu Song from *All Men Are Brothers*, whose method for dealing with desiring/desirable women was to physically eliminate them. To an audience raised in such a historical context, the Bruce Lee persona, far from being wooden, exudes much sexuality.

The interface between race and sex finds its most interesting expression in the Chinese interpreter who works for the Italian mafia in *Way of the Dragon*. He is depicted as a camped-up queer. In one scene, he tucks Bruce's belt down the latter's trousers, and leeringly keeps his hand inside. In another scene, he puts his hands on Bruce's body, massaging it and sighing 'what a beautiful torso'. This character is interesting because he is Chinese, but he works for the evil Europeans. He has therefore crossed the racial barrier. This transgression is mirrored in his sexual preferences. Despite the perceived transgression, there is no doubting that he finds Bruce Lee's body sexually very desirable. By contrast, it would be difficult to find such explicit homo-eroticism in James Bond, whose hyper-masculinity allows him to blow many handsome men away, but he is never demonstratively the object of another man's desire.

In examining Bruce Lee's films, Jachinson Chan argues that 'Lee's characters seem to encourage a homoerotic desire for his body' and that 'an ambivalent or ambiguous model of masculinity is a more effective way to counter a hegemonic model of masculinity'.[26]

The Bruce Lee films have thus in their own way crossed cultural boundaries and their depictions of masculinity have accordingly been modified to suit the new hybrid culture of the diaspora Chinese. With the advent of the movie industry, this had to happen. Furthermore, the star as represented by the gossip columns is often more influential than his screen persona, and this was true of Bruce Lee. His fans knew that he had lots of affairs, which *wu* heroes are not supposed to do. In *wen-wu* terms, the scholar, not the fighter, is supposed to bed the girl. His admirers have, like worshippers of Guan Yu before, re-invented their idol so now Bruce Lee is recast as a philosopher and teacher as well as kung fu expert.[27] He is thus both *wen* and *wu*. The sexual puritanism of the *wu* warrior can therefore be relaxed. In fact, some Chinese biographers such as Lu Yue say that because his wife Linda was white, she was open-minded and 'didn't mind' his continued friendships with women![28] This writer mixes race and sex in claiming that Bruce Lee's womanising behaviour was like a '*laowai*', referring to his being part-Caucasian (his mother was half-Chinese) and being born in America.

After Bruce Lee, kung fu became something more than just lion dancing and fireworks. Many men (and women) all over the world learnt a little bit of Eastern martial arts or *wu* masculinity and did not think twice about its Chinese origins. Bruce Lee's masculinity found a wildly receptive audience because it produced a male model which filled a sorely felt vacuum in the last decades of the twentieth century. In a recent astute and insightful paper, David Desser points out that:

> The kung fu craze is just one cinematic signifier of a post-Vietnam stress dis-order on the cultural level. Other signifiers include the spate of films focusing on troubled returning Vietnam vets ... and, more precisely, the rise of the white male martial arts stars who, in a sense, co-opt the Asian martial arts for the American action hero, for the American movie star, for the American man.[29]

This is one interpretation of the consequences of the Bruce Lee phenomenon taken from an American perspective.[30] It points to the insecurities of the American male psyche and its subsequent incorporation of aspects of Chinese masculinity.[31]

Conversely, from the Chinese perspective, the Bruce Lee phenomenon can be interpreted as a reassertion of a Chinese *wu* masculinity in the international arena. As we have seen in the last chapter, the affirmation of a Chinese masculinity was a major concern in Chinese contacts with the

West throughout the twentieth century. In a recent book on Chinese martial arts, the author voices the nationalist sentiments of those who practise *wu* by concluding the book with Huo Yuanjia's challenge to martial artists of all nationalities in 1909. He insists that this spirit must be maintained if the Chinese are to be kung fu champions.[32] Competing racial masculinities therefore play a big part in the rise of the kung fu genre. Bruce Lee literally punches and kicks his way into recognition. In *The Big Boss*, he beats the living daylights out of Southeast Asian bullies. In *Fist of Fury*, he does the same to the Japanese. In *Way of the Dragon*, he defeats the white guy Chuck Norris, who in real life *was* a karate champion. By *The Game of Death*, he defeats the black basketball star Abdul-Jabbar. In keeping with all *wu* heroes, he is especially popular among men in the lower classes and minority groups, such as the blacks and hispanics in America and Maoris in New Zealand. He also has legions of fans in non-Western countries such as Egypt and other Middle Eastern nations.[33]

Mr Nice Guy, Jackie Chan

Of course, Bruce Lee was most popular in Hong Kong, so much so that when he died at the young age of 32, a series of Hong Kong actors changed their names to Lee-alikes such as Bruce Lie, Bruce Le, Bruce Liang, Bruce Leung and Dragon Lee. All but one failed to make any impact. The one exception was Jackie Chan. In English, the names Jackie Chan and Bruce Lee do not seem to have anything in common. But Bruce Lee's Chinese stage name is Li Xiaolong, 'Lee the Little Dragon'. Although Jackie Chan's real name is Chen Gangsheng, 'Chen the Hong Kong born', Director Lo Wei changed it to Sing Lung (Cheng Long), 'To Become A Dragon', a direct reference to the wish to inherit the mantle of Bruce Lee.[34] These names are central to masculinity. As we have indicated in chapter 2, the dragon, as well as being a symbol for China, is also a phallic symbol, with its ability to expand and shrink, soften and harden. 'Little Dragon' and 'Becoming Dragon' are therefore not accidental, but point clearly to male ideals. Two of Bruce Lee's movie titles have dragons in them. In fact, many kung fu and action movies have dragon in their titles, from Samo Hung's recent TV series *Martial Law* (*Guo jiang long*), 'A Dragon That's Crossed the Waters', to Ang Lee's *Crouching Tiger, Hidden Dragon.*

   In the beginning, Chan imitated Lee in more ways than just in the name. Jackie had actually acted as a stuntman in *Enter the Dragon*, where he was hit full in the face by Bruce's nunchakus.[35] Far from bearing a grudge, Jackie Chan acknowledges that Bruce Lee 'brought the martial arts movie to the attention of the world – and without him, I don't think anyone would have heard of Jackie Chan'.[36] In *City Hunter*, Jackie pays homage to Bruce by showing the Lee vs. Abdul-Jabbar fight scene within his own movie. In the middle of a particularly difficult fight, the Jackie Chan character glances up at the movie screen, sees Bruce Lee's clever tactic and employs it to full effect in his real-time fight.

Jackie Chan, like all the other would-be dragons, spent nearly ten years after Bruce Lee's death trying to imitate the master. But his early career was as undistinguished as most of the other Bruce Lee wannabes. As Richard Dyer observes in the case of Hollywood actors such as Clint Eastwood, it is difficult for them to maintain their hard macho masculinity in a straight-faced manner without wanting to send it up.[37] Jackie Chan became phenomenally successful only when he abandoned the macho image and took on another kind of masculinity, that of the 'kung fu comedian'. Like the dragon, Jackie Chan is famous for his ability to use his body in the most amazing ways. One of his trademarks is showing out-shots of himself doing his own stunts and often sustaining injuries.[38] Unlike Bruce Lee, who does not even flinch when hit or knifed, Jackie Chan uses every opportunity to show that his nerve endings are as sensitive as any New Age guy. While paying homage to the machismo of Bruce Lee, Chan's deflation of the tough man image ultimately has the effect of further diluting traditional *wu* masculinity as exemplified by the uptight Guan Yu.

Jackie Chan's irony is therefore also a re-ordering and de-emphasis of the macho aspect in *wu*. Unlike Bruce Lee who trained in martial arts and was himself a martial arts instructor,[39] Jackie Chan was trained in a traditional Peking Opera school to be a *wusheng* (a *wu* actor).[40] Consequently, the choreography for the unarmed combat sequences in his films is much more stylised. The combatants often strike up poses reminiscent of Peking Opera, and the fights, though spectacular, are essentially set pieces designed for their entertainment value as much as for the martial arts skills involved. Peking Opera, like the kung fu movie, is a performance for the audience's pleasure. In the early 1970s, Hong Kong audiences derived satisfaction from seeing a Chinese fighter dominating men with more political and economic clout. By the end of the decade, the colony's re-integration into China was a tangible reality, and Hong Kong people knew they were powerless to influence the outcome in any way, and many chose to take flight and migrate.[41] They would still derive pleasure from a spectacle, but instead of flattening an army of men with his nunchaku, the hero now had to know his limitations, and to ease the audience's anxieties by making them laugh.[42]

Jackie Chan does this by injecting a heavy dose of humour in his movies. As well as the slapstick acrobatics for which he is famous, Chan also dissolves the stereotypical notions of *wu* by mocking it. This does not mean he is not respectful towards the traditional values – he simply shows that to win, some orthodoxies will have to be altered. This insight can be seen in *Drunken Master* (*Zuiquan*) (1978), the first in the Jackie Chan repertoire which struck the right chord among audiences. Jackie Chan plays the role of a young Wong Fei-Hung (Huang Feihong), a Cantonese martial arts hero around whom a whole cycle of popular movies had already been developed.[43] Chan's Wong Fei-Hung is taking kung fu lessons from an alcoholic uncle, Beggar Su. But Wong is mischievous and lazy. Worse still, the routine he is learning is called the Drunken Eight Immortals Kung Fu. It consists of eight segments, one of which is modelled on the only female member of the Eight Immortals, Lady He. Jackie's Wong Fei-Hung considers it too womanlike and does not bother to master it well. This nearly costs him his life at the final showdown with the arch-villain, and he is only saved by getting 'really drunk'.

This brief plot summary does not do justice to what is a hilarious and beautifully crafted film. However, the transformations of the *wu* concept can readily be discerned. The *wu* hero here is not of the inflexible, all-powerful type found in the Bruce Lee characters. Indeed, he is portrayed in the beginning as a fun-loving prankster. Jackie Chan uses self-mockery to great effect in the comment about Wong Fei-Hung's reluctance to learn a 'sissy style' of kung fu which imitates a woman. It would indeed be inconceivable to imagine Guan Yu or Bruce Lee prancing around in public in drag. Yet this is precisely what Jackie Chan does in several of his movies.[44] The box office is a leveller of power, and the buying power of the female and juvenile audiences means entertainment cannot cater only for the adult male gaze.

In a recent study of the male dancer, Ramsay Burt observes that the convention of having the audience only adopt a male point of view has resulted in: 'first, the range of male dancing being largely limited to the expression of male dominance and control over the female bodies, and, second, in a tough, hard vocabulary of macho movements and gestures'.[45] While Bruce Lee appealed to young, marginalised males, Jackie Chan deliberately made movies to suit the whole family. And many of his most ardent fans are young women.[46] As a consequence, his body movements while spectacular are fluid, and they disrupt many of the conventional understandings about what it is to be a real man. His body is not quite the 'physical body' of Bruce Lee, and when his naked body is shown (and he's got a very nice one indeed) we are invited to look and giggle. For example, in one scene in *First Strike*, the Chan character has been ordered to strip all his clothes off, when a group of middle-aged white women tourists walk past, happily taking photos of him, one even pinching his cute butt. The playful action on screen is an invitation to voyeurism, and the object of the women's gaze on screen and that of the audience off screen is the nude hero. It would be difficult for him to regain macho sexual dominance and control after such a display of abnegation of male power.

This does not mean that the Jackie Chan type masculinity is less attractive to women than Bruce Lee's. In fact, by making himself the cute object for women's gaze, he may be more desirable for those with buying power, such as the women in Japan, where he was consistently the most popular foreign actor for over ten years.[47] As we saw in chapter 6, women are quite happy to patronise and fantasise about coy young men, especially if they are good-looking. Jackie Chan is also no less moralistic and self-righteous than Bruce Lee.[48] On the contrary, in many of his movies, the hero lectures gangsters and thugs about being good and responsible citizens. In interviews and in his biographies, he emphasises that his movies are clean: no sex and no bad language. He also avoids politics.[49] Such a strategy ensures that he will be accepted by children and by the Chinese authorities in re-integrated Hong Kong. And he has succeeded. As early as 1993, some of his films were already officially sanctioned in the Mainland.[50] In September 1999, a conference was convened in Beijing to celebrate his achievements. At this conference, his morality and righteousness (*zhengyi*) were highly eulogised.[51]

Throughout the late 1970s and 1980s, Jackie Chan's movies were immensely successful in Southeast Asia. Some, such as *Five Lucky Stars* (1983) and *Police Story* (1985), were such smash hits that sequel after sequel was produced. However, like Bruce Lee before him, Jackie wanted to break into the American (international) market. In 1980, Chan worked in two Hollywood movies, *The Big Brawl* and *Cannonball Run*, but they were flops. For Jackie Chan, the worst aspect of this experience was that he discovered the Americans saw him as a curiosity, and wanted him 'to perform like a trained dog', doing things like smashing bricks with his fists.[52] In retrospect, he decided that:

> I wasn't going to jump through any more hoops for patronizing reporters or feel any shame for being Chinese ... I know who I am; I am Jackie Chan. I may not have perfect English, but tell me, how many talk show hosts can speak Chinese?[53]

After this experience, Jackie Chan more or less stayed out of Hollywood productions for over ten years. In the mid-1990s, he tried again. After a successful *Rumble in the Bronx* (1994) and a winning *First Strike* (1996) in Australia, both produced by Barbie Tung and directed by Stanley Tong but distributed by New Line Cinema for the international market, New Line signed Jackie Chan in a Hollywood studio production in *Rush Hour* (1998). Directed by Brett Ratner, this is a buddy action comedy in which Jackie provides the action and Chris Tucker provides the comedy. It grossed over US$100 million and was one of the most successful films in terms of 'transnational Chinese cinemas'.[54] Its success was much more than financial. The teaming of a Chinese and a black as mismatched buddies is revolutionary.[55] By taking on the comic role, Chris Tucker allowed Jackie Chan to be more 'serious', so instead of his usual casual attire, Chan is dressed in a suit and behaves accordingly. This is an important shift, because, for the first time, he is now officially a policeman of the People's Republic of China, and his duty is to look after the interests of the Chinese ambassador against a bleached-hair Chinese crook and his British boss. Both American and Hong Kong audiences can now collectively leave behind their fears that 1997 would turn nasty. Nevertheless, the blond Chinese criminal is inserted in the film as a reminder that transgression of racial and cultural boundaries is not desirable and that these boundaries should be maintained for the sake of social order.

As well as these political and moral messages, Jackie Chan is also able to say on screen what he has been wanting to tell the Americans for over ten years. In the final scene, as the credits roll, Jackie Chan tries to sing a rap song but produces only a humorous imitation, even though in real life he is musical, being quite a famous canto pop singer. Chris Tucker feigns horror at Chan's attempt. Then when Chris Tucker tries to say 'thank you' in Chinese, he couldn't say that simple phrase (although in the movie itself he does so adequately). Jackie laughs and says, 'you see, I speak English. You try Chinese. You see how difficult it is. You see how difficult I am.' He means, of course, you see how great I am to have been able to make a movie in English and you can't even say such a simple thing as 'thank you'. The audience knows what Jackie means: he is wonderful not only for speaking English, but also for his heroism, which, though tinged with laughter, is terrific. He does his own stunts, boasting that practically every bone in his body has been broken once. Now he is boasting he can control the language of another culture, conquering America by making its audiences laugh and giving moralistic homilies.

In 2000, Jackie Chan teamed up with Owen Wilson to make another buddy action comedy, *Shanghai Noon*. Again, Jackie Chan plays the role of a government agent sent to America to rescue a Chinese princess. By setting the movie in the late nineteenth century, the film gives plenty of scope for Jackie to show that China, too, must change its old ways. However, the movie also presents us with ample scope for exploring racialised depictions of masculinity. The comic, or at least troublesome, buddy in this instance is Owen Wilson's Roy, the white guy. Though tongue-in-cheek, Roy begins to talk like a wise Chinaman by the end of the movie. He is partly Sinicised. Jackie is shown to be a 'better man' than other men, whether they be yellow, black and white. He does so not by a fist of fury or a game of death, but moralistic comedy.

By the turn of the millennium, then, it seems that Chinese masculinity has succeeded in becoming part of the global consciousness of masculinity. Certainly, journalists such as one *Newsweek* reporter were beginning to opine that 'Asian guys are on a roll'.[56] Interestingly, journalists regard Chan as having lived up to his name of being heir to Bruce Lee. His on-screen kinetic energy was superb, but he is still too much of a man's man. He is still very much a stereotype:

> Charlie Chan was one early stereotype, formal and inscrutable. There were servants, and sneaky villains, and Bruce Lee – who, superman that he was, never got the girl on screen. Then came Jackie Chan, heir to Lee's tradition. 'He's a funny martial artist, but are you going to sleep with him?' asks sociology professor Rebecca Chiyoko King of the University of San Francisco.[57]

This question can be put in terms of *wen-wu*. While Jackie Chan is less uptight about his masculinity, he nevertheless relies to a very large extent on kung fu sequences, in using his body as spectacle. The problem with kung fu films is that like their Bruce Willis and Sylvester Stallone equivalents, the formulaic plots and action leave them open to being seen as 'dumb movies for dumb people'.[58] In the modern world, 'dumb people', including uneducated women, can have buying power, and they can find a brainless body sexually attractive. However, in the traditional *wen-wu* scheme, it is the *wen* man who always attracts the girl. The sociology professor's question here echoes a *wen-wu* sentiment. Chinese critics, too, have been advocating the idea that 'martial arts (*wu*) performances should be harmonised by cultured (*wen*) scripts' (*wu xi wen chang*).[59] Jackie Chan himself has expressed the wish that he wants to be '*wen*' as well as '*wu*'.[60] To date, however, he has not succeeded.

Chow Yun Fat, The Coolest Man Alive

Dismissing Bruce Lee and Jackie Chan, the *Newsweek* article proposes several Asian actors as sexy idols, one being the Hong Kong action star Chow Yun Fat. In his fansites, he is variously described as 'God of Actors', 'The Coolest Man Alive', 'the most sumptuous Babe' and so on. And in *People's Magazine* of November 1999, Chow was voted 'Sexiest Action Star'. Of all the Hong Kong actors, he is the only one whose fame rivals that of Bruce Lee and Jackie Chan. Unlike Bruce's and Jackie's, however, Chow Yun Fat's cult status is not built on his kung fu (*wu*) prowess. As Anne Ciecko observes, his (via John Woo) *A Better Tomorrow* (*Yingxiong bense*) (1986) is a 'catalyst that marked the emergence of a truly transnational action genre'.[61] Ciecko does not disparage Jackie Chan, noting that his 'physical stunts were long imitated by Hollywood action filmmakers'.[62] However, this still acknowledges that Chan is only a *wusheng*. Chow Yun Fat's screen presence by contrast does not rely solely on his body or gymnastic skills.

In a pioneering study of action cinema, Yvonne Tasker identifies three types of action heroes: the star, the performer and the actor.[63] Stars dominate the screen by their physicality, and they tend to be body-building types like Stallone. Performers excel in some form of athletic skill, especially in the martial arts, and the actor has the ability to portray a complex character. While Bruce Lee does not have the excessive bulk of a Schwarzenegger and Stallone, his semi-nude body dominates the screen, and it is a body which is groped, kissed and stabbed in his films. As if his one body is not enough, we have an infinite number of half-naked Bruce Lee bodies in the famous reflecting mirrors scene towards the end of *Enter the Dragon*. Bruce is a star. As Steve Fore observes, Jackie Chan is a performer by virtue of his athleticism.[64] Chow Yun Fat, whose brooding and ebullient presence 'embraces life so unselfconsciously that he becomes vulnerable to all kinds of suffering and heartache',[65] is a good illustration of an actor.

As Ciecko points out, 'Chow Yun-fat's visage rather than his body is used expressively to develop character (via "acting"); he is certainly not a "poser" à la bodybuilding culture and aesthetics'.[66] While the modern urban setting and the absence of kung fu in Chow's trademark action films such as *A Better Tomorrow*, *The Killer* (*Diexue shuangxiong*) (1989) and *Hard Boiled* (*Lashou shentan*) (1992) should mean that they are less 'Chinese' and therefore less *wu* in the masculinity they glorify, this is in fact not the case. In all three movies, the Chow Yun Fat character observes a code of conduct not very different to that of the Liangshan heroes in *All Men Are Brothers*. In particular, homosocial bonds are an important and pervasive element in these movies, with the heroes ready and willing to sacrifice their lives for their mates and honour. The 'buddies' here aren't thrown in for comic relief, they are deadly serious rivals or 'brothers' of the Liu Bei–Guan Yu kind.

In a discussion on the director John Woo, Tony Williams points out that films such as *A Better Tomorrow* and *Hard Boiled* – signature movies for Chow Yun Fat as well – present the 'heroes as twentieth-century versions of Chinese knights with traditional codes of loyalty and friendship yet still relevant to the contemporary world'.[67] Guan Yu's shrine appears consistently in the police departments of these films. Williams notes that in the final scene of *A Better Tomorrow II* (*Yinxiong bense II*) (1988), the three mortally wounded heroes are seated exactly in the way that the three 'brothers' Guan Yu, Liu Bei and Zhang Fei would be positioned, with Liu Bei in the middle and the others on either side.[68] This mythic dimension is verbalised by the hero Mark (Chow Yun Fat) himself. In *A Better Tomorrow*, Ho (played by Ti Lung) asks Mark whether he believes in god. The answer is, 'I am a god. Anyone can be a god if he can control his life.' The paramount importance attached to self-control is the core of the *wen-wu* ideal. The problem for the *wu* god, as indicated in chapter 3, is that the self-control turns tragically wrong. These films were made in Hong Kong for a Chinese audience, so the Guan Yu motif would have been immediately identifiable.

Moreover, homage to Guan Yu's *wu* masculinity is also underlined in *The Corruptor* (1999), one of the first films that heralded Chow Yun Fat's Hollywood career. Apart from having Chow as the lead, this box-office hit was directed, written and produced by non-Chinese, so the extent of the Guan Yu presence is all the more remarkable. Chow Yun Fat plays Nick Chan, the police lieutenant in charge of New York's Asian Gang Unit in Chinatown. He is a corrupt cop, and in the beginning of the movie, his partner rookie Danny Wallace is introduced to him as he burns incense to the Guan Yu altar in the police station. Towards the end when Nick discusses 'business' with Henry Lee in Lee's newly acquired office after he has betrayed and killed his boss, Uncle Benny, Guan Yu's statue is again in the background. Thus, while Chinatown is used, as in early representations, in an Orientalist fashion to signify mystery, sex and violence, this Orientalism is now framed by a more informed setting. *The Corruptor* is about righteousness, loyalty and betrayal. The Guan Yu idol literally watches over the dramatisation and bastardisation of these masculine codes.

Like *Three Kingdoms* and *All Men Are Brothers*, the most important issue that needed resolution in the movie is whether primacy should be given to brotherly loyalty or brotherhood loyalty. In the classic manifestations, the brotherhood is the gang, the clan or the nation, so that the 'great righteousness' (*dayi*), such as patriotism and loyalty to one's lord, is supposed to take precedence over one's kin and mate. In *The Corruptor*, race becomes the great loyalty. References are made throughout the movie to how the Chinese do not trust the whites and vice versa. However, Nick and Danny, having gone through the rituals of saving each other's lives and even sharing a couple of women (whose one-night intrusion into their lives begins their undoing), develop a strong bond. That bond is first questioned by Nick when he discovers Danny is also on the take from the Triad boss Henry Lee. In this encounter, in the shop of a Malaysian drug-dealer, Nick tells Danny, 'you're dead, your life is over' in yet another attempt to get him to stop being corrupted. This discussion again occurs under a portrait of Guan Yu. The *wu* god of loyalty is watching over mateship negotiations, but the audience knows that Danny's betrayal is more multifaceted than the 'corruptor' Nick can anticipate given his allegiance to the *wu* ideals of personal honour and trust.

Danny is not just taking money from the criminals, he is in fact sent by Internal Affairs to build a case against Nick. However, even when told of Danny's mission, Nick decides to opt for mateship loyalty rather than racial loyalty. Like Guan Yu who chooses mateship loyalty above 'national' loyalty when faced with Cao Cao at Hua Rong Pass, Nick turns his back on the Triads and remains loyal to his white, and treacherous, partner. Instead of killing Danny, he saves him at the final shoot-out with Triad members. Here, the two heroes annihilate the gangsters in a blaze of gunfire. However, when the last Triad member shoots at Danny, Nick covers Danny's body with his own before killing the criminal. As Nick lies dying in Danny's arms, Danny cries out, 'Nick, Nick, it's just you and me, your partner.' A partner dying for his mate is a ritualistic routine in Chow Yun Fat's Hong Kong action buddy movies. In this case, however, the buddy is a white, and 'it's just you and me' is a desperate and plaintive cry for salvation from a 'marriage' of racial others, and neither race would save them. As Cynthia J. Fuchs remarks in the context of Hollywood mixed-race buddy movies, 'caught inside conventions of "male bonding" and outside racist, heterosexist norms, the buddy politic can only implode'.[69]

The Corruptor therefore does not stray far from the conventions of the mixed-race buddy politic. With racial honour and loyalty as one of the 'great righteousnesses', the *wu* masculinity in this Hollywood production is maintained. However, its maintenance is only possible because it has been transformed. The hero's relationship to women, too, has softened. In this film, Chow's Nick is extremely tender and caring to his prostitute girlfriend May, treating her almost as a little sister. In one scene while May is recovering from a drug overdose, Nick lovingly feeds her broth by the spoonful. This scene, needless to say, is not watched over by a Guan Yu effigy of any kind. Situated in a New York context, Chow Yun Fat's *wu* hero can be a sensitive soul.

Although we rarely see Chow Yun Fat's naked body (even though he could easily have been half-naked when he played the King of Siam in *Anna and the King* as Yul Brynner had done when he played the role), this sensitive image ensures that even modern urbane women would swoon around him. In fact, in *The Replacement Killers* (1998) and *Anna and the King*, we have Mira Sorvino's Meg and Jodie Foster's Anna falling for him. No wonder *Newsweek* thinks Asian men are on a roll! However, in both cases, Chow does not make love to the women. Some Chinese critics are disappointed by the fact that the Chow Yun Fat character does not go to bed with Mira Sorvino, 'as any white male hero would do with a non-white heroine in a typical Hollywood movie'.[70] This is the same concern voiced by those who attack Bruce Lee as wooden and lacking in the sex appeal of James Bond. However, the lack of explicit sexual intercourse in the screen persona of Bruce Lee, Jackie Chan and Chow Yun Fat should be placed in the conventions of the traditional *wu* hero as much as remnants of the Fu Manchu syndrome. As I have indicated in chapter 1, *wu* heroes regarded women as obstacles to true brotherhood. The *wenren* made love to women, *wu* heroes only made love (Platonic or otherwise) to their sworn brothers.

In fact, this convention has been followed right from the outset in *wuxia* (*wu* complemented by chivalry) films.[71] *Wu* masculinity is premised on the brotherhood ideal where women had to be one of the boys if they were to be heroic. For there to be sexual attraction, the men should really be *wen*. In Hollywood, it is difficult not to have heterosexual desire at least hinted at if the film is to be mainstream. Thus, *The Replacement Killers* already has a very strong heterosexual (and interracial) bond established. But again, apart from a Chinese lead actor and the evil presence of Chinatown, the film is basically a non-Chinese production. As Jillian Sandell observes regarding the films of John Woo, there is a price to be paid for this 'reinvention' of Chinese masculinity. The cost is that 'his vision of intimacy between men[,] falls by the wayside'.[72] When director Ang Lee announced that he was to make a *wuxia* film, *Crouching Tiger, Hidden Dragon*, based on a novel by Wang Dulu (1909–1977), starring Chow Yun Fat and Michelle Yeoh, there was general rejoicing among action movie fans. These artists have not disappointed. As well as being a huge commercial success, the movie had received awards at Cannes and has won four Academy Awards including Best Foreign Language Film. Rave reviews, of which there are hundreds, have appeared in many countries.

The isolated negative ones, such as that by the *Guardian*'s Charlotte Raven, who found the movie so boring she walked out before it was finished, have met with disbelief and indignation.[73] Nonetheless, it is true that the film did not rate as highly in China and Hong Kong as expected.[74] Stephen Teo alludes to some of the problems in this epic. Because *Crouching Tiger* is a *wuxia* film, it 'comes loaded with significant cultural and genre baggage'.[75] Part of that baggage is that the hero is weighed down with all the notions associated with *yi* – righteousness, loyalty and no romance – discussed above. By adding his romantic vision and wanting to explore notions of love and emotion in this film, Ang Lee produced a film where 'the heroic prototype is considerably watered down'. Chinese audiences, saturated in the conventions of the *wuxia* and kung fu genres, may object to this mix. However, it is undeniable that *Crouching Tiger* has been enthusiastically welcomed in the West. This may be the most significant contribution that the film will make in terms of the internationalisation of *wen-wu* masculinity. If Western audiences are to accept a subtitled movie on a mass scale, sacrifices will need to be made. And the *wen-wu* dyad will have to be reconstituted.

As Hollywood hegemony shows no signs of abating, and constructions of basic human features such as masculinity and femininity are powerfully packaged on celluloid, ideal constructs must be encased in these packages if they are to have effect across the world. Kung fu is now so widely accepted as part of action cinema that Hollywood's formal credit bestowed on 'Yuen Wo Ping as the "kung fu choreographer" for his outstanding contribution to *The Matrix* ... is a long overdue recognition of HK kung fu film's unique contribution to film aesthetics'.[76] But Yuen Wo Ping's is an invisible face.[77] His impact further shows that Chinese influence on perceptions of human activity is a whole package, not all the elements of which are readily discernible. In this chapter, we have examined three actors who are highly visible. Each in his own way, Bruce Lee, Jackie Chan and Chow Yun Fat, has added additional Chinese content to the package. In their personal histories, these actors illustrate how the West was won. Bruce was born in America. Jackie's parents live in Canberra and he himself spent some of his youth there. Both have English names. You would think that with a name like Fat, Chow would change his English name at least. But he stuck to it. He didn't even change his Chinese name to include any Dragons. The fact that Chinese and Western audiences accept him as a sexy male icon indicates that indeed Chinese masculinity is changing Western notions of masculinity while it itself is also transformed by Western masculinity.

9 *Wen-wu* Reconstructed: Chinese Masculinity Hybridised and Globalised

Robotic contestants fighting under the sign '*Wen-wu* Temple'. From the 1999 PlayStation game *Wu-Tang Shaolin Style*.

I have advanced the dyad *wen-wu* as an analytical tool and theoretical construct for conceptualising the Chinese masculinity matrix. Because *wen-wu* manifests itself in many different forms and carries many different meanings over space and time, I have tried to capture its core qualities inductively by way of paradigmatic male figures throughout Chinese history rather than by a more detailed and discursive examination of one text or one historical period. I have also used sources and methodologies from a diverse range of disciplines such as philosophy, literature and cinema studies. One consequence of this approach is that the slippage between the ideal and the performance can manifest itself in a variety of ways. The core meaning of *wen-wu* still revolves around cultural attainment and martial valour. However, in practice *wen* can refer to a whole range of attributes such as literary excellence, civilised behaviour, and general education, while *wu* can refer to just as many different sets of descriptors, including a powerful physique, fearlessness and fighting skills. This is only to be expected. I have shown that as a cultural construct, the *wen-wu* ideal must reflect the multifarious social conditions that produce it. The one theme that appears consistently is that like all ideals, it masks all the contradictions of class, sex and race that exist in all societies. The analysis of Chinese masculinity therefore ultimately brings us back to the perennial issues of how different groups of people relate to each other. This in turn raises questions of dominance, subordination, nationalism and hegemony.

In the first three chapters of this book, in which I discussed masculinity in traditional contexts as well as Guan Yu and Confucius, I have presented a changing *wen-wu* – one that is driven mainly by internal dynamics. The last five chapters show the transformations of this dyad that result from external forces such as communism and Western capitalism. The nationalist impulse of 'training the body for China' and the Communist insistence that able-bodied citizens work for social construction have had tremendous influence on the way physicality is constructed in China.[1] This has generated idealised images of workers and peasants, whose physical and moral composition is closer to the *wu* heroes than the *wen*. With the advent of the consumer society in the late twentieth century, the traditional predominance of the *wen* over *wu* within the *wen-wu* model is further destabilised. Capitalism is concerned with production and profits. Male ideals are increasingly those imbued with buying power. The result is that images of masculinity are moving away from their traditional core attributes of literary and cultural learning and martial expertise.

The democratisation process resulting from the social changes in the last century is also beginning to change the gender-bound nature of *wen-wu*. Whereas women who excelled in *wen-wu* skills in the past had either to disguise themselves as men, or, when they were idealised as soul-mates (*zhiji*), to become 'gender hybrids, for a part of their lives at least assume a male persona',[2] they can now assume the *wen-wu* attributes publicly and formally. They were not able to formally qualify for *wen-wu* status in the past because they were barred from the civil and military service examinations (the *wenju* and the *wuju*) which bestowed official recognition on *wen* and *wu* achievements. By opening up many of the traditional male preserves, male–female relations must also become less restrictive. That in turn should reduce the gynophobia that was once so characteristic of the many man-only organisations such as the academies, the military and the secret societies that have existed in Chinese society. As a social construct which provides the key to understanding Chinese masculinity, *wen-wu* may dissolve in time to reveal its true purpose without all the ambiguities and slipperiness that surround it: a power tool to consolidate the interests of certain classes of people and to exclude others.

As well as women, other people who have been excluded for centuries were foreigners and minorities. Non-Chinese men, like the weird human-oids that appear in the *Classic of Mountains and Seas* (*Shanhai jing*)[3] and their progenies such as those in the novel *Flowers in the Mirror*, were all portrayed as needing Han civilisation to become genuinely human. Out-side the realm of the civilising influence of Han culture, men simply could not have *wen-wu*. This xenophobia, too, was formalised by the fact that foreigners did not sit for the civil or military service examinations. And again, this system began to disintegrate in the twentieth century. Chinese Central Television now regularly shows foreign students who have mastered the traditional *wen-wu* arts such as poetry recitations and martial arts. Chinese language schools and kung fu academies have also become established outside China and are producing certified graduates who have mastered these disciplines. The Chinese of the diaspora, who have often themselves suffered racial discrimination, have in no small measure contributed to this trend towards hybridity,[4] as we have dis-cussed in this and the previous chapter.

Hybridity in the twenty-first century is much more than just 'a mix-ture of two social languages' or an encounter 'between two linguistic consciousnesses'.[5] In today's internationalised world, it is common for several languages and consciousnesses to form a multilayered and multi-faceted hybrid. In terms of *wen-wu*, Jim Jarmusch's recent film *Ghost Dog* provides an excellent illustration of this postmodern hybridisation process.[6] Living in the slums of New York, Ghost Dog is an African-American contract assassin who tries to adhere to the code of conduct in the eighteenth-century Japanese text *Hagakure*. As I have indicated in chapter 1, this text has been popularised in the West by Yukio Mishima as *The Way of the Samurai*, a book with a set of principles for reviving traditional masculine ideals. In order to live by this code, Ghost Dog devotes himself to a small-time Mafia boss, who in turn is bound by an anachronistic set of laws. Ghost Dog does not interact with many people in any sort of meaningful way, except with a French-speaking Caribbean ice-cream hawker and a black girl to whom he lends the *Hagakure*. In order to fulfil his destiny, Ghost Dog forces his reluctant Italian-American 'lord' to kill him in the end. However, before that happens, the African-American girl whom he has befriended has read the *Hagakure* and it has been passed to the daughter of the Mafia godfather – presumably the old warrior code will live on in these young women.

This film is a perfect example of the postmodern hybrid because here, not only do we have the confluence of a number of languages and cultural consciousnesses (the ice-cream vendor speaks no English, yet Ghost Dog and he 'communicate' by uttering the same sentiments for different occasions almost simultaneously), but also the past and the present have merged into a timeless dimension. Living and dying by a masculine code that comes from another place and another time, Ghost Dog's nostalgia for that imagined past is heroic but misplaced. He believes that he is maintaining the 'ancient ways', but, as Ryoko Otomo shows, the *Hagakure* is less than 300 years old. In its attempt to use the Confucian philosophy of Wang Yangming (1472–1529) 'to legitimate the position of the samurai class at the top of a social hierarchy',[7] it was already anachronistic when it was first written. But such misplacement arises frequently from the multiplicity of voices and consciousnesses in the film. Everything, from the incongruity of a young African-American girl and a young Italian-American woman being entrusted to carry on the samurai code to Ghost Dog's acting out of *seppuku* in a Western-style shoot-out, is incongruous. Yet, all these contradictory elements gel together. As Ryoko Otomo observes, the movie does not 'privilege a particular meaning among others. It instead, offers a *style* that is elected out of many, a method of eclecticism'.[8] While *wen-wu* in Wang Yangming's time might have had a very culturally specific import, it is now a *style* that can be 'inherited' by anybody in any place and at any time.[9]

Even the music of *Ghost Dog* shows the promiscuous manner in which *wen-wu* has been incorporated into popular culture. The music is by the RZA. RZA is the pseudonym of Robert Diggs, founder of the phenomenally successful rap group Wu-Tang Clan. Ghost Dog plays their CDs every time he goes out on an assignment. Robert Diggs is said to have gone to the Wudang (Wu-Tang) Mountains in China (it and the Shaolin Temples are the two sacred sites of martial arts) where he was received by some kung fu masters.[10] His urban-gangster-warrior image is thus like that of Ghost Dog: a postmodern man imbued with traditional

Asian martial arts ethics. His music is 'an ominous blend of creepy piano riffs, whiny horns, wailing fiddles and kung-fu movie samples'.[11] As Gina Marchetti observes in another context, 'Black music and Chinese kung fu share a common cultural currency that circulates internationally.'[12] As well as music, the Wu-Tang Clan has a large crop of Wu-branded products such as the Wu-Wear clothing line and the Wu comic-book line. It also has a line of kung fu video games, the first of which is called *Wu-Tang Shaolin Style* (released in 1999). In this game, the contestants fight each other in kung fu style under a pavilion with the Chinese characters '*Wen-wu* Temple' (*wen wu miao*) inscribed on its main beam.[13] This game alone quickly sold over 600,000 units for Sony PlayStation. *Wen-wu* has truly become part of the international consciousness.

The advent of mass education and mass consumption of technologies such as the internet and computer games has no doubt brought un-foreseen problems. However, they have also brought benefits. Ideals are now becoming more accessible and more heterogeneous. While good brains will no doubt continue to be important, audiences will also want to see performances by good bodies. It is also possible that they will want to see 'everyman', that is, themselves, as the heroes. The film and tele-vision industries, despite all their inadequacies, may serve to democratise *wen* and *wu* in even more exciting directions yet. Here, Chinese mascu-linity has shown that it could move to being more multi-gendered as well as being more international. As early as 1993, Ang Lee's highly successful comedy *A Wedding Banquet* already dealt with the question of the Chinese gay in an American setting.[14] And in Mainland China itself, as Lisa Rofel observes, 'Avant-garde filmmakers are fascinated with the possibilities that a gay sexuality offers for challenging the official regime. Gay men mock the masculinity of the market while carving out new paths toward a transnational gay imaginary.'[15] A good example of such an attempt is in Liu Bingjian's independently made 1999 film *Man Man Man, Woman Woman Woman* (*Nannannan, nününü*). The depiction of gay men as ordinary people living mundane lives provides models for masculine behaviour that had previously been marginalised or caricatured. The democratisation process allows not just women and 'foreigners' to shape masculinity ideals, but working-class and gay men as well.

By democracy, then, I do not mean reducing male ideals to a case of 'dumb masculinity for dumb people'. I mean a truly multicultural and multi-gender hybrid encompassing but improving existing ideals. Michael Kimmel observes that 'All masculinities are not created equal; or rather, we are all *created* equal, but any hypothetical equality evaporates quickly because our definitions of masculinity are not equally valued in society.'[16] Kimmel is referring to different groups of people within one culture. The statement is even more true when viewed cross-culturally.[17]

To value the different definitions, we have to know their meanings, implications and significance. Until we are at least aware of the meanings of the codes and symbols they use to represent ideal manhood, we are talking at cross-purposes.

If ethnographers like David Gilmore are correct, there are fundamental elements of manhood that seem to be common in most societies. However, there are also differences. Traditional Chinese and American conceptions of masculinity, for example, certainly had many divergent elements. The transformations of *wen-wu* as stated above seem to indicate that at least in the Chinese versus Western scenario, a sort of convergence and mutual appreciation is happening. This does not mean, of course, that differences will be eliminated. Nonetheless, it is possible that globalisation and gender equalisation will make the traditional uses of *wen-wu* as a tool to divide people redundant. This goal is difficult to achieve, given the structures of societies and continuing hegemonic international relations that exist at present. I have attempted to add to the efforts made by those who are working towards that end. At the very least, my hope is that this book will make the hitherto undisclosed parts of ideal Chinese masculinity more decipherable to a broader range of people and less effective for the few who have used them for dominance and control.

Notes

1 INTRODUCING *WEN-WU*: TOWARDS A DEFINITION OF CHINESE MASCULINITY

1 This point is made clearly in the title of the book Trinh T. Minh-ha, *Woman, Native, Other*, Bloomington: Indiana University Press, 1989.

2 See for example Christina K. Gilmartin, Gail Hershatter, Lisa Rofel and Tyrene White (eds), *Engendering China: Women, Culture and the State*, Cambridge, Mass: Harvard University Press, 1994; Judith Stacey, *Patriarchy and the Socialist Revolution in China*, Berkeley: University of California Press, 1983; Louise Edwards, 'Women in the People's Republic of China: New challenges to the grand gender narrative', in Louise Edwards and Mina Roces (eds), *Women in Asia: Tradition, Modernity and Globalisation*, Ann Arbor: University of Michigan Press, 2000, pp. 59–82.

3 In a provocative review of recent scholarship on Chinese gender and sexuality, William Jankowiak points out that the exclusive focus on women has the unfortunate consequence of the overlooking of the role of social class in the formulation of people's lives and the significance of emotional bonds and the failure to interpret the erotic fully. William Jankowiak, 'Chinese Women, Gender, and Sexuality: A Critical Review of Recent Studies', *Bulletin of Concerned Asian Scholars* 31.1 (1999), pp. 31–37.

4 David D. Gilmore, *Manhood in the Making: Cultural Concepts of Masculinity*, New Haven: Yale University Press, 1990, pp. 222–223.

5 Michael S. Kimmel (ed.), *The Politics of Manhood: Profeminist Men Respond to the Mythopoetic Men's Movement*, Philadelphia: Temple University Press, 1995.

6 See for example the discussions in Michael S. Kimmel and Michael A. Messner (eds), *Men's Lives*, Boston: Allyn and Bacon, 1995. This book covers a large range of issues related to men, including Black, Chicano and Jewish perspectives in part I. However, the experiences are all drawn from contemporary America.

7 Ibid., p. xxi.

8 The Chinese term for 'mankind' is *renlei* ('peoplekind'). Even linguistically, the Chinese gendered categorisation of the world is quite different to that of the English.

9 Kenneth Clatterbaugh, *Contemporary Perspectives on Masculinity: Men, Women and Politics in Modern Society*, Boulder, CO: Westview Press, 1990.

10 Edward Said, *Orientalism*, London: Routledge & Kegan Paul, 1978, p. 207.

11 For example, although it is meant to be a book about communication in male–female relationships, the title of the bestseller by John Grey, *Men Are from Mars, Women Are from Venus*, London: Harper Collins, 1992, harks back to the view that men are by nature hard and warlike while women are soft and supportive.

12 Susan Mann, 'The Male Bond in Chinese History and Culture', *The American Historical Review* 105.5 (2000), p. 1601.

13 See for example Xiaomingxiong, *Zhongguo tongxingai shilu* (History of Homosexuality in China), rev. edn, Hong Kong: Rosa Winkel Press, 1997.

14 See Li Bihua, *Zhongguo nanren* (Chinese Males), Hong Kong: Tiandi tushu, 1993; Xie Pengxiong, *Wenxue zhong de nanren* (Men in Literature), Taipei: Jiuge chubanshe, 1992.

15 I should add that the journal *Nan nü: Men, Women and Gender in Early and Imperial China* began publishing in 1999. While not exclusively on men, it has excellent articles about masculinity in traditional China and there is no reason why this should not continue.

16 Zhong Xueping, *Masculinity Besieged? Issues of Modernity and Male Subjectivity in Chinese Literature of the Late Twentieth Century*, London: Duke University Press, 2000.

17 Susan Brownell and Jeffrey N. Wasserstrom (eds), *Chinese Femininities and Masculinities: A Reader*, Berkeley: University of California Press, forthcoming.

18 Ibid., from the 'Introduction'. I would like to thank Susan Brownell for so generously sending me the manuscript.

19 For example, Margery Wolf, *Revolution Postponed: Women in Contemporary China*, Stanford University Press, 1985; Emily Honig and Gail Hershatter, *Personal Voices: Chinese Women in the 1980's*, Stanford University Press, 1988; William R. Jankowiak, *Sex, Death, and Hierarchy in a Chinese City: An Anthropological Account*, New York: Columbia University Press, 1993; Elisabeth Croll, *Changing Identities of Chinese Women*, London: Zed Books, 1995; and Tamara Jacka, *Women's Work in Rural China*, Cambridge University Press, 1997.

20 The paucity of material on *wen-wu* is not confined to English language material. It is true in the Chinese case as well. For example, Liu Dalin's mammoth and definitive *Zhongguo gudai xing wenhua* (The Sex Culture of Ancient China), Yinchuan: Ningxia renmin chubanshe, 1993, and *Zhongguo dangdai xing wenhua* (Sexual Behaviour in Modern China), Shanghai: Sanlian shudian, 1992, deal with sexuality and men ranging from eunuchs to gigolos, but there is no discussion of masculinity as '*wen-wu*'.

21 Kenneth Henshall characterises Japanese masculine ideals in terms of 'soft' and 'hard', and the descriptions read much like those describing *wen* and *wu*. Kenneth G. Henshall, *Dimensions of Japanese Society: Gender, Margins and Mainstream*, New York: St Martin's Press, 1999, pp. 1–8.

22 For an evocative account of Mishima's defence of traditional masculine ways, see Yukio Mishima, *The Way of the Samurai: Yukio Mishima on Hagakure in Modern Life* (trans. Kathryn Sparling), New York: Basic Books, 1977.

23 See for example the essays in Lin Foxhall and John Salmon (eds), *When Men Were Men: Masculinity, Power and Identity in Classical Antiquity*, London: Routledge, 1998.

24 See Daniel Boyarin, *Unheroic Conduct: The Rise of Heterosexuality and the Invention of the Jewish Man*, Berkeley: University of California Press, 1997, pp. 1–80.
25 See for example the essays on male romantic passion in William Jankowiak (ed.), *Romantic Passion: A Universal Experience?*, New York: Columbia University Press, 1995, especially Jankowiak, 'Romantic Passion in the People's Republic of China', pp. 166–183.
26 David D. Gilmore, *Manhood in the Making: Cultural Concepts of Masculinity*, New Haven: Yale University Press, 1990, p. 4.
27 Ibid., p. 170.
28 See for example the writings of influential eugenicists such as J. Philippe Rushton, who believe that in measures such as brain size, reproductive behaviour and sex hormones, 'people of east Asian ancestry ... and people of African ancestry ... define opposite ends of the spectrum, with people of European ancestry ... falling intermediately', in *Race, Evolution, and Behaviour: A Life History Perspective*, New Brunswick: Transaction Publishers, 1997, p. xiii.
29 See Ann Oakley's pioneering work *Sex, Gender and Society*, Aldershot: Gower/Temple Smith, 1972.
30 For a brief survey of this debate see *Australian Feminist Studies* 10 (1989). More detail is provided in Elizabeth Grosz, *Volatile Bodies: Towards a Corporeal Feminism*, Sydney: Allen & Unwin, 1994.
31 For a glimpse of the various forms of the ideal male body in the West, see Kenneth R. Dutton, *The Perfectible Body: The Western Ideal of Physical Development*, St Leonards, NSW: Allen & Unwin, 1995.
32 John Stoltenberg, *Refusing to Be a Man*, Portland, Ore.: Breitenbush Books, 1989.
33 See Angela Zito and Tani E. Barlow (eds), *Body, Subject & Power in China*, University of Chicago Press, 1994 for excellent discussions of the cultural manifestations of the Chinese human body.
34 R.H. Van Gulik, *Sexual Life in Ancient China*, Leiden: E.J. Brill, 1974, p. 188.
35 Ibid., pp. 295–296.
36 The literature on sociobiology and psychobiology is immense, and we clearly cannot discuss the sometimes heated debates that this literature has produced in any depth in this book. For an influential and persuasive account, see Donald Symons, *The Evolution of Human Sexuality*, Oxford University Press, 1979.
37 See for example Louisa Schein, *Minority Rules: The Miao and the Feminine in China's Cultural Politics*, Durham, NC: Duke University Press, 2000.
38 Of course, there have been 'men's magazines' such as *Playboy* and *Penthouse* in existence prior to this time and these are still popular today. However, where they are *for* the men as consumers, the new breed is *about* men as objects to be studied as well as being for them as readers.
39 See discussion in Chilla Bulbeck, *One World Women's Movement*, London: Pluto Press, 1988, and *Re-orienting Western Feminisms: Women's Diversity in a Postcolonial World*, Cambridge University Press, 1998.
40 For a discussion of the evolution of sexual identities in modern China, see Frank Dikötter, *Sex, Culture and Modernity in China*, London: Hurst & Co, 1995.

41 See the studies of Michael S. Kimmel (ed.), *Changing Men: New Directions in Research on Men and Masculinity*, Newbury Park, CA: Sage Publications, 1987, especially Gregory M. Herek, 'On Heterosexual Masculinity: Some Physical Consequences of the Social Construction of Gender and Sexuality', pp. 68–82; M. Kaufman, *Beyond Patriarchy: Essays by Men on Pleasure, Power, and Change*, Toronto: Oxford University Press, 1987; J.L. Dubbert, *A Man's Place: Masculinity in Transition*, London: Prentice Hall, 1979.

42 See for example Gail Sheehy, *Passages for Men: Discovering the New Map of Men's Lives*, London: Simon & Schuster, 1998; Anne and Bill Moir, *Why Men Don't Iron: The Real Science of Gender Studies*, London: Harper-Collins, 1998.

43 Ronald F. Levant, 'The Masculinity Crisis', *The Journal of Men's Studies* 5.3 (1997), pp. 221–31.

44 See Steve Biddulph, *Manhood: A Book about Setting Men Free*, Sydney: Finch Publishing, 1994 and Robert Bly, *Iron John: a Book about Men*, Rockport, Mass.: Element, 1991.

45 Michael-David Gordon, 'Why Is This Men's Movement So White?' *Changing Men* 26 (1993), pp. 15–17.

46 See Allan Luke, 'Representing and Reconstructing Asian Masculinities: This is not a Movie Review', *Social Alternatives* 16.31 (1997), pp. 32–34 and Tony Ayres, 'Undesirable Aliens', *HQ* 57 (1998), pp. 110–115.

47 See W.J.F. Jenner's discussion of the '*haohan*' in *The Tyranny of History: The Roots of China's Crisis*, London: Allen Lane, 1992, pp. 203–206. *Yingxiong* will be described in detail in the next chapter.

48 Sun Longji, *Zhongguo wenhua de 'shenceng jiegou'* (The 'Deep structure' of Chinese Culture), Hong Kong: Jixianshe, 1983, p. 210.

49 Ibid., p. 206.

50 See for example Charles Humana and Wang Wu, *The Ying-Yang: The Chinese Way of Love*, London: Tandem, 1971.

51 Sima Xiaomeng, *Nanzi shenghuo daquan* (Encyclopedia for Men), Zhengzhou: Henan kexuejishu chubanshe, 1996. The quotation is the title to the preface of the book.

52 R.H. Van Gulik gives several examples of this, including explanations in his *Sexual Life in Ancient China*, pp. 158–60. See also Charlotte Furth's comments on these techniques in her 'Rethinking Van Gulik: Sexuality and Reproduction in Traditional Chinese Medicine', in Gilmartin et al. (eds), pp. 125–146.

53 Charlotte Furth's work on androgyny points out this split between the *yin-yang* cosmology and Confucian ideas in her article, 'Androgynous Males and Deficient Females: Biology in Sixteenth and Seventeenth Century China', *Late Imperial China* 9.2 (December 1988), pp. 1–31. Her more recent *A Flourishing Yin: Gender in China's Medical History, 960–1665*, Berkeley: University of California Press, 1999, gives a very detailed and erudite account of gender and the uses of *yin-yang* in Chinese medicine.

54 Luo Zhufeng (ed.), *Hanyu da cidian* (The Great Chinese Dictionary), vol. 6, Shanghai: Hanyu da cidian chubanshe, 1990, pp. 1512–1513.

55 Herrlee G. Creel, *The Origins of Statecraft in China*, vol. I: *The Western Zhou Empire*, Chicago University Press, 1970, p. 67.

56 Luo Zhufeng (ed.), *Hanyu da cidian*, vol. 5, pp. 338–339.

57 Chen Shan, *Zhongguo wuxia shi* (History of the Chinese Chivalrous Knights), Shanghai: Sanlian shudian, 1992, pp. 298–310.

58 Ibid., pp. 10–13.

59 *Analects*, XIX.22. This translation is D.C. Lau's from his *Confucius: The Analects*, Harmondsworth: Penguin, 1979, p. 156.

60 The Chinese is 'Wen wang yi wen zhi, Wu wang yi wu gong'. *Li ji: jifa* in *Gu jin Hanyu chengyu cidian* (Dictionary of Chinese Idioms Past and Present), Taiyuan: Shanxi renmin chubanshe, 1986, p. 176. Legge has translated this as 'King Wen, who by his peaceful rule, and King Wu who by his martial achievements, delivered the people from their afflictions', F. Max Muller (ed.), *The Sacred Books of the East*, vol. XXVIII, *The Texts of Confucianism Part IV The Li Ki, XI–XLVI* (trans. James Legge), Oxford: Clarendon Press, 1885, p. 209. This translation does not quite give the full flavour of the term *wen*.

61 Li Ruzhen, *Jinghua yuan*, Taipei: Xuehai chubanshe, 1985 (first published 1828). For an abridged English translation see Li Ju-chen, *Flowers in the Mirror* (trans. Lin Tai-yi), Berkeley: University of California Press, 1965.

62 See the cases in Susan Mann, *Precious Records: Women in China's Long Eighteenth Century*, Stanford University Press, 1997.

63 Louise Edwards has also argued that the very existence of these women in men's roles – female scholars and warriors – framed as they are within the 'disruptive', 'immoral' reign of Empress Wu, simply serve to further create the impression of social disorder within the text of *Jinghua yuan*. See chapter 6 of Louise Edwards, *Men and Women in Qing China: Gender in the 'Red Chamber Dream'*, Leiden: E.J. Brill, 1994.

64 Anne-Marie Hsiung, 'A Feminist Re-Vision of Xu Wei's *Ci Mulan* and *Nü Zhuangyuan*', in Yingjin Zhang (ed.), *China in a Polycentric World*, Stanford University Press, 1998, p. 78.

65 While Empress Wu of the Tang Dynasty had instituted martial arts examinations (*wuju*), they were held irregularly and unlike the civil service examinations (*wenju*), success in the *wuju* was not an automatic path to power and privilege. Most who passed did not obtain government positions and those who did were always subordinate to their *wen* counterparts. See discussion in Ying-jen Chang, 'The Rise of Martial Arts in China and America', unpublished PhD dissertation, Graduate Faculty of Political and Social Science, New School for Social Research, 1978, pp. 61–71.

66 Frank Dikötter, *The Discourse of Race in Modern China*, Hong Kong University Press, 1992, pp. 44–47.

67 The historiography of Empress Wu's 'irregular' reign and that of Jiang Qing's attempted 'reign' confirm the extreme distrust of women who dare to usurp this ultimate 'masculine' power.

68 Wu Jingzi, *Rulin waishi*, Beijing: Zuojia chubanshe, 1954. For an English translation see Wu Ching-tzu, *The Scholars* (trans. by Gladys Yang and Yang Hsien-yi), Beijing: Foreign Languages Press, 1957.

69 D.L. McMullen, 'The Cult of Ch'i T'ai-kung and T'ang Attitudes to the Military', *T'ang Studies* 7 (1989), p. 68.

70 Edwin G. Pulleyblank, 'The An Lu-Shan Rebellion and the Origins of Chronic Militarism in Late T'ang China', in John Curtis Perry and Bardwell L. Smith (eds), *Essays on T'ang Society*, Leiden: E.J. Brill, 1976, p. 33.

71 Hereafter *Three Kingdoms*. An English translation is found in Luo Guan-zhong, *Three Kingdoms: A Historical Novel* (trans. Moss Roberts), 3 vols, Beijing: Foreign Languages Press, 1994.

72 The literal translation of '*shuihu*' is 'water margin'. I have adopted Pearl Buck's more suggestive translations here. Shi Nai'an, *All Men Are Brothers* (trans. Pearl S. Buck), 2 vols, London: Methuen, 1957.

73 It is interesting to note that popular depictions of the *wu* god, Guan Yu, describe him reading the Confucian classic *The Spring and Autumn Annals* despite the fact that he was probably illiterate.

74 'Liu Jingshu sun tong liezhuan', *Shiji: di ba ce: 99 juan*, Beijing: Zhonghua shuju, 1959, p. 2723.

75 '*Guojia bi you wen wu, guan zhi bi you shang fa*', *Han Feizi ji shi: shang*, Shanghai: Renmin chubanshe, 1974, p. 377.

76 '*Wen wu bing yong, chang jiu zhi shu*', *Shiji: di ba ce: 97 juan*, p. 2699.

77 Quoted in McMullen, 'The Cult of Ch'i T'ai-kung', p. 75.

78 McMullen, 'The Cult of Ch'i T'ai-kung', p. 75.

79 Jonathan D. Spence, *Ts'ao Yin and the Kang-hsi Emperor*, New Haven: Yale University Press, 1966, p. 157. See also p. 130 where Spence again discusses the Kangxi Emperor's bids to impress both the military and literary elite.

80 Angela Zito, *Of Body & Brush: Grand Sacrifices as Text/Performance in Eighteenth-Century China*, University of Chicago Press, 1997, pp. 17–26.

81 See Richard Kraus, *Brushes with Power: Modern Politics and the Chinese Art of Calligraphy*, Berkeley: University of California Press, 1991 for an in-depth study of the relationship between calligraphy and power.

82 Mao Zedong, 'The Snow', in Kai-yu Hsu (trans. and ed.), *Twentieth Century Chinese Poetry: An Anthology*, Ithaca: Cornell University Press, 1970, pp. 363–64.

83 Lau, 'Introduction', *Confucius: The Analects*, p. 39.

84 *Confucius: The Analects*, III.25 (trans. D.C. Lau), p. 71.

85 Huang Kuanzhong, *Nan Song junzheng yu wenxian tansuo* (Explorations into Military Administration and Documents of the Southern Song), Taipei: Xinwen feng chubanshe, 1980, p. 391.

86 McMullen, 'The Cult of Ch'i T'ai-kung', p. 80.

87 Ibid., p. 82.

88 Ibid., p. 68.

89 Huang Kuanzhong, *Nan Song junzheng*, p. 397.

90 Wang Shifu, *Xixiang ji* (Story of the West Wing), reissued Shanghai: Shanghai guji chubanshe, 1978.

91 For a description of the Chen Shimei image see Liu Lanying et al. (eds), *Zhongguo gudai wenxue cidian: dier juan*, Nanning: Guangxi jiaoyu chubanshe, 1989, p. 721.

92 Anonymous, *The Golden Lotus* (trans. Clement Egerton) 4 vols, London: Routledge and Kegan Paul Ltd, 1939.

93 Susan Brownell documents the difficulties of overcoming the old prejudices encapsulated in the old adage that 'Those who work with their brains rule; those who work with their brawn are ruled' even for the sports academies, when parents are reluctant to let their children enter such a profession. See Susan Brownell, *Training the Body for China: Sports in the Moral Order of the People's Republic*, University of Chicago Press, 1995, pp. 180–209.

94 This novel has been translated by Chen Hanming and James O. Belcher, New York: Garland, 1991.
95 Zhu Hong titled her translation of this style of tale *The Chinese Western*, New York: Ballantine, 1988.
96 A good illustration can be found in Kam Louie (ed. and introd.), *Strange Tales From Strange Lands: Stories by Zheng Wanlong*, Ithaca: Cornell East Asia Series, 1993.
97 Although it does not use the *wen-wu* concept, one of the most insightful discussions that links class, race and the manipulations of discourses in power struggles between men can be found in Donald M. Nonini, 'The Dialectics of "Disputatiousness" and "Rice-Eating Money": Class Confrontation and Gendered Imaginaries Among Chinese Men in West Malaysia', *American Ethnologist* 26.1 (1999), pp. 47–68.

2 PORTRAIT OF THE GOD OF WAR GUAN YU: SEX, POLITICS AND *WU* MASCULINITY

1 For example James J.Y. Liu, *The Chinese Knight-Errant*, London: Routledge & Kegan Paul, 1967; Cui Fengyuan, *Zhongguo gudian duanpian xiayi xiaoshuo yanjiu* (A Study of Classical Chinese Short Stories on Knight-Errantry), Taipei: Lianjing chuban shiye gongsi, 1986.
2 Zhou Zhongming, *Zhongguo de xiaoshuo yishu* (The Art of Chinese Fiction), reprinted Taipei: Guanya wenhua, 1990, pp. 25–37.
3 Liu, p. 204. Neither Liu nor Cui, for example, mentions sex in their books.
4 It is of course very difficult to give a precise definition of 'hero', especially when we are dealing with different cultures. For the purposes of this chapter, it refers to the variety encapsulated in the Chinese terms *yingxiong* and *haohan*. Other varieties such as the 'moral' kind are better dealt with in later chapters.
5 See for example Keith McMahon, *Misers, Shrews and Polygamists: Sexuality and Male–Female Relations in Eighteenth-century Chinese Fiction*, Durham, NC: Duke University Press, 1995; Tani E. Barlow (ed.), *Gender Politics in Modern China: Writing and Feminism*, Durham: Duke University Press, 1993; Louise Edwards, 'Gender Imperatives in *Honglou meng*: Jia Baoyu's Bisexuality', *Chinese Literature: Essays, Articles and Reviews* 12 (1990), pp. 69–81, and the Special Issue on women in *Late Imperial China* 13.1 (1992) and modern sex in *Positions* 13.2 (1994).
6 Keith McMahon, *Causality and Containment in Seventeenth-Century Chinese Fiction*, Leiden: E.J. Brill, 1988.
7 Zhu Zhengming, *Legends about Guan Yu of China*, Beijing: China Today Press, 1996, p. 2.
8 I should note here that in this book, homosexuality, bisexuality and heterosexuality are terms describing erotic behaviour between people only, with none of the modern pathological connotations attached to these terms. I fully agree with David Halperin's view that these terms were constructed completely differently in antiquity. David M. Halperin, 'Sex Before Sexuality: Pederasty, Politics, and Power in Classical Athens', in Martin Bauml Duberman et al. (eds), *Hidden From History: Reclaiming the Gay and Lesbian Past*, Harmondsworth: Penguin Books, 1991, p. 48.

9 For the case of Japan, see for example Ihara Saikaku, *The Great Mirror of Male Love* (trans. and introd. Paul Gordon Schalow), Stanford University Press, 1990. For the Greek case, see for example K.J. Dover, *Greek Homosexuality*, London: Duckworth, 1978. Classical Greek homosexuality was not without its problems. Pederasty, for example, has recently received negative assessment in Enid Bloch, 'Sex between Men and Boys in Classical Greece: Was It Education for Citizenship or Child Abuse?', *The Journal of Men's Studies* 9.2 (2001), pp. 183–204.

10 This is documented in Xiao Mingxiong, *Zhongguo tongxing'ai shilu*. In English, see Bret Hinsch, *Passions of the Cut Sleeve: The Homosexual Tradition in China*, Berkeley: University of California Press, 1990. A discussion of more contemporary relevance can be found in Chris Berry, *A Bit on the Side: East–West Topographies of Desire*, Sydney: EmPress, 1994.

11 In some circles, men holding hands would be seen as a sexual act.

12 Eve Kosofsky Sedgwick, *Between Men: English Literature and Male Homosocial Desire*, New York: Columbia University Press, 1985, p. 1.

13 Sedgwick, p. 2.

14 The novel *Sanguo yanyi* (*Romance of the Three Kingdoms*) is the first major novel in Chinese literature. The earliest extant edition dates from 1522 and it still ranks in the top three of the most read and influential novels in China.

15 For the sake of clarity, I will use *Three Kingdoms* when I refer to the novel and Three Kingdoms for all texts including the novel that relate to the cycle of stories about this period.

16 R. H. Van Gulik, *Sexual Life in Ancient China*, Leiden: E.J. Brill, 1974, pp. 278–279.

17 Robert Ruhlmann, in his survey of heroes in traditional fiction, singles out Guan Yu for a separate discussion: Ruhlmann, 'Traditional Heroes in Chinese Popular Fiction', in Arthur Wright (ed.), *The Confucian Persuasion*, Stanford University Press, 1960, pp. 141–176. Also, Xie Pengxiong begins his book on men in literature with a chapter on Guan Yu: Xie, *Wenxue zhong de nanren* (Men in Literature), Taipei: Jiuge chubanshe, 1992, pp. 11–18.

18 Li Xifan, 'Lüe lun *Sanguo yanyi* li de Guan Yu de xingxiang' (A Brief Discussion of Guan Yu's Image in Three Kingdoms), in Henan sheng shehui kexueyuan (ed.), *Sanguo yanyi yanjiu lunwen ji* (Collected Essays on *Romance of the Three Kingdoms*), Beijing: Zhonghua shuju, 1991, p. 408.

19 He is often placed alongside Confucius in temples as the *wu* (military) god, with Confucius the *wen* (civil) god. See discussion of him in Huang Huajie, *Guan Yu de renge yu shenge* (The Human and Godlike Characteristics of Guan Yu), Taipei: Taiwan shangwu yinshuguan, 1967.

20 A discussion of Guan Yu's titles can be found in Gordon Victor Ross, 'Guan Yu in Drama: Translations and Critical Discussions of Two Yuan Plays', unpublished PhD Dissertation, University of Texas at Austin, 1976, pp. 19–25.

21 Examples of new year paper cuts, temple paintings, etc., are found in Wang Shucun (ed.), *Guan Gong baitu* (One Hundred Images of Duke Guan), Guangzhou: Lingnan meishu chubanshe, 1996.

22 For a discussion of Guan Yu's impact on popular culture and the diaspora, see Bob Hodge and Kam Louie, *The Politics of Chinese Language and Culture*, London: Routledge, 1998, pp. 119–142.

23 This description of the power of the dragon is a very old one. See for example the Han definition in *Shuowen jiezi zhu* (Annotated Shuowen jiezi), Shanghai: Guji chubanshe, 1981, p. 582.

24 The association of the dragon with male sexuality is very common, vividly illustrated in the title of the book on the history of Chinese sexuality, Eric Chou, *The Dragon and The Phoenix*, London: Corgi Books, 1973.

25 In many martial arts (*wuxia*) novels such as *Ernü yingxiong zhuan*, we do find cases where the small win over the big and strong, but in such cases, the winners are often women, and when men are involved, the size reversion seems to suggest that largeness is reserved for powerful men.

26 Qin and Han law required the shaving of beards and hair as punishment for serious offences. Having a shaven head and wearing an iron collar seemed to have been signs of unforgivable criminality. See A.F.P. Hulsewé, 'Han-time Documents', *T'oung Pao* 45 (1957), pp. 36–37. The emphasis on Guan Yu's beard could therefore be seen in historical terms as an exaggerated projection of his indestructible virtue and masculinity.

27 Zhu Yixuan and Liu Yuchen (eds), *Sanguo yanyi ziliao huibian* (Compilation of Reference Materials on *The Romance of the Three Kingdoms*), Guangzhou: Baihua wenyi chubanshe, 1983, pp. 735–736.

28 For one version of this story, see Qiu Zhensheng, *Sanguo yanyi zongheng tan* (Random Notes on *The Romance of the Three Kingdoms*), pp. 46–47. The Heavenly Queen Mother is supposed to have retained her youthful vigour by sexual vampirism – sucking the *yang* essence out of her young male sex partners. It is therefore possible that her 'water' contains this *yang* essence. See Van Gulik, p. 158.

29 See for example the Greek parallel in Dover, pp. 133–134.

30 In the novel, it is Liu Bei who bestows the sword on Guan Yu. This is a significant innovation as it confirms Liu Bei's imperial (dragon motif) legitimacy as well as his right to confer political and sexual power.

31 For a discussion of Diao Chan's fate, see Liu Zhijian, *'Sanguo yanyi' xinlun* (A New Discussion of *Romance of the Three Kingdoms*), Chongqing: Chongqing chubanshe, 1985, pp. 93–96.

32 For a discussion of the Diao Chan/Guan Yu episode in *zaju*, see Jiang Xingyu, *Zhongguo xiqushi gouchen* (Explorations in the History of Chinese Drama), Henan: Zhengzhou shuhuashe, 1982, pp. 240–244.

33 Luo Guanzhong, *Sanguo yanyi* (Romance of the Three Kingdoms), vol. 1. Taipei: Guiguan tushu, 1988, p. 177.

34 See *The Story of Hua Guan Suo* (trans. Gail Oman King), Arizona State University, Center for Asian Studies, 1989.

35 Another well-known translated version for *Shuihu* is Pearl Buck's *All Men Are Brothers*. Chapter 5 discusses this novel in some more detail.

36 C.T. Hsia, *The Classic Chinese Novel*, Bloomington: Indiana University Press, 1980, p. 106.

37 In Yuan Shao's wife Lady Liu, for example, we have one of the most needless sadistic murderers in the novel: she kills Yuan's five consorts, shaves their heads, tattoos their faces and mutilates their bodies and kills their whole families. See Luo Guanzhong, p. 281.

38 Both Yang Xiong and Wu Song are known for their orgiastic killings – the former, for example, for slicing his own wife up into pieces and the latter for the gruesome slaying of the famous Golden Lotus.

39 The expression 'Guan Yunchang du *Chunqiu*' (Guan Yu reads the *Spring and Autumn Annals*) indicating that Guan Yu was a staunch Confucian scholar has become a popular dictum. Tan Liangxiao and Zhang Dake (eds), *Sanguo renwu pingzhuan* (Critical Biographies of Characters from the Three Kingdoms), Taipei: Shuiniu, 1992, p. 177.

40 Moss Roberts (trans. and ed.), *Three Kingdoms: China's Epic Drama by Lo Kuan-chung*, New York: Pantheon Books, 1976, p. 303.

41 For a translation of this episode, see James Legge, *The Ch'un Tsew with The Tso Chuen*, reprinted Taipei: Southern Materials Center, 1985 (originally published 1935), pp. 81–82. This story makes the popular dictum that Guan Yu was well-versed in the *Chunqiu* (Spring and Autumn Annals) much more significant, as the *Zuozhuan* and *Chunqiu* are normally read as one book.

42 As late as 1985, Chinese critics continued to highlight this episode. See Liu Zhijian, *'Sanguo yanyi' xinlun*, p. 128.

43 Other critics have also taken such an interpretation of Guan Yu's actions at this point. See for example Paul Kimlicka, 'The Novel *San Kuo chih Tung-su yen-i* As Literature: Uses of Irony by Its Author Lo Kuan-chung', unpublished MA thesis, Indiana University, 1986.

44 I am aware that this Freudian interpretation of the dream may present cultural problems. However, even without this interpretation, Guan Yu's actions following the dream justify my assertion that his irrational behaviour is very much a consequence of his unease with his quest for power, a quest that could threaten his loyalty to Liu Bei.

45 For example, Liu Bei's outburst at Guan Yu's death, and his wanting to take revenge at the cost of his kingdom.

46 Of course, it could be argued that homosocial desire was so much part of the lives of traditional scholars that it was never taken as a problem needing discussion. If this is the case, modern interpreters have certainly failed in making this point explicit.

47 Yuan Mei, 'Double Blossom Temple', in Kam Louie and Louise Edwards (eds and trans.), *Censored by Confucius: Ghost Stories by Yuan Mei*, Armonk, NY: M.E. Sharpe, 1996, pp. 206–208. It is interesting that in the 'jottings' of less tolerant scholars of the Qing period, explicit homosexuality is seen as vile and Guan Yu the God is the one to condemn it. See for example Vivien W. Ng, 'Homosexuality and the State in Late Imperial China', in Martin Bauml Duberman, pp. 86–87.

48 Not to mention more specifically homosexual romances like the *Bian er chai* and *Yichun xiangzhi*. See Keith McMahon's discussion of these in his *Causality and Containment*, p. 69.

49 The expression 'peach orchard pledge' (*taoyuan jieyi*) is commonly used to refer to forming brotherhoods and other acts of loyalty. The ceremony was widely imitated in China until the People's Republic. See for example Lee McIsaac, '"Righteousness Fraternities" and Honorable Men: Sworn Brotherhoods in Wartime Chongqing', *American Historical Review* 105.5 (2000), p. 1648.

50 Wolfram Eberhard, *Dictionary of Chinese Symbols*, Singapore: Federal Publications, 1990, pp. 227–228. 'Sharing the peach', like 'cutting the sleeve', also refers to homosexual behaviour. See Eric Chou, pp. 21–23.

51 It is significant that the source of this phrase is the *Sanguo zhi*. It is absent at the corresponding point in the novel (immediately after the brothers joined forces).

52 Both *tongchuang* and *tongta* mean sharing the same bed. Han Feizi, however, had already referred to the term *tongchuang* as one of the eight vices because it entailed being sexually bewitched by women and young boys.

53 Wu Cuncun notes that in the Ming-Qing period, verbs that describe homosexual relations (for example *bi, chong, xing*, all meaning to favour) generally carry connotations of hierarchy such as lord to servant and elder to younger, whereas the equivalent heterosexual verbs (for example *ai, yue and mu*) are more equal. Wu Cuncun, *Ming Qing shehui xing'ai fengqi* (Trends in Sexual Love in Ming-Qing Society), Beijing: Renmin chubanshe, 2000, p. 8.

54 For examples of the use of '*tongta*' throughout history, see Luo Zhufeng (ed.), *Hanyu da cidian* (The Great Chinese Dictionary), vol. 3, Hong Kong: Sanlian chubanshe, 1989, p. 122.

55 Luo Guanzhong, vol. 1, pp. 321–322.

56 Ibid., p. 347.

57 Reasons for this imbalance have been indicated in the last chapter. They will be discussed in more detail in later chapters.

58 See for example Su Dongpo's poem 'Tune: "The Charms of Nian-nu"' (trans. Ch'u Ta-kao), in Cyril Birch (ed.), *Anthology of Chinese Literature*, Harmondsworth: Penguin, 1967, p. 361.

59 In fact the term '*tongta*', used for so many couples in the novel, is not used for Guan Yu's relationship even with Liu Bei.

60 Michel Foucault, *The Use of Pleasure* (trans. Robert Hurley), Harmondsworth: Penguin, 1987, p. 20.

61 Ibid.

62 It should be noted here that in the context of the story cycle, Guan Yu is never the most powerful politically. His influence and god-like status were bestowed on him posthumously. In popular iconography, Guan Yu is usually portrayed in the company of his two subordinates Guan Ping and Zhang Jie. This grouping mirrors the trio Liu, Guan and Zhang, but it is the former icon that dominates the popular imagination, thus displaying the superiority of Guan Yu over Liu Bei among the populace.

63 Some critics, such as Andrew Lo, prefer to see the title 'to mean a playing out of the various implications of moral principle'. See William H. Nienhauser Jr (ed.), *The Indiana Companion to Traditional Chinese Literature*, Indiana University Press, 1986, p. 669. *Yi* is so central to historical romances of this sort that many later novels also take *yanyi* as part of the title.

64 For a detailed discussion of the uses of *zhong* and *yi* in the *Three Kingdoms*, see Gao Mingge, *Sanguo yanyi lungao* (On *The Romance of the Three Kingdoms*), Shenyang: Liaoning daxue chubanshe, 1986, pp. 185–215.

65 Both *zhong* and *yi* are Confucian concepts. In a recent study on Confucian writings on male friendship, Norman Kusher makes the interesting observation that the Confucians were very wary of egalitarian affective bonds between men because they were seen to have the potential to disrupt the traditional hierarchical social order. Norman Kusher, 'The Fifth Relationship: Dangerous Friendships in the Confucian Context', *The American Historical Review* 105.5 (2000), pp. 1615–1629.

66 Zhu Yixuan and Liu Yuchen, p. 116. Interestingly, one of the turning moments in ancient Greek portrayals of male self-control is depicted in Plato's description of Socrates' deathbed scene, in which Socrates forbids his friends to weep. See Hans van Wees, 'A Brief History of Tears: Gender Differentiation in Archaic Greece', in Lin Foxhall and John Salmon (eds), *When Men Were Men: Masculinity, Power and Identity in Classical Antiquity*, London: Routledge, 1998, p. 16.

67 Mao Zonggang, 'Di yi caizi shu' (Number One Work of Genius), published under the title *Sanguo yanyi de zhengzhi yu molüe guan* (Politics and strategy in *The Romance of the Three Kingdoms*), Taipei: Laogu wenhua shiye, 1985, p. 130.

68 See Qiu Zhensheng, *Sanguo yanyi zongheng tan* (Random Essays on *The Romance of the Three Kingdoms*), Taipei: Xiaoyuan chubanshe, 1991, pp. 111–113.

69 Mao Zonggang, 'Di yi caizi shu', p. 129.

70 Zhou Zhaoxin, *Sanguo yanyi kaoping* (Evaluation and Criticism of the *Romance of the Three Kingdoms*), Beijing: Beijing daxue chubanshe, 1990, p. 169.

71 For a discussion of Guan Yu's tragic delusions of grandeur, see Andrew Plaks, *The Four Masterworks of the Ming Novel*, Princeton University Press, 1987, pp. 406–413.

72 Sedgwick, p. 15.

73 Keith McMahon in *Causality and Containment* correctly points out that fiction can be 'noisy' (p. 12) compared to more orthodox literary genres. However, in this chapter, we are contrasting a literati novel with texts which show even less restraint in erotic descriptions.

3 CONFUCIUS AS SAGE, TEACHER, BUSINESSMAN: TRANSFORMATIONS OF THE *WEN* ICON

1 Bob Hodge and Kam Louie, *The Politics of Chinese Language and Culture*, London: Routledge, 1998, pp. 119–142.

2 Andrew J. Nathan, *China's Transition*, New York: Columbia University Press, 1997, pp. 136–151.

3 David L. Hall and Roger T. Ames, *Thinking Through Confucius*, Albany: State University of New York Press, 1987, pp. 182–192.

4 For a discussion of the relationship between *wen* and *junzi* and its manifestations by the Song Dynasty, see Brian E. McKnight, *Law and Order in Sung China*, Cambridge University Press, 1992, pp. 191–193.

5 Yang Bojun, *Lunyu Yizhu* (The *Analects* Translated and Annotated), Beijing: Zhonghua shuju, 1958, p. 68.

6 Ibid., p. 65.

7 See for example D.C. Lau (trans.), *Confucius: The Analects*, Harmondsworth: Penguin Books, 1979, pp. 37–38.

8 Yang Bojun, p. 78.

9 Ibid., p. 42.

10 Wu Jingzi, *Rulin waishi* (The Scholars), Hong Kong: Zhonghua shuju, 1972 reprint.

11 Yang Bojun, p. 198.

12 C.T. Hsia, *The Classic Chinese Novel*, New York: Columbia University Press, 1968, pp. 75–114.

13 In fact, unlike Guan Yu who is often depicted with two men on his side, Confucius is usually shown in iconography as a solitary and dominating figure, beyond other human comparisons. This portrayal only became standard after his apotheosis in the Han Dynasty. See the fascinating account in Deborah Sommer, 'The Unlearned Sage? The Early Iconography of Confucius and Its Textual Referents', unpublished paper presented at the XXXVIth International Congress of Asian and North African Studies (September 2000).

14 Joseph R. Allen, 'Dressing and Undressing the Chinese Woman Warrior', *Positions* 4.2 (1996), p. 346.

15 See for example Donald J. Munro, *The Concept of Man in Early China*, Stanford University Press, 1969.

16 Yang Bojun, p. 68.

17 James D. Sellmann and Sharon Rowe, 'The Feminine in Confucius', *Asian Culture* 26.3 (1998), p. 1.

18 Sellmann and Rowe, 1998, p. 4.

19 Cai Shangsi, *Zhongguo chuantong sixiang zong pipan* (A Comprehensive Criticism of Traditional Chinese Thought), Shanghai: Tangdai chubanshe, 1950.

20 Zhao Jibin, *Lunyu xintan* (A New Exploration of the *Analects*), Beijing: Renmin chubanshe, 1962.

21 See Kam Louie, *Critiques of Confucius in Contemporary China*, Hong Kong: Chinese University Press, 1980.

22 Chen Shigai, 'Kongzi de lunli sixiang yu zichan jieji rendao zhuyi zhi bijiao yanjiu' (A comparative study of Confucius' ethical thinking and the humanism of the bourgeoisie), *Hubei daxue xuebao* (Hubei University Journal) 2 (1986), pp. 31–36.

23 Kang Youwei, *Kongzi gaizhi kao* (A Study of Confucius as Reformer), first published 1897, reissued Taipei: Taiwan shangwu yinshuguan, 1968.

24 Roger T. Ames, *The Art of Rulership: A Study in Ancient Chinese Political Thought*, Honolulu: University of Hawai'i Press, 1983, p. 4.

25 See Kam Louie, 'In Search of Socialist Capitalism and Chinese Modernisation', *Australian Journal of Chinese Affairs* 12 (1984), pp. 87–96.

26 Xu Mengying, 'Kongzi de jiaoyu sixiang' (Confucius' Educational Thought), *Guangming ribao* (Guangming Daily), 14 June 1954.

27 Chen Jingpan, *Kongzi de jiaoyu sixiang* (Confucius' Educational Thought), Wuhan: Hubei renmin chubanshe, 1957.

28 Liu Shaoqi, *Lun Gongchandang yuan de xiuyang* (On the Self-cultivation of a Communist Party Member), Beijing: Renmin chubanshe, 1962 reprint.

29 Xin Lan, 'Kongzi zai tiyu fangmian de shijian he zhuzhang' (Confucius' Practice and Principles in the Field of Sport), *Xin tiyu* (New Sports) 8 (1962), pp. 13–16.

30 Li Yinnong, 'Lun Kongzi dui laodong de taidu' (On Confucius' Attitudes Towards Labour), *Yangcheng wanbao* (Guangzhou Evening News), 22 March 1962.

31 Liu Xinwu, 'Ban zhuren' (Class Teacher), *Renmin wenxue* (People's Literature) 11 (1977), pp. 16–29.

32 Liu Fudao, 'Yanjing' (Glasses), *Aiqing xiaoshuo ji* (Collected Love Stories), Shanghai: Shanghai wenyi chubanshe, 1979, pp. 1–21.

33 Zhang Xianliang, *Half of Man Is Woman* (trans. Martha Avery), London: Penguin Books, 1989.

34 Xu Quanxing, 'Kongzi yu Mao Zedong: Gujin weida "jiaoyuan"' (Confucius and Mao Zedong: Great 'Teachers' of the Past and Present), *Kongzi yanjiu* (Confucius Research) 4 (1993), p. 4.

35 Ibid., p. 6.

36 Ibid.

37 Liang Xin, 'Shenme jiao "dangdai xin rujia"' (What is a 'Contemporary Neo-Confucianist'?), *Wenhui bao* (Wenhui Daily), 10 June 1986.

38 Tu Wei-ming (ed.), *Confucian Traditions in East Asian Modernity: Moral Education and Economic Culture in Japan and the Four Mini-Dragons*, Cambridge, Mass: Harvard University Press, 1996.

39 Geert Hofstede, *Cultures and Organizations: Software of the Mind*, New York: McGraw-Hill, 1997.

40 Song Zhongfu et al., *Ruxue zai xiandai Zhongguo* (Confucianism in Modern China), Zhengzhou: Zhengzhou guji chubanshe, 1991, p. 353.

41 Kuang Yaming, *Kongzi pingzhuan* (A Critical Biography of Confucius), Jinan: Qilu shushe, 1985.

42 See for example Wang Ruisheng, 'Rujia sixiang yu dongya de xiandaihua' (Confucian Thought and East Asian Modernisation), *Zhongguo zhexueshi* (History of Chinese Philosophy) 4 (1996), pp. 7–11 and 31; and Li Xianghai, 'Rujia lunli yu Dongya xiandaihua' (Confucian Ethics and East Asian Modernisation), *Zhongzhou xuekan* (Zhongzhou Journal) 1 (1997), pp. 64–69.

43 Louie, 'In Search of Socialist Capitalism and Chinese Modernisation'.

44 The conservatism of Chinese intellectuals in the 1990s compared to the previous decade is also evident in other aspects of cultural politics. See Ben Xu, *Disenchanted Democracy: Chinese Cultural Criticism After 1989*, Ann Arbor: University of Michigan Press, 1999.

45 In Europe, a similar transformation took place within Protestantism at the beginning of the Industrial Revolution, indicating that such changes may be symptomatic of a more general capitalist modernity.

46 Kam Louie, *Inheriting Tradition: Interpretations of the Classical Philosophers in Communist China 1949–1966*, Hong Kong: Oxford University Press, 1986.

47 Zang Hong, 'Lüelun rujia de yili guan' (On the Confucians' Attitude Towards Yi-Li), *Xuexi yuekan* (Study Monthly) 4 (1986), p. 21.

48 Miao Runtian, 'Qianlun Kongzi de yili guan ji qi xiandai yiyi' (On Confucius' Attitude Towards Yi-Li and its Modern Significance), *Qilu xuekan* (Qilu Journal) 1 (1989), pp. 55–59.

49 Cited in Song Zhongfu et al., pp. 358–359.

50 Hu Dongyuan, 'Zhongguo chuantong wenhua, shichang jingji, daode jianshe' (Traditional Chinese Culture, The Market Economy, Moral Development), *Xuehai* (Sea of Learning) 1 (1996), pp. 52–54.

51 See for example Ye Ruixin, 'Kongzi de yili guan' (Confucius' Attitudes Towards Yi-Li), *Shanxi daxue xuebao* (Shanxi University Journal) 4 (1998), pp. 33–37.

52 Liu Minghua, 'Rujia yili guan yu fazhan shehuizhuyi shichang jingji' (On the Confucians' Attitudes Towards Yi-Li and the Developing Socialist Market Economy), *Guizhou daxue xuebao* (Guizhou University Journal) 1 (1996), p. 29.

53 Song Xiren, 'Rujia chuantong yili guan yu qingshaonian daode jiaoyu' (On the Confucians' Attitudes Towards Yi-Li and the Moral Education of the Young), *Jiangsu shehui kexue* (Jiangsu Social Sciences) 6 (1993), pp. 119–123.

54 Zhao Jing, 'Kongzi de guanli sixiang he xiandai jingying guanli' (Confucius' Management Ideas and Modern Administration and Management), *Kongzi yanjiu* (Confucius Research) 1 (1989), p. 34.

55 Xu Qixian, 'Lun rujia lunli yu daode guanli' (On Confucian Ethics and Moral Management), *Zhongguo renmin daxue xuebao* (Chinese People's University Journal) 1 (1998), pp. 48–54.

56 Kam Louie and Cheung Chiu-yee, 'Three Kingdoms: The Chinese Cultural Scene Today', in Joseph Y.S. Cheng (ed.), *China Review 1998*, Hong Kong: Chinese University Press, 1998, pp. 543–575.

57 Luo Guojie, 'Guanyu Kongzi yili guan de yidian sikao' (Some Considerations on Confucius' Attitudes Towards Yi-Li), *Xueshu yanjiu* (Academic Research) 3 (1994), pp. 51–53.

58 Pavel Korchagin is the protagonist from the novel *How The Steel Was Tempered*. He represents the 'New Man, the man of the socialist epoch who dares all and achieves all'. Nikolai Ostrovsky, *How The Steel Was Tempered*, part 1, Moscow: Foreign Languages Press, 1952, p. 9.

59 Zhao Weimin (ed.), 'Gaici: Baoer de jiu chuanpiao hainengfou dengshang Bier de kechuan?' (Gates: Can Pavel's Old Ticket Be Used to Board Bill's Passenger Liner?), 8 (2000) *Zhongguo qingnian* (China Youth), pp. 14–15.

60 See Kong Xiangjin and Wang Xinhong, 'Qufu choujian Kongzi wenhua guangchang' (Qufu Raises Money to Build Confucius Culture Square), *Renmin ribao* (People's Daily), 9 April 1999, and Yu Xuecai, 'Rujia sixiang yu Zhongguo lüyou wenhua chuantong' (Confucian Thinking and Traditional Chinese Tourist Culture), *Kongzi yanjiu* (Confucius Research) 2 (1990), pp. 29–33.

61 Michael Backman, *Asian Eclipse: Exposing the Dark Side of Business in Asia*, Singapore: John Wiley & Sons, 1999.

4 SCHOLARS AND INTELLECTUALS: REPRESENTATIONS OF *WEN* MASCULINITY PAST AND PRESENT

1 There are a number of studies of the *caizi jiaren* genre in English. As well as discussions of this genre in the two books by Keith McMahon, he has also written an article which summarises some of his main observations about this genre. Keith McMahon, 'The Classic "Beauty-Scholar" Romance and the Superiority of the Talented Woman', in Angela Zito and Tani E. Barlow (eds), *Body, Subject & Power in China*, University of Chicago Press, 1994, pp. 227–252. See also Richard C. Hessney, 'Beyond Beauty and Talent: The Moral and Chivalric Self in The Fortunate Union', in Robert E. Hegel and Richard C. Hessney (ed.), *Expressions of Self in Chinese Literature*, New York: Columbia University Press, 1985, pp. 214–250.

2 Yin Guoguang and Ye Junyuan (eds), 'Qianyan' (Preface), *Ming Qing yanqing xiaoshuo daguan* (Comprehensive Collection of Romantic Fiction from the Ming and Qing Dynasties), vol. 1. Beijing: Huaxia chubanshe, 1993, p. iii.

3 Wang Zejun and Long Tao (eds), 'Qianyan' (Preface), *Zhongguo yanqing xiaoshuo daguan* (Comprehensive Collection of Chinese Romantic Fiction), Chengdu: Chengdu chubanshe, 1992, p. 1.

4 The love story between the talented scholar Sima Xiangru and the beautiful widow Zhuo Wenjian, recorded by Sima Qian (145–90BC), for example, is collected in ibid., pp. 6–11.

5 John Minford and Joseph S.M. Lau (eds), *Classical Chinese Literature: An Anthology of Translations*, vol, 1: *From Antiquity to the Tang Dynasty*, New York: Columbia University Press, 2000, p. 1047.

6 The *chuanqi* is a short story form that flourished in the Tang Dynasty. It is written in the classical language and is quite short, of around one or two thousand characters. It is highly stylised and the narrator usually assumes an 'objective' viewpoint, so that the story gives the impression of truthfulness and verifiability.

7 Wang Shifu, *Xixiang ji* (The Story of the West Wing) (annotated Wang Jisi), Shanghai: Shanghai guji chubanshe, 1978. Little is known about Wang Shifu, but it is believed that he lived in the Yuan Dynasty in the thirteenth century and composed about fourteen plays.

8 See Huang Qiang, 'Ming Qing "Xi xiang re" de yige zhongyao yuanyin' (One Important Reason for the Continuance of the 'West Wing Fever' of the Ming and Qing Dynasties), *Hebei xuekan* (Hebei Journal) 3 (1999), pp. 69–73.

9 For a modern feminist and humorous re-interpretation of the classic scholar–beauty tales in which the women do things like spotting talents and sponsoring them (in the plural) to take the examinations in the hope that one of them will pass the examinations and return to pay the 'dividends', see Kong Huiyi (Eva Hung), *Fujie xiandaiban caizi jiaren* (Women's Liberation Modern Edition Talented Scholars and Beautiful Women), Hong Kong: Maitian wenxue, 1996.

10 Martin W. Huang, *Literati and Self-Re/Presentation: Autobiographical Sensibility in the Eighteenth-Century Chinese Novel*, Stanford University Press, 1995, p. 29.

11 Ibid., p. 31.

12 Quoted in the *Hanyu dazidian* (The Chinese Character Dictionary), Chengdu: Sichuan cishu chubanshe, 1993, p. 766.

13 In the civil service examination process, a graduate of the first degree is called the *xiucai*, with *xiu* meaning 'refined' or 'accomplished'. Thus, the most common literati, the *xiucai* (often translated simply as scholar), who normally would be pursuing further study, were people whose *cai* was 'refined' by the primary examination.

14 See Gansu shifan daxue zhongwenxi (ed.), *Hanyu chengyu huishi* (A Compendium of Chinese Idioms and Their Explanations), no publisher or date given, p. 536.

15 Collected in Wang Zejun and Long Tao (eds), *Zhongguo yanqing xiaoshuo daguan*, pp. 138–156. James R. Hightower's translation is used here. Hightower, 'Yüan Chen and "The Story of Yingying"', *Harvard Journal of Asiatic Studies* 33 (1973), p. 93.

16 Ibid., p. 94.
17 Ibid., p. 123.
18 Ibid., p. 122.
19 Ibid., p. 103.
20 Ibid., p. 97.
21 It is interesting that neither Miss Ren nor Xiaoyu are from respectable families. Ren is a fox-fairy and Xiaoyu a courtesan. The heroes, too, cannot be considered *junzi*. Zheng Liu is good at martial arts while Li Yi has no self-control whatsoever. In the context of *wen-wu*, they 'deserve' their fates. The stories are collected in Wang Zejun and Long Tao (eds), pp. 60–63 and pp. 90–103.
22 Hightower, p. 96.
23 Ibid., p. 102.
24 Hsu Pi-ching, 'Courtesans and Scholars in the Writings of Feng Menglong: Transcending Status and Gender', *Nan-nü: Men, Women and Gender in Early and Imperial China* 2.1 (2000), p. 77. This article has an excellent section on Ming appreciation of the Tang stories.
25 First published in 1657, the *Rou putuan* has been translated a number of times. The latest English rendition is Li Yu, *The Carnal Prayer Mat* (trans. Patrick Hanan), London: Arrow Books, 1990.
26 Robert E. Hegel, *The Novel in Seventeenth Century China*, New York: Columbia University Press, 1981, pp. 166–187.
27 Although it is derived from 'The Story of Yingying', the immediate source for *The Story of the West Wing* is the *Xixiang ji zhugongdiao* by Dong Jieyuan (fl. 1189–1208). An introduction and translation to this work is available. Ch'en Li-li (trans.), *Master Tung's Western Chamber Romance: A Chinese Chantefable*, Cambridge University Press, 1976. The *zhugongdiao* is a form of story-telling with verse (for singing) and prose (for narration). It flourished in the twelfth century.
28 For a standard Chinese interpretation of the new versions of this story, see the entries in Ma Liangchun and Li Futian (eds), *Zhongguo wenxue dacidian* (Dictionary of Chinese Literature), vol. 3. Tianjin: Tianjin renmin chubanshe, 1991, pp. 1840–1842.
29 Song Geng, 'Wax Spear-head: The Construction of Masculinity in Yuan Drama', *Tamkang Review* 30.1 (2000), p. 220. I should acknowledge that I have benefited from the many insights of this paper in the writing of this section.
30 Even the published editions of the text had undergone a number of transformations so that some were targeted at 'ignorant men and women'. See the account in Anne McLaren, *Chinese Popular Culture and Ming Chantefables*, Leiden: E.J. Brill, 1998, pp. 49–52.
31 Song Geng, p. 209.
32 Ibid., pp. 242–243.
33 C.T. Hsia, 'A Critical Introduction' in Wang Shifu, *The Romance of the Western Chamber* (trans. S.I. Hsiung), New York: Columbia University Press, 1968, p. xv.
34 All the examples of the *caizi* cited in Zhang Wenhong & Ji Dejun, 'Caizi xingxiang moshi de wenhua xinli chanshi' (A Cultural Psychological Interpretation of the Image Pattern of the *caizi*), *Zhongshan daxue xuebao*

(Zhongshan University Journal) 5 (1996), p. 111, for example, obtain a degree in their careers.

35 From the blurb in the back cover of Zhang Xianliang, *Getting Used to Dying* (trans. Martha Avery), London: HarperCollins, 1991.

36 See for example Jeffrey C. Kinkley, 'A Bettelheimian Interpretation of Chang Hsien-liang's Concentration-Camp Novels', *Asia Major* 4.2 (1991), pp. 83–113. Kinkley argues that Zhang Yonglin, the protagonist of *Half of Man Is Woman*, is in effect a 'concentration camp survivor' (p. 100). Other 'labour-camp' articles on Zhang appear in the same issue of *Asia Major*. See Yenna Wu, 'Women as Sources of Redemption in Chang Hsien-liang's Labor-Camp Fiction', pp. 115–131; and Philip F. Williams, '"Remolding" and the Chinese Labor Camp Novel', pp. 133–149.

37 Martha Avery, 'Translator's Introduction', in Zhang Xianliang, *Half of Man Is Woman*, p. xii.

38 Other critics have also noted the connection between the beautiful women in Zhang Xianliang's fiction and Yingying. See Yenna Wu, 'Women as Sources of Redemption', p. 129.

39 Zhang Xianliang, 'Ling yu rou' (Flesh and Soul), first published in *Shuofang* in 1980; reprinted in Zhang Xianliang, *Zhang Xianliang xuanji* (Selected Works of Zhang Xianliang), vol. I, Tianjin: Baihua wenyi chubanshe, 1985, pp.138–165. This short story was part of the campaign to attack the 'blood-line' theory that class loyalty is passed from one generation to the next, a campaign which was waged around 1980.

40 Gang Yue, *The Mouth That Begs: Hunger, Cannibalism, and the Politics of Eating in Modern China*, Durham: Duke University Press, 1999, p. 195.

41 Ibid., p. 197

42 Zhang Xianliang, 'Lühua shu' (Mimosa), reprinted in *Zhang Xianliang xuanji*, vol. 3, p. 291.

43 Zhang Xianliang, 'Mimosa' (trans. Gladys Yang), in *Mimosa*, Beijing: Chinese Literature, 1985, p.137. Yang translates '*rourou*' as 'pudgy', which is more idiomatic but 'meat' is more accurate.

44 Ibid., p. 135.

45 Ibid., p. 171.

46 Ibid., p. 132.

47 Ibid., p. 55.

48 Gao Song, *Zhang Xianliang xiaoshuo lun* (On Zhang Xianliang's fiction), Chengdu: Sichuan wenyi chubanshe, 1986, p. 101.

49 Zhang Xianliang, *Mimosa*, p. 151.

50 Ibid.

51 See for example Zhou Weibo, 'Zhang Yonglin shi ge wei junzi' (Zhang Yonglin is a Fake Gentleman). Originally published in *Wenhui bao* (Wenhui Daily), 7 October 1985, reprinted in Ningxia renmin chubanshe (ed.), *Ping 'Nanren de yiban shi nüren'* (Criticisms of 'Half of Man Is Woman'), Yinchuan: Ningxia renmin chubanshe, 1987, pp. 4–6. For an opposing view, see Cai Kui, 'Xiguan yu congrong de tanlun ta' (Getting Used to Talking About It in a Calm Manner), originally published in *Dangdai zuojia pinglun* (Critiques of Contemporary Writers) 2 (1986), reprinted in Ningxia renmin chubanshe (ed.), pp. 100–110.

52 See for example Yenna Wu, 'The Interweaving of Sex and Politics in Zhang Xianliang's *Half of Man Is Woman*', *Journal of the Chinese Language Teachers Association* 27.1/2 (1992), pp. 1–27.

53 Zhong Xueping, 'Male Suffering and Male Desire: The Politics of Reading *Half of Man Is Woman*', in Christina K. Gilmartin, Gail Hershatter, Lisa Rofel, Tyrene White (eds), *Engendering China: Women, Culture, and the State*, Cambridge, Mass: Harvard University Press, 1994, p. 191.

54 Martha L. Wagner, 'Reviews: *Half of Man Is Woman*', *Modern Chinese Literature* 5.1 (1989), p. 142.

55 See for example Huang Ziping, 'Zhengmian zhankai ling yu rou de bodou' (Directly Open Up a Struggle Between Flesh and Mind), originally published in *Wenyi bao*, 7 October 1985, reprinted in Ningxia renmin chubanshe (ed.), pp. 1–3; and Feng Gu, 'Women kan *Nanren de yiban shi nüren*' (Looking at *Half of Man Is Woman*), *Dangdai zuojia pinglun* 4 (1986), pp. 112–115.

56 Kwok-kan Tam, 'Sexuality and Power in Zhang Xianliang's Novel *Half of Man Is Woman*', *Modern Chinese Literature* 5.1 (1989), p. 69.

57 Ibid.

58 See my discussion of this phenomenon in the early years of the Communist regime in Kam Louie, *Inheriting Tradition: Interpretations of the Classical Philosophers in Communist China 1949–1966*, Oxford University Press, 1986, pp. 91–128.

59 A recent example can be seen in Gao Xingjian's novel, *Lingshan*, first published in Taiwan in 1990. English translation, *Soul Mountain* (trans. Mabel Lee), Sydney: HarperCollins, 2000.

60 See my essay on *Soul Mountain*. Kam Louie, 'In Search of the Chinese Soul in the Mountains of the South', *The China Journal* 45 (2001), pp. 145–149.

61 Xueping Zhong, *Masculinity Besieged?* Durham, NC: Duke University Press, 2000, p. 65.

62 The identification of orgasm with death is not that uncommon. The French expression 'la petite mort', for example, refers to the denouement of sexual climax. As Xueping Zhong has shown, however, Zhang's conflation of sex and death has the effect of justifying a misogynistic view of women (ibid., pp. 71–75).

63 Geremie R. Barmé, 'To Screw Foreigners Is Patriotic: China's Avant-Garde Nationalists', *The China Journal* 34 (1995), pp. 209–34.

64 Zhang Xianliang, *Getting Used to Dying* (trans. Martha Avery), p. 301.

65 The most controversial and best-known is Jia Pingwa's *Defunct Capital*, in which a writer is highly attractive sexually although he doesn't seem to do very much socially to deserve that attractiveness. The depiction of this writer is very much like a typical *wenren* of traditional literature except that he doesn't have to pass any imperial examinations. Jia Pingwa, *Feidu* (Defunct Capital), first published in Beijing in 1993, reprinted Hong Kong: Tiandi tushu youxiangongsi, 1996.

66 Zhang Xianliang, *Getting used to Dying* (trans. Martha Avery), p. 212.

67 The intense emotionalism caused by sexual competition between the different racial groups is illustrated well by the uproar following an article published in Australia in January 1994. The author, a Chinese woman living in Sydney, claimed that white men were better lovers than Chinese men. The

article generated a huge backlash in the Sydney media. For a summary of the controversy, see Yong Zhong, 'What's Behind White Masks and Yellow Skin: A Postcolonial Critique of a Chinese Sex Debate in Sydney', in Wenche Ommundsen (ed.), *Bastard Moon: Essays on Chinese-Australian Writing*, Special Issue of *Otherland* 7 (2001), pp. 56–72.

68 *Beijingers in New York* (*Beijingren zai Niuyue*) (dir. Zheng Xiaolong and Feng Xiaogang, CCTV and Beijing TV, 1993); *Foreign Babes in Beijing* (*Yangniu zai Beijing*) (dir. Wang Binglin and Li Jianxin, Beijing Film Studio, 1996).

69 Sheldon H. Lu, 'Soap Opera in China: The Transnational Politics of Visuality, Sexuality, and Masculinity', *Cinema Journal* 30.1 (2000), p. 37.

70 Zhang Xianliang, *Getting Used to Dying* (trans. Martha Avery), pp. 70–71. This use of a 'bought' woman for male bonding is similar to that described by Anne Allison's ethnography of the workings of a Japanese nightclub. See Allison, *Nightwork: Sexuality, Pleasure, and Corporate Masculinity in a Tokyo Hostess Club*, Chicago University Press, 1996.

71 Zhang Xianliang, *Getting Used to Dying* (trans. Martha Avery), p. 285.

72 Jiang Zilong, 'Manager Qiao Assumes Office' (trans. Wang Mingjie), *All the Colours of the Rainbow*, Beijing: Chinese Literature, 1983, pp. 130–178. This collection contains other stories by Jiang on the theme of reforms.

73 Zhang Xianliang, *Nanren de fengge* (Man's Style), first published in 1983, Taiwanese edition, Taipei: Yuanjing chubanshiye gongsi, 1988.

74 Jing Wang, *High Culture Fever: Politics, Aesthetics, and Ideology in Deng's China*, Berkeley: University of California Press, 1996, p. 264.

75 Cliff Cheng, '"We Choose Not To Compete": The "Merit" Discourse in the Selection Process, and Asian and Asian American Men and Their Masculinity', in Cliff Cheng (ed.), *Masculinities in Organizations*, Thousand Oaks, CA: Sage Publications, 1996, pp. 177–200.

5 THE WORKING-CLASS HERO: IMAGES OF *WU* IN TRADITIONAL AND POST-MAO FICTION

1 The issue of who belonged to what class was a contentious one in the early years of the Chinese Communist movement. Mao Zedong's 1927 Report on the Hunan peasantry effectively 'Sinicised' Marxism by giving the poor peasants a proletarian status in the Marxist class schema. Mao Zedong, 'Report on an Investigation of the Peasant Movement in Hunan', *Selected Works of Mao Tse-tung*, vol. 1, Beijing: Foreign Languages Press, 1967, pp. 23–59. In post-Mao China, class is no longer a key concept to interpret and change the world, and 'working-class hero' carries more a John Lennon style emotional impact than any specific, scientific entity.

2 C.T. Hsia, *The Classic Chinese Novel: A Critical Introduction*, New York: Columbia University Press, 1968, p. 86.

3 W.J.F. Jenner, 'A Knife in My Ribs for a Mate: Reflections on Another Chinese Tradition', The Fifty-fourth George Ernest Morrison Lecture in Ethnology 1993, Canberra: Australian National University.

4 A national campaign was waged against Song Jiang's 'capitulationism' in 1975. For an example of the way his 'crimes' were dissected, see Zhang Peiheng and Huang Lin, *Song Jiang xi* (An Analysis of Song Jiang), Shanghai: Renmin chubanshe, 1975.

5 Song Jiang is also one of the very few members of the Liangshan gang with no martial arts skills. The others are Chai Jin and Wu Yong. However, not having *wu* only means that these men take the leadership role very 'naturally'.

6 See Wolfram Eberhard, *Dictionary of Chinese Symbols*, Singapore: Federal Publications, 1990, pp. 237–238.

7 It should be remembered that apart from a handful of names in the novel which may have a historical basis (and Wu Song's is not one of them), the novel is mostly fiction, so that the heroes' names may not be entirely incidental.

8 Shi Nai'an, *Shuihu zhuan* (*All Men Are Brothers*), vol. 1. Taipei: Lianjing chuban shiye gongsi, 1987, pp. 304–305. There are of course numerous translations of this classic novel. I have used my own translation here because the word *haohan* is understandably interpreted into English in a variety of ways.

9 I have quoted from Shapiro's translation here. Shi Nai'an and Luo Guanzhong, *Outlaws of the Marsh*, vol. 1 (trans. Sidney Shapiro), Beijing: Foreign Languages Press, 1980, p. 356.

10 Zhou Guangkuo, '*Shuihu* zenyang miaoxie Wu Song da hu' (How Does *All Men Are Brothers* Describe Wu Song Killing the Tiger), in Zuojia chubanshe bianjibu (ed.), *Shuihu yanjiu lunwen ji* (Research Articles on *All Men Are Brothers*), Beijing: Zuojia chubanshe, 1957, pp. 180–188.

11 Hsia, p. 100.

12 It should be remembered that in the Chinese consciousness, tigers are often associated with dragons and have gained mythological status. This is seen in common idioms like '*longteng huyue*' (dragons leap and tigers bound) and '*longzheng hudou*' (contest of dragon and tiger).

13 The author of this classic novel published in the late sixteenth century is unknown. Clement Egerton has translated the entire novel into English with the help of Lao She: *The Golden Lotus*, 4 vols, London: Routledge & Kegan Paul Ltd, 1939.

14 Shi Nai'an and Luo Guangzhong, p. 364.

15 Shi Nai'an, p. 368. I have used the translation by Maram Epstein, 'Inscribing the Essentials: Culture and the Body in Ming-Qing Fiction', *Ming Studies* 41 (1999), p. 25.

16 Ibid.

17 The Cultural Revolution is the culmination of this trend. For a list of these characteristics, see Lan Yang, *Chinese Fiction of the Cultural Revolution*, Hong Kong University Press, 1998, pp. 33–120.

18 Sun Shaoxian, *Nüxing zhuyi wenxue* (Feminist Literature), Shenyang: Liaoning daxue chubanshe, 1987, p. 68.

19 Zhang Jie, 'The Ark' (trans. Stephen Hallett), in Chinese Literature (eds), *Love Must Not Be Forgotten*, Beijing: Panda, 1987, p. 152

20 Fan Yang, *Yanggang de huichen* (The Decline of Masculine Power), Beijing: Guoji wenhua chubanshe, 1988, p. 200.

21 Sun Longji, *Zhongguo wenhua de 'shenceng jiegou'* (The 'Deep Structure' of Chinese culture), Hong Kong: Jixianshe, 1983, p. 213. The 'emasculation' of men due to the advances of feminism was of course a common complaint in the West as well. See for example Susan Faludi, *Stiffed: The Betrayal of the Modern Man*, London: Chatto & Windus, 1999.

22 See for example Scott Donaldson, *By Force of Will: The Life and Art of Ernest Hemingway*, New York: Viking, 1977, for a discussion of Hemingway's attitudes to love and sex. I have chosen Hemingway here as an illustration because he has often been cited by Chinese critics as a Western writer who best embodies the spirit of the 'real man'.

23 S. Moore, 'Getting a bit of the other: The pimps of postmodernism', in Rowena Chapman and Jonathan Rutherford (eds), *Male Order: Unwrapping Masculinity*, London: Lawrence & Wishart, 1988, pp. 165–166.

24 Cao Wenxuan, *Zhongguo bashi niandai wenxue xianxiang yanjiu* (A Study of Chinese Literature in the 1980s), Beijing: Beijing daxue chubanshe, 1988, pp. 251–267.

25 Emily Honig and Gail Hershatter note that the craze to find the 'real man' was so strong in the 1980s that a magazine devoted exclusively to this issue, titled *Nanzihan* (Real Men), was established. Honig and Hershatter, *Personal Voices: Chinese Women in the 1980's*, Stanford University Press, 1988, p. 101.

26 Jia Pingwa, a native of Shangzhou in Shanxi province, was born in 1952. During the Cultural Revolution, he worked in the villages as a peasant. He entered university in 1972 and began writing the year after. He has written numerous novels, novelettes, and collections of short stories, poetry, and essays. He won the Mobil Pegasus Prize with his 1987 novel Jia Pingwa, *Turbulence: A novel* (trans. Howard Goldblatt), Baton Rouge: Louisiana State University Press, 1991. 'Renji' first appeared in *Wenhui yuekan* (Literary Monthly) 10 (1985), pp. 2–12. It is translated as 'How Much Can A Man Bear?' by Zhu Hong (in Zhu Hong (ed. and trans.), *The Chinese Western*, New York: Ballantine, 1988, pp. 1–52). Except for the title, I have used Zhu Hong's translation throughout.

27 Zhu Hong (ed. and trans.).

28 Curiously, *La Condition Humaine* is in its Penguin translation masculinised into English as *Man's Estate*. See André Malraux, *Man's Estate* (trans. Alastair Macdonald), Harmondsworth: Penguin Books, 1961.

29 Jia Pingwa, *Feidu* (Defunct Capital), first published in Beijing in 1993, reissued Hong Kong: Tiandi tushu youxian gongsi, 1996.

30 Jia Pingwa, 'How Much Can A Man Bear?' in Zhu Hong (ed. and trans.), pp. 3–4.

31 For a detailed and scholarly treatment of the development of *yin-yang* and its relationship to the Five Elements Theory, see Joseph Needham, *Science and Civilisation in China*, vol. 2: *History of Scientific Thought*, Cambridge University Press, 1954, pp. 216–345.

32 Baishui, the other female character in the story, is unambiguously named 'Plain Water'. The author must have deliberately chosen this name to show how this character, who is the most pathetic and most defenceless in the story, is not more than just plain water, the female essence, transformed into human shape.

33 Zheng Wanlong, 'Xiagu' (The Canyon), in Zheng Wanlong, *You ren qiao men* (Somebody is Knocking on the Door), Shenyang: Chunfeng wenyi chubanshe, 1986, p. 71.

34 Ibid., p. 15.

35 Shi Nai'an and Luo Guangzhong, p. 170.

36 Hsia, pp. 75–114.

37 Kam Louie, *Between Fact and Fiction: Essays on Post-Mao Chinese Literature & Society*, Sydney: Wild Peony, 1989, pp. 76–102.

38 Guangzi's extreme mood swings reflect the conflicting ideologies encased in the whole fraternity ideal. In a recent article in which he examines three fratricide cases in late Qing, Adrian Davis argues convincingly that the opposing demands of fraternity (from egalitarian love to hierarchical obedience) can, when there is competition for scarce resources, lead to murder. Adrian Davis, 'Fraternity and Fratricide in Late Imperial China', *The American Historical Review* 105.5 (2000), pp. 1630–1640. Guangzi does not murder Lamao here, but the implicit competition over Liangliang causing the latter's death is obvious.

39 Many of these tales are collected in Pu Songling, *Liaozhai zhiyi* (Strange Tales from the Leisure Studio), Hong Kong: Shangwu yinshuguan, 1963. See in particular 'Hongyu' (Red Jade, pp. 103–107) and 'Nie Xiaoqian' (pp. 54–59).

40 Jia Pingwa, 'How Much Can A Man Bear?', p. 19.

41 Ye Weilin, 'Five girls and one rope' (trans. Zhou Shizong and Diane Simmons), *Fiction* 8 (2 and 3) 1987, pp. 96–114.

42 Charles Humana and Wang Wu, *The Ying-Yang: The Chinese Way of Love*, London: Tandem, 1971, pp. 62–80.

43 Jiang Yinxiang (ed.), *Shijing yizhu* (Book of Songs Translated and Annotated), Beijing: Zhongguo shudian, 1982, pp. 4–6.

44 Humana and Wang, p. 68.

45 Michel Foucault, *The Use of Pleasure: The History of Sexuality*, vol. 2 (trans. Robert Hurley), Harmondsworth: Penguin, 1987, pp. 80–81.

46 Jia Pingwa, 'How Much Can A Man Bear?', p. 10

47 Liu Dalin, *Xing shehuixue* (Sociology of Sex), Ji'nan: Shandong renmin chubanshe, 1988, p. 62.

48 Generally regarded as the best classic novel of manners, *The Dream of Red Mansions* first appeared in the mid-eighteenth century. It is also translated as *Dream of Red Chambers* and *Story of the Stone*. An easily accessible recent edition is Cao Xueqin, *Honglou meng: yi–si* (The Dream of Red Mansions: vols 1–4), Beijing: Beijing shifan daxue chubanshe, 1987.

49 R.H. Van Gulik, *Sexual Life in Ancient China*, Leiden: E.J. Brill, 1974, p. 296.

50 Michael S. Kimmel (ed.), *Changing Men: New Directions in Research on Men and Masculinity*, Newbury Park, CA: Sage Publications, 1987, p. 124.

51 See Marilyn Young, 'Chicken Little in China: Some Reflections on Women', in Arif Dirlik and Maurice Meisner (eds), *Marxism and the Chinese Experience*, Armonk, NY: M.E. Sharpe, 1989, pp. 253–268. She observes that women face similar dilemmas in the restoration of traditional gender roles in the post-Mao era.

52 Andy Metcalf and Martin Humphries (eds), *The Sexuality of Men*, London: Pluto Press, 1985, p. 1.

53 Louie, pp. 38–48.

54 For example, see the treatment of the PLA soldiers in Li Cunbao, *Gaoshan xia de huahuan* (The Wreath at the Foot of the Mountain), Ji'nan: Shandong wenyi chubanshe, 1984.

6 WOMEN'S VOICES: THE IDEAL 'WOMAN'S MAN' IN THE TWENTIETH
CENTURY

1 Yue Ming-Bao, 'Gendering the Origins of Modern Chinese Fiction', in Tongling Lu (ed.), *Gender and Sexuality in Twentieth-Century Chinese Literature and Society*, Albany: State University of New York Press, 1993, p. 48.

2 Louise Edwards, 'Consolidating a Socialist Patriarchy: The Women Writers' Industry and "Feminist" Literary Criticism', in Antonia Finnane and Anne McLaren (eds), *Dress, Sex and Text in Chinese Culture*, Clayton: Monash Asia Institute, 1999, pp. 183–197.

3 Tani E. Barlow, 'Introduction', in Tani E. Barlow (ed.), *I Myself Am a Woman: Selected Writings of Ding Ling*, Boston: Beacon Press, 1989, p. 25.

4 David Der-wei Wang, 'Feminist Consciousness in Modern Male Fiction', in Michael Duke (ed.), *Modern Chinese Women Writers: Critical Appraisals*, Armonk, NY: M.E. Sharpe, 1989, p. 254.

5 For a discussion of the relationship between the 'new woman' and literature, see Wendy Larson, *Women and Writing in Modern China*, Stanford University Press, 1998, pp. 131–165.

6 Further evidenced, as we saw earlier, by the appearance of magazines in the 1980s such as *Nanzihan* (Real Men).

7 For details about these authors, see Bonnie S. McDougall and Kam Louie, *The Literature of China in the Twentieth Century*, London: Hurst, 1997.

8 Ding Ling, 'Miss Sophia's Diary' (trans. Tani E. Barlow), in Barlow (ed.), pp. 49–81.

9 Ru Zhijuan, 'Lilies' (trans. Gladys Yang), in *Lilies and Other Stories*, Beijing: Panda Books, 1985, pp. 7–19.

10 Wang Anyi, *Brocade Valley* (trans Bonnie S. McDougall and Chen Maiping), New York: New Directions, 1992.

11 Some critics take a more unkind interpretation by casting Sophia as being doubly vicitimised by being trapped between feudal and bourgeois thinking. Zhang Yongquan, 'Zai heianzhong xunqiu guangming de nüxing – Shafei xingxiang de zai pingjia' (Women Who Search for Light in the Midst of Darkness – A Reappraisal of the Sophia Image), *Ding Ling zuopin pinglunji* (Critical Essays on Ding Ling's Works), Beijing: Zhongguo wenlian chubangongsi, 1984, pp. 143–163.

12 See for example Rou Shi, 'A Hired Wife' in Lu Xun and Others, *Masterpieces of Modern Chinese Fiction 1919–1949*, Beijing: Foreign Languages Press, 1983, pp. 205–229, and Shen Congwen, 'The Husband', in ibid., pp. 398–417.

13 For its workings in Western literature, see Elisabeth Ermarth, 'Fictional Consensus and Female Casualties', in C.G. Heilbrun and M.H. Higgonet (eds), *The Representation of Women*, Baltimore: Johns Hopkins University Press, 1983, pp. 1–18.

14 Bonnie S. McDougall, 'Disappearing Women and Disappearing Men in May Fourth Narrative: A Post-Feminist Survey of Short Stories by Mao Dun, Bing Xin, Ling Shuhua and Shen Congwen', *Asian Studies Review* 22.4 (1998), p. 451. See also Louise Edwards, 'Policing the Modern Woman in Republican China', *Modern China* 26.2 (2000), pp. 115–147.

15 Understandably, this trend is reflected in the literary analyses of these works. Furthermore, as Jankowiak observes, this tendency is also evident in much of

the scholarship on Chinese gender. William Jankowiak, 'Chinese Women, Gender, and Sexuality: A Critical Review of Recent Studies', *Bulletin of Concerned Asian Scholars* 31.1 (1999), p. 31. Although this observation seems fairly incontestable, it is interesting to see that it has obviously displeased some scholars in the field. See Jude Howell et al., 'Responses', *Bulletin of Concerned Asian Scholars* 31.1 (1999), pp. 37–47.

16　For examples, see the stories in the 'superhuman maiden' and 'ghost wife' sections in Y.W. Ma and Joseph S.M. Lau (eds), *Traditional Chinese Stories: Themes and Variations*, New York: Columbia University Press, 1978, pp. 337–409.

17　Fatima Wu, 'Foxes in Chinese Supernatural Tales (Part I)', *Tamkang Review* 17.2 (1986), p. 141.

18　Cited in Yi-tsi Mei Feuerwerker, *Ding Ling's Fiction: Ideology and Narrative in Modern Chinese Literature*, Cambridge, Mass: Harvard University Press, 1982, p. 30.

19　Amy Tak-yee Lai, 'Liberation, Confusion, Imprisonment: The Female Self in Ding Ling's "Diary of Miss Sophie" and Zhang Jie's "Love Must Not be Forgotten"', *Comparative Literature and Culture* 3 (1998), pp. 95–96.

20　Ding Ling, 'Miss Sophia's Diary', in Barlow, p. 52.

21　Lydia H. Liu, 'Invention and Intervention: The Making of a Female Tradition in Modern Chinese Literature', in Ellen Widmer and David Der-wei Wang (eds), *From May Fourth to June Fourth: Fiction and Film in Twentieth-Century China*, Cambridge, MA: Harvard University Press, 1993, p. 207.

22　Li Daxuan, *Ding Ling yu Shafei xilie xingxiang* (Images of Ding Ling and Sophia), Changsha: Hunan wenyi chubanshe, 1991, p. 15.

23　Ding Ling, 'Miss Sophia's Diary', in Barlow, p. 55.

24　Lydia H. Liu, 'Invention and Intervention', p. 201.

25　Lydia H. Liu, *Translingual Practice: Literature, National Culture, and Translated Modernity – China, 1900–1937*, Stanford University Press, 1995, p. 174.

26　The idea that overseas Chinese men could only be successful in making money (and so having neither *wen* nor *wu*) was a widely accepted one, giving rise to the stereotypes discussed in the next chapter.

27　Ding Ling, 'Miss Sophia's Diary', in Barlow, p. 71.

28　Ibid., p. 73.

29　This is the argument advanced by critics such as Shunzhu Wang, 'The Double-Voiced Feminine Discourses in Ding Ling's "Miss Sophie's Diary" and Zora Neale Hurston's *Their Eyes Were Watching God*', *Tamkang Review* 28.1 (1997), pp. 131–158.

30　Feuerwerker, p. 50.

31　Zheng Daqun, 'Nüxing jinji yu hou xinshiqi nüxing xiezuo' (The Prohibition on Women and Post-neo-feminist writing), *Wenyi pinglun* (Literary and Art Criticism) 2 (2000), p. 35. See also Ziyun Li, 'The Disappearance and Revival of Feminine Discourse', *Tamkang Review* 30.2 (1999), pp. 55–69.

32　See discussion in Antonia Finnane, 'What Should Chinese Women Wear? A National Problem', *Modern China* 22.2 (1996), pp. 99–131.

33　Deng Youmei, 'At the Precipice' (trans. Hua-yua Li Mowry), in Vivian Ling Hsu (ed.), *Born of the Same Roots: Stories of Modern Chinese Women*, Bloomington: Indiana University Press, 1981, pp. 94–127.

34 See Zong Pu, 'Red Beans' (trans. Geremie Barmé), in W.J.F. Jenner (ed.), *Fragrant Weeds – Chinese Short Stories Once Labelled as 'Poisonous Weeds'*, Hong Kong: Joint Publishing, 1983, pp. 195–228.

35 Details on these military models can be found in *Cihai* (Sea of Words), Shanghai: Shanghai cishu chubanshe, 1980, pp. 599 and 2056.

36 Ru Zhijuan, 'How I Came to Write "Lilies on a Comforter"', in Helen Siu (ed.), *Furrows: Peasants, Intellectuals, and the State*, Stanford University Press, 1990, pp. 297–303.

37 This was later debated by some critics, who accused Ru Zhijuan of not portraying 'heroes of the modern age' (*dangdai yingxiong*). Ouyang Wenbin, 'Shilun Ru Zhijuan de yishu fengge' (On Ru Zhijuan's Artistic Style), in Sun Luxi and Wang Fengbo (eds), *Ru Zhijuan yanjiu zhuanji* (Anthology on Ru Zhijuan Research), Hangzhou: Zhejiang renmin chubanshe, 1982, p. 118.

38 Mao Dun, 'Tan zuijin de duanpian xiaoshuo' (On a Recent Short Story), in ibid., pp. 247–251.

39 Shi Jingping, 'Gechang putongren de xinlingmei' (In Praise of the Beautiful Souls of the Common People'), in ibid., pp. 265–270.

40 Bob Hodge and Kam Louie, *The Politics of Chinese Language and Culture*, London: Routledge, 1998, p. 66.

41 Ru Zhijuan, 'How I Came to Write "Lilies on a Comforter"', p. 297.

42 See for example Lü Yi, 'Chunpu de shipian' (Simple Poetry), in Sun Luxi and Wang Fengbo (eds), pp. 255–280; and Tang Ming, 'Meili de huaduo, chunpu de shipian' (Beautiful Flower, Simple Poetry), in ibid., pp. 261–264.

43 This is in the original Chinese, but not in the English translation. See Ru Zhijuan, 'Baihehua' (Lilies), *Zhongguo dangdai zuopin xuanbian 1949–1986* (Readings from Chinese Writers 1949–1986), vol. 1, Beijing: Sinolingua, 1989, p. 166.

44 Robert E. Hegel, 'Political Integration in Ru Zhijuan's "Lilies"', in Theodore Huters (ed.), *Reading the Modern Chinese Short Story*, Armonk, NY: M.E. Sharpe, 1990, p. 99.

45 Ru Zhijuan, 'Lilies' (trans. Gladys Yang), p. 8.

46 Xueping Zhong, *Masculinity Besieged? Issues of Modern and Male Subjectivity in Chinese Literature of the Late Twentieth Century*, London: Duke University Press, 2000.

47 Margaret Hillenbrand, 'Beleaguered Husbands: Representations of Marital Breakdowns in Some Recent Chinese Fiction', *Tamkang Review* 30.2 (1999), pp. 112–150.

48 Ru Zhijuan, 'Ernü qing', translated as 'Sons and Successors' by Ellen Klempner, in Lee Yee (ed.), *The New Realism: Writings from China After the Cultural Revolution*, New York: Hippocrene Books, 1983, pp. 17–30.

49 Zhang Kangkang, 'Beiji guang' (Northern Lights), *Shouhuo* (Harvest) 3 (1980), pp. 4–61.

50 Chi Li, *Apart from Love*, Beijing: Panda Books, 1994, p. 159.

51 All three stories have been collected in Wang Anyi, *Huangshan zhi lian* (Love in a Barren Mountain), Hong Kong: Nanyue chubanshe, 1988.

52 Chen Xinyuan, 'Xing'ai yu xungen' (Sexual Love and Seeking Roots), in Bo Yang (ed.), *Xiaocheng zhi lian* (Love in a Small Town), Taipei: Linbai chubanshe, 1988, p. 10.

53 Qian Hong, 'Youmei shiluo zhihou' (After Gracefulness Has Declined), *Guangming ribao* (Guangming Daily), 21 August 1987.

54 I will be using the translation by Bonnie S. McDougall and Chen Maiping for this chapter. Wang Anyi, *Brocade Valley*, New York: New Directions, 1992, p. 17.

55 Ibid.

56 Ibid., p. 2.

57 Ibid., p. 3.

58 Yu Dafu, 'Nights of Spring Fever', in *Nights of Spring Fever and Other Stories*, Beijing: Panda Books, 1984, pp. 7–17.

59 Wang Anyi, p. 33.

60 Ibid., p. 64.

61 Ibid., p. 45.

62 Wang Anyi, *Huangshan zhi lian*, p. 94. Wu Liang also makes his point in his critique of *Brocade Valley*. See Wu Liang, 'Ai de jieju yu chulu' (The Way Out for Love), *Shanghai wenxue* (Shanghai Literature) 4 (1987), p. 89.

63 Peng Bin, 'Lun Wang Anyi yishu de fengge de yanbian' (On the Changes in Wang Anyi's Artistic Techniques), *Shehuikexuejia* (The Social Scientist) 6 (1989), pp. 74–78.

64 Quoted in Guo Li, 'Wang Anyi hua "San lian"' (Wang Anyi on the 'Three Loves'), *Zuopin yu zhengming* (Literary Works and Controversy) 3 (1988), p. 76.

65 Helen H. Chen, 'Gender, Subjectivity, Sexuality: Defining a Subversive Discourse in Wang Anyi's Four Tales of Sexual Transgression', in Yingjin Zhang (ed.), *China in a Polycentric World: Essays in Chinese Comparative Literature*, Stanford University Press, 1998, p. 106.

66 Most of the male characters in Chen Ran's work are nearly as bad as the men denounced by the American feminist Andrea Dworkin, *Woman Hating*, New York: E.P. Dutton, 1974.

67 See in particular her novel Chen Ran, *Siren shenghuo* (A Private Life), Beijing: Zuojia chubanshe, 1996.

68 This is also true for the younger writers, those born in the 1970s, a generation of women that I have not considered in this chapter. A recent controversial novel of self-exposure from this generation is Wei Hui, *Shanghai Baby* (trans. Bruce Humes), London: Constable Publishers, 2001.

69 Xiaojiang Li, 'Resisting While Holding the Tradition: Claims for Rights Raised in Literature by Chinese Women Writers in the New Period', *Tamkang Review* 30.2 (1999), p. 108.

70 See Inge Nielsen, 'Modern Chinese Literature Sells Out', *Tamkang Review* 30.3 (2000), p. 100.

71 See discussion in Kam Louie and Chiu-yee Cheung, 'Three Kingdoms: The Chinese Cultural Scene Today', in Joseph Y.S. Cheng (ed.), *China Review* 1998, Hong Kong: Chinese University Press, 1998, p. 550.

72 Kaja Silverman, *The Subject of Semiotics*, Oxford University Press, 1983, p. 185.

73 Judith Butler, *Gender Trouble: Feminism and the Subversion of Identity*, London: Routledge, 1990, p. 25.

7 LAO SHE'S *THE TWO MAS* AND FOREIGN WIVES: CONSTRUCTING *WEN* MASCULINITY FOR THE MODERN WORLD

1 Since Edward Said published his influential *Orientalism* in 1978, there have been a number of excellent studies of the 'feminisation' of indigenous men in the colonies. See for example Mrinalini Sinha, *Colonial Masculinity: The 'Manly Englishman' and the 'Effeminate Bengali' in the Late Nineteenth Century*, Manchester University Press, 1995. On China, however, there is none.

2 Lao She, 'Er Ma' (The Two Mas), in Shu Ji and Shu Yi (eds), *Lao She xiaoshuo quanji* (Complete Stories by Lao She), vol. 2, Wuhan: Changjiang wenyi chubanshe, 1993, pp. 1–250. Unless otherwise stated, I will use the English translation by Kenny K. Huang and David Finkelstein, *The Two Mas*, Hong Kong: Joint Publishing, 1984 (cited henceforth as 'Huang translation').

3 Hu Shi made this call in 1929. For a discussion of this and the controversy which surrounded it, see his 1935 essay 'Chongfen shijiehua yu quanpan xihua' (Total Globalisation and Wholesale Westernisation), in *Hu Shi wencun* (Collected Works of Hu Shi), vol. 4, no. 2, Taipei: Yuandong tushu, 1971, pp. 541–544.

4 Renamed School of Oriental and African Studies in 1938.

5 In fact, after his return from Europe and Singapore, Lao She did not go back to live in Beijing until the People's Republic was established. Many of his short stories in this period do have non-Beijing settings. See discussion in David Wang, 'Lao She's Wartime Fiction', *Modern Chinese Literature* 5.2 (1989), pp. 197–218.

6 Song Yongyi, *Lao She yu Zhongguo wenhua guannian* (Lao She and Chinese Culture), Shanghai: Xuelin chubanshe, 1988, p. 20.

7 V.G. Kiernan, *The Lords of Human Kind: Black Man, Yellow Man, and White Man in an Age of Empire*, New York: Columbia University Press, 1986, p. 164.

8 J.P. May, 'The Chinese in Britain, 1860–1914', in Colin Holmes (ed.), *Immigrants and Minorities in British Society*, London: George Allen & Unwin, 1978, p. 113.

9 Thomas Burke, 'The Chink and the Child', in *Limehouse Nights: Tales of Chinatown*, London: Grant Richards Limited, 1916. The book was extremely popular, reaching its seventh reprint by 1920.

10 Robert Bickers, *Britain in China: Community, Culture and Colonialism 1900–1949*, Manchester University Press, 1999, p. 44. I will return to the film version in the next chapter.

11 Ibid. Bickers gives an excellent summary and analysis of the significant works which shaped British ideas of the Chinese in chapter 4 of his book, pp. 22–66.

12 Quoted in ibid., p. 43.

13 The literature on Sax Rohmer's Fu Manchu is immense. As well as films and stories inspired by this image, there are literally thousands of items such as restaurants, toys and games with this name. There are also numerous websites devoted to this icon. One of the best is probably 'The Page of Fu Manchu' (http://www.njin.net/~knapp/NewsOfFu.htm).

14 Bickers, p. 23.

15 Yu Dafu, 'Sinking' (Chenlun), in *Yu Dafu wenji* (Collected Works of Yu Dafu), vol. 1, Hong Kong: Sanlian shudian, 1982, p. 53.

16 Ma Liangchun and Li Futian (eds), *Zhongguo wenxue dacidian* (Dictionary of Chinese Literature), vol. 2, Tianjin: Tianjin renmin chubanshe, 1991, p. 44.

17 For example, John Fitzgerald, *Awakening China: Politics, Culture, and Class in the Nationalist Revolution*, Stanford University Press, 1996, p. 126.

18 C.T. Hsia, *A History of Modern Chinese Fiction: 1917–1957*, New Haven: Yale University Press, 1971, pp. 171–172.

19 The literature on the diaspora hybrid identity is extensive. For a couple of short introductory essays, see Homi K. Bhabha, 'Culture's In-Between', in Stuart Hall and Paul du Gay (eds), *Questions of Cultural Identity*, London: Sage Publications, 1996, pp. 53–60 and Stuart Hall, 'Cultural Identity and Diaspora' in Patrick Williams and Laura Chrisman (eds), *Colonial Discourse and Post-colonial Theory: A Reader*, New York: Harvester Wheatsheaf, 1993, pp. 392–403.

20 Li Mingguang, 'Chen Daoming shuo "Er Ma"' (Chen Daoming on *The Two Mas*), *Renmin ribao* (People's Daily), 23 February 1999.

21 Ouyang Yu, *Moon Over Melbourne: Poems*, Upper Ferntree Gully, Vic.: Papyrus Publishing, 1997, p. 16.

22 See discussion in Bob Hodge and Kam Louie, *The Politics of Chinese Language and Culture*, London: Routledge, 1998, pp. 143–172.

23 Lu Xun, 'Kung I-chi', in *Selected Stories of Lu Hsun*, Peking: Foreign Languages Press, 1960, pp. 19–24.

24 For information on the lives of these writers, see Bonnie McDougall and Kam Louie, *The Literature of China in the Twentieth Century*, London: Hurst, 1997.

25 Chow Tse-tsung, *The May Fourth Movement: Intellectual Revolution in Modern China*, Stanford University Press, 1967, pp. 45–47.

26 See Kam Louie, *Critiques of Confucius in Contemporary China*, Hong Kong: Chinese University Press, 1980, pp. 1–16.

27 Lu Xun, 'An Incident', in *Selected Stories of Lu Hsun*, pp. 42–44.

28 Zhao Xiaqiu and Zeng Qingrui, *Zhongguo xiandai xiaoshuo shi* (History of Modern Chinese Fiction), Vol. 2, Beijing: Zhongguo renmin daxue chubanshe, 1985, p. 290.

29 Wang, Der-wei David, *Fictional Realism in Twentieth-Century China: Mao Dun, Lao She, Shen Congwen*, New York: Columbia University Press, 1992, p. 126.

30 Leo Oufan Lee, *The Romantic Generation of Modern Chinese Writers*, Cambridge, MA: Harvard University Press, 1973, p. 38.

31 Quoted in ibid., p. 250.

32 See discussion in Hsiao-yen Peng, 'Sex Histories: Zhang Jingsheng's Sexual Revolution', *Tamkang Review* 30.2 (1999), pp. 71–98.

33 Leo Lee, p. 265.

34 Lydia H. Liu, 'Invention and Intervention: The Making of a Female Tradition in Modern Chinese Literature', in Ellen Widmer and David Der-wei Wang (eds), *From May Fourth to June Fourth: Fiction and Film in Twentieth-Century China*. Cambridge, Mass: Harvard University Press, 1993, pp. 194–220.

35 Kang Youwei, *Datong shu* (The Great Commonwealth), first published 1935, reissued Beijing: Guji chubanshe, 1956.

36 Laurence G. Thompson, '*Ta-t'ung Shu* and the *Communist Manifesto*: Some Comparisons', in Jung-pang Lo (ed.), *K'ang Yu-wei: A Biography and a Symposium*, Tucson: University of Arizona Press, 1967, p. 79.

37 Lu Xun, 'My Views on Chastity', in *Lu Xun: Selected Works*, vol. 2, Beijing: Foreign Languages Press, 1980, p. 20.

38 A good illustration is found in Lu Xun, 'The New Year's Sacrifice', *Selected Stories of Lu Hsun*, pp. 125–143.

39 In England in the 1920s and 1930s, there were, at maximum, only around 2000 Chinese. See David Parker, *Through Chinese Eyes: The Cultural Identities of Young Chinese People in Britain*, Aldershot: Avebury, 1995, p. 55.

40 Interestingly, Mrs Winter in the novel observes that they are from the same class (Huang translation, p. 270), demonstrating by the remark her belief that educated, relatively well-off Chinese men are the same as British women of her background.

41 Han Suyin, *The Crippled Tree*, London: Jonathan Cape, 1965. While this novel may not be a factual account of the difficulties faced by a Chinese man married to a white woman in a period of social unrest in China, it does illustrate the added hardships brought on by racial and linguistic difference. I am not arguing that 'mixed marriages' were disasters. Indeed, for many, Chinese men 'won the reputation of making good husbands to women of more races than any other men could' (Kiernan, p. 164). Such findings make the fictional constructions of Chinese men being potential rapists and drug addicts even more poignant.

42 A summary and discussion of the story can be found in McDougall and Louie, pp. 90–93.

43 For information on Sai Jinhua's life and some of the literary works about her, see Lily Xiao Hong Lee, A.D. Stefanowska and Clara Wing-chung Ho (eds), *Biographical Dictionary of Chinese Women: The Qing Period, 1644–1911*, Armonk, NY: M.E. Sharpe, 1998, pp. 182–184.

44 Parker, pp. 59–60.

45 Huang translation, p. 263.

46 Lao She himself later claimed that in the novel, 'none showed any humanity'. Quoted in Zhao Xiaqiu and Zeng Qingrui, p. 290.

47 The literature on race is immense, and this is not the place to engage in the debate on whether it has any scientific merit. For a recent discussion, see *History and Anthropology* 11.2–3 (1999), especially Christine Dureau and Morris Low, 'The Politics of Knowledge: Science, Race and Evolution in Asia and the Pacific' (pp. 131–156) and Morris Low, 'The Japanese Nation in Evolution: W.E. Griffis, Hybridity and the Whiteness of the Japanese Race' (pp. 203–234). In Chinese studies, Frank Dikötter's *The Discourse of Race in Modern China*, London: C. Hurst, 1992, remains a standard reference. While I agree with Dikötter that race 'is a cultural construct', I am less convinced that it bears 'no relationship to objective reality' (p. viii). Whether it corresponds to an objective reality or not, Lao She's novel is a good example of how an apparently nationalist discourse can so easily drift into a racial one.

48 'Race' and 'ethnicity' are often used interchangeably. Again, this is not the place to debate their uses. For the sake of convenience, I use 'ethnic' as meaning belonging to a minority group within a wider cultural (national) population. Like 'race', its use as discourse is important here, and not whether it has an objective referent.

49 See the table of major occupations of Chinese in England between 1901 and 1931 in Parker, p. 55.

50 Herman Scheffauer, 'The Chinese in England: A Growing National Problem', *The London Magazine* June, July (1911). Quoted in Parker, p. 59. While 'workers' and 'Chinatown' may be misnomers, I will adopt these terms as they are used by Lao She in the novel.

51 See in particular the long and bitter indictment in Lao She, pp. 12–13.

52 Lao She, p. 12. I have used my own more literal translation here instead of Huang's.

53 Although Lao She does not mention this icon in the novel, Sax Rohmer's popular Fu Manchu stories were published in Britain around this time. As well as the Fu Manchu websites indicated in n. 13, a more scholarly treatment of the Fu Manchu phenomenon can be found in Jenny Clegg, *Fu Manchu and The 'Yellow Peril': The Making of a Racist Myth*, Stoke-on-Trent: Trentham Books, 1994.

54 Huang translation, p. 297.

55 'Ugly Chinaman' and 'Commie Bastard' probably do more justice to the intended connotations of these names.

56 Lao She, p. 192.

57 Burke, 'Tai Fu and Pansy Greers', in *Limehouse Nights*, pp. 149–168.

58 Zou Rong, 'Geming jun', cited in Ranbir Vohra, *Lao She and the Chinese Revolution*, Cambridge, Mass: East Asian Research Center, Harvard University Press, 1974, p. 7.

59 Vohra, p. 9.

60 Lao She, *Beneath the Red Flag* (trans. Don J. Cohn), Beijing: Panda Books, 1982.

61 Huang translation, p. 159.

62 Ibid., p. 81.

63 Ibid., p. 250.

64 Lu Xun, 'Preface to the First Collection of Short Stories, "Call to Arms"', *Selected Stories of Lu Hsun*, pp. 1–6.

65 The European image of the Chinese was not a static one. However, it reached its most Orientalist depths in late nineteenth and early twentieth centuries. As well as the discussion in Robert Bickers mentioned above, see the changing perceptions described in Raymond Dawson, *The Chinese Chameleon: An Analysis of European Conceptions of Chinese Civilization*, London: Oxford University Press, 1967 and Colin Mackerras, *Western Images of China*, Hong Kong: Oxford University Press, 1989.

66 Benedict Anderson, *Imagined Communities: Reflections on the Origin and Rise of Nationalism*, London: Verso, 1991.

67 Hall, 'Cultural Identity and Diaspora', p. 395.

68 Ralph A. Litzinger, 'Questions of Gender: Ethnic Minority Representations in Post-Mao China', *Bulletin of Concerned Asian Scholars* 32.4 (2000), p. 11.

69 I quote here, with thanks, one of the many perceptive comments by an anonymous reader of this chapter: 'The two Mas are running a "curio" shop. "Curio" was a belittling term for Chinese-produced cultural artefacts which treaty port Westerners collected. The "curio" was the acceptable face of Chinese culture which was otherwise denigrated. Not only are the Mas therefore selling Chinese culture, but they're not even selling it very well'.

70 Lao She, p. 242. I have used my own more literal translation here.

71 Mary C. Wright, *The Last Stand of Chinese Conservatism: The T'ung-chih Restoration, 1862–1874*, Stanford University Press, 1957.

72 Indeed, David Wang quite astutely refers to him as 'even more a dupe than the two Mas'. Wang, *Fictional Realism*, p. 131.

73 Wang Huiyun and Su Qingchang, *Lao She pingzhuan* (A Critical Biography of Lao She), Shijiazhuang: Huashanwenyi chubanshe, 1985, p. 56.

74 Lao She, 'Wo zenyang xie Er Ma' (How I Wrote *The Two Mas*), quoted in ibid.

75 The distinction between 'old' and 'new' money is important, most particularly in Britain before World War II, but this distinction is often glossed over in Chinese writings.

76 For a summary of Asian student numbers in Australia in the 1990s, see Department of Education, Employment and Training table given in Curtis Andressen, 'The Location and Characteristics of Asia-born Overseas Students in Australia', in James E. Coughlan and Deborah J. McNamara (eds), *Asians in Australia: Patterns of Migration and Settlement*, Melbourne: Macmillan, 1997, p. 95.

77 Edmund S.K. Fung and Chen Jie, *Changing Perceptions: The Attitudes of the PRC Chinese Towards Australia and China, 1989–1996*, Brisbane: Griffith University Centre for the Study of Australia Asia Relations, 1996, p. 8.

78 See discussion in C. Lever-Tracy, D. Ip, J. Kitay, I. Phillips and N. Tracy, *Asian Entrepreneurs in Australia, Ethnic Small Business in the Chinese and Indian Communities of Brisbane and Sydney: Report to the Office of Multicultural Affairs*, Department of the Prime Minister and Cabinet, Canberra: Australian Government Publishing Service, 1991.

79 Wu Li, *Qu ge waiguo nüren zuo taitai* (He Married a Foreign Woman), Tianjin: Renmin chubanshe, 1993.

80 Ibid., pp. 4–5.

81 Ibid., p. 8.

82 Ibid., p. 9.

83 However, it could have been, and was, said by men who were from a different class background, and at a much earlier period. See the 'Chinese Impressions of the West', special issue of *Renditions*, 53/54 (2000), especially the section 'My Eyes Were Opened' (statement by Wang Tao, 1828–1897), pp. 159–230.

84 For the case of Australia, see some of the descriptions in Eric Rolls, *Sojourners: The Epic Story of China's Centuries-Old Relationship with Australia*, St Lucia: University of Queensland Press, 1992.

85 Qian Ning, 'Liuxue Meiguo' (Studying in USA), in *Xinhua wenzhai* (New China Digest) 10 (1996), p. 90.

86 Ibid., p. 91.

87 Ibid., p. 95.

88 Edmund Fung and Colin Mackerras, 'Chinese Students in Australia: An Attitudinal Study', in Anthony Milner and Mary Quilty (eds), *Australia in Asia: Episodes*, Melbourne: Oxford University Press, 1998, p. 214.

89 Fung and Mackerras do not make clear what 'Australian' refers to in this article, but the context seems to imply white Australian.

90 Ibid., p. 215.

91 Peter Chua and Diane C. Fujino, 'Negotiating New Asian-American Mascu-linities: Attitudes and Gender Expectations', *Journal of Men's Studies* 7.3 (1999), p. 391.

92 Such favourable typecasting of Asian men is reminiscent of the way Japanese women treat gay men as 'beautiful boys'. See Mark J. McLelland, *Male Homosexuality in Modern Japan: Cultural Myths and Social Realities*, Richmond, UK: Curzon, 2000.

93 See for example Carmen Luke and Allan Luke, 'Interracial Families: Difference within Difference', *Ethnic and Racial Studies* 21.4 (1998), pp. 728–754.

94 The rise of One Nation in the last years of twentieth-century Australia is one example. In America, a much more vitriolic discourse is found in the discourse on blacks. See for example Abby L. Ferber, '"Shame of White Men": Interracial Sexuality and the Construction of White Mascu-linity in Contemporary White Supremacist Discourse', *Masculinities* 3.2 (1995), pp. 1–24.

95 Carmen Luke and Vicki Carrington, 'Race Matters', *Journal of Intercultural Studies* 21.1 (2000), pp. 5–24.

96 See Jan Ryan, '"She Lives with a Chinaman": Orient-ing "White" Women in the Court of Law', *Journal of Australian Studies* 18 (1999), pp. 149–159, 216–218.

97 Carmen Luke, 'White Women in Interracial Families: Reflections on Hybridization, Feminine Identities, and Racialized Othering', *Feminist Issues* 14.2 (1994), p. 52.

98 Carmen Luke and Allan Luke, 'Theorizing Interracial Families and Hybrid Identity: An Australian Perspective', *Educational Theory* 49.2 (1999), p. 231.

99 See for example Tony Ayres, 'China Doll – The Experience of Being a Gay Chinese Australian', *Journal of Homosexuality* 36.3/4 (1999), pp. 87–97.

100 See for example the essays in David L. Eng and Alice Y. Hom (eds), *Q&A: Queer in Asian America*, Philadelphia: Temple University Press, 1998.

101 I should point out that the writings I have discussed in this chapter were originally written in Chinese for Chinese readers. They therefore repre-sent self-images the authors want Chinese readers to see. In recent years, many books have been published in English describing happy white–Asian marital relations. Curiously, Asian women wrote most of these books. In a review of recent bestsellers by authors such as Nien Cheng, Jung Chang, Aiping Mu and Anhua Gao, Suh-kyung Yoon points out that these Chinese women writers have been successful because they have stuck to the formula: 'A young woman struggles but survives the Cultural Revolution in China … to find health, happiness – and a husband – in the West'. Suh-kyung Yoon, 'The Crying Game', *Far Eastern Economic Review* 164.14 (2001), p. 64. Yoon argues that these heartbreaking memoirs pander to Western preconceptions, whereby 'Red China is the evil enemy that treats its people like beasts, denying them freedom and happiness, which can only be found in the West' (p. 66). In these popular memoirs and novels, the saviour husbands are always white and the wife Chinese. Thus, while social forces are breaking down stereotypes in some areas, opposing forces are also at work.

8 BRUCE LEE, JACKIE CHAN AND CHOW YUN FAT: INTERNATIONALISING
  WU MASCULINITY

1 The position of the genre is further indicated by the fact that most video
  rental outlets now have designated aisles for martial arts films, featuring
  white actors such as Chuck Norris, Jean-Claude Van Damme and Steven
  Seagal as well as other Chinese kung fu favourites such as Jet Li, Samo Hung
  and Michelle Yeoh.
2 Stanley E. Henning, 'Academia Encounters the Chinese Martial Arts', *China
  Review International* 6.2 (1999), p. 319. A description of martial arts 'as a
  confluence of ... physical combat, Buddho-Taoist religion, and theater' can
  be found in Charles Holcombe, 'Theater of Combat: A Critical Look at the
  Chinese Martial Arts', *The Historian* 52.3 (1990), p. 431.
3 For example, search engines on the internet generate more than 200,000
  sites for the keyword 'kung fu'. These include martial arts clubs, fansites,
  books as well as training schools.
4 Jenny Kwok Wah Lau (also romanised as Loh in the book), 'A Cultural
  Interpretation of the Popular Cinema of China and Hong Kong', in Chris
  Berry (ed.), *Perspectives on Chinese Cinema*, London: British Film Institute,
  1991, p. 173.
5 Sax Rohmer, *The Insidious Dr Fu-Manchu*, New York: Pyramid Books, 1961,
  p. 17.
6 Gary Hoppenstand, 'Yellow Devil Doctors and Opium Dens: A Survey of
  the Yellow Peril Stereotypes in Mass Media Entertainment', in Christopher
  D. Geist and Jack Nachbar (eds), *The Popular Culture Reader*, Bowling Green,
  Ohio: Bowling Green University Popular Press, 1983, p. 174.
7 See discussion in Gina Marchetti, *Romance and the 'Yellow Peril': Race, Sex,
  and Discourse Strategies in Hollywood Fiction*, Berkeley: University of
  California Press, 1993, pp. 32–45.
8 Ibid., p. 37.
9 Gloria Heyung Chun, *Of Orphans and Warriors: Inventing Chinese American
  Culture and Identity*, New Brunswick, NJ: Rutgers University Press, 2000,
  p. 19. A good introduction to the Charlie Chan cycle with pictures and
  biographies of the actors who played Chan can be found on the website
  CharlieChan.net: http://www.charliechan.net/.
10 Gloria Chun, p. 19.
11 This was not due to a lack of Chinese actors who could speak pidgin English.
  For example, Charlie Chan's sons were played by American-Chinese actors.
  It is interesting to note that in Lao She's *The Two Mas*, the riot at the Mas'
  curio shop was a result of Ma Senior's acting in a film which was insulting to
  the Chinese.
12 Hoppenstand, p. 174.
13 Tae Kwon Do was included for the first time in the Sydney Olympics in
  2000.
14 From a summary of the episode provided in http://www.dm.net/~karen/
  kungfu/kungfu1.html.
15 Lan Chao, *Li Xiaolong quanzhuan* (The Complete Biography of Bruce Lee),
  Hong Kong: Mingliu chubanshe, 1999, pp. 199–201.
16 From the fansite 'The Shrine to Bruce Lee', http://www.ocf.berkeley.edu/
  ~chenj/brucelee/bruce_timeline.html, p. 4.

17 Cited in John R. Little (ed.), *Bruce Lee: Words from a Master*, Chicago: Contemporary Books, 1999, p. 82.

18 Very little is known about Huo. He was born in 1869 and defeated a Japanese martial arts expert in 1910. His whereabouts after that are unknown.

19 Good discussions of the making of these movies can be found in Bey Logan, *Hong Kong Action Cinema*, London: Titan Books, 1995, pp. 22–43.

20 Ibid., p. 37.

21 See the chart for the Hong Kong box-office rundown in ibid., p. 37.

22 Ibid.

23 Wu Jianping, 'Haolaiwu yu choulou de Zhongguoren' (Hollywood and the Ugly Chinamen), in Li Xiguang and Liu Kang (eds), *Yaomohua Zhongguo de beihou* (Behind the Demonised China), Beijing: Zhongguo shehuikexue chubanshe, 1996, p. 252.

24 Yvonne Tasker, 'Fists of Fury: Discourses of Race and Masculinity in the Martial Arts Cinema', in Harry Stecopoulos and Michael Uebel (eds), *Race and the Subject of Masculinities*, Durham, NC: Duke University Press, 1997, p. 324.

25 I refer to the pre-*Enter the Dragon* films here.

26 Jachinson W. Chan, 'Bruce Lee's Fictional Models of Masculinity', *Men and Masculinities* 2.4 (2000), p. 385.

27 See for example the autobiography which details the way that Bruce Lee inspires the spiritual and personal development of the biographer in David Miller, *The Tao of Bruce Lee*, London: Vintage, 2000.

28 Lu Yue, *Li Xiaolong chuanqi* (Biography of Bruce Lee), Hong Kong: Huangguan chubanshe, 1996, p. 67.

29 David Desser, 'The Kung Fu Craze: Hong Kong Cinema's First American Reception', in Poshek Fu and David Desser (eds), *The Cinema of Hong Kong: History, Arts, Identity*, Cambridge University Press, 2000, p. 39.

30 The macho New Right cinematic response to the 'trauma of Vietnam' is also analysed cogently in the chapter 'Anxieties of the Masculine Sublime', in John Orr, *Contemporary Cinema*, Edinburgh University Press, 1998, pp. 188–209.

31 For an insightful analysis of the ways in which kung fu movies such as Corey Yuen's *No Retreat, No Surrender* (1985) and Rob Cohen's *Dragon: The Bruce Lee Story* (1993) have incorporated the Bruce Lee legend, see Meagan Morris, 'Learning from Bruce Lee: Pedagogy and Political Correctness in Martial Arts Cinema', in Matthew Tinkcom and Amy Villarejo (eds), *Keyframes: Popular Cinema and Cultural Studies*, London: Routledge, 2001, pp. 171–186.

32 Lu Cao, *Zhongguo wushu* (China's *wu* techniques, translated on the cover as 'China's Gongfu (kung fu)'), Guangzhou: Guangdong lüyou chubanshe, 1996, pp. 271–273.

33 Fansites from these countries are easily accessed on the internet.

34 For a discussion on the various names adopted by Jackie Chan, see Shi Qi (Sek Kei), *Shi Qi yinghua ji: Shiba ban wuyi* (Collected Essays on Sek Kei's Film Reviews: The 18 Martial Arts Styles), vol. 1, Hong Kong: Ciwenhua youxian gongsi, 1999, pp. 35–36.

35 Jackie Chan, with Jeff Yang, *I Am Jackie Chan: My Life in Action*, St Leonards, NSW: Allen & Unwin, 1998, pp. 173–174.

36 Ibid., p. 169.

37 Richard Dyer, *Heavenly Bodies: Film Stars and Society*, London: Macmillan, 1987, p. 12.

38 His injuries on set are so renowned that they are described and enumerated for his fans. See for example Liang Jian, *Cheng Long* (Jackie Chan), Hong Kong: Xingli youxian gongsi, 1997, p. 391.

39 Lee founded a martial arts school before he entered the film industry. He continued to teach and philosophise on jeet kune do, his brand of martial arts, throughout his life. Among his followers were Steve McQueen and James Coburn. Jeet kune do flourished after his death, and there are now many books (for example, John Little (ed.), *Jeet Kune Do: Bruce Lee's Commentaries on the Martial Way*, Boston: Tuttle Publishing, 1997) and magazines (for example, *Bruce Lee*, published by the Jun Fan Jeet Kune Do Nucleus in Burbank, California) that are devoted to this school of martial arts.

40 For a description of Jackie Chan's life at the Yu Jim-yuen China Drama Academy, see Chan, *I Am Jackie Chan*, pp. 20–122.

41 Mark Gallagher observes that as part of his masculine mastery over events, 'in virtually all of his films, Chan uses flight as a survival strategy'. Mark Gallagher, 'Masculinity in Translation: Jackie Chan's Transcultural Star Text', *The Velvet Light Trap* 39 (1997), p. 28. Gallagher discusses this device in terms of a 'feminine logic' and its appeal. It can also be seen as Han Feizi's 'flight strategy' mentioned in chapter 4.

42 A different perspective on why Jackie Chan's style is more 'relaxed' is often put forward by Chinese scholars, who believe 'Bruce Lee had a heavier historical burden to bear, and so could not relax', in Hu Ke, 'Cheng Long dianyingzhong de xijuxing dongzuo yu baoli' (Comic Elements and Violence in Jackie Chan's Films), *Dangdai dianying* (Contemporary Cinema) 1 (2000), p. 69.

43 For a description of the Wong Fei-Hung series and its impact on the Hong Kong film industry, see 'Xianggang wuxia dianying de fazhan yu yanbian' (The Development and Evolution of Hong Kong Martial Arts Movies), *Dangdai dianying* (Contemporary Cinema) 3 (1997), pp. 44–52. To see how Jackie Chan changed the Wong Fei-Hung image, see Chen Mo, 'Gongfu Cheng Long: Cong Gangdao zouxiang shijie' (Kung fu and Jackie Chan: From Hong Kong to the World), *Dangdai dianying* (Contemporary Cinema) 1 (2000), p. 74.

44 For a description of some of these, see Wade Major, *Jackie Chan*, New York: MetroBooks, 1999, p. 41.

45 Ramsay Burt, *The Male Dancer: Bodies, Spectacle, Sexualities*, London: Routledge, 1995, p. 8.

46 One sensational incident involved a Japanese female fan, who threw herself in front of a speeding train when she discovered Chan was married.

47 See details in Liang Jian, pp. 130, 203–210.

48 As with Bruce Lee, however, recent scandals about Chan's private life such as having an illegitimate daughter suggest that his morality is also a performance.

49 See Renée Witterstaetter, *Dying for Action: The Life and Films of Jackie Chan*, London: Ebury Press, 1998, p. 202.

50 Fredric Dannen and Barry Long, *Hong Kong Babylon: An Insider's Guide to the Hollywood of the East*, New York: Miramax Books, 1997, p. 55.

51 Cai Hongsheng, 'Cheng Long de dianying shijie' (Jackie Chan's Movie World), *Dangdai dianying* (Contemporary Cinema) 1 (2000), p. 65.

52 Chan, *I Am Jackie Chan*, p. 262.

53 Ibid., p. 263.

54 This is the title of a book published not long before *Rush Hour* was released. The essays in the book are excellent works illustrating the trend towards 'transnationalism' as well as great scholarly pieces. It contains a good analysis of *Rumble in the Bronx*, in Steve Fore, 'Jackie Chan and the Cultural Dynamics of Global Entertainment', in Sheldon Hsiao-peng Lu (ed.), *Transnational Chinese Cinemas: Identity, Nationhood, Gender*, University of Hawai'i Press, 1997, pp. 239–262.

55 For a brilliant analysis of this movie and Jackie Chan's relationship to black audiences, see Gina Marchetti, 'Jackie Chan and the Black Connection', in Matthew Tinkcom and Amy Villarejo (eds), *Keyframes: Popular Cinema and Cultural Studies*, London: Routledge, 2001, pp. 136–158.

56 Esther Pan, 'Why Asian Guys Are on a Roll', *Newsweek* 135.8 (2000), p. 50.

57 Ibid.

58 Yvonne Tasker, 'Dumb Movies for Dumb People: Masculinity, the body, and the voice in contemporary action cinema', in Steven Cohan and Ina Rae Hark (eds), *Screening the Male: Exploring Masculinities in Hollywood Cinema*, London: Routledge, 1993, pp. 230–244.

59 Yu Zhonghua, 'Wuda pian yao "wu xi wen chang"' (Martial Arts Movies Should be 'Martial Arts Performances Harmonised by Cultured Scripts'), *Dianying yishu* (Film Art) 2 (1996), pp. 65–66.

60 Chen Ye, 'Cheng Long tan Cheng Long dianying' (Jackie Chan on Jackie Chan Films), *Dianying yishu* (Film Art) 2 (2000), p. 62.

61 Anne T. Ciecko, 'Transnational Action: John Woo, Hong Kong, Hollywood', in Sheldon Hsiao-peng Lu (ed.), p. 234.

62 Ibid., p. 232.

63 Yvonne Tasker, *Spectacular Bodies: Gender, Genre, and the Action Cinema*, London: Routledge, 1993, pp. 73–75.

64 Fore, p. 252.

65 From David Chute, *Film Comment*, quoted in Stefan Hammond and Mike Wilkins, *Sex and Zen & A Bullet in the Head: The Essential Guide to Hong Kong's Mind-Bending Films*, New York: A Fireside Book, 1996, p. 44.

66 Ciecko, p. 227.

67 Tony Williams, 'Space, Place, and Spectacle: The Crisis Cinema of John Woo', in Fu and Desser, p. 148.

68 Ibid.

69 Cynthia J. Fuchs, 'The Buddy Politic', in Cohan and Hark, p. 195.

70 Quoted in Leo Ou-fan Lee, 'Hong Kong Movies in Hollywood: An Informal Comment on Asian "Influences" in American Popular Culture', *Harvard Asia Pacific Review* Winter Issue (1998–89), http://hcs.harvard.edu/~hapr/winter98/people.htm/.

71 The *wuxia* genre, epitomised by the director King Hu (1931–97), is different to the kung fu variety. Whereas the former are based more on traditional novels in which the sword-wielding hero (or heroine) has such superhuman skills that s/he can scale walls and fly over rooftops, the kung fu hero, such as Bruce Lee and Jackie Chan, speaks in Cantonese and specialises in unarmed

combat with little or no superhuman qualities. See discussion in Stephen Teo, *Hong Kong Cinema: The Extra Dimensions*, London: The British Film Institute, 1997, pp. 87–134.

72 Jillian Sandell, 'Reinventing Masculinity: The Spectacle of Male Intimacy in the Films of John Woo', *Film Quarterly* 49.4 (1996), p. 30.

73 See Charlotte Raven, 'Crashing Bore, Wooden Drama', *Guardian*, 16 January 2001. As well as letters from readers of the *Guardian* on 19 and 20 January 2001, outraged comments can be found in the 'Perspective' page of the *Dimsum: Food for Thought* website: http://www.dimsum.co.uk/perspective/chen_yoursay2.html.

74 Henry Chu, '"Crouching Tiger" Can't Hide From Bad Reviews in China', *Los Angeles Times*, 29 January 2001.

75 Stephen Teo, 'Love and Swords: The Dialectics of Martial Arts Romance', *Senses of Cinema*, http://www.sensesofcinema/00/11/crouching.html.

76 Evans Chan, 'Postmodernism and Hong Kong Cinema', in Arif Dirlik and Xudong Zhang (eds), *Postmodernism and China*, Durham, NC: Duke University Press, 2000, p. 311.

77 In this book, I have not highlighted the influence of other 'invisible' men such as the directors John Woo, Tsui Hark, Wong Kar-wai and Ang Lee. Their impact on the internationalisation of *wen-wu* masculinity is less obvious but so important that they deserve detailed and individual study.

9 *WEN-WU* RECONSTRUCTED: CHINESE MASCULINITY HYBRIDISED AND GLOBALISED

1 As well as her book *Training the Body for China*, Susan Brownell has written a number of articles on the importance of physical competition (via sport) for the nationalist enterprise. Her particular interest is on how women's bodies and sports were glorified when the women won international events. But ultimately, the old gender hierarchies take precedence. See Susan Brownell, 'Strong Women and Impotent Men: Sports, Gender, and Nationalism in Chinese Public Culture', in Mayfair Mei-hui Yang (ed.), *Spaces of Their Own: Women's Public Sphere in Transnational China*, Minneapolis: University of Minnesota Press, 1999, pp. 207–231; and 'Gender and Nationalism in China at the Turn of the Millennium', in Tyrene White (ed.), *China Briefing 1997–1999*, Armonk, NY: M.E. Sharpe, 2000, pp. 195–232.

2 See Vitielli's fascinating account of how this hybridisation can be imagined, in Giovanni Vitielli, 'Exemplary Sodomites: Chivalry and Love in Late Ming Culture', *Nan Nü: Men, Women and Gender in Early and Imperial China* 2.2 (2000), p. 234.

3 The *Shanhai jing* is so old that its authorship is attributed to the legendary Yi and Yü who are said to have lived about three and a half thousand years ago. An English translation is found in Hsiao-Chieh Cheng et al. (eds and trans.), *Shan Hai Ching: Legendary Geography and Wonders of Ancient China*, Taipei: National Institute for Compilation and Translation, 1985.

4 By hybridity, I refer to Homi Bhabha's *inter*national kind, and not just a multicultural or diverse variety. See Homi K. Bhabha, *The Location of Culture*, London: Routledge, 1994, p. 38.

5 Mikhail Bakhtin (trans. Caryl Emerson and Michael Holquist), 'Discourse in the Novel', in Michael Holquist (ed.), *The Dialogic Imagination: Four Essays by M.M. Bakhtin*, Austin: University of Texas Press, 1981, p. 358.

6 Directed by Jim Jarmusch, *Ghost Dog: The Way of the Samurai* stars Forest Whitaker as Ghost Dog and was filmed in 1999

7 Ryoko Otomo, '"The Way of the Samurai": Ghost Dog, Mishima, and Modernity's Other', *Japanese Studies* 21.1 (2001), p. 33.

8 Ibid., p. 36.

9 See my *Inheriting Tradition: Interpretations of the Classical Philosophers in Communist China* for a discussion of the way the Chinese have debated this issue of appropriating a 'style' as 'abstract inheritance'.

10 Mike Eskenazi, 'Remaking Wu: The Diggs Brothers are Part of a Famous Rap Group, But They'd Rather Run a Profitable Conglomerate', *Time* 156.24 (2000), pp. 82–83.

11 N'Gai Croal, 'Bring in 'da Ruckus: Rap's Wu-Tang Clan Takes Over', *Newsweek* 129.24 (1997), p. 58.

12 Gina Marchetti, 'Jackie Chan and the Black Connection', in Matthew Tinkcom and Amy Villarejo (eds), *Keyframes: Popular Cinema and Cultural Studies*, London: Routledge, 2001, p. 150.

13 See an illustration of this at http://www.activision.com/games/wutang/ss10.html, reproduced in this book on p. 160.

14 See my discussion of this film in Bob Hodge and Kam Louie, *The Politics of Chinese Language and Culture*, London: Routledge, 1998, pp. 143–172.

15 Lisa Rofel, *Other Modernities: Gendered Yearnings in China After Socialism*, Berkeley: University of California Press, 1999, pp. 283–284.

16 Michael S. Kimmel, 'Masculinities as Homophobia: Fear, Shame and Silence in the Construction of Gender Identity', in Harry Brod and M. Kaufman (eds), *Theorising Masculinities*, Thousand Oaks, CA: Sage, 1994, p. 124.

17 In an essay on the Japanese gay identity, for example, Mark McLelland concludes that: 'It is unlikely that the local specificities of gay and lesbian liberation in the US or Europe can illuminate, except in very general ways, the lives and experiences of same-sex desiring Japanese'. Mark McLelland, 'Is There a Japanese "Gay Identity"?', *Culture, Health and Sexuality* 2.4 (2000), p. 469.

Bibliography

Allen, Joseph R. 'Dressing and Undressing the Chinese Woman Warrior', *Positions* 4.2 (1996), pp. 343–397.

Allison, Anne. *Nightwork: Sexuality, Pleasure, and Corporate Masculinity in a Tokyo Hostess Club*. University of Chicago Press, 1996.

Ames, Roger T. *The Art of Rulership: A Study in Ancient Chinese Political Thought*. Honolulu: University of Hawai'i Press, 1983.

Anderson, Benedict. *Imagined Communities: Reflections on the Origin and Rise of Nationalism*. London: Verso, 1991.

Andressen, Curtis. 'The Location and Characteristics of Asia-born Overseas Students in Australia', in James E. Coughlan and Deborah J. McNamara (eds), *Asians in Australia: Patterns of Migration and Settlement*. Melbourne: Macmillan, 1997, pp. 75–98.

Anonymous. *The Golden Lotus* (trans. Clement Egerton), 4 vols. London: Routledge & Kegan Paul Ltd, 1939.

Avery, Martha. 'Translator's Introduction', *Half of Man Is Woman*. London: Penguin Books, 1989, pp. xi–xiv.

Ayres, Tony. 'China Doll – The Experience of Being a Gay Chinese Australian', *The Journal of Homosexuality* 36.3/4 (1999), pp. 87–97.

Ayres, Tony. 'Undesirable Aliens', *HQ* 57 (1998), pp. 110–115.

Backman, Michael. *Asian Eclipse: Exposing the Dark Side of Business in Asia*. Singapore: John Wiley & Sons, 1999.

Bakhtin, Mikhail. 'Discourse in the Novel' (trans. Caryl Emerson and Michael Holquist), in Michael Holquist (ed.), *The Dialogic Imagination: Four Essays by M.M. Bakhtin*. Austin: University of Texas Press, 1981, pp. 259–422.

Barlow, Tani E. (ed.). *Gender Politics in Modern China: Writing and Feminism*. Durham, NC: Duke University Press, 1993.

Barlow, Tani E. (ed.). *I Myself Am a Woman: Selected Writings of Ding Ling*. Boston: Beacon Press, 1989.

Barmé, Geremie R. 'To Screw Foreigners Is Patriotic: China's Avant-Garde Nationalists', *The China Journal* 34 (1995), pp. 209–34.

Berry, Chris. *A Bit on the Side: East–West Topographies of Desire*. Sydney: EmPress, 1994.

Berry, Chris (ed.). *Perspectives on Chinese Cinema*. London: British Film Institute, 1991.

Bhabha, Homi K. 'Culture's In-Between', in Stuart Hall and Paul du Gay (eds), *Questions of Cultural Identity*. London: Sage Publications, 1996, pp. 53–60.

Bhabha, Homi K. *The Location of Culture*. London: Routledge, 1994.

Bickers, Robert. *Britain in China: Community, Culture and Colonialism 1900–1949*. Manchester University Press, 1999.

Biddulph, Steve. *Manhood: A Book about Setting Men Free*. Sydney: Finch Publishing, 1994.

Birch, Cyril (ed.). *Anthology of Chinese Literature*. Harmondsworth: Penguin, 1967.

Bloch, Enid. 'Sex between Men and Boys in Classical Greece: Was It Education for Citizenship or Child Abuse?', *Journal of Men's Studies* 9.2 (2001), pp. 183–204.

Bly, Robert. *Iron John: A Book about Men*. Rockport, Mass.: Element, 1991.

Bo Yang (ed.). *Jia Pingwa juan* (Volume on Jia Pingwa). Taipei: Linbai chubanshe, 1988.

Boyarin, Daniel. *Unheroic Conduct: The Rise of Heterosexuality and the Invention of the Jewish Man*. Berkeley: University of California Press, 1997.

Brod, H. and M. Kaufman (eds). *Theorising Masculinities*. Thousand Oaks, CA: Sage, 1994.

Brownell, Susan. 'Gender and Nationalism in China at the Turn of the Millennium', in Tyrene White (ed.), *China Briefing 1997–1999*. Armonk, NY: M.E. Sharpe, 2000, pp. 195–232.

Brownell, Susan. 'Strong Women and Impotent Men: Sports, Gender, and Nationalism in Chinese Public Culture', in Mayfair Mei-hui Yang (ed.), *Spaces of Their Own: Women's Public Sphere in Transnational China*. Minneapolis: University of Minnesota Press, 1999, pp. 207–231.

Brownell, Susan. *Training the Body for China: Sports in the Moral Order of the People's Republic*. University of Chicago Press, 1995.

Brownell, Susan and Jeffrey N. Wasserstrom (eds). *Chinese Femininities and Masculinities: A Reader*. Berkeley: University of California Press, forthcoming.

Bulbeck, Chilla. *One World Women's Movement*. London: Pluto Press, 1988.

Bulbeck, Chilla. *Re-orienting Western Feminisms: Women's Diversity in a Postcolonial World*. Cambridge University Press, 1998.

Burke, Thomas. 'The Chink and the Child', in *Limehouse Nights: Tales of Chinatown*. London: Grant Richards Ltd, 1916, pp. 13–37.

Burke, Thomas. *Limehouse Nights: Tales of Chinatown*. London: Grant Richards Ltd, 1916.

Burke, Thomas. 'Tai Fu and Pansy Greers', in *Limehouse Nights: Tales of Chinatown*. London: Grant Richards Ltd, 1916, pp. 149–168.

Burt, Ramsay. *The Male Dancer: Bodies, Spectacle, Sexualities*. London: Routledge, 1995.

Butler, Judith. *Gender Trouble: Feminism and the Subversion of Identity*. London: Routledge, 1990.

Cai Hongsheng. 'Cheng Long de dianying shijie' (Jackie Chan's Movie World), *Dangdai dianying* (Contemporary Cinema) 1 (2000), pp. 65–68.

Cai Kui. 'Xiguan yu congrong de tanlun ta' (Getting Used to Talking About It in a Calm Manner). Originally published in *Dangdai zuojia pinglun* (Critiques of Contemporary Writers) 2 (1986). Reprinted in Ningxia renmin chubanshe (ed.), *Ping 'Nanren de yiban shi nüren'* (Criticisms of 'Half of Man Is Woman'). Yinchuan: Ningxia renmin chubanshe, 1987, pp. 100–110.

Cai Shangsi. *Zhongguo chuantong sixiang zong pipan* (A Comprehensive Criticism of Traditional Chinese Thought). Shanghai: Tangdai chubanshe, 1950.

Cao Wenxuan. *Zhongguo bashi niandai wenxue xianxiang yanjiu* (A Study of Chinese Literature in the 1980s). Beijing: Beijing daxue chubanshe, 1988.

Cao Xueqin. *Honglou meng: yi–si* (A Dream of Red Mansions: vols 1–4). Beijing: Beijing shifan daxue chubanshe, 1987.

Cao Xueqin (romanised as Tsao Hsueh-chin). *A Dream of Red Mansions* (trans. Yang Hsien-yi and Gladys Yang), 2 vols. Beijing: Foreign Languages Press, 1978.

Chan, Evans. 'Postmodernism and Hong Kong Cinema', in Arif Dirlik and Xudong Zhang (eds), *Postmodernism and China*. Durham, NC: Duke University Press, 2000, pp. 294–322.

Chan, Jachinson W. 'Bruce Lee's Fictional Models of Masculinity', *Men and Masculinities* 2.4 (2000), pp. 371–387.

Chan, Jackie with Jeff Yang. *I Am Jackie Chan: My Life in Action*. St Leonards, NSW: Allen & Unwin, 1998.

Chang, Ying-jen. The Rise of Martial Arts in China and America. Unpublished PhD dissertation, Graduate Faculty of Political and Social Science, New School for Social Research, 1978.

Chen, Helen H. 'Gender, Subjectivity, Sexuality: Defining a Subversive Discourse in Wang Anyi's Four Tales of Sexual Transgression', in Yingjin Zhang (ed.), *China in a Polycentric World: Essays in Chinese Comparative Literature*. Stanford, CA: Stanford University Press, 1998, pp. 90–109.

Chen Jingpan. *Kongzi de jiaoyu sixiang* (Confucius' Educational Thought). Wuhan: Hubei renmin chubanshe, 1957.

Ch'en Li-li (ed. and trans.). *Master Tung's Western Chamber Romance: A Chinese Chantefable*. Cambridge University Press, 1976.

Chen Mo. 'Gongfu Cheng Long: Cong Gangdao zouxiang shijie' (Kung fu and Jackie Chan: From Hong Kong to the World), *Dangdai dianying* (Contemporary Cinema) 1 (2000), pp. 72–78.

Chen Ran. *Siren shenghuo* (A Private Life). Beijing: Zuojia chubanshe, 1996.

Chen Shan. *Zhongguo wuxia shi* (History of the Chinese Chivalrous Knights). Shanghai: Sanlian shudian, 1992.

Chen Shigai. 'Kongzi de lunli sixiang yu zichan jieji rendao zhuyi zhi bijiao yanjiu' (A Comparative Study of Confucius' Ethical Thinking and the Humanism of the Bourgeoisie), *Hubei daxue xuebao* (Hubei University Journal) 2 (1986), pp. 31–36.

Chen Xinyuan. 'Xing'ai yu xungen' (Sexual Love and Seeking Roots), in Bo Yang (ed.), *Xiaocheng zhi lian* (Love in a Small Town). Taipei: Linbai chubanshe, 1988, pp. 7–11.

Chen Ye. 'Cheng Long tan Cheng Long dianying' (Jackie Chan on Jackie Chan Films), *Dianying yishu* (Film Art) 2 (2000), pp. 60–62, 14.

Cheng, Cliff (ed.). *Masculinities in Organizations*. Thousand Oaks, CA: Sage Publications, 1996.

Cheng, Cliff. '"We Choose Not To Compete": The "Merit" Discourse in the Selection Process, and Asian and Asian American Men and Their Masculinity', in Cliff Cheng (ed.), *Masculinities in Organizations*. Thousand Oaks, CA: Sage Publications, 1996, pp. 177–200.

Cheng, Hsiao-Chieh et al. (eds and trans.). *Shan Hai Ching: Legendary Geography and Wonders of Ancient China*. Taipei: National Institute for Compilation and Translation, 1985.

Chi Li. *Apart from Love*. Beijing: Panda Books, 1994.

Chou, Eric. *The Dragon and The Phoenix*. London: Corgi Books, 1973.

Chow Tse-tsung. *The May Fourth Movement: Intellectual Revolution in Modern China*. Stanford, CA: Stanford University Press, 1967.

Chu, Henry. '"Crouching Tiger" Can't Hide From Bad Reviews in China', *Los Angeles Times*, 29 January 2001.

Chua, Peter and Diane C. Fujino. 'Negotiating New Asian-American Masculinities: Attitudes and Gender Expectations', *The Journal of Men's Studies* 7.3 (1999), pp. 391–413.

Chun, Gloria Heyung. *Of Orphans and Warriors: Inventing Chinese American Culture and Identity*. New Brunswick, NJ: Rutgers University Press, 2000.

Chute, David. 'Film Comment', in Stefan Hammond and Mike Wilkins, *Sex and Zen & A Bullet in the Head: The Essential Guide to Hong Kong's Mind-Bending Films*. New York: A Fireside Book, 1996, p. 44.

Ciecko, Anne T. 'Transnational Action: John Woo, Hong Kong, Hollywood', in Sheldon Hsiao-peng Lu (ed.), *Transnational Chinese Cinemas: Identity, Nationhood, Gender*. Honolulu: University of Hawai'i Press, 1997, pp. 221–237.

Cihai (Sea of Words). Shanghai: Shanghai cishu chubanshe, 1980.

Clatterbaugh, Kenneth. *Contemporary Perspectives on Masculinity: Men, Women and Politics in Modern Society*. Boulder, CO: Westview Press, 1990.

Clegg, Jenny. *Fu Manchu and The 'Yellow Peril': the Making of a Racist Myth*. Stoke-on-Trent, UK: Trentham Books, 1994.

Cohan, Steven and Ina Rae Hark (eds). *Screening the Male: Exploring Masculinities in Hollywood Cinema*. London: Routledge, 1993.

Coughlan, James E. and Deborah J. McNamara (eds). *Asians in Australia: Patterns of Migration and Settlement*. Melbourne: Macmillan, 1997.

Coward, Rosalind. *Female Desire: Women's Sexuality Today*. London: Paladin Grafton, 1984.

Creel, Herrlee G. *The Origins of Statecraft in China*, vol. I: *The Western Zhou Empire*. University of Chicago Press, 1970.

Croal, N'Gai. 'Bring in 'da Ruckus: Rap's Wu-Tang Clan Takes Over', *Newsweek* 129.24 (1997), p. 58.

Croll, Elisabeth. *Changing Identities of Chinese Women*. London: Zed Books, 1995.

Cui Fengyuan, *Zhongguo gudian duanpian xiayi xiaoshuo yanjiu* (A Study of Classical Chinese Short Stories on Knight-Errantry). Taipei: Lianjing chuban shiye gongsi, 1986.

Dannen, Fredric and Barry Long. *Hong Kong Babylon: An Insider's Guide to the Hollywood of the East*. New York: Miramax Books, 1997.

Davis, Adrian. 'Fraternity and Fratricide in Late Imperial China', *The American Historical Review* 105.5 (2000), pp. 1630–1640.

Dawson, Raymond. *The Chinese Chameleon: an Analysis of European Conceptions of Chinese Civilization*. Oxford University Press, 1967.

Deng Youmei. 'At the Precipice' (trans. Hua-yua Li Mowry), in Vivian Ling Hsu (ed.), *Born of the Same Roots: Stories of Modern Chinese Women*. Bloomington: Indiana University Press, 1981, pp. 94–127.

Desser, David. 'The Kung Fu Craze: Hong Kong Cinema's First American Reception', in Poshek Fu and David Desser (eds), *The Cinema of Hong Kong: History, Arts, Identity*. Cambridge University Press, 2000, pp. 19–43.

Dikötter, Frank. *The Discourse of Race in Modern China*. London: C. Hurst, 1992.

Dikötter, Frank. *Sex, Culture and Modernity in China*. London: Hurst & Co, 1995.

Ding Ling. 'Miss Sophia's Diary' (trans. Tani E. Barlow), in Tani E. Barlow (ed.), *I Myself Am a Woman: Selected Writings of Ding Ling*. Boston: Beacon Press, 1989, pp. 49–81.

Dirlik, Arif and Xudong Zhang (eds). *Postmodernism and China*. Durham, NC: Duke University Press, 2000.

Donaldson, Scott. *By Force of Will: The Life and Art of Ernest Hemingway*. New York: Viking, 1977.

Dover, K.J. *Greek Homosexuality*. London: Duckworth, 1978.

Dubbert, J.L. *A Man's Place: Masculinity in Transition*. London: Prentice Hall, 1979.

Duberman, Martin Bauml et al. (eds). *Hidden From History: Reclaiming the Gay and Lesbian Past*. Harmondsworth: Penguin Books, 1991.

Duke, Michael (ed.). *Modern Chinese Women Writers: Critical Appraisals*. Armonk, NY: M.E. Sharpe, 1989.

Dureau, Christine and Morris Low. 'The Politics of Knowledge: Science, Race and Evolution in Asia and the Pacific', *History and Anthropology* 11.2–3 (1999), pp. 131–156.

Dutton, Kenneth R. *The Perfectible Body: The Western Ideal of Physical Development*. St Leonards, NSW: Allen & Unwin, 1995.

Dworkin, Andrea. *Woman Hating*. New York: E.P. Dutton, 1974.

Dyer, Richard. *Heavenly Bodies: Film Stars and Society*. London: Macmillan, 1987.

Eberhard, Wolfram. *Dictionary of Chinese Symbols*. Singapore: Federal Publications, 1990.

Edwards, Louise. 'Consolidating a Socialist Patriarchy: The Women Writers' Industry and "Feminist" Literary Criticism', in Antonia Finnane and Anne McLaren (eds), *Dress, Sex and Text in Chinese Culture*. Clayton, Vic.: Monash Asia Institute, 1999, pp. 183–197.

Edwards, Louise. 'Gender Imperatives in *Honglou meng*: Jia Baoyu's Bisexuality', *Chinese Literature: Essays, Articles and Reviews* 12 (1990), pp. 69–81.

Edwards, Louise. *Men and Women in Qing China: Gender in the 'Red Chamber Dream'*. Leiden, Netherlands: E.J. Brill, 1994.

Edwards, Louise. 'Policing the Modern Woman in Republican China', *Modern China* 26.2 (2000), pp. 115–147.

Edwards, Louise. 'Women in the People's Republic of China: New Challenges to the Grand Gender Narrative', in Louise Edwards and Mina Roces (eds), *Women in Asia: Tradition, Modernity and Globalisation*. Ann Arbor: University of Michigan Press, 2000, pp. 59–82.

Edwards, Louise and Mina Roces (eds). *Women in Asia: Tradition, Modernity and Globalisation*. Ann Arbor: University of Michigan Press, 2000.

Eng, David L. and Alice Y. Hom (eds). *Q&A: Queer in Asian America*. Philadelphia: Temple University Press, 1998.

Epstein, Maram. 'Inscribing the Essentials: Culture and the Body in Ming-Qing Fiction', *Ming Studies* 41 (1999), pp. 6–36.

Ermarth, Elisabeth. 'Fictional Consensus and Female Casualties', in C.G. Heilbrun and M.H. Higgonet (eds), *The Representation of Women*. Baltimore: Johns Hopkins University Press, 1983, pp. 1–18.

Eskenazi, Mike. 'Remaking Wu: The Diggs Brothers are Part of a Famous Rap Group, But They'd Rather Run a Profitable Conglomerate', *Time* 156.24 (2000), pp. 82–83.

Faludi, Susan. *Stiffed: The Betrayal of the Modern Man*. London: Chatto & Windus, 1999.

Fan Yang. *Yanggang de huichen* (The Decline of Masculine Power). Beijing: Guoji wenhua chubanshe, 1988.

Feng Gu. 'Women kan *Nanren de yiban shi nüren*' (Looking at *Half of Man Is Woman*), *Dangdai zuojia pinglun* 4 (1986), pp. 112–115.

Ferber, Abby L. '"Shame of White Men": Interracial Sexuality and the Construction of White Masculinity in Contemporary White Supremacist Discourse', *Masculinities* 3.2 (1995), pp. 1–24.

Feuerwerker, Yi-tsi Mei. *Ding Ling's Fiction: Ideology and Narrative in Modern Chinese Literature*. Cambridge, MA: Harvard University Press, 1982.

Finnane, Antonia. 'What Should Chinese Women Wear? A National Problem', *Modern China* 22.2 (1996), pp. 99–131.

Finnane, Antonia and Anne McLaren (eds). *Dress, Sex and Text in Chinese Culture*. Clayton, Vic.: Monash Asia Institute, 1999.

Fitzgerald, John. *Awakening China: Politics, Culture, and Class in the Nationalist Revolution*. Stanford University Press, 1996.

Fore, Steve. 'Jackie Chan and the Cultural Dynamics of Global Entertainment', in Sheldon Hsiao-peng Lu (ed.), *Transnational Chinese Cinemas: Identity, Nationhood, Gender*. University of Hawai'i Press, 1997, pp. 239–262.

Foucault, Michel. *The Use of Pleasure: The History of Sexuality*, vol. 2 (trans. Robert Hurley). Harmondsworth: Penguin, 1987.

Foxhall, Lin and John Salmon (eds). *When Men Were Men: Masculinity, Power and Identity in Classical Antiquity*. London: Routledge, 1998.

Fu, Poshek and David Desser (eds). *The Cinema of Hong Kong: History, Arts, Identity*. Cambridge University Press, 2000.

Fuchs, Cynthia J. 'The Buddy Politic', in Steven Cohan and Ina Rae Hark (eds), *Screening the Male: Exploring Masculinities in Hollywood Cinema*. London: Routledge, 1933, pp. 194–210.

Fung, Edmund and Colin Mackerras. 'Chinese Students in Australia: An Attitudinal Study', in Anthony Milner and Mary Quilty (eds), *Australia in Asia: Episodes*. Melbourne: Oxford University Press, 1998, pp. 210–230.

Fung, Edmund S.K. and Chen Jie. *Changing Perceptions: The Attitudes of the PRC Chinese Towards Australia and China, 1989–1996*. Brisbane: Griffith University Centre for the Study of Australia Asia Relations, 1996.

Furth, Charlotte. 'Androgynous Males and Deficient Females: Biology in Sixteenth and Seventeenth Century China', *Late Imperial China* 9.2 (December 1988), pp. 1–31.

Furth, Charlotte. *A Flourishing Yin: Gender in China's Medical History, 960–1665*. Berkeley: University of California Press, 1999.

Furth, Charlotte. 'Rethinking Van Gulik: Sexuality and Reproduction in Traditional Chinese Medicine', in Christina K. Gilmartin et al. (eds), *Engendering China: Women, Culture and the State*. Cambridge, Mass: Harvard University Press, 1994, pp. 125–146.

Gallagher, Mark. 'Masculinity in Translation: Jackie Chan's Transcultural Star Text', *The Velvet Light Trap* 39 (1997), pp. 23–41.

Gang Yue. *The Mouth That Begs: Hunger, Cannibalism, and the Politics of Eating in Modern China*. Durham, NC: Duke University Press, 1999.

Gansu shifan daxue zhongwenxi (ed.). *Hanyu chengyu huishi* (A Compendium of Chinese Idioms and Their Explanations), no publisher or date given.

Gao Mingge. *Sanguo yanyi lungao* (On *The Romance of the Three Kingdoms*). Shenyang: Liaoning daxue chubanshe, 1986.

Gao Song. *Zhang Xianliang xiaoshuo lun* (On Zhang Xianliang's Fiction). Chengdu: Sichuan wenyi chubanshe, 1986.

Gao Xingjian. *Lingshan*, first published in Taiwan in 1990. English translation, *Soul Mountain* (trans. Mabel Lee), Sydney: HarperCollins, 2000.

Geist, Christopher D. and Jack Nachbar (eds). *The Popular Culture Reader*. Bowling Green, Ohio: Bowling Green University Popular Press, 1983.

Gilmartin, Christina K., Gail Hershatter, Lisa Rofel and Tyrene White (eds). *Engendering China: Women, Culture and the State*. Cambridge, Mass: Harvard University Press, 1994.

Gilmore, David D. *Manhood in the Making: Cultural Concepts of Masculinity*. New Haven: Yale University Press, 1990.

Gordon, Michael-David. 'Why Is This Men's Movement So White?', *Changing Men* 26 (1993), pp. 15–17.

Grey, John. *Men Are from Mars, Women Are from Venus*. London: Harper Collins, 1992. *V*

Grosz, Elizabeth. *Volatile Bodies: Towards a Corporeal Feminism*. Sydney: Allen & Unwin, 1994.

Gu jin Hanyu chengyu cidian (A Dictionary of Chinese Idioms Past and Present) (no author provided). Taiyuan: Shanxi renmin chubanshe, 1986.

Guo Li. 'Wang Anyi hua "San lian"' (Wang Anyi on the 'Three Loves'). *Zuopin yu zhengming* (Literary Works and Controversy) 3 (1988), p. 76.

Hall, David L. and Roger T. Ames. *Thinking Through Confucius*. Albany: State University of New York Press, 1987.

Hall, Stuart. 'Cultural Identity and Diaspora', in Patrick Williams and Laura Chrisman (eds), *Colonial Discourse and Post-colonial Theory: A Reader*. New York: Harvester Wheatsheaf, 1993, pp. 392–403.

Hall, Stuart and Paul du Gay (eds). *Questions of Cultural Identity*. London: Sage Publications, 1996.

Halperin, David M. 'Sex Before Sexuality: Pederasty, Politics, and Power in Classical Athens', in Martin Bauml Duberman et al. (eds), *Hidden From History: Reclaiming the Gay and Lesbian Past*. Harmondsworth: Penguin Books, 1991, pp. 37–53.

Hammond, Stefan and Mike Wilkins. *Sex and Zen & A Bullet in the Head: The Essential Guide to Hong Kong's Mind-Bending Films*. New York: A Fireside Book, 1996.

Han Suyin. *The Crippled Tree*. London: Jonathan Cape, 1965.

Hanyu dazidian (The Chinese Character Dictionary, author not given). Chengdu: Sichuan cishu chubanshe, 1993.

Hawkes, David (ed. and trans.). *The Songs of the South*. Harmondsworth: Penguin, 1985.

Hegel, Robert E. *The Novel in Seventeenth Century China*. New York: Columbia University Press, 1981.

Hegel, Robert E. 'Political Integration in Ru Zhijuan's "Lilies"', in Theodore Huters (ed.), *Reading the Modern Chinese Short Story*. Armonk, NY: M.E. Sharpe, 1990, pp. 92–104.

Hegel, Robert E. and Richard C. Hessney (eds). *Expressions of Self in Chinese Literature*. New York: Columbia University Press, 1985.

Heilbrun, C.G. and M.H. Higgonet (eds). *The Representation of Women*. Baltimore: Johns Hopkins University Press, 1983.

Henan sheng shehui kexueyuan (ed.). *Sanguo yanyi yanjiu lunwen ji* (Collected Essays on *Romance of the Three Kingdoms*). Beijing: Zhonghua shuju, 1991.

Henning, Stanley E. 'Academia Encounters the Chinese Martial Arts', *China Review International* 6.2 (1999), pp. 319–332.

Henshall, Kenneth G. *Dimensions of Japanese Society: Gender, Margins and Mainstream*. New York: St Martin's Press, 1999.

Herek, Gregory M. 'On Heterosexual Masculinity: Some Physical Consequences of the Social Construction of Gender and Sexuality', in Michael S. Kimmel (ed.), *Changing Men: New Directions in Research on Men and Masculinity*. Newbury Park, CA: Sage Publications, 1987, pp. 68–82.

Hessney, Richard C. 'Beyond Beauty and Talent: The Moral and Chivalric Self in The Fortunate Union', in Robert E. Hegel and Richard C. Hessney (eds), *Expressions of Self in Chinese Literature*. New York: Columbia University Press, 1985, pp. 214–250.

Hightower, James R. 'Yüan Chen and "The Story of Yingying"', *Harvard Journal of Asiatic Studies* 33 (1973), pp. 90–123.

Hillenbrand, Margaret. 'Beleaguered Husbands: Representations of Marital Breakdowns in Some Recent Chinese Fiction', *Tamkang Review* 30.2 (1999), pp. 112–150.

Hinsch, Bret. *Passions of the Cut Sleeve: The Homosexual Tradition in China*. Berkeley: University of California Press, 1990.

Hodge, Bob and Kam Louie. *The Politics of Chinese Language and Culture*. London: Routledge, 1998.

Hofstede, Geert. *Cultures and Organizations: Software of the Mind*. New York: McGraw-Hill, 1997.

Holcombe, Charles. 'Theater of Combat: A Critical Look at the Chinese Martial Arts', *The Historian* 52.3 (1990), pp. 411–431.

Holmes, Colin (ed.). *Immigrants and Minorities in British Society*. London: George Allen & Unwin, 1978.

Holquist, Michael (ed.). *The Dialogic Imagination: Four Essays by M.M. Bakhtin*. Austin: University of Texas Press, 1981.

Honig, Emily and Gail Hershatter, *Personal Voices: Chinese Women in the 1980's*. Stanford University Press, 1988.

Hooper, B. 'China's Modernization: Are Young Women Going to Lose Out?', *Modern China* 10.3 (1984), pp. 317–343.

Hoppenstand, Gary. 'Yellow Devil Doctors and Opium Dens: A Survey of the Yellow Peril Stereotypes in Mass Media Entertainment', in Christopher D. Geist and Jack Nachbar (eds), *The Popular Culture Reader*. Bowling Green, Ohio: Bowling Green University Popular Press, 1983, pp. 171–185.

Howell, Jude et al. 'Responses', *Bulletin of Concerned Asian Scholars* 31.1 (1999), pp. 37–47.

Hsia, C.T. *The Classic Chinese Novel*. New York: Columbia University Press, 1968.

Hsia, C.T. 'A Critical Introduction', in Wang Shifu, *The Romance of the Western Chamber* (trans. S.I. Hsiung). New York: Columbia University Press, 1968, pp. ix–xxxvii.

Hsia, C.T. *A History of Modern Chinese Fiction: 1917–1957*. New Haven: Yale University Press, 1971.

Hsiung, Anne-Marie. 'A Feminist Re-Vision of Xu Wei's *Ci Mulan* and *Nü Zhuangyuan*', in Yingjin Zhang (ed.), *China in a Polycentric World*. Stanford University Press, 1998, pp. 73–89.

Hsu Kai-yu (ed. and trans.). *Twentieth Century Chinese Poetry: An Anthology*. Ithaca, NY: Cornell University Press, 1970.

Hsu Pi-ching. 'Courtesans and Scholars in the Writings of Feng Menglong: Transcending Status and Gender', *Nan-nü: Men, Women and Gender in Early and Imperial China* 2.1 (2000), pp. 40–77.

Hsu, Vivian Ling (ed.). *Born of the Same Roots: Stories of Modern Chinese Women*. Bloomington: Indiana University Press, 1981.

Hu Dongyuan. 'Zhongguo chuantong wenhua, shichang jingji, daode jianshe' (Traditional Chinese Culture, The Market Economy, Moral Development), *Xuehai* (Sea of Learning) 1 (1996), pp. 52–54.

Hu Ke. 'Cheng Long dianyingzhong de xijuxing dongzuo yu baoli' (Comic Elements and Violence in Jackie Chan's Films), *Dangdai dianying* (Contemporary Cinema) 1 (2000), pp. 68–72.

Hu Shi. 'Chongfen shijiehua yu quanpan xihua' (Total Globalisation and Wholesale Westernisation), in *Hu Shi wencun* (Collected Works of Hu Shi), vol. 4, no. 2. Taipei: Yuandong tushu, 1971, pp. 541–544.

Hua Shiping (ed.). *Chinese Political Culture: 1989–2000*. Armonk, NY: M.E. Sharpe, 2001.

Huang Huajie. *Guan Yu de renge yu shenge* (The Human and Godlike Characteristics of Guan Yu). Taipei: Taiwan shangwu yinshuguan, 1967.

Huang Kuanzhong. *Nan Song junzheng yu wenxian tansuo* (Explorations into Military Administration and Documents of the Southern Song). Taipei: Xinwen feng chubanshe, 1980.

Huang, Martin W. *Literati and Self-Re/Presentation: Autobiographical Sensibility in the Eighteenth-Century Chinese Novel*. Stanford University Press, 1995.

Huang Qiang. 'Ming Qing "Xi xiang re" de yige zhongyao yuanyin' (One Important Reason for the Continuance of the 'West Wing Fever' of the Ming and Qing Dynasties), *Hebei xuekan* (Hebei Journal) 3 (1999), pp. 69–73.

Huang Ziping. 'Zhengmian zhankai ling yu rou de bodou' (Directly Open Up a Struggle Between Flesh and Mind), originally published in *Wenyi bao*, 7 October 1985, reprinted in Ningxia renmin chubanshe (ed.), *Ping 'Nanren de yiban shi nüren'* (Criticisms of 'Half of Man Is Woman'). Yinchuan: Ningxia renmin chubanshe, 1987, pp. 1–3.

Hulsewé, A.F.P. 'Han-time Documents', *T'oung Pao* 45 (1957), pp. 1–50.

Humana, Charles and Wang Wu. *The Ying-Yang: The Chinese Way of Love*. London: Tandem, 1971.

Huters, Theodore (ed.). *Reading the Modern Chinese Short Story*. Armonk, NY: M.E. Sharpe, 1990.

Jacka, Tamara. *Women's Work in Rural China*. Cambridge University Press, 1997.

Jankowiak, William. 'Chinese Women, Gender, and Sexuality: A Critical Review of Recent Studies', *Bulletin of Concerned Asian Scholars* 31.1 (1999), pp. 31–37.

Jankowiak, William. 'Romantic Passion in the People's Republic of China', in William Jankowiak (ed.), *Romantic Passion: A Universal Experience?* New York: Columbia University Press, 1995, pp. 166–183.

Jankowiak, William R. *Sex, Death, and Hierarchy in a Chinese City: An Anthropological Account.* New York: Columbia University Press, 1993.

Jankowiak, William (ed.). *Romantic Passion: A Universal Experience?* New York: Columbia University Press, 1995.

Jenner, W.J.F. 'A Knife in My Ribs for a Mate: Reflections on Another Chinese Tradition', The Fifty-fourth George Ernest Morrison Lecture in Ethnology 1993, Canberra: Australian National University.

Jenner, W.J.F. *Tyranny of History: The Roots of China's Crisis.* London: Allen Lane, 1992.

Jia Pingwa. *Feidu* (Defunct Capital). First published in Beijing in 1993, reprinted Hong Kong: Tiandi tushu youxian gongsi, 1996.

Jia Pingwa. 'How Much Can a Man Bear?', in Zhu Hong (ed. and trans.), *The Chinese Western.* New York: Ballantine, 1988, pp. 1–52.

Jia Pingwa. 'Renji' (Human Extremities), *Wenhui yuekan* (Literary Monthly) 10 (1985), pp. 2–12.

Jia Pingwa. 'Tian Gou' (Heavenly Hound), in Bo Yang (ed.), *Jia Pingwa juan* (Volume on Jia Pingwa). Taipei: Linbai chubanshe, 1988, pp. 59–122.

Jia Pingwa. *Turbulence: A Novel* (trans. Howard Goldblatt). Baton Rouge: Louisiana State University Press, 1991.

Jiang Xingyu. *Zhongguo xiqushi gouchen* (Explorations in the History of Chinese Drama). Henan: Zhengzhou shuhuashe, 1982.

Jiang Yinxiang (ed.). *Shijing yizhu* (Book of Songs Translated and Annotated). Beijing: Zhongguo shudian, 1982.

Jiang Zilong. 'Manager Qiao Assumes Office' (trans. Wang Mingjie), in *All the Colours of the Rainbow.* Beijing: Chinese Literature, 1983, pp. 130–178.

Kang Youwei. *Datong shu* (The Great Commonwealth). First published 1935, reissued Beijing: Guji chubanshe, 1956.

Kang Youwei. *Kongzi gaizhi kao* (A Study of Confucius as Reformer). First published 1897, reissued Taipei: Taiwan shangwu yinshuguan, 1968.

Kaufman, M. *Beyond Patriarchy: Essays by Men on Pleasure, Power, and Change.* Toronto: Oxford University Press, 1987.

Kiernan, V.G. *The Lords of Human Kind: Black Man, Yellow Man, and White Man in an Age of Empire.* New York: Columbia University Press, 1986.

Kimlicka, Paul. The Novel *San Kuo chih Tung-su yen-i* As Literature: Uses of Irony By Its Author Lo Kuan-chung. Unpublished MA thesis, Indiana University, 1986.

Kimmel, Michael S. 'Masculinities as Homophobia: Fear, Shame and Silence in the Construction of Gender Identity', in Harry Brod and M. Kaufman (eds), *Theorising Masculinities.* Thousand Oaks, CA: Sage, 1994, pp. 119–141.

Kimmel, Michael S. (ed.). *Changing Men: New Directions in Research on Men and Masculinity.* Newbury Park, CA: Sage Publications, 1987.

Kimmel, Michael S. (ed.). *The Politics of Manhood: Profeminist Men Respond to the Mythopoetic Men's Movement.* Philadelphia: Temple University Press, 1995.

Kimmel, Michael S. and Michael A. Messner (eds). *Men's Lives*. Boston: Allyn and Bacon, 1995.

Kinkley, Jeffrey C. 'A Bettelheimian Interpretation of Chang Hsien-liang's Concentration-Camp Novels', *Asia Major* 4.2 (1991), pp. 83–113.

Kong Huiyi (Eva Hung). *Fujie xiandaiban caizi jiaren* (Women's Liberation Modern Edition Talented Scholars and Beautiful Women). Hong Kong: Maitian wenxue, 1996.

Kong Xiangjin and Wang Xinhong, 'Qufu choujian Kongzi wenhua guangchang' (Qufu Raises Money to Build Confucius Culture Square), *Renmin ribao* (People's Daily), 9 April 1999.

Kraus, Richard. *Brushes with Power: Modern Politics and the Chinese Art of Calligraphy*. Berkeley: University of California Press, 1991.

Kuang Yaming. *Kongzi pingzhuan* (A Critical Biography of Confucius). Jinan: Qilu shushe, 1985.

Kusher, Norman. 'The Fifth Relationship: Dangerous Friendships in the Confucian Context', *The American Historical Review* 105.5 (2000), pp. 1615–1629.

Lai, Amy Tak-yee. 'Liberation, Confusion, Imprisonment: The Female Self in Ding Ling's "Diary of Miss Sophie" and Zhang Jie's "Love Must Not be Forgotten"', *Comparative Literature and Culture* 3 (1998), pp. 88–103.

Lan Chao. *Li Xiaolong quanzhuan* (The Complete Biography of Bruce Lee). Hong Kong: Mingliu chubanshe, 1999.

Lan Yang. *Chinese Fiction of the Cultural Revolution*. Hong Kong University Press, 1998.

Lao She. *Beneath the Red Flag* (trans. Don J. Cohn). Beijing: Panda Books, 1982.

Lao She. 'Er Ma' (The Two Mas), in Shu Ji and Shu Yi (eds), *Lao She xiaoshuo quanji* (Complete Stories by Lao She), vol. 2. Wuhan: Changjiang wenyi chubanshe, 1993, pp. 1–250.

Lao She. *The Two Mas* (trans. Kenny K. Huang and David Finkelstein). Hong Kong: Joint Publishing, 1984.

Larson, Wendy. *Women and Writing in Modern China*. Stanford University Press, 1998.

Lau, D.C. 'Introduction', *Confucius: The Analects*. Harmondsworth: Penguin Books, 1979, pp. 9–55.

Lau, D.C. (trans.). *Confucius: The Analects*. Harmondsworth: Penguin Books, 1979.

Lau, Jenny Kwok Wah (also romanised as Loh). 'A Cultural Interpretation of the Popular Cinema of China and Hong Kong', in Chris Berry (ed.), *Perspectives on Chinese Cinema*. London: British Film Institute, 1991, pp. 166–174.

Lee, Leo Ou-fan. 'Hong Kong Movies in Hollywood: An Informal Comment on Asian "Influences" in American Popular Culture', *Harvard Asia Pacific Review*, Winter Issue (1998–89), http://hcs.harvard.edu/~hapr/winter98/people.htm/.

Lee, Leo Oufan. *The Romantic Generation of Modern Chinese Writers*. Cambridge, MA: Harvard University Press, 1973.

Lee, Lily Xiao Hong, A.D. Stefanowska and Clara Wing-chung Ho (eds). *Biographical Dictionary of Chinese Women: The Qing Period, 1644–1911*. Armonk, NY: M.E. Sharpe, 1998.

Lee Yee (ed.). *The New Realism: Writings from China After the Cultural Revolution*. New York: Hippocrene Books, 1983.

Legge, James (ed. and trans.). *The Ch'un Tsew with The Tso Chuen*. Originally published 1935, reprinted Taipei: Southern Materials Center, 1985.

Levant, Ronald F. 'The Masculinity Crisis', *The Journal of Men's Studies* 5.3 (1997), pp. 221–31.

Lever-Tracy, C., D. Ip, J. Kitay, I. Phillips and N. Tracy. *Asian Entrepreneurs in Australia, Ethnic Small Business in the Chinese and Indian Communities of Brisbane and Sydney: Report to the Office of Multicultural Affairs*. Department of the Prime Minister and Cabinet, Canberra: Australian Government Publishing Service, 1991.

Li Bihua. *Zhongguo nanren* (Chinese Males). Hong Kong: Tiandi tushu, 1993.

Li Cunbao. *Gaoshan xia de huahuan* (The Wreath at the Foot of the Mountain). Ji'nan: Shandong wenyi chubanshe, 1984.

Li Cunbao. *The Wreath at the Foot of the Mountain* (trans. Chen Hanming and James O. Belcher). New York: Garland, 1991.

Li Daxuan. *Ding Ling yu Shafei xilie xingxiang* (Images of Ding Ling and Sophia). Changsha: Hunan wenyi chubanshe, 1991.

Li Ju-chen. *Flowers in the Mirror* (trans. Lin Tai-yi). Berkeley: University of California Press, 1965.

Li Mingguang. 'Chen Daoming shuo "Er Ma"' (Chen Daoming on *The Two Mas*), *Renmin ribao* (People's Daily), 23 February 1999.

Li Ruzhen. *Jinghua yuan*. First published 1828, reissued Taipei: Xuehai chubanshe, 1985.

Li Xianghai. 'Rujia lunli yu Dongya xiandaihua' (Confucian Ethics and East Asian Modernisation), *Zhongzhou xuekan* (Zhongzhou Journal) 1 (1997), pp. 64–69.

Li Xiaojiang. 'Resisting While Holding the Tradition: Claims for Rights Raised in Literature by Chinese Women Writers in the New Period', *Tamkang Review* 30.2 (1999), pp. 99–109.

Li Xifan. 'Lüe lun *Sanguo yanyi* li de Guan Yu de xingxiang' (A Brief Discussion of Guan Yu's Image in *Romance of the Three Kingdoms*), in Henan sheng shehui kexueyuan (ed.), *Sanguo yanyi yanjiu lunwen ji* (Collected Essays on *The Romance of the Three Kingdoms*). Beijing: Zhonghua shuju, 1991, pp. 395–411.

Li Xiguang and Liu Kang (eds). *Yaomohua Zhongguo de beihou* (Behind the Demonised China). Beijing: Zhongguo shehuikexue chubanshe, 1996.

Li Yinnong. 'Lun Kongzi dui laodong de taidu' (On Confucius' Attitudes Towards Labour). *Yangcheng wanbao* (Guangzhou Evening News), 22 March 1962.

Li Yu. *Rou putuan: The Carnal Prayer Mat* (trans. Patrick Hanan). London: Arrow Books, 1990.

Li Ziyun. 'The Disappearance and Revival of Feminine Discourse', *Tamkang Review* 30.2 (1999), pp. 55–69.

Liang Jian. *Cheng Long* (Jackie Chan). Hong Kong: Xingli youxian gongsi, 1997.

Liang Xin. 'Shenme jiao "dangdai xin rujia"?' (What is a 'Contemporary Neo-Confucianist'?), *Wenhui bao* (Wenhui Daily), 10 June 1986.

Little, John R. (ed.). *Bruce Lee: Words from a Master*. Chicago: Contemporary Books, 1999.

Little, John (ed.). *Jeet Kune Do: Bruce Lee's Commentaries on the Martial Way*. Boston: Tuttle Publishing, 1997.

Litzinger, Ralph A. 'Questions of Gender: Ethnic Minority Representations in Post-Mao China', *Bulletin of Concerned Asian Scholars* 32.4 (2000), pp. 3–14.

Liu Dalin. *Xing shehuixue* (Sociology of Sex). Ji'nan: Shandong renmin chubanshe, 1988.

Liu Dalin. *Zhongguo dangdai xing wenhua* (Sexual Behaviour in Modern China). Shanghai: Sanlian shudian, 1992.

Liu Dalin. *Zhongguo gudai xing wenhua* (The Sex Culture of Ancient China). Yinchuan: Ningxia renmin chubanshe, 1993.

Liu Fudao. 'Yanjing' (Glasses), in *Aiqing xiaoshuo ji* (Collected Love Stories). Shanghai: Shanghai wenyi chubanshe, 1979, pp. 1–21.

Liu, James J.Y. *The Chinese Knight-Errant*. London: Routledge and Kegan Paul, 1967.

Liu Lanying et al. (eds). *Zhongguo gudai wenxue cidian: dier juan*. Nanning: Guangxi jiaoyu chubanshe, 1989.

Liu, Lydia H. 'Invention and Intervention: The Making of a Female Tradition in Modern Chinese Literature', in Ellen Widmer and David Derwei Wang (eds), *From May Fourth to June Fourth: Fiction and Film in Twentieth-Century China*. Cambridge, Mass: Harvard University Press, 1993, pp. 194–220.

Liu, Lydia H. *Translingual Practice: Literature, National Culture, and Translated Modernity – China, 1900–1937*. Stanford University Press, 1995.

Liu Minghua. 'Rujia yili guan yu fazhan shehuizhuyi shichang jingji' (On the Confucians' Attitudes Towards Yi-Li and the Developing Socialist Market Economy), *Guizhou daxue xuebao* (Guizhou University Journal) 1 (1996), pp. 24–29.

Liu Shaoqi. *Lun Gongchandang yuan de xiuyang* (On the Self-cultivation of a Communist Party Member). Beijing: Renmin chubanshe, 1962 reprint.

Liu Wu-Chi. *An Introduction to Chinese Literature*. Bloomington: Indiana University Press, 1966.

Liu Xinwu. 'Ban zhuren' (Class Teacher), *Renmin wenxue* 11 (1977), pp. 16–29.

Liu Zhijian. '*Sanguo yanyi* xinlun (A New Discussion of *The Romance of the Three Kingdoms*). Chongqing: Chongqing chubanshe, 1985.

Lo Jung-pang (ed.). *K'ang Yu-wei: A Biography and a Symposium*. Tucson: University of Arizona Press, 1967.

Logan, Bey. *Hong Kong Action Cinema*. London: Titan Books, 1995.

Louie, Kam. *Between Fact and Fiction: Essays on Post-Mao Chinese Literature & Society*. Sydney: Wild Peony, 1989.

Louie, Kam. 'Constructing Chinese Masculinity for the Modern World: with Particular Reference to Lao She's *The Two Mas*', *China Quarterly*, 164 (2000), pp. 1062–1078.

Louie, Kam. *Critiques of Confucius in Contemporary China*. Hong Kong: Chinese University Press, 1980.

Louie, Kam. 'I Married a Foreigner: Recovering Chinese Masculinity in Australia', in Wenche Ommundsen (ed.), *Bastard Moon: Essays on Chinese-Australian Writing*, Special Issue of *Otherland* 7 (2001), pp. 39–56.

Louie, Kam. 'In Search of Socialist Capitalism and Chinese Modernisation', *Australian Journal of Chinese Affairs* 12 (1984), pp. 87–96.

Louie, Kam. 'In Search of the Chinese Soul in the Mountains of the South', *The China Journal* 45 (2001), pp. 145–149.

Louie, Kam. *Inheriting Tradition: Interpretations of the Classical Philosophers in Communist China 1949–1966*. Hong Kong: Oxford University Press, 1986.

Louie, Kam. 'Sage, Teacher, Businessman: Confucius as a Model Male', in Shiping Hua (ed.), *Chinese Political Culture: 1989–2000*. Armonk, NY: M.E. Sharpe, 2001, pp. 21–41.

Louie, Kam. 'Salvaging Confucian Education (1949–1983)', *Comparative Education* 20.1 (1984), pp. 27–38.

Louie, Kam. 'Sexuality, Masculinity and Politics in Chinese Culture: The Case of the *Sanguo* Hero Guan Yu', *Modern Asian Studies* 33.4 (1999), pp. 835–860.

Louie, Kam (ed. and introd.). *Strange Tales from Strange Lands: Stories by Zheng Wanlong*. Ithaca, NY: Cornell East Asian Series, 1993.

Louie, Kam. 'The Macho Eunuch: The Politics of Masculinity in Jia Pingwa's "Human Extremities"', *Modern China* 17.2 (1991), pp. 163–187.

Louie, Kam and Cheung Chiu-yee. 'Three Kingdoms: The Chinese Cultural Scene Today', in Joseph Y.S. Cheng (ed.), *China Review 1998*. Hong Kong: Chinese University Press, 1998, pp. 543–575.

Louie, Kam and Louise Edwards. 'Chinese Masculinity: Theorizing *Wen* and *Wu*', *East Asian History* 8 (1994), pp. 135–148.

Low, Morris. 'The Japanese Nation in Evolution: W.E. Griffis, Hybridity and the Whiteness of the Japanese Race', *History and Anthropology* 11.2–3 (1999), pp. 203–234.

Lu Cao. *Zhongguo wushu* (China's *wu* techniques, translated on the cover as 'China's Gongfu [kung fu]'). Guangzhou: Guangdong lüyou chubanshe, 1996.

Lu, Sheldon H. 'Soap Opera in China: The Transnational Politics of Visuality, Sexuality, and Masculinity', *Cinema Journal* 30.1 (2000), pp. 25–47.

Lu, Sheldon Hsiao-peng (ed.). *Transnational Chinese Cinemas: Identity, Nationhood, Gender*. Honolulu: University of Hawai'i Press, 1997.

Lu Tongling (ed.). *Gender and Sexuality in Twentieth-Century Chinese Literature and Society*. Albany: SUNY, 1993.

Lu Hsun (Lu Xun). 'An Incident', in *Selected Stories of Lu Hsun*. Peking: Foreign Languages Press, 1960, pp. 42–44.

Lu Hsun (Lu Xun). 'Kung I-chi', in *Selected Stories of Lu Hsun*. Peking: Foreign Languages Press, 1960, pp. 19–24.

Lu Hsun (Lu Xun). 'Preface to the First Collection of Short Stories, "Call to Arms"', in *Selected Stories of Lu Hsun*. Peking: Foreign Languages Press, 1960, pp. 1–6.

Lu Hsun (Lu Xun). *Selected Stories of Lu Hsun*. Peking: Foreign Languages Press, 1960.

Lu Hsun (Lu Xun). 'The New Year's Sacrifice', in *Selected Stories of Lu Hsun*. Peking: Foreign Languages Press, 1960, pp. 125–143.

Lu Xun. 'My Views on Chastity', in *Lu Xun: Selected Works*, vol. 2. Beijing: Foreign Languages Press, 1980, pp. 13–25.

Lu Xun. *Lu Xun: Selected Works*, vol. 2. Beijing: Foreign Languages Press, 1980.

Lu Xun and Others. *Masterpieces of Modern Chinese Fiction 1919–1949*. Beijing: Foreign Languages Press, 1983.

Lü Yi. 'Chunpu de shipian' (Simple Poetry), in Sun Luxi and Wang Fengbo (eds), *Ru Zhijuan yanjiu zhuanji* (Anthology on Ru Zhijuan Research). Hangzhou: Zhejiang renmin chubanshe, 1982, pp. 255–280.

Lu Yue. *Li Xiaolong chuanqi* (Biography of Bruce Lee). Hong Kong: Huangguan chubanshe, 1996.

Luke, Allan. 'Representing and Reconstructing Asian Masculinities: This is not a Movie Review', *Social Alternatives* 16.31(1997), pp. 32–34

Luke, Carmen. 'White Women in Interracial Families: Reflections on Hybridization, Feminine Identities, and Racialized Othering', *Feminist Issues* 14.2 (1994), pp. 49–72.

Luke, Carmen and Allan Luke. 'Interracial Families: Difference within Difference', *Ethnic and Racial Studies* 21.4 (1998), pp. 728–754.

Luke, Carmen and Allan Luke. 'Theorizing Interracial Families and Hybrid Identity: An Australian Perspective', *Educational Theory* 49.2 (1999), pp. 223–249.

Luke, Carmen and Vicki Carrington. 'Race Matters', *Journal of Intercultural Studies* 21.1 (2000), pp. 5–24.

Luo Guanzhong. *Sanguo yanyi* (Romance of the Three Kingdoms), 2 vols. Taipei: Guiguan tushu, 1988 reprint.

Luo Guanzhong. *Three Kingdoms: A Historical Novel* (trans. Moss Roberts), 3 vols. Beijing: Foreign Languages Press, 1994.

Luo Guojie. 'Guanyu Kongzi yili guan de yidian sikao' (Some Considerations on Confucius' Attitudes Towards Yi-Li), *Xueshu yanjiu* (Academic Research) 3 (1994), pp. 51–53.

Luo Zhufeng (ed.). *Hanyu da cidian* (The Great Chinese Dictionary), 13 vols and index. Shanghai: Hanyu da cidian chubanshe, 1988–1994.

Ma Liangchun and Li Futian (eds). *Zhongguo wenxue dacidian* (Dictionary of Chinese Literature), 8 vols. Tianjin: Tianjin renmin chubanshe, 1991.

Ma, Y.W. and Joseph S.M. Lau (eds). *Traditional Chinese Stories: Themes and Variations*. New York: Columbia University Press, 1978.

McDougall, Bonnie S. 'Disappearing Women and Disappearing Men in May Fourth Narrative: A Post-Feminist Survey of Short Stories by Mao Dun, Bing Xin, Ling Shuhua and Shen Congwen', *Asian Studies Review* 22.4 (1998), pp. 427–458.

McDougall, Bonnie S. and Kam Louie. *The Literature of China in the Twentieth Century*. London: Hurst, 1997.

McIsaac, Lee. '"Righteousness Fraternities" and Honorable Men: Sworn Brotherhoods in Wartime Chongqing', *The American Historical Review* 105.5 (2000), pp. 1614–1655.

Mackerras, Colin. *Western Images of China*. Hong Kong: Oxford University Press, 1989.

McKnight, Brian E. *Law and Order in Sung China*. Cambridge University Press, 1992.

McLaren, Anne. *Chinese Popular Culture and Ming Chantefables*. Leiden, Netherlands: E.J. Brill, 1998.

McLelland, Mark. 'Is There a Japanese "Gay Identity"?', *Culture, Health and Sexuality* 2.4 (2000), pp. 459–472.

McLelland, Mark J. *Male Homosexuality in Modern Japan: Cultural Myths and Social Realities*. Richmond, UK: Curzon, 2000.

McMahon, Keith. 'The Classic "Beauty-Scholar": Romance and the Superiority of the Talented Woman', in Angela Zito and Tani E. Barlow (eds), *Body, Subject & Power in China*. University of Chicago Press, 1994, pp. 227–252.

McMahon, Keith. *Causality and Containment in Seventeenth-Century Chinese Fiction*. Leiden, Netherlands: E.J. Brill, 1988.

McMahon, Keith. *Misers, Shrews and Polygamists: Sexuality and Male–Female Relations in Eighteenth-century Chinese Fiction*. Durham, NC: Duke University Press, 1995.

McMullen, D.L. 'The Cult of Ch'i T'ai-kung and T'ang Attitudes to the Military', *T'ang Studies* 7 (1989), pp. 59–103.

Major, Wade. *Jackie Chan*. New York: MetroBooks, 1999.

Malraux, André. *Man's Estate* (trans. Alastair Macdonald). Harmondsworth: Penguin Books, 1961.

Mann, Susan. 'The Male Bond in Chinese History and Culture', *The American Historical Review* 105.5 (2000), pp. 1600–1614.

Mann, Susan. *Precious Records: Women in China's Long Eighteenth Century*. Stanford University Press, 1997.

Mao Dun. 'Tan zuijin de duanpian xiaoshuo' (On a Recent Short Story), in Sun Luxi and Wang Fengbo (eds), *Ru Zhijuan yanjiu zhuanji* (Anthology on Ru Zhijuan Research). Hangzhou: Zhejiang renmin chubanshe, 1982, pp. 247–251.

Mao Zedong. 'Report on an Investigation of the Peasant Movement in Hunan', *Selected Works of Mao Tse-tung*, vol. 1. Beijing: Foreign Languages Press, 1967, pp. 23–59.

Mao Zedong. 'The Snow', in Kai-yu Hsu (trans. and ed.), *Twentieth Century Chinese Poetry: An Anthology*. Ithaca, NY: Cornell University Press, 1970, pp. 363–364.

Mao Zonggang. 'Di yi caizi shu' (Number One Work of Genius), published under the title *Sanguo yanyi de zhengzhi yu molüe guan* (Politics and Strategy in *The Romance of the Three Kingdoms*). Taipei: Laogu wenhua shiye, 1985.

Marchetti, Gina. 'Jackie Chan and the Black Connection', in Matthew Tinkcom and Amy Villarejo (eds), *Keyframes: Popular Cinema and Cultural Studies*. London: Routledge, 2001, pp. 136–158.

Marchetti, Gina. *Romance and the 'Yellow Peril': Race, Sex, and Discourse Strategies in Hollywood Fiction*. Berkeley: University of California Press, 1993.

May, J.P. 'The Chinese in Britain, 1860–1914', in Colin Holmes (ed.), *Immigrants and Minorities in British Society*. London: George Allen & Unwin, 1978, pp. 111–124.

Metcalf, Andy and Martin Humphries (eds). *The Sexuality of Men*. London: Pluto Press, 1985.

Miao Runtian. 'Qianlun Kongzi de yili guan ji qi xiandai yiyi' (On Confucius' Attitude Towards Yi-Li and its Modern Significance), *Qilu xuekan* (Qilu Journal) 1 (1989), pp. 55–59.

Miller, David. *The Tao of Bruce Lee*. London: Vintage, 2000.

Milner, Anthony and Mary Quilty (eds). *Australia in Asia: Episodes*. Melbourne: Oxford University Press, 1998.

Minford, John and Joseph S.M. Lau (eds). *Classical Chinese Literature: An Anthology of Translations, volume 1: From Antiquity to the Tang Dynasty*. New York: Columbia University Press, 2000.

Minh-ha, Trinh T. *Woman, Native, Other*. Bloomington: Indiana University Press, 1989.

Mishima, Yukio. *The Way of the Samurai: Yukio Mishima on Hagakure in Modern Life* (trans. Kathryn Sparling). New York: Basic Books, 1977.

Moir, Anne and Bill. *Why Men Don't Iron: The Real Science of Gender Studies.* London: Harper-Collins, 1998.

Moore, S. 'Getting a Bit of the Other: The Pimps of Postmodernism', in Rowena Chapman and Jonathan Rutherford (eds), *Male Order: Unwrapping Masculinity*. London: Lawrence & Wishart, 1988, pp. 165–192.

Morris, Meagan. 'Learning from Bruce Lee: Pedagogy and Political Correctness in Martial Arts Cinema', in Matthew Tinkcom and Amy Villarejo (eds), *Keyframes: Popular Cinema and Cultural Studies*. London: Routledge, 2001, pp. 171–186.

Muller, F. Max (ed.). *The Sacred Books of the East*, vol. XXVIII: James Legge (trans.), *The Texts of Confucianism Part IV The Li Ki, XI–XLVI*. Oxford: Clarendon Press, 1885.

Munro, Donald J. *The Concept of Man in Early China*. Stanford University Press, 1969.

Nathan, Andrew J. *China's Transition*. New York: Columbia University Press, 1997.

Needham, Joseph. *Science and Civilization in China*, vol. 2: *History of Scientific Thought*. Cambridge University Press, 1954.

Ng, Vivien W. 'Homosexuality and the State in Late Imperial China', in Martin Bauml Duberman et al. (eds), *Hidden From History: Reclaiming the Gay and Lesbian Past*. Harmondsworth: Penguin Books, 1991, pp. 86–87.

Nielsen, Inge. 'Modern Chinese Literature Sells Out', *Tamkang Review* 30.3 (2000), pp. 89–109.

Nienhauser Jr, William H. (ed.). *The Indiana Companion to Traditional Chinese Literature*. Bloomington: Indiana University Press, 1986.

Ningxia renmin chubanshe (ed.). *Ping 'Nanren de yiban shi nüren'* (Criticisms of 'Half of Man Is Woman'). Yinchuan: Ningxia renmin chubanshe, 1987.

Nonini, Donald M. 'The Dialectics of "Disputatiousness" and "Rice-Eating Money": Class Confrontation and Gendered Imaginaries Among Chinese Men in West Malaysia', *American Ethnologist* 26.1 (1999), pp. 47–68.

Oakley, Ann. *Sex, Gender and Society*. Aldershot, UK: Gower/Temple Smith, 1972.

Ommundsen, Wenche (ed.). *Bastard Moon: Essays on Chinese-Australian Writing*, Special Issue of *Otherland* 7, 2001.

Orr, John. *Contemporary Cinema*. Edinburgh University Press, 1998.

Ostrovsky, Nikolai. *How The Steel Was Tempered Part 1*. Moscow: Foreign Languages Press, 1952.

Otomo, Ryoko. '"The Way of the Samurai": Ghost Dog, Mishima, and Modernity's Other', *Japanese Studies* 21.1 (2001), pp. 31–43.

Ouyang Wenbin. 'Shilun Ru Zhijuan de yishu fengge' (On Ru Zhijuan's Artistic Style), in Sun Luxi and Wang Fengbo (eds), *Ru Zhijuan yanjiu zhuanji* (Anthology on Ru Zhijuan Research). Hangzhou: Zhejiang renmin chubanshe, 1982, pp. 111–122.

Ouyang Yu. *Moon Over Melbourne: Poems*. Upper Ferntree Gully, Vic.: Papyrus Publishing, 1997.

Pan, Esther. 'Why Asian Guys Are on a Roll', *Newsweek* 135.8 (2000), p. 50.

Parker, David. *Through Chinese Eyes: The Cultural Identities of Young Chinese People in Britain*. Aldershot, UK: Avebury, 1995.

Paz, Octavio. *The Labyrinth of Solitude* (trans. Lysander Kemp). New York: Grove, 1961.

Peng Bin. 'Lun Wang Anyi yishu de fengge de yanbian' (On the Changes in Wang Anyi's Artistic Techniques), *Shehuikexuejia* (The Social Scientist) 6 (1989), pp. 74–78.

Peng, Hsiao-yen. 'Sex Histories: Zhang Jingsheng's Sexual Revolution', *Tamkang Review* 30.2 (1999), pp. 71–98.

Perry, John Curtis and Bardwell L. Smith (eds). *Essays on T'ang Society*. Leiden, Netherlands: E.J. Brill, 1976.

Plaks, Andrew. *The Four Masterworks of the Ming Novel*. Princeton: Princeton University Press, 1987.

Pu Songling. *Liaozhai zhiyi* (Strange Tales from the Leisure Studio). Hong Kong: Shangwu yinshuguan, 1963.

Pulleyblank, Edwin G. 'The An Lu-Shan Rebellion and the Origins of Chronic Militarism in Late T'ang China', in John Curtis Perry and Bardwell L. Smith (eds), *Essays on T'ang Society*. Leiden, Netherlands: E.J. Brill, 1976, pp. 32–60.

Qian Hong. 'Youmei shiluo zhihou' (After Gracefulness Has Declined), *Guangming ribao* (Guangming Daily), 21 August 1987.

Qian Ning. 'Liuxue Meiguo' (Studying in USA), in *Xinhua wenzhai* (New China Digest) 10 (1996), pp. 85–97.

Qiu Zhensheng. *Sanguo yanyi zongheng tan* (Random Essays on *The Romance of the Three Kingdoms*). Taipei: Xiaoyuan chubanshe, 1991.

Qu Yuan. 'Li Sao' (On Encountering Trouble), in David Hawkes (ed. and trans.), *The Songs of the South*. Harmondsworth: Penguin, 1985, pp. 67–95.

Raven, Charlotte. 'Crashing Bore, Wooden Drama', *The Guardian*, 16 January 2001.

Roberts, Moss (trans. and ed.). *Three Kingdoms: China's Epic Drama by Lo Kuan-chung*. New York: Pantheon Books, 1976.

Rofel, Lisa. *Other Modernities: Gendered Yearnings in China After Socialism*. Berkeley: University of California Press, 1999.

Rohmer, Sax. *The Insidious Dr Fu-Manchu*. New York: Pyramid Books, 1961.

Rolls, Eric. *Sojourners: The Epic Story of China's Centuries-Old Relationship with Australia*. St Lucia: University of Queensland Press, 1992.

Ross, Gordon Victor. Guan Yu in Drama: Translations and Critical Discussions of Two Yuan Plays. Unpublished PhD dissertation, University of Texas at Austin, 1976.

Rou Shi. 'A Hired Wife', in Lu Xun and Others, *Masterpieces of Modern Chinese Fiction 1919–1949*. Beijing: Foreign Languages Press, 1983, pp. 205–229.

Ru Zhijuan. 'Baihehua' (Lilies), *Zhongguo dangdai zuopin xuanbian 1949–1986* (Readings from Chinese Writers 1949–1986), vol. 1. Beijing: Sinolingua, 1989, pp. 165–182.

Ru Zhijuan. 'Ernü qing' (trans. Ellen Klempner as 'Sons and Successors'), in Lee Yee (ed.), *The New Realism: Writings from China After the Cultural Revolution*. New York: Hippocrene Books, 1983, pp. 17–30.

Ru Zhijuan. 'How I Came to Write "Lilies on a Comforter"', in Helen Siu (ed.), *Furrows: Peasants, Intellectuals, and the State*. Stanford University Press, 1990, pp. 297–303.

Ru Zhijuan. 'Lilies' (trans. Gladys Yang), in *Lilies and Other Stories*. Beijing: Panda Books, 1985, pp. 7–19.

Ruhlmann, Robert. 'Traditional Heroes in Chinese Popular Fiction', in Arthur Wright (ed.), *The Confucian Persuasion*. Stanford University Press, 1960, pp. 141–176.

Rushton, J. Philippe. *Race, Evolution, and Behaviour: A Life History Perspective*. New Brunswick, NJ: Transaction Publishers, 1997.

Ryan, Jan. '"She Lives with a Chinaman": Orient-ing "White" Women in the Court of Law', *Journal of Australian Studies* 18 (1999), pp. 149–159, 216–218.

Said, Edward. *Orientalism*. London: Routledge & Kegan Paul, 1978.

Saikaku, Ihara. *The Great Mirror of Male Love* (trans. and introd. Paul Gordon Schalow). Stanford University Press, 1990.

Sandell, Jillian. 'Reinventing Masculinity: The Spectacle of Male Intimacy in the Films of John Woo', *Film Quarterly* 49.4 (1996), pp. 23–34.

Schein, Louisa. *Minority Rules: The Miao and the Feminine in China's Cultural Politics*. Durham, NC: Duke University Press, 2000.

Sedgwick, Eve Kosofsky. *Between Men: English Literature and Male Homosocial Desire*. New York: Columbia University Press, 1985.

Sellmann, James D. and Sharon Rowe, 'The Feminine in Confucius', *Asian Culture* 26.3 (1998), pp. 1–8.

Sheehy, Gail. *Passages for Men: Discovering the New Map of Men's Lives*. London: Simon & Schuster, 1998.

Shen Congwen. 'The Husband', in Lu Xun and Others, *Masterpieces of Modern Chinese Fiction 1919–1949*. Beijing: Foreign Languages Press, 1983, pp. 398–417.

Shi Jingping. 'Gechang putongren de xinlingmei' (In Praise of the Beautiful Souls of the Common People), in Sun Luxi and Wang Fengbo (eds), *Ru Zhijuan yanjiu zhuanji* (Anthology on Ru Zhijuan Research), Hangzhou: Zhejiang renmin chubanshe, 1982, pp. 265–270.

Shi Nai'an. *All Men Are Brothers* (trans. Pearl S. Buck), 2 vols. London: Methuen, 1957.

Shi Nai'an. *Shuihu zhuan* (Water Margin), 2 vols. Taipei: Lianjing chuban shiye gongsi, 1987.

Shi Nai'an and Luo Guanzhong, *Outlaws of the Marsh*, vol. 1 (trans. Sidney Shapiro). Beijing: Foreign Languages Press, 1980.

Shi Qi (Sek Kei). *Shi Qi yinghua ji: Shiba ban wuyi* (Collected Essays on Sek Kei's Film Reviews: The 18 Martial Arts Styles), vol. 1. Hong Kong: Ciwenhua youxian gongsi, 1999.

Shu Ji and Shu Yi (eds). *Lao She xiaoshuo quanji* (Complete Stories by Lao She), vol. 2. Wuhan: Changjiang wenyi chubanshe, 1993.

Shuowen jiezi zhu (Annotated *Shuowen jiezi*). Shanghai: Guji chubanshe, 1981.

Silverman, Kaja. *The Subject of Semiotics*. Oxford University Press, 1983.

Sima Xiaomeng. *Nanzi shenghuo daquan* (*Encyclopedia for Men*). Zhengzhou: Henan kexuejishu chubanshe, 1996.

Sinha, Mrinalini. *Colonial Masculinity: The 'Manly Englishman' and the 'Effeminate Bengali' in the Late Nineteenth Century*. Manchester University Press, 1995.

Siu, Helen (ed.). *Furrows: Peasants, Intellectuals, and the State*. Stanford University Press, 1990.

Sommer, Deborah. The Unlearned Sage? The Early Iconography of Confucius and Its Textual Referents. Unpublished paper presented at the XXXVIth International Congress of Asian and North African Studies (September 2000).

Song Geng. 'Wax Spear-head: The Construction of Masculinity in Yuan Drama', *Tamkang Review* 30.1 (2000), pp. 209–254.

Song Xiren. 'Rujia chuantong yili guan yu qingshaonian daode jiaoyu' (On the Confucians' Attitudes Towards Yi-Li and the Moral Education of the Young), *Jiangsu shehui kexue* (Jiangsu Social Sciences) 6 (1993), pp. 119–123.

Song Yongyi. *Lao She yu Zhongguo wenhua guannian* (Lao She and Chinese Culture). Shanghai: Xuelin chubanshe, 1988.

Song Zhongfu et al. *Ruxue zai xiandai Zhongguo* (Confucianism in Modern China). Zhengzhou: Zhengzhou guji chubanshe, 1991.

Spence, Jonathan D. *Ts'ao Yin and the Kang-hsi Emperor.* New Haven, CT: Yale University Press, 1966.

Stacey, Judith. *Patriarchy and the Socialist Revolution in China.* Berkeley: University of California Press, 1983.

Stecopoulos, Harry and Michael Uebel (eds). *Race and the Subject of Masculinities.* Durham, NC: Duke University Press, 1997.

Stoltenberg, John. *Refusing to Be a Man.* Portland, Or: Breitenbush Books, 1989.

Story of Hua Guan Suo, The (trans. Gail Oman King). Phoenix: Center for Asian Studies, Arizona State University, 1989.

Su Dongpo. 'Tune: "The Charms of Nian-nu"' (trans. Ch'u Ta-kao), in Cyril Birch (ed.), *Anthology of Chinese Literature.* Harmondsworth: Penguin, 1967, p. 361.

Sun Longji. *Zhongguo wenhua de 'shenceng jiegou'* (The 'Deep Structure' of Chinese Culture). Hong Kong: Jixianshe, 1983.

Sun Luxi and Wang Fengbo (eds). *Ru Zhijuan yanjiu zhuanji* (Anthology on Ru Zhijuan Research). Hangzhou: Zhejiang renmin chubanshe, 1982.

Sun Shaoxian. *Nüxing zhuyi wenxue* (Feminist Literature). Shenyang: Liaoning daxue chubanshe, 1987.

Symons, Donald. *The Evolution of Human Sexuality.* Oxford University Press, 1979.

Tam, Kwok-kan. 'Sexuality and Power in Zhang Xianliang's Novel *Half of Man Is Woman*', *Modern Chinese Literature* 5.1 (1989), pp. 55–72.

Tan Liangxiao and Zhang Dake (eds). *Sanguo renwu pingzhuan* (Critical Biographies of Characters from the Three Kingdoms). Taipei: Shuiniu, 1992.

Tang Ming. 'Meili de huaduo, chunpu de shipian' (Beautiful Flower, Simple Poetry), in Sun Luxi and Wang Fengbo (eds), *Ru Zhijuan yanjiu zhuanji* (Anthology on Ru Zhijuan Research). Hangzhou: Zhejiang renmin chubanshe, 1982, pp. 261–264.

Tasker, Yvonne. 'Dumb Movies for Dumb People: Masculinity, the Body, and the Voice in Contemporary Action Cinema', in Steven Cohan and Ina Rae Hark (eds), *Screening the Male: Exploring Masculinities in Hollywood Cinema.* London: Routledge, 1993, pp. 230–244.

Tasker, Yvonne. 'Fists of Fury: Discourses of Race and Masculinity in the Martial Arts Cinema', in Harry Stecopoulos and Michael Uebel (eds), *Race and the Subject of Masculinities.* Durham, NC: Duke University Press, 1997, pp. 315–336.

Tasker, Yvonne. *Spectacular Bodies: Gender, Genre, and the Action Cinema*. London: Routledge, 1993.

Teo, Stephen. *Hong Kong Cinema: The Extra Dimensions*. London: The British Film Institute, 1997.

Teo, Stephen. 'Love and Swords: The Dialectics of Martial Arts Romance', *Senses of Cinema*, http://www.sensesofcinema/00/11/crouching.html.

Thompson, Laurence G. '*Ta-t'ung Shu* and the *Communist Manifesto*: Some Comparisons', in Jung-pang Lo (ed.), *K'ang Yu-wei: A Biography and a Symposium*. Tucson: University of Arizona Press, 1967, pp. 341–356.

Tinkcom, Matthew and Amy Villarejo (eds). *Keyframes: Popular Cinema and Cultural Studies*. London: Routledge, 2001.

Tsao Hsueh-chin (Cao Xueqin). *A Dream of Red Mansions* (trans. Yang Hsien-yi and Gladys Yang), 2 vols. Beijing: Foreign Languages Press, 1978.

Tu Wei-ming (ed.). *Confucian Traditions in East Asian Modernity: Moral Education and Economic Culture in Japan and the Four Mini-Dragons*. Cambridge, Mass: Harvard University Press, 1996.

Van Gulik, R.H. *Sexual Life in Ancient China*. Leiden, Netherlands: E.J. Brill, 1974.

van Wees, Hans. 'A Brief History of Tears: Gender Differentiation in Archaic Greece', in Lin Foxhall and John Salmon (eds), *When Men Were Men: Masculinity, Power and Identity in Classical Antiquity*. London: Routledge, 1998, pp. 10–53.

Vitielli, Giovanni. 'Exemplary Sodomites: Chivalry and Love in Late Ming Culture', *Nan Nü: Men, Women and Gender in Early and Imperial China* 2.2 (2000), pp. 207–257.

Vohra, Ranbir. *Lao She and the Chinese Revolution*. Cambridge, Mass: East Asian Research Center, Harvard University Press, 1974.

Wagner, Martha L. 'Reviews: *Half of Man Is Woman*', *Modern Chinese Literature* 5.1 (1989), pp. 137–143.

Wang Anyi. *Brocade Valley* (trans. Bonnie S. McDougall and Chen Maiping). New York: New Directions, 1992.

Wang Anyi. *Huangshan zhi lian* (Love in a Barren Mountain). Hong Kong: Nanyue chubanshe, 1988.

Wang, David. 'Lao She's Wartime Fiction', *Modern Chinese Literature* 5.2 (1989), pp. 197–218.

Wang, David Der-wei. 'Feminist Consciousness in Modern Male Fiction', in Michael Duke (ed.), *Modern Chinese Women Writers: Critical Appraisals*. Armonk, NY: M.E. Sharpe, 1989, pp. 236–261.

Wang, Der-wei David. *Fictional Realism in Twentieth-Century China: Mao Dun, Lao She, Shen Congwen*. New York: Columbia University Press, 1992.

Wang Huiyun and Su Qingchang. *Lao She pingzhuan* (A Critical Biography of Lao She). Shijiazhuang: Huashanwenyi chubanshe, 1985.

Wang Jing. *High Culture Fever: Politics, Aesthetics, and Ideology in Deng's China*. Berkeley: University of California Press, 1996.

Wang Ruisheng. 'Rujia sixiang yu dongya de xiandaihua' (Confucian Thought and East Asian Modernisation), *Zhongguo zhexueshi* (History of Chinese Philosophy) 4 (1996), pp. 7–11 and 31.

Wang Shifu. *The Romance of the Western Chamber* (trans. S.I. Hsiung). New York: Columbia University Press, 1968.

Wang Shifu (annotated by Wang Jisi). *Xixiang ji* (The Story of the West Wing). Reprinted Shanghai: Shanghai guji chubanshe, 1978.

Wang Shucun (ed.). *Guan Gong baitu* (One Hundred Images of Duke Guan). Guangzhou: Lingnan meishu chubanshe, 1996.

Wang, Shunzhu. 'The Double-Voiced Feminine Discourses in Ding Ling's "Miss Sophie's Diary" and Zora Neale Hurston's *Their Eyes Were Watching God*', *Tamkang Review* 28.1 (1997), pp. 131–158.

Wang Yong. *Guanxin nanren* (Take Care of Men). Beijing: Zhongguo chengshi chubanshe, 1997.

Wang Zejun and Long Tao (eds). 'Qianyan' (Preface), *Zhongguo yanqing xiaoshuo daguan* (Comprehensive Collection of Chinese Romantic Fiction). Chengdu: Chengdu chubanshe, 1992, pp. 1–12.

Wei Hui. *Shanghai Baby* (trans. Bruce Humes). London: Constable Publishers, 2001.

White, Tyrene (ed.). *China Briefing 1997–1999*. Armonk, NY: M.E. Sharpe, 2000.

Widmer, Ellen and David Der-wei Wang (eds). *From May Fourth to June Fourth: Fiction and Film in Twentieth-Century China*. Cambridge, Mass: Harvard University Press, 1993.

Williams, Patrick and Laura Chrisman (eds). *Colonial Discourse and Post-colonial Theory: A Reader*. New York: Harvester Wheatsheaf, 1993.

Williams, Philip F. '"Remolding" and the Chinese Labor Camp Novel', *Asia Major* 4.2 (1991), pp. 133–149.

Williams, Tony. 'Space, Place, and Spectacle: The Crisis Cinema of John Woo', in Poshek Fu and David Desser (eds), *The Cinema of Hong Kong: History, Arts, Identity*. Cambridge University Press, 2000, pp. 137–157.

Witterstaetter, Renée. *Dying for Action: The Life and Films of Jackie Chan*. London: Ebury Press, 1998.

Wolf, Margery. *Revolution Postponed: Women in Contemporary China*. Stanford University Press, 1985.

Wright, Arthur (ed.). *The Confucian Persuasion*. Stanford University Press, 1960.

Wright, Mary C. *The Last Stand of Chinese Conservatism: The T'ung-chih Restoration, 1862–1874*. Stanford University Press, 1957.

Wu Ching-tzu (Wu Jingzi). *The Scholars* (trans. by Gladys Yang and Yang Hsien-yi). Beijing: Foreign Languages Press, 1957.

Wu Cuncun. *Ming Qing shehui xing'ai fengqi* (Trends in Sexual Love in Ming-Qing Society). Beijing: Renmin chubanshe, 2000.

Wu, Fatima. 'Foxes in Chinese Supernatural Tales (Part I)', *Tamkang Review* 17.2 (1986), pp. 121–153.

Wu Jianping. 'Haolaiwu yu choulou de Zhongguoren' (Hollywood and the Ugly Chinamen), in Li Xiguang and Liu Kang (eds), *Yaomohua Zhongguo de beihou* (Behind the Demonised China). Beijing: Zhongguo shehuikexue chubanshe, 1996, pp. 222–261.

Wu Jingzi. *Rulin waishi* (The Scholars). Hong Kong: Zhonghua shuju, 1972 reprint.

Wu Li. *Qu ge waiguo nüren zuo taitai* (He Married a Foreign Woman). Tianjin: Renmin chubanshe, 1993.

Wu Liang. 'Ai de jieju yu chulu' (The Way Out for Love), *Shanghai wenxue* (Shanghai Literature) 4 (1987), pp. 88–91 & p. 96.

Wu, Yenna. 'The Interweaving of Sex and Politics in Zhang Xianliang's *Half of Man Is Woman*', *Journal of the Chinese Language Teachers Association* 27.1/2 (1992), pp. 1–27.

Wu, Yenna. 'Women as Sources of Redemption in Chang Hsien-liang's Labor-Camp Fiction', *Asia Major* 4.2 (1991), pp. 115–131.

Xiao Mingxiong. *Zhongguo tongxing'ai shilu* (History of Homosexuality in China). Revised edition, Hong Kong: Rosa Winkel Press, 1997.

Xie Pengxiong. *Wenxue zhong de nanren* (Men in Literature). Taipei: Jiuge chubanshe, 1992.

Xin Lan. 'Kongzi zai tiyu fangmian de shijian he zhuzhang' (Confucius' Practice and Principles in the Field of Sport), *Xin tiyu* (New Sports) 8 (1962), pp. 13–16.

Xu, Ben. *Disenchanted Democracy: Chinese Cultural Criticism After 1989*. Ann Arbor: University of Michigan Press, 1999.

Xu Mengying. 'Kongzi de jiaoyu sixiang' (Confucius' Educational Thought), *Guangming ribao* (Guangming Daily), 14 June 1954.

Xu Qixian. 'Lun rujia lunli yu daode guanli' (On Confucian Ethics and Moral Management), *Zhongguo renmin daxue xuebao* (Chinese People's University Journal) 1 (1998), pp. 48–54.

Xu Quanxing. 'Kongzi yu Mao Zedong: Gujin weida "jiaoyuan"' (Confucius and Mao Zedong: Great 'Teachers' of the Past and Present), *Kongzi yanjiu* (Confucius Research) 4 (1993), pp. 3–9.

Yang Bojun. *Lunyu Yizhu* (The *Analects* Translated and Annotated). Beijing: Zhonghua shuju, 1958.

Yang, Mayfair Mei-hui (ed.). *Spaces of Their Own: Women's Public Sphere in Transnational China*. Minneapolis: University of Minnesota Press, 1999.

Ye Ruixin. 'Kongzi de yili guan' (Confucius' Attitudes Towards Yi-Li), *Shanxi daxue xuebao* (Shanxi University Journal) 4 (1998), pp. 33–37.

Ye Weilin. 'Five girls and one rope' (trans. Zhou Shizong and Diane Simmons), *Fiction* 8 (2 and 3) 1987, pp. 96–114.

Yin Guoguang and Ye Junyuan (eds). 'Qianyan' (Preface), *Ming Qing yanqing xiaoshuo daguan* (Comprehensive Collection of Romantic Fiction from the Ming and Qing Dynasties), vol. 1. Beijing: Huaxia chubanshe, 1993, pp. iii–xiii.

Yoon, Suh-kyung. 'The Crying Game', *Far Eastern Economic Review* 164.14 (2001), pp. 64–66.

Young, Marilyn. 'Chicken Little in China: Some Reflections on Women', in Arif Dirlik and Maurice Meisner (eds), *Marxism and the Chinese Experience*. Armonk, NY: M.E. Sharpe, 1989, pp. 253–268.

Yu Dafu. 'Nights of Spring Fever', in *Nights of Spring Fever and Other Stories*. Beijing: Panda Books, 1984, pp. 7–17.

Yu Dafu. 'Chenlun' (Sinking), in *Yu Dafu wenji* (Collected Works of Yu Dafu), vol. 1. Hong Kong: Sanlian shudian, 1982, pp. 16–53.

Yu Xuecai. 'Rujia sixiang yu Zhongguo lüyou wenhua chuantong' (Confucian Thinking and Traditional Chinese Tourist Culture), *Kongzi yanjiu* (Confucius Research) 2 (1990), pp. 29–33.

Yu Zhonghua. 'Wuda pian yao "wu xi wen chang"' (Martial Arts Movies Should be 'Martial Arts Performances Harmonised by Cultured Scripts'), *Dianying yishu* (Film Art) 2 (1996), pp. 65–66.

Yuan Mei. 'Double Blossom Temple', in Kam Louie and Louise Edwards (eds and trans.), *Censored by Confucius: Ghost Stories by Yuan Mei*. Armonk, NY: M.E. Sharpe, 1996, pp. 206–208.

Yue Ming-Bao. 'Gendering the Origins of Modern Chinese Fiction', in Tongling Lu (ed.), *Gender and Sexuality in Twentieth-Century Chinese Literature and Society*. Albany: State University of New York Press, 1993, pp. 47–65.

Zang Hong. 'Lüelun rujia de yili guan' (On the Confucians' Attitude Towards Yi-Li), *Xuexi yuekan* (Study Monthly) 4 (1986), pp. 16–21.

Zhang Jie. 'The Ark' (trans. Stephen Hallett), in Chinese Literature (eds), *Love Must Not Be Forgotten*. Beijing: Panda, 1987, pp. 125–222.

Zhang Kangkang. 'Beiji guang' (Northern Lights), *Shouhuo* (Harvest) 3 (1980), pp. 4–61.

Zhang Peiheng and Huang Lin. *Song Jiang xi* (An Analysis of Song Jiang). Shanghai: Renmin chubanshe, 1975.

Zhang Wenhong and Ji Dejun. 'Caizi xingxiang moshi de wenhua xinli chanshi' (A Cultural Psychological Interpretation of the Image Pattern of the *caizi*), *Zhongshan daxue xuebao* (Zhongshan University Journal) 5 (1996), pp. 110–118.

Zhang Xianliang. *Getting Used to Dying* (trans. Martha Avery). London: HarperCollins, 1991.

Zhang Xianliang. 'Ling yu Rou' (Flesh and Soul). First published in *Shuofang* in 1980. Reprinted in Zhang Xianliang, *Zhang Xianliang xuanji* (Selected Works of Zhang Xianliang), vol. I. Tianjin: Baihua wenyi chubanshe, 1985, pp. 138–165.

Zhang Xianliang. 'Lühua shu' (Mimosa), reprinted in *Zhang Xianliang xuanji*, vol. 3, pp. 161–338.

Zhang Xianliang. 'Mimosa' (trans. Gladys Yang) in *Mimosa*. Beijing: Chinese Literature, 1985, pp. 7–181.

Zhang Xianliang. *Nanren de fengge* (Man's Style). First published in 1983. Taiwanese edition, Taipei: Yuanjing chubanshiye gongsi, 1988.

Zhang Xianliang. *Zhang Xianliang xuanji* (Selected Works of Zhang Xianliang), 3 vols. Tianjin: Baihua wenyi chubanshe, 1985.

Zhang Yongquan. 'Zai heianzhong xunqiu guangming de nüxing – Shafei xingxiang de zai pingjia' (Women Who Search for Light in the Midst of Darkness – A Reappraisal of the Sophia Image), *Ding Ling zuopin pinglunji* (Critical Essays on Ding Ling's Works). Beijing: Zhongguo wenlian chubangongsi, 1984, pp. 143–163.

Zhao Jibin. *Lunyu xintan* (A New Exploration of the *Analects*). Beijing: Renmin chubanshe, 1962.

Zhao Jing. 'Kongzi de guanli sixiang he xiandai jingying guanli' (Confucius' Management Ideas and Modern Administration and Management), *Kongzi yanjiu* (Confucius Research) 1 (1989), pp. 26–37.

Zhao Weimin (ed.). 'Gaici: Baoer de jiu chuanpiao hainengfou dengshang Bier de kechuan' (Gates: Can Pavel's Old Ticket Be Used to Board Bill's Passenger Liner?), 8 (2000) *Zhongguo qingnian* (China Youth), pp. 14–15.

Zhao Xiaqiu and Zeng Qingrui. *Zhongguo xiandai xiaoshuo shi* (History of Modern Chinese Fiction), vol. 2. Beijing: Zhongguo renmin daxue chubanshe, 1985.

Zheng Daqun. 'Nüxing jinji yu hou xinshiqi nüxing xiezuo' (The Prohibition on Women and Post-neo-feminist writing), *Wenyi pinglun* (Literary and Art Criticism) 2 (2000), pp. 33–40.

Zheng Wanlong. 'Xiagu' (The Canyon), in Zheng Wanlong, *You ren qiao men* (Somebody is Knocking on the Door). Shenyang: Chunfeng wenyi chubanshe, 1986, pp. 59–72.

Zheng Wanlong, *You ren qiao men* (Somebody is Knocking on the Door). Shenyang: Chunfeng wenyi chubanshe, 1986.

Zhong Xueping. 'Male Suffering and Male Desire: The Politics of Reading *Half of Man Is Woman*', in Christina K. Gilmartin, Gail Hershatter, Lisa Rofel, Tyrene White (eds), *Engendering China: Women, Culture, and The State*. Cambridge, Mass: Harvard University Press, 1994, pp. 175–191.

Zhong Xueping. *Masculinity Besieged? Issues of Modernity and Male Subjectivity in Chinese Literature of the Late Twentieth Century*. Durham, NC: Duke University Press, 2000.

Zhong, Yong. 'What's Behind White Masks and Yellow Skin: A Postcolonial Critique of a Chinese Sex Debate in Sydney', in Wenche Ommundsen (ed.), *Bastard Moon: Essays on Chinese-Australian Writing*, Special Issue of *Otherland* 7 (2001), pp. 56–72.

Zhongguo dangdai zuopin xuanbian 1949–1986 (Readings from Chinese Writers 1949–1986), vol. 1 (no editor provided). Beijing: Sinolingua, 1989.

Zhou Guangkuo. '*Shuihu* zenyang miaoxie Wu Song da hu' (How Does *All Men Are Brothers* Describe Wu Song Killing the Tiger), in Zuojia chubanshe bianjibu (ed.), *Shuihu yanjiu lunwen ji* (Research Articles on *All Men Are Brothers*). Beijing: Zuojia chubanshe, 1957, pp. 180–188.

Zhou Weibo. 'Zhang Yonglin shi ge wei junzi' (Zhang Yonglin is a Fake Gentleman). Originally published in *Wenhui bao* (Wenhui Daily), 7 October 1985. Reprinted in Ningxia renmin chubanshe (ed.), *Ping 'Nanren de yiban shi nüren'* (Criticisms of *Half of Man Is Woman*). Yinchuan: Ningxia renmin chubanshe, 1987, pp. 4–6.

Zhou Zhaoxin. *Sanguo yanyi kaoping* (Evaluation and Criticism of *The Romance of the Three Kingdoms*). Beijing: Beijing daxue chubanshe, 1990.

Zhou Zhongming. *Zhongguo de xiaoshuo yishu* (The Art of Chinese Fiction). Reprinted Taipei: Guanya wenhua, 1990.

Zhu Hong. *The Chinese Western*. New York: Ballantine, 1988.

Zhu Yixuan and Liu Yuchen (eds). *Sanguo yanyi ziliao huibian* (Compilation of Reference Materials on *The Romance of the Three Kingdoms*). Guangzhou: Baihua wenyi chubanshe, 1983.

Zhu Zhengming. *Legends about Guan Yu of China*. Beijing: China Today Press, 1996.

Zito, Angela. *Of Body & Brush: Grand Sacrifices as Text/Performance in Eighteenth-Century China*. University of Chicago Press, 1997.

Zito, Angela and Tani E. Barlow (eds). *Body, Subject & Power in China*. University of Chicago Press, 1994.

Zong Pu. 'Red Beans' (trans. Geremie Barmé), in W.J.F. Jenner (ed.), *Fragrant Weeds – Chinese Short Stories Once Labelled as 'Poisonous Weeds'*. Hong Kong: Joint Publishing, 1983, pp. 195–228.

Zuojia chubanshe bianjibu (ed.). *Shuihu yanjiu lunwen ji* (Research Articles on *All Men Are Brothers*). Beijing: Zuojia chubanshe, 1957.

Index

References in bold type, e.g. **140–59**, indicate the most detailed discussion of the topic. References to endnotes are in the form 187n.32.

LaVergne, TN USA
07 April 2010
178399LV00003B/73/P